PALGRAVE STUDIES IN CULTURAL AND INTELLECTUAL HISTORY
Series Editors
Anthony J. La Vopa, North Carolina State University
Suzanne Marchand, Louisiana State University
Javed Majeed, King's College, London

The Palgrave Studies in Cultural and Intellectual History series has three primary aims: to close divides between intellectual and cultural approaches, thus bringing them into mutually enriching interactions; to encourage interdisciplinarity in intellectual and cultural history; and to globalize the field, both in geographical scope and in subjects and methods. This series is open to work on a range of modes of intellectual inquiry, including social theory and the social sciences; the natural sciences; economic thought; literature; religion; gender and sexuality; philosophy; political and legal thought; psychology; and music and the arts. It encompasses not just North America but also Africa, Asia, Eurasia, Europe, Latin America, and the Middle East. It includes both nationally focused studies and studies of intellectual and cultural exchanges between different nations and regions of the world, and encompasses research monographs, synthetic studies, edited collections, and broad works of reinterpretation. Regardless of methodology or geography, all books in the series are historical in the fundamental sense of undertaking rigorous contextual analysis.

Published by Palgrave Macmillan

Indian Mobilities in the West, 1900–1947: Gender, Performance, Embodiment
By Shompa Lahiri

The Shelley-Byron Circle and the Idea of Europe
By Paul Stock

Culture and Hegemony in the Colonial Middle East
By Yaseen Noorani

Recovering Bishop Berkeley: Virtue and Society in the Anglo-Irish Context
By Scott Breuninger

The Reading of Russian Literature in China: A Moral Example and Manual of Practice
By Mark Gamsa

Rammohun Roy and the Making of Victorian Britain
By Lynn Zastoupil

Carl Gustav Jung: Avant-Garde Conservative
By Jay Sherry

Law and Politics in British Colonial Thought: Transpositions of Empire
Edited by Shaunnagh Dorsett and Ian Hunter

Sir John Malcolm and the Creation of British India
By Jack Harrington

The American Bourgeoisie: Distinction and Identity in the Nineteenth Century
Edited by Sven Beckert and Julia B. Rosenbaum

Benjamin Constant and the Birth of French Liberalism
By K. Steven Vincent

The Emergence of Russian Liberalism: Alexander Kunitsyn in Context, 1783–1840
By Julia Berest

The Gospel of Beauty in the Progressive Era: Reforming American Verse and Values
By Lisa Szefel

Knowledge Production, Pedagogy, and Institutions in Colonial India
Edited by Indra Sengupta and Daud Ali

Religious Transactions in Colonial South India: Language, Translation, and the Making of Protestant Identity
By Hephzibah Israel

Cultural History of the British Census: Envisioning the Multitude in the Nineteenth Century
By Kathrin Levitan

Character, Self, and Sociability in the Scottish Enlightenment
Edited by Thomas Ahnert and Susan Manning

The European Antarctic: Science and Strategy in Scandinavia and the British Empire
By Peder Roberts

Isaiah Berlin: The Journey of a Jewish Liberal
By Arie Dubnov

The Origins of Modern Historiography in India: Antiquarianism and Philology, 1780–1880
By Rama Sundari Mantena

At the Edges of Liberalism: Junctions of European, German, and Jewish History
By Steven E. Aschheim

Making British Indian Fictions: 1772–1823
By Ashok Malhotra

Alfred Weber and the Crisis of Culture, 1890–1933
By Colin Loader

Monism: Science, Philosophy, Religion, and the History of a Worldview
Edited by Todd H. Weir

The French Enlightenment and Its Others: The Mandarin, the Savage, and the Invention of the Human Sciences
By David Allen Harvey

Nature Engaged: Science in Practice from the Renaissance to the Present
Edited by Mario Biagioli and Jessica Riskin

History and Psyche: Culture, Psychoanalysis, and the Past
Edited by Sally Alexander and Barbara Taylor

The Scottish Enlightenment: Race, Gender, and the Limits of Progress
By Silvia Sebastiani

Art and Life in Modernist Prague: Karel Čapek and His Generation, 1911–1938
By Thomas Ort

Music and Empire in Britain and India: Identity, Internationalism, and Cross-Cultural Communication
By Bob van der Linden

Geographies of the Romantic North: Science, Antiquarianism, and Travel, 1790–1830
By Angela Byrne

Fandom, Authenticity, and Opera: Mad Acts and Letter Scenes in Fin-de-Siècle Russia
By Anna Fishzon

Memory and Theory in Eastern Europe
Edited by Uilleam Blacker, Alexander Etkind, and Julie Fedor

The Philosophy of Life and Death: Ludwig Klages and the Rise of a Nazi Biopolitics
By Nitzan Lebovic

The Dream of a Democratic Culture: Mortimer J. Adler and the Great Books Idea
By Tim Lacy

German Freedom and the Greek Ideal: The Cultural Legacy from Goethe to Mann
By William J. McGrath and edited by Celia Applegate, Stephanie Frontz, and Suzanne Marchand

Beyond Catholicism: Heresy, Mysticism, and Apocalypse in Italian Culture
Edited by Fabrizio De Donno and Simon Gilson

Translations, Histories, Enlightenments: William Robertson in Germany, 1760–1795
By László Kontler

Translations, Histories, Enlightenments

William Robertson in Germany, 1760–1795

László Kontler

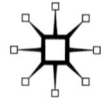

TRANSLATIONS, HISTORIES, ENLIGHTENMENTS
Copyright © László Kontler, 2014.

All rights reserved.

First published in 2014 by
PALGRAVE MACMILLAN®
in the United States—a division of St. Martin's Press LLC,
175 Fifth Avenue, New York, NY 10010.

Where this book is distributed in the UK, Europe and the rest of the world, this is by Palgrave Macmillan, a division of Macmillan Publishers Limited, registered in England, company number 785998, of Houndmills, Basingstoke, Hampshire RG21 6XS.

Palgrave Macmillan is the global academic imprint of the above companies and has companies and representatives throughout the world.

Palgrave® and Macmillan® are registered trademarks in the United States, the United Kingdom, Europe and other countries.

ISBN: 978–1–137–37171–3

Library of Congress Cataloging-in-Publication Data

Kontler, László.
   Translations, histories, enlightenments : William Robertson in Germany, 1760–1795 / László Kontler.
      pages cm.—(Palgrave studies in cultural and intellectual history)
   Includes bibliographical references and index.
   ISBN 978–1–137–37171–3 (hardback : alk. paper)
     1. Robertson, William, 1721–1793. 2. Germany—Intellectual life—18th century. 3. Scotland—Intellectual life—18th century. 4. Europe—Intellectual life—18th century. 5. Enlightenment—Germany. 6. Enlightenment—Scotland. 7. Enlightenment—Europe. I. Title. II. Title: William Robertson in Germany, 1760–1795.

DA759.7.R63K66 2014
907.2′02—dc23   2013046855

A catalogue record of the book is available from the British Library.

Design by Newgen Knowledge Works (P) Ltd., Chennai, India.

First edition: June 2014

Contents

Preface ix

Introduction 1
   Robertson in Scotland and in Europe 2
   Translation, reception, "influence" 6
   Spaces and places, regional and institutional contexts 9
   Situating Robertson, situating the Enlightenment 13

1 **Politics, Literature, and Science: William Robertson and Historical Discourses in Eighteenth-Century Scotland and Germany** 19
   Stages, conjectures, narratives: Scottish history and the science of man 20
   Varieties of *Geschichte*, toward *Wissenschaft* 31

2 **Time and Progress, Time as Progress: History by Way of Enlightened Preaching** 41
   Agency and event, Christian and other times: "progressive revelation" 42
   An unnoticed translation 53
   Baumgarten and Semler: history and the religious Enlightenment in Germany 56
   Lessing: progressive revelation remastered 62
   Michaelis: Göttingen and the cultural approach to Christianity 67

3 **A Different *View of the Progress of Society in Europe*** 73
   Manners and sociocultural dynamics 74
   An "exotic" interlude 78
   Some interlocutors 81
   Sitten and ethnocultural specifics 84

4 **Scottish Histories and German Identities** 95
   Scotland and *Charles V*: Robertson's making of modern Europe 95
   Rendering "national" history 106
   German Robertsons? 117

5 Maps of Mankind	**125**
Robertson's "global histories"	125
America: savages and "imperfectly civilized"	126
India: civilization subdued	140
Translating the history of mankind: terminologies and interlocutors	146
Landlocked gazes at the new worlds and Oriental lures	150
Robertson and Forster: strange bedfellows?	164
Conclusion	**179**
Notes	185
Bibliography	227
Index	251

Preface

The idea of this book dates back to many years. As is often the case, at its origins it was a far more ambitious project. Its completion has been delayed by a great variety of other pursuits and commitments. When it began, its central concerns were—or seemed so to me—fresh and relevant. I can only hope that during the long gestation period not all of the freshness and relevance have been lost.

The debts I have incurred while working on this book are commensurate with the length of time spent on it. The research and writing has been supported by gratefully received grants from the Hungarian National Research Fund, the Central European University Research Fund, and fellowships from the Herzog August Bibliothek in Wolfenbüttel, the Andrew Mellon Foundation, the Deutsches Akademisches Austauschdienst (DAAD), the Max-Planck-Gesellschaft, and the European Commission (Marie Curie Fellowship). Their generous support has enabled me, at various periods, to do library and archival research, and enjoy the academic ambience, as a guest of the Herzog August Bibliothek, the Max-Planck-Institut für Geschichte (Göttingen), the Institute for Advanced Studies in the Humanities (Edinburgh), the University of Cambridge, and the European University Institute (Florence). For their logistic help, I would like to express my thanks to the excellent staff at each of these institutions, as well as the National Library of Scotland and the University Library in Edinburgh, the University Library in Cambridge, the Niedersächsische Staats- und Universitätsbibliothek and the Universitätsarchiv in Göttingen, the Niedersächsisches Staatsarchiv in Wolfenbüttel, and the Österreichische Nationalbibliothek in Vienna. While in Budapest, I have been able to continue research on the topics of this book, thanks mainly to the collections in the libraries of Eötvös Lóránd University, the Hungarian Academy of Sciences, and my own institutional home, Central European University (CEU), with its remarkable journal holdings and smooth interlibrary loan services.

Over the years, at each of these places and elsewhere—including CEU, with its ever-challenging intellectual atmosphere—I have benefited enormously from general support and specific feedback in the form of conversation or correspondence from many wonderful colleagues and friends. Some of them may not be aware of their imprint on this manuscript (though hopefully they would not repudiate it), and some of them, sadly, have not lived to see it in full. I would like to specifically mention and express my thanks to Guido Abbattista, Thomas Ahnert, Éva H. Balázs, György Bence, Gillian Bepler, Hans

Erich Bödeker, Stuart J. Brown, Harry T. Dickinson, Roger Emerson, Tibor Frank, Gábor Gángó, Martin van Gelderen, Istvan Hont, Ferenc Horkay Hörcher, Edward J. Hundert, Girolamo Imbruglia, Peter Jones, Anthony LaVopa, Mária Ludassy, Rolando Minuti, Fania Oz-Salzberger, László Péter, Mark Salber Phillips, Nicholas Phillipson, John Pocock, János Poór, Peter Hanns Reill, John Robertson, Antonella Romano, Gordon Schochet, Silvia Sebastiani, Richard B. Sher, Sabine Solf, Endre Szécsényi, István Szijártó, Zoltán Gábor Szűcs, Anne Thomson, Zsuzsanna Török, Balázs Trencsényi, Benedek Varga, Rudolf Vierhaus, and Hanna Orsolya Vincze. I am also grateful to Palgrave's two anonymous reviewers, hoping to have turned their advice to the advantage of this book, and, last but not least, to Tom Szerecz for editorial suggestions and polishing the English prose. Needless to say, the author bears the sole responsibility for all remaining shortcomings of the ensuing text.

As always, those closest to the author have borne the bulk of the burden of completing this book, with indulgence and understanding. It is dedicated to them: to the memory of my parents, and to my wife and two daughters.

* * *

Earlier versions of several portions of this manuscript have been published as journal articles or contributions to collective volumes. Each of these has been severely revised, both in substantive aspects and with a view to monographic consistency. I am grateful to the publishers for permitting me to reuse material from these publications. The details are as follows:

Chapter 2 has its remote origins in "Time and Progress—Time as Progress: An Enlightened Sermon by William Robertson," in *Given World and Time: Temporalities in Context*, ed. Tyrus Miller, 195–220 (Budapest, Central European University Press, 2008).

Chapter 3 builds on "William Robertson's History of Manners in German 1770–1795," *Journal of the History of Ideas* 58/1 (1997): 125–44. Copyright 1997 by Journal of the History of Ideas, Inc., adapted by permission of the University of Pennsylvania Press.

Chapter 4 has been expanded from "Germanizing Scottish Histories: The Case of William Robertson," *Cromohs* 12 (2007): 1–9, http://www.cromohs.unifi.it/12_2007/kontler_robertson.html. © Digidocs

Chapter 5 includes material from "William Robertson and His German Audience on European and Non-European Civilisations," *Scottish Historical Review* 80/1 (2001): 63–89, © Edinburgh University Press, and "Mankind and Its Histories: William Robertson, Georg Forster and a Late Eighteenth-Century German Debate," *Intellectual History Review* 23/3 (2013): 411–29, www.tandfonline.com © 2013 International Society for Intellectual History.

Unless otherwise indicated, translations of German quotations into English are mine throughout the text.

Budapest, October 2013
László Kontler

Introduction

The work I have had in preparing this new edition of Robertson's History of Charles V has not been very agreeable. To compare an already existing translation line by line with the original, in order to be convinced of its accuracy; to alter a deficient phrase in a period while retaining the idiom already used, instead of deleting it altogether; to be ceaselessly alert, in order to avoid being led astray by the old translation and becoming familiar with its defects to such a degree as to overlook them; all this costs more trouble than a new translation would require. I do not flatter myself that I have noticed everything that could have been improved, and would hardly ever again undertake such a task, which causes more difficulties than it would seem at first sight.[1]

Anybody familiar with the frustrating side of editorial work can only sympathize with the sentiments expressed in these sentences by Julius August Remer, the editor of the 1779 second German edition of William Robertson's *History of Charles V*. What makes this complaint peculiar is that its author shortly earlier had spoken very highly about its target: "The translator, the late councilor Mittelstedt had too much wisdom and common sense, and was too proficient in both languages...to produce a translation that is not faithful" and the "excellent book" only needed to be supplemented with a handful of notes in order to improve its accuracy.[2] Nevertheless, just over a decade later Remer decided to revise the second edition, too. The revision concerned especially the book's celebrated introductory volume, *A View of the Progress of Society in Europe, from the Subversion of the Roman Empire, to the Beginning of the Sixteenth Century*; in the 1792 German edition, its structure and organizing principles became radically transformed, and its size was also substantially expanded.

Remer's complaint and his procedure—its context, causes, and consequences are examined in detail in chapter 3—serve as a forceful illustration of the central themes and endeavors of this book. The eighteenth century signaled the advent of multilingual modernity in European culture, in which there arose a sizable body of literate men and women, with adequate schooling and an appetite for novelties in all areas of learned and polite letters, who could comfortably read but one language, their own mother tongue. Humans may have been forced to "live by translation" ever since the *confusio linguarum*.[3] But making available texts originally conceived in one vernacular rendered into another had never before seemed so essential as in the Age of Enlightenment—which, at the same time, was fashioned and understood by its adherents and many later students as a unitary intellectual and cultural universe, conjoined by shared values and a dense network of print communication. However, Remer's grumblings express some concern, even doubt, about the potential of translation as a suitable vehicle of the processes of transmission on which the constitution of modern learning seemed to depend. In a more remote sense, it also points to the question of the transferability of intellectual products across linguistic and cultural barriers in a supposedly unified world of ideas—and still further, how unified that world actually was.

My book addresses this dilemma by way of a case study in comparative intellectual and conceptual history, reception and intellectual communication. In particular, it aims to contribute to the study of cultural and ideological unity versus diversity in the European Enlightenment by assessing the limits and possibilities of intellectual transfer through the translation and commentary of the works of one of the central figures of the Scottish Enlightenment in contemporary Germany. It elaborates on and hopes to enrich a research tradition according to which, besides the approximate unity of aspirations and questions shared by "the enlightened" of the eighteenth century across Europe, the answers depended on a great variety of contingent and context-dependent factors and thus pointed in rather different directions.

Robertson in Scotland and in Europe

William Robertson (1721–1793)[4] wrote some of the historical bestsellers of the eighteenth century, and his thought developed in close dialogue with the foremost thinkers of the Scottish Enlightenment, including David Hume, Adam Smith, John Millar, Adam Ferguson, Henry Home Lord Kames, and others. He emerged as a central figure of the Edinburgh intellectual scene in the company of several of these friends in the famous Select Society, founded in 1754 for civilized discussion and debate on literary, scholarly, and social matters; about the same time, he was also one of the founders and authors of the short-lived *Edinburgh Review*, the embodiment of the same endeavors in print media. Besides being a uniquely financially successful author and an intellectual celebrity of public and official recognition, appointed to the newly revived office of Historiographer Royal for Scotland in 1763, he was also a remarkably powerful man. As principal of the University of Edinburgh (where he had studied in the 1730s) from 1762 until his death, he promoted several successful projects—from the creation of a botanical garden and a natural history museum to the overhaul of teaching premises and implementing a routine of merit-based appointment to professorial chairs—that consolidated the university's status as a leading European institution of higher learning. Starting his career in the Scottish Presbyterian *Kirk* as a minister in 1744, by the early 1760s he emerged as its uncontested leader, with his "administration"[5] asserting the values of the "Moderate Party" (briefly, preserving authority, order, and discipline within the Church, and making it an instrument of promoting civility, sympathy, and benevolence outside) until his retirement from ecclesiastical politics in 1780.

Robertson was thus both an establishment public figure and a participant in some of the most interesting intellectual innovations in the arising social and human sciences. His works on themes from national, European, and global history addressed major questions of the Enlightenment as an intellectual movement that embraced the whole spectrum of efforts to confront the challenges of commercial modernity, and of the erosion of the Christian and republican ethical foundations of Western societies from the late seventeenth century to the era of the French Revolution—at least those segments of the spectrum that were not confined to a mere repudiation or negation of these challenges. How is it possible to alleviate the religious and political conflict inspired by the extremes of "superstition" and "enthusiasm" that had marred the social and political atmosphere of the sixteenth and seventeenth centuries? How is it possible to accommodate commerce, which had become inevitable and indispensable for modern societies but equally inevitably reinforced the self-regarding impulses inherent in human nature, with the moral imperatives of cooperation, sympathy, public spirit, and the pursuit of happiness in human collectives? How is it possible to enshrine the dignity of man in constitutions that also allow for strong government and stability? These, and a great many other questions, defined themes, fields, and endeavors in eighteenth-century intellectual inquiry that were central to what we now know as Enlightenment: religious toleration and the "natural history" of religion, political economy and conjectural history, natural law, and so forth.

Such an understanding of the Enlightenment, as the sum of the debates provoked by these questions and many more, conducted with considerable ardor and sometimes even venom but for the most part imbued on all sides with the values of "humanity," is spacious and open-ended, allowing for many borderline cases that will always be cited with relish by those who prefer tighter definitions (and also those irremediably skeptical of the possibility of such definitions).[6] The answers to the questions were diverse, and this is what introduced plurality amidst unity in the Enlightenment. Those answers developed or implied in Robertson's contributions to the enlightened "narratives of civil government" (John Pocock) and "cosmopolitan history" (Karen O'Brien)[7] were conceived from the vantage point of one of the most influential men in an economically and politically, but especially culturally ever more robustly emerging "minor partner" within a composite monarchy; while that monarchy itself struggled with the major challenges of rising as a leading imperial power in commercial and military terms between the 1750s and the 1790s. These decades coincided both with Robertson's activity as a historian and the heyday of the Scottish Enlightenment. The main historical themes presented by this vantage point included the internal dynamics that led to the Anglo-Scottish Union of 1707; the phenomenon of international competition and the balance of power within the emerging European commonwealth recognized as a system of states; and the broadening global interface between the civilization peculiar to this system and its counterparts in other continents that were now opening themselves to the gaze of Europeans. Robertson's oeuvre addressed each of these themes extensively. In the *History of Scotland* (1759), he sought to show how and why Scotland, although already making its appearance on the horizon of European history by the sixteenth century, did not share in processes that were taking place elsewhere, such as the curtailing of feudalism, which in Scotland was in effect postponed until the parliamentary union with England. By doing so, he attempted to refocus Scottish historiography, to supersede its shallow ancient constitutionalism, insularity, and the partisan debates between the adherents and adversaries of Mary Queen of Scots, and endeavored instead to place Scottish history on the map of Europe. The chief ambition of *The History of Charles V* (1769) was to show how Europe in the same period—before high-taxing territorial monarchies maintaining large standing armies could have become internally mitigated by checks and balances and externally by balance of power and the idea of toleration reconciled people to religious plurality—experienced the trials of absolutism, universal monarchy, and religious wars. Robertson then explored the ties forged through commercial and cultural exchange as well as imperialism between Europe and the rest of the globe (*History of America*, 1777; *An Historical Disquisition of the Knowledge which the Ancients Had of India*, 1791) in terms that, while certainly "Eurocentric," were marked by a great deal of sensitivity toward cultural difference, as well as by empirical richness and theoretical sophistication. As far as theory is concerned, it must be added that while the writing of history was, both for Robertson himself and his environment, still conceived as a literary pursuit as well as a form of political discourse, he was a pioneer in grafting on it the qualities of a field of inquiry with the claims of a scientific discipline, anxious as he was to cultivate it with the methodological tools provided by the new "science of man" that was becoming an Edinburgh trademark during his lifetime.

All over Europe, Robertson's combination of narrative and philosophical history evoked widespread interest. After a relatively "measured response" by the public to the 1764 French translation by N. P. Besset de La Chapelle of the *History of Scotland*, largely thanks to the good offices of Hume and his *philosophe* friends, the *History of Charles V* and the *History of America* were translated into French (and published in 1771 and 1779, respectively) by the renowned *encyclopédiste* Jean-Baptiste-Antoine Suard.[8] Each of Robertson's four great histories were also made available in Italian (some of them translated from the French) soon after their publication in the original, and he was elected a foreign member of the Academy of Sciences of Padua.[9] As the *History of Charles V* and the *History of America* tackled subjects of central concern for Spain, they were avidly discussed both in the Iberian kingdom and its colonial dependencies. A Spanish translation of the latter book was prepared by Ramón de Guevara Vasconcelos, a member of the Real Academia de Historia de Madrid (of which Robertson also became a foreign member). It received King Charles III's authorization for publication on January 8, 1778, but was never published, because a strong opposition within the Academia convinced the king of the need for a "Spanish" perspective on the history of the New World. Juan Bautista Muñoz, who was commissioned to execute this work, published a volume of his *Historia del Nuevo Mundo* in 1793, but then interrupted his work. His interpretation was very close to Robertson's.[10] In Central Europe, parts of the *History of America* appeared (based on the French translation) in Polish in 1789 and in Hungarian in 1809. But more lively interest was shown toward Robertson's works in Russia, where Catherine II's Scottish physician John Rogerson reported to the principal that "[a]ll your historical productions have ever been favorite parts of her reading."[11] The Tsarina's admiration undoubtedly played a part in the permission for Rogerson to supply Robertson with ethnographic information culled from Russian expeditions to the Far East, to be used by the historian in the *History of America*. Robertson also became an external member of the Imperial Academy of Sciences of Saint Petersburg and a Russian translation of the *History of Charles V* (based on the 1775 French edition) was published in 1775–1778. Even before then, Catherine commissioned the German tutor of Grand Duke Paul, Ludwig Heinrich Nicolay, to translate the introductory volume of the *History of Charles V*, the *View of the Progress of Society in Europe*, into German to serve as a tool for the political education of the heir to the Russian imperial throne.[12]

Yet, perhaps nowhere in the continent was the reception of Robertson as enthusiastic as in contemporary Germany. All of his books (both the English editions and the German translations) became valued items on the shelves of public and private libraries[13] and were nearly immediately reviewed in important journals. Translations appeared just a few months after the publication of the originals in each case (some of them in several versions simultaneously by different hands, others being revised again and again during the course of several decades). German authors exploring similar themes demonstrated a keen awareness of Robertson's work, referring to it and engaging with it critically. On account of his moderation and strong Protestant credentials, he was considered in Germany a respectable alternative to like-minded skeptical historians, such as Voltaire or Hume or Gibbon, and enjoyed great popularity among princes and authority among the educated.[14] The political and moral theorist Thomas Abbt planned to write a history of Braunschweig on the model of Robertson's *History of Scotland*,[15] while Julius August Remer, who edited, annotated, and adapted *The History of Charles V* for the German public, dreamed of writing a "View of the Progress of Society" about the post-Reformation period that would be a match to Robertson's tableau of the growth of European civilization before it.[16] The young Friedrich Schiller, whose uncle translated Robertson's *History of America* into German, thought that Robertson wrote history "in a poetical spirit" and confessed to a friend that he was keen on preparing a universal history following Robertson's path, besides Gibbon and (oddly enough) Bossuet. He also invoked Robertson as an authority in notes to the preface of his 1783 play *Verschwörung des Fiesco zu Genua* (Fiesco's Conspiracy in Genoa) and solutions used in Mittelstedt's translation are echoed in this republican tragedy as well as in *Mary Stuart* (1800).[17]

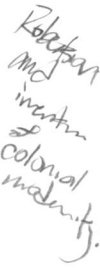

For the modern historian, the chief interest of the "Robertson in Germany" theme lies elsewhere. Arguably, the translations and the interpretation of his works contributed to, as well as reflected, the shaping of the linguistic and analytical tools employed to cope with the complexities of modernity in the German *Sattelzeit*. Robertson's grand theme—the simultaneous growth of the commercial and colonial system; the resulting advance of enlightenment and improvement of manners in the Western world; their contribution to a better understanding of the Christian revelation; the rise of modern national (as against universal) monarchy that accommodated the rule of law; the combination of monarchical and republican states in Europe as a system whose internal relationships were based on emulation as well as cooperation—had a specific relevance to the German experience and predicament. For different reasons, but on the whole not unlike the case of post-1707 Scotland, the challenges of an age of mercantile and maritime expansion caused uneasiness in the economic backwaters that constituted a majority of Germany throughout most of the early modern period. At the same time, the settlement of Westphalia in 1648 after the Thirty Years' War, which thwarted the Habsburgs' endeavor to impose political and religious homogeneity on the Holy Roman Empire, raised the issues of universal monarchy versus territorial state, of balance of power, and of religious moderation in a highly complex manner. Robertson's texts were, therefore, particularly suitable for generating interest and reflection in Germany.

Translation, reception, "influence"

The fact that amidst this extensive attention the amount of "impact" Robertson had in Germany remained rather limited, especially on the character of German historical studies, is all the more noteworthy and by itself indicative of the above-mentioned complexities of intellectual communication and reception in the Enlightenment. These complexities are examined on several levels in this present book, both in general terms and by reference to the particular texts of Robertson. The first level is that of translation as the "construction of comparables" with the aim of both linguistic and cultural transmission, and the pursuit of goals peculiar to the recipient environment. As I have argued more extensively elsewhere,[18] in the study of such processes it is of central importance to emphasize the amount of intellectual and conceptual adjustment, adaptation, and transformation occurring as a result of the combination of linguistic and discursive, sociocultural and political parameters with the agency of translators. Thus, the "(un)translatability of concepts/ideas/texts" may be a misleading term because it suggests that concepts/ideas/texts tend to resist translation *in spite of* whatever efforts translators may be making to render them faithfully. The second part of this assumption would be clearly a fallacious one. Regardless of the resisting power of concepts, keywords, and vocabularies to translation, in most historically documented cases translators could have hardly cared less about their faithful rendering. The outcome has sometimes been described as "mistranslation" or "misreception,"[19] which is technically accurate, but as it has a tendency to represent the agent of translation or reception as blameworthy of oversight, incompetence, or malicious manipulation, it should be used with caution. Its uncompromising use risks association with a tradition of research that understood reception as a unilinear process of "passing on" ideal-typical meanings from authoritative creators to inferior recipients, whose task would be faithful copying, except out of inability or unwillingness produce only faint or distorted replicas. In contrast to this limited perspective, recent studies of translation in cultural and intellectual history—even ones that employ the "mis-" prefix—have led us a long way toward restoring active agency to the translator-recipient and the environment of reception by translation, to the extent that it might be helpful to exchange the term "reception" with "confrontation" and "negotiation." To invoke Friedrich Schleiermacher's famous formulation of the two ways of bringing "those two separated persons, author and reader, truly together," the vast majority of translators of texts that are of potential interest for intellectual and conceptual historians have preferred "leav[ing] the reader in peace, as much as possible, and mov[ing] the author towards him."[20] In other words, the contexts and agendas in the target culture and on the recipient side of the translation process must be of paramount interest. One of the endeavors of my book is thus to provide, by means of a contextualized case study, some correctives to the received interpretation of and theoretical assumptions about processes of intellectual transmission and reception across linguistic and cultural frontiers.

In full compliance with a broad range of theoretical reflection on the tasks and methods of translation in the period, and similarly to widely pursued translating practices, some of the German translators of Robertson took extensive liberties in rendering his texts, tacitly or explicitly putting them in the service of indigenous academic, intellectual, political, or personal agendas. This leads to the second level of analysis, which is constituted by the personal character, the academic and institutional allegiances, and the specific endeavors of the individuals involved in the process of reception. Most of these individuals derive their significance from representing sociocultural types. These include Protestant pastors, mainly interested in Robertson's providentialism; professionals of the expanding German publishing business, for whom translating was part of earning a livelihood; provincial university professors, for whom the engagement with the text was an exercise in emulation; as well as academics and intellectuals of national stature, including one emblematic, hard-to-classify figure of the German Enlightenment whose participation in this story is as astonishing as it is predictable: the Anglophile, cosmopolitan, circumnavigator, "Jacobin" Georg Forster. Together, these figures and types represent an interesting cross section of the contemporary German academic–intellectual scene. The scope and the genre of this present work hardly allows a full-scale reliance on the recently revived biographical approach in historical studies. Still, at this stage of the investigation, I also attempt to provide glimpses into the range of the highly variegated aspirations and stakes that prompted the respective agents, in a remarkably contingent manner, to participate in a shared history of intellectual transfer. The fact that among all of these figures the restless and radical Forster was the one to demonstrate the greatest amount of intellectual empathy in engaging Robertson also places the above-mentioned "unity versus diversity" issue in a particularly interesting light.

However, the transformations that Robertson's texts underwent in the process of translation arose not only from intended interventions by consciously acting agents, but also from the differences of the linguistic and conceptual tools at their disposal. In investigating these aspects of the topic, I rely on "linguistic contextualism" (the "Cambridge" or "Collingwoodian" approach to the history of ideas), the history of concepts (*Begriffsgeschichte*), and reception history (*Rezeptionsgeschichte*). If the capacity of language to provide tools for the competent user to attain specific goals is asserted in the act of translation as described above, its character as a paradigm imposing constraints by defining the range of what is capable of expression can also be fruitfully studied in the rich history of Robertson's German reception. This aspect of the level of exploring "transmission through translation" brings us to the consideration of the compatibility of the conceptual apparatus, together with the coherence of the vocabulary employed to give expression to this apparatus, that was available for Robertson in his contemporary Scottish setting, on the one hand, and for his German interlocutors, on the other hand. No degree of inventiveness on the part of the latter would have served fully to convey the consistency of the etymological associations possible to detect in the language of Scottish stadial and conjectural history, with which even the purely narrative portions of Robertson's oeuvre are interspersed.

Next, beyond individual agency and the linguistic barrier, differences of perspective also arose from the different modes of historical inquiry and their places on the contemporary map of learning, tied up with their peculiar public–political valence in eighteenth-century Scotland and Germany. An examination of the sociocultural practices associated with the production of historical knowledge constitutes yet another level of analysis.[21] In both cases, history was cultivated predominantly in order to show how the present arose from the past, and, consequently, how the nature of the present—and the future—can be better understood through the study of the past. What was different was the present, or rather the vision of the present and its aspects, which history was expected to highlight. These stakes were "enlightened" in both cases, concerned as they were with the growth and chances of political stability, denominational peace, legal security, and material improvement; with conquering or taming the "violent passions" responsible for the calamities of the previous two centuries though the cultivation of the virtues of reason and moderation. For many eighteenth-century Germans, such chances seemed to be predicated to a considerable extent on the specific structure of the Holy Roman Empire of the German Nation, as it became consolidated, indeed enshrined, after the traumas of the Thirty Years' War, in the peace settlement of Münster and Osnabrück in 1648. As a counterpart of Robertson's modern Europe on a broader scale, the Westphalian system was conceived as one of the equilibrium of larger and smaller states *within* Germany, characterized by the plurality of political and religious establishments, for which the existence of an "imperial constitution," that eschewed universal monarchy and vested the composite parts of the assemblage with considerable powers to provide for the civil, spiritual, and material well-being of their subjects, was deemed essential. From Robertson's continent-wide preoccupations it followed that the assumptions of large-scale sociological analysis underlay most of his works and history's closest neighbor-disciplines were the Edinburgh-style sciences of man. While the latter were also emerging in Germany, the main genres in which history was cultivated there—whether *Landesgeschichte*, *Reichshistorie*, or *Universalgeschichte*—had their gaze on public law and the state sciences. The demand for both an anthropological perspective informed by the arising sciences of man and a literary quality in historical works came to Germany with a phase displacement, while the early signs of the emergence of the "critical-philological method" made Robertson's somewhat cavalier treatment of the sources a target of criticism even among sympathizers of his grand design. Through tracing the reception of Robertson in Germany, this book thus intends to offer new perspectives on the history of eighteenth-century historiography, an intellectual pursuit whose practitioners voiced in the period of the Enlightenment ever more forceful but culturally complex and varied claims on behalf of its status as a scientific discipline with its own theory and methodology.

Spaces and places, regional and institutional contexts

Yet another level of analysis is introduced in the approach to the Enlightenment from a regional perspective and the implicit presence throughout this work of Edinburgh and Göttingen as "cities of Enlightenment,"[22] with their special status in the British and German intellectual and cultural scenes and the European network for communicating enlightened knowledge.[23] Many of the individuals involved in the German reception of Robertson's works as translators, reviewers, or independent authors who were regarded as the Scottish historian's counterparts, maintained more or less intimate ties with the University of Göttingen. The list includes former students, professors of various faculties, as well as their friends and family members. Both Edinburgh and Göttingen were medium-sized urban centers and seats of prestigious universities with tightly knit academic communities, modernized curricula, and scholars of international renown, a combination that represented a considerable appeal far and wide. The two cities were also alike in their capacity to exploit strategic advantages in their cultural–intellectual emulation with regional rivals (Glasgow, Aberdeen, and St. Andrews, and Halle and Jena, respectively) and in regard to the integrity they maintained vis-à-vis metropolitan centers of the broader cultural area (London and Berlin). The two universities therefore deserve some attention in the account that follows.

The University of Edinburgh[24]—or "college," as the jealous town councilors who formally still possessed administrative authority over the school preferred to call it in order to downplay its corporate academic status—was the emblem as well as the instrument of the "Moderate revolution" carried out by Robertson and his associates in the early 1760s.[25] "Moderatism" has been characterized as the Enlightenment of Presbyterian clerics who sought to revamp the *Kirk*—one of the two institutional frameworks that still embodied Scotland's integrity after the Union of Parliaments—as a community of tolerant and undogmatic patriots whose zeal was of a non-confessional kind and aimed at national unification on the basis of Erastianism and improvement. These enlightened churchmen, significantly aided by intellectual ammunition from their extra-ecclesiastical comrades, promoted polite manners, rational religious practices, rights secured by the rule of law, and "a cosmopolitan species of nationalism that sought to raise the status of Scotland in the eyes of the world by demonstrating its superiority according to universally accepted standards of morality and taste."[26] They found no difficulty in accommodating a Stoic, Ciceronean—moralist rather than constitutionalist—commitment to civic virtue and an emphasis on the public duty of clerics with an appreciation for the progressive, civilizing functions of self-interest, commerce, and luxury. The degree of control which the Moderates gained in the early 1760s over Scotland's academic and ecclesiastical establishment enabled them to vigorously disseminate these cultural values. Several of them were invested in prestigious parish churches, and besides Robertson's taking over as principal in 1762, Hugh Blair and Adam Ferguson were appointed to the important chairs of rhetoric and belles lettres and moral philosophy, respectively, at the University of Edinburgh. They were soon joined by further sympathizers and also had influential allies at other Scottish universities. As the universities were entitled to send a considerable number of delegates to the General Assembly of the *Kirk*, the national "program" of the Moderates could be pursued not only by shaping the profile of the future educated elite of the country, but also via direct engagement in church politics.

This synoptic characterization of the University of Edinburgh under the Moderate regime of the decades after 1760 has been inserted here on the basis of the now respectable amount of literature in order to point to some possible parallels with the outlook of the Georgia Augusta in Göttingen. Founded by the decree of George II of Great Britain in his capacity as Elector of Hanover in 1734, and opened for studies in 1737, the new university was in many ways a natural home for the reception of an author whose oeuvre, personality, and career stands for much that was distinctive about the Edinburgh Enlightenment. From the very outset, the Georgia Augusta was deliberately and explicitly conceptualized and planned as a "modern" university, which in the given circumstances meant a university serving the goals of a society ordered by post-confessional secular governments. This was in strict conformity with the idea that the university was a *Staatsanstalt*, a state institution to be supervised through *Polizey*, that is, the ordering functions of the state, expressed by the famous cameralist thinker Johann Heinrich Gottlob von Justi (1717–1771).[27] The principal goal of the Enlightenment university in the German lands was to supply students with a sufficient understanding of scholarship and theoretical principles in order for them to succeed in the professions and perform socially useful service in their office (*Amt*). Relegating religious concerns into the background, and especially suppressing extremist and intolerant as well as ignorant forms of religion, was crucial to this agenda of supplanting traditional forms of authority with bureaucratic rationality. Germany already had a university whose foundation was motivated by such concerns of a rising state, and therefore "offered academics extraordinary intellectual latitude in relation to Lutheran orthodoxy, yet inside an institution that was strictly controlled by a monarchical court bent on using it to provide the state with a de-confessionalizing ruling elite."[28] That university was Halle, founded in 1694 by Frederick I of Prussia, where the Hanoverian prime minister Gerlach Adolph von Münchhausen, the *spiritus movens* behind the foundation of the Georgia Augusta, and several of the first Göttingen professors received their education or worked during the earlier stages of their career. To a considerable extent, the Georgia Augusta was patterned after Halle, with its emphasis on academic praxis, vocational training, a freer theological atmosphere, and the abandonment of the medieval *Autoritätsprinzip*. However, it strove to avoid falling victim, as Halle did, to the tensions of three "rival Enlightenments" represented by the anti-scholastic civil philosophy of Christian Thomasius, the Pietist "theological Enlightenment," and the neoscholastic Leibnizian metaphysics of Christian Wolff.[29] If institutional cohesiveness, an indispensable condition for the cohesiveness of the social elite that the university strove to secure, was to be achieved, such tensions were impermissible.

Therefore, a kind of philosophical and theological irenicism was central to the founders' vision. At Göttingen, the theological faculty did not possess the right of censorship: it was controversy, faction, rancor, and excessive disagreement inspired by religious polemic that became subject to censure.

Controversial ideologies ("naturalism, indifferentism, Socinianism, enthusiasm, chiliasm, the doctrine of *apocatastasis*, mystical theology, Machiavellianism, Hobbesianism, alchemy, Ramism, Cartesianism, or pure Aristotelianism") were to be kept at bay.[30] Apart from this, the Georgia Augusta secured an unprecedented degree of academic freedom for its teaching faculty (the *Lehrfreiheit* also including the suppression of scholarly monopolies: professors were free, even encouraged, to test themselves outside their disciplines and experiment with courses in nontraditional fields like statistics or ethnography). This was partly also a means of avoiding compartmentalization and "factionalism" (though not one to preclude personal jealousies[31]), and partly a trademark of the Enlightenment university as the seat of rational, open-ended inquiry. The implications were twofold. On the one hand, Göttingen took pride in being a "research university," one whose fame was based on the excellence of the academic output of the celebrity professors it assembled.[32] On the other hand, as far as the recipients of its educational program are concerned, there was a purpose to the abandonment of scholasticism, overarching systems, and traditional disciplines and to the focus on new and practical disciplines dictated by the current needs of the social and political order, together with the ethos and method of instruction applied. This higher end was *Bildung*, that is, education and formation for the whole person, in which the specific technical competences to be acquired were closely wedded to the virtues of public-mindedness and social adeptness (to which professors themselves were supposed to set an example by their own commitment to human betterment under a rational order). In their ideals, the lettered statesman Cicero took precedence over Plato the dogmatist, as explained by Samuel Christian Hollmann, the first professor of philosophy, in his inaugural lectures of 1734 (still held in a temporary building).[33]

Göttingen occupied an important place in the path toward the full *Verwissenschaftlichung, Professionalisierung, Entkonfessionalisierung,* and *Verstaatlichung* of the German (Protestant) university scene.[34] While "scientization" and "professionalization" are by no means negligible, in the present context the relationship between "de-confessionalization" and "statization" seems to be of greater importance.[35] At Göttingen, the de-confessionalization of academic life by removing it from the orbit of the churches, understood as crucial in order to create the conditions of the rational government of society with a view to public happiness by a cohesive elite, could be plausibly carried out by founding a university "under the sway of the state." The absence of a Scottish state is, of course, only one reason among many why this was inconceivable in Edinburgh. There enlightened churchmen, with similar ends in mind, embarked on the de-confessionalization of their own church—whose significance as a national institution loomed especially large because of the lack of an independent political state—by pursuing the same agenda within the educational establishment. Yet, to a striking extent, the enlightened professors, who were *Staatsbeamter* in the one case and clerics in the other, shared an ethos that emphasized order and moderation combined with improvement and enlightenment.

Further differences between the two environments must be mentioned, too. These include the fact that while in addition to the academic elite, Edinburgh also had sizeable elite groups in the legal, military, and ecclesiastical professions to an extent with which Göttingen could not compete. To some extent, at least, this may have been due to the fact that in the latter there were no traditions of a national capital, even though both universities were closely integrated with the establishment of the day, and both of them issued a steady supply of well-trained professionals and specialists who populated public services and bureaucratic machineries, educational and medical institutions, in an entire imperial space: the British colonial empire in the one case, and the German *Reich* in the other. The stimuli deriving from Edinburgh's identity as representing a Scottish Lowland culture, dramatically wedged between the underdeveloped Highlands and a dynamic England, were also lacking in the German town. Nevertheless, in addition to the parallels mentioned above, there were two other factors that offered opportunities as well as incentives for a substantial critical reception of an author like Robertson. One of these was the superb library resources of the University of Göttingen, growing from c. 12 thousand volumes in 1737 and 60 thousand in 1764, to about 200 thousand in 1802 (double the holdings of the University of Cambridge), including virtually all the important works of the Scottish Enlightenment.[36] The other was the unique mechanism provided by the review journal *Göttingische Anzeigen von gelehrten Sachen* for the wider dissemination of knowledge accumulated on the library's shelves: it was one of the obligations of the university's professors to systematically give an account of the library's new acquisitions in the journal (and all books received by and reviewed in the journal went into the library).[37] Altogether, in view of the amalgam of commonalities as well as differences, the two cities constitute an ideal unit of comparison, both as a background through which Robertson's reception could be approached, and as a topic in its own right that can be better understood in light of that reception. In other words, this aspect of the investigation points toward a refinement of the spatial structures in which the varieties in the production and consumption of enlightened knowledge are conceptualized.

Situating Robertson, situating the Enlightenment

This multilayered investigation, thanks to the inherently comparative framework adopted in it, will hopefully put into sharper relief the work and character of a figure of the Edinburgh Enlightenment whose importance is now widely acknowledged, but who still lacks a monographic study. It must be emphasized that in this sense this book is as much an interpretation of Robertson and his works as a study of the reception of these works in Germany. At this point, let me resume the discussion of the significance of inquiry into translation in intellectual history. A fundamental feature of the comparative endeavor inherent in the current historical literature on translation is that it emphasizes the difference arising at the target end of the translatorial process: the focus of attention of virtually all of this literature is the considerable amount we may learn from the comparisons inherent in the study of translation about the cultural–intellectual–conceptual milieu into which the text is transferred by translation. Not contesting the value of this perspective, but going beyond it, I suggest—and hope to illustrate in the chapters that follow—that the difference of meaning emerging through translation in the recipient environment can be turned to contributing to significant discussions and to sorting out disagreements about the character and status of authors, their texts, and their concepts as they exist in their "home" culture. My premise is a simple one: whatever aspect in the work of an author or in a concept, or whatever thread in a text, is overlooked, set aside, or redescribed in order to better suit the peculiarities of the target language, the purposes of the translator and/or the (actual or presumed) cultural sensibilities of the recipient environment must be regarded as peculiar to and distinctive of the "original." This may sound trivial, but there are cases in which it may have important consequences. At least in cases where the translation dates not long after the publication of the original, the "difference" arising at the recipient end is quite likely to highlight the *differentia specifica* of the translated text. We may not learn much about Aristotle from a study of early modern translations of the *Politics*; but what eighteenth-century translators of, say, *Le siècle de Louis XIV* miss, misunderstand, or neglect in rendering Voltaire's text may reveal something about Voltaire in his original context.

I believe that the translations and reception of Robertson in late eighteenth-century Germany is a case that both confirms this premise and can be helpfully explored by employing it. To anticipate some of the conclusions of this comparative analysis, the profile of Robertson that emerges from it is closer to the avant-garde historian we have been accustomed to recognize in him than the more traditionalist one, as he has been described in some more recent studies. The cultivation of narrative and character analysis undoubtedly remained central to Robertson's historical endeavors, and his political and ecclesiastical commitments may have been closer to the Scottish patriotic and Presbyterian mainstream than has been often represented. Nevertheless, his intellectual distinctiveness arose from his determination both to enrich his professional pursuits and to enhance the credibility of his consequent public agendas through the application of methodological principles derived from the Scottish "sciences of man." This is confirmed by the fact that besides many other interesting themes in the history of the German reception, this was the aspect of Robertson's oeuvre that constituted the greatest challenge—in some cases leading to perplexity, in others to critical response, and in yet others providing fruitful intellectual stimuli.

The agenda outlined thus far is ambitious enough and perhaps even immodest. Yet, finally, the study of the translation and reception of Robertson in late eighteenth-century Germany, combined with the application of the comparative approach to the history of historical thought and social theory in the period, not only builds on but also further elucidates a number of relatively recent developments in Enlightenment studies, to which much of the continuing dynamism of the field may be ascribed.[38] The first of these is the view of the Enlightenment not as a sterile forward movement, or contrariwise, the corruption of "progressive" ideas, but as a complex web of communicative processes and practices of sociability: "the Enlightenment as communication." Recognizing the merits of the "social history of ideas," my signposts here are not the investigations of the diffusion of ideas and their "agency," but the notion of the Enlightenment republic of letters as an "echo chamber": a communicative space marked by a plurality of voices in a reciprocal, even if asymmetric relationship with one another.[39] The approach to translation, briefly outlined above but enunciated in detail elsewhere, is congenial to this understanding of the Enlightenment in a climate of inquiry where the focus is no longer on the construction of canons, on assigning the place of periods and intellectual heroes in them, and on following their "impact"—necessarily, on an ever weakening scale from "centers" to "peripheries"—but on active and context-dependent engagements with a generally accessible pool of ideas, in order to transform them into ways of living in local life-worlds. Second, and not unrelated, the discussion of Robertson and his German reception must be comprehended within the debate about the plurality of the (regional, ideological, academic, professional, and other) contexts of the Enlightenment. "Unity versus diversity" in the Enlightenment is an old theme in whose exploration we no longer understand unity as conformity with a putative model of Parisian freethinking and diversity as more or less hopeless endeavors to emulate it elsewhere (the chances of success decreasing with greater geographic distance). True, the proposition to study the Enlightenment in "national context"[40] has received sound criticism, as did constructions of "conservative," "Arminian," "Utrecht" Enlightenments.[41] But even in the enterprise that has recently forcefully restated "radicalism" as the *differentia specifica* of "the" Enlightenment, which we ought to regard as the fountainhead of the secularist and democratic modernity of the western world, the existence of a more cautious, "magisterial" Enlightenment is also readily acknowledged.[42] For the present study, the most helpful recent proposition—as hinted above—seems to be that while the Enlightenment was unitary in the questions its protagonists asked, the answers they gave differed widely.[43] Third, it must be noted briefly that recent applications of postcolonialist studies, the concept of orientalism, and global history to research on the Enlightenment are also of obvious relevance to the discussion of the implications and impact of the output of an author who dedicated two out of his four great historical works to the problem of encounter between European and other civilizations.

Besides specialized studies, concise as well as more bulky syntheses exist that attempt to do justice to the enormous diversification of Enlightenment

16 *Translations, Histories, Enlightenments*

studies in the past few decades.[44] Amidst the variety of approaches to the Enlightenment, one question that certainly might be asked with good reason is whether the term still preserves any other meaning than a generic reference to "the eighteenth century." But it may equally be asked whether this was an unwelcome development in the first place. Students of the eighteenth century have recently been urged to provide "a sound and stable sense of the Enlightenment" for their colleagues focusing on different periods, even in different disciplines, with which to work.[45] This purpose is served well if any attempt to answer such calls by proposing "strong points" is made against a canvas depicting the richness of contemporary thought and experience.

A study of the contemporary reception of Robertson's works in Germany has a solid potential to provide an answer of this kind. The questions which Robertson the historian asked about the past of his own nation in the context of continent-wide developments and about the past of Europe in its global entanglements were typically "enlightened" in the sense that they were centrally relevant to the assessment of the chances of human betterment. They were ultimately questions about the persistent features of human nature, the contingencies of individual character, and the determinants of sociability as fundamental conditions of such betterment. The questions and the solutions which he proposed reflected not only his intellectual commitments, but also his personal inclinations, positions, and distinctions in church and university, as well as his intense presence on the scenes of enlightened sociability in eighteenth-century Edinburgh. His practice as an author of historical works— the research, the writing, and the promotion of these works—depended in part on the social capital he possessed, thanks to his status among the establishment of the day. Members of the diplomatic and colonial service as well as expatriate Scots—from Thomas Hutchinson, governor of Massachusetts Bay, to Robert Waddilove, chaplain of the British embassy in Madrid, to John Rogerson, the physician of the Empress of Russia in Saint Petersburg—assisted him in obtaining answers to his famous questionnaire on native civilizations in the Americas and in Siberia.[46] But equally important was the role of the opportunities opened by the Enlightenment culture of communication. Robertson actively used such opportunities in a highly proficient manner: it has already been mentioned that his success in France depended to a considerable extent on the inlets through Hume and other Scottish mediators to the Parisian *le monde*.[47] The same types of connections also rounded off the information network Robertson built to collect material for the *History of America* and, as we shall see, he had them in Germany, too. Nevertheless, from the point of view of the German reception it was a different aspect of the Enlightenment public sphere that was paramount. Thanks to the immensely increased volume and accelerated pace of the circulation of printed works and commentary on them in publications specifically destined for this end, as a practice that at least in its endeavor was systematic and all-embracing, there was also an increase in the likelihood that the text of an author would be reviewed, evaluated, appreciated, or criticized, even turned to purposes different from his or her own by someone at a geographically remote location, unconnected with and unknown to him or her. The consequences of what has been illustrated by the above-mentioned "echo chamber" metaphor of Enlightenment communication operated powerfully in the case of the history of Robertson's works in Germany—significantly, without the active promotion encountered in the French case. This is a factor which not even a study in purely intellectual history, such as the present one, can afford to disregard entirely.

But as this is a study in intellectual history, in the empirically based chapters of this book I shall be preoccupied with the ways in which Robertson's confrontations with the challenges of molding his Scottish, European, and global topics into the frame of the "enlightened narrative" were engaged by enlightened men in a different cultural and linguistic environment, in which his questions were, by and large, shared, but in which several aspects of his texts started to live their own lives, where the texts as wholes were understood to contribute to debates and dilemmas with a local flavor. Before the specific texts are examined in detail, however, chapter 1 will continue the general line of inquiry pursued in this introduction. Its task is to embed the central theme in the universe of eighteenth-century historical writing in relation to its three different but interlocking forms: as political thought, as literary pursuit and aesthetic expression, and as a branch of knowledge with the nascent claim to the status of a scientific discipline. The sketch attempted in this chapter is intended as an overall framework of interpretation for the case studies that follow: each of its paragraphs call for further elaboration, which I hope to provide in the rest of the chapters, which conform to a roughly identical structure. First, in each of them I offer an interpretation of Robertson's individual texts, which is followed and hopefully further nuanced by tracing their reception in late eighteenth-century Germany—or, in cases where translation is not accompanied by a substantial reception, a comparative perspective is adopted in order to highlight parallel structures in German enlightened discourse. Chapter 2, the first of four devoted to detailed textual analysis, is a case in point. On the basis of Robertson's first published work and his only sermon to appear in print, it assesses Robertson's status as a Christian thinker who was at the same time embarking on a career as a secular historian, ambitious to employ recent advances in the Enlightenment science of man to enrich the providentialist account of human progress (and vice versa). It then attempts to place the German translation of this text in the context of contemporary German religious thought. Somewhat in violation of the chronology, chapter 3 analyses translations and responses to Robertson's overview of European development from late antiquity to early modern times in *A View of the Progress of Society in Europe*, the lengthy introduction to the *History of Charles V*. This piece receives separate treatment from the main text of the three-volume work in part as the text that established Robertson's reputation for the combination of historical narrative with the perspectives opened by stadial history and structural analysis; and also because of the particular vicissitudes it underwent in the course of the very complicated German translation history. In chapter 4, I turn to the translations and the reception of the *History of Scotland* and volumes 2 and 3 (the narrative portions) of the *History of Charles V*, with a special emphasis on Robertson's treatment of the context provided for national histories by the rise of the international European state system; his account of political agency, relations, and institutions; as well as his representation of religious and civil conflict. His commitment to a peculiar ideal of "impartiality" and the ways in which this resonated in the German reception receives attention, as well as the works on the same range of topics by some scholars, some of them active in mediating Robertson, who were proposed by their contemporaries as his counterparts on the German intellectual scene. Confronting the character of the works of these authors with those of Robertson gives occasion for reflection on the peculiar political–constitutional conditions of the Holy Roman Empire as a further context for the history of reception. My last case study, in chapter 5, is the most extensive because of the rich complexity of both of the texts of Robertson explored in it and the story of their German reception. It brings together in a common discussion the translations and reception of Robertson's works devoted to the history of Europeans' relations with non-European peoples: the *History of America* and the *Historical Disquisition on...India*. Salient topics, such as expansion, empire, race, etc., which Robertson explored in stadial–conjectural as well as narrative terms, are placed in the course of the reception into an interesting light by the fact that Germany as a geographic and cultural entity was sealed off from a direct confrontation with these issues, while demonstrating a steadily increasing interest in them. The involvement of Johann Reinhold Forster and Georg Forster, Anglophiles and experts (as well as fieldworkers) in natural history and ethnology, in this episode of the complicated story of reception, receive special attention, and is exploited to add further color to the exploration of "unity and diversity" in the Enlightenment.

1
Politics, Literature, and Science: William Robertson and Historical Discourses in Eighteenth-Century Scotland and Germany

As proposed at the end of the Introduction, before any attempt to analyze the German reception of Robertson's individual texts, it is indispensable to take a more general look at the various modes in which history was engaged in Robertson's Scottish environment and in which it was practiced in contemporary Germany. It is from a comparative assessment of such variables that one might expect to arrive at the understanding of an apparent paradox. The German reception of Robertson, in regard to both its extent and immediacy—the volume of translations, of critical response, and reference—was, if anything, avid. Each of the four great histories appeared in, and was borrowed from, important academic libraries in Germany within a few months of publication. Each of them were equally promptly reviewed in German periodicals, and became swiftly translated into German, occasionally by several different hands simultaneously, and were republished and reedited in new versions over a period of several decades. The intensity of reception apparently contradicts the fact that it would be difficult to claim for Robertson a dramatic influence on the character of contemporary German historiography. This contradiction, however, makes the history of reception no less instructive.

In seeking to resolve this paradox, which is far from being exceptional in histories of reception, I propose to delve into the character of eighteenth-century historical writing in three different but interlocking forms: as political thought, as literary pursuit and aesthetic expression, and as a branch of knowledge with the emerging claim to the status of an academic discipline. These forms of appearance converged in Robertson's histories, while each of them were equally relevant in the Scottish environment where those histories were produced and the German one in which they were appropriated. The paradox both arises from, and is explained by, the rather different substances that filled each of these forms of cultivating history in the two cases. In unraveling such complexities, I shall predominantly rely on "state-of-the-art" research on eighteenth-century Scottish, German, and European historiography. But the comparative perspective I adopt may refine our understanding of the broader subject of this book: the possibilities and the limits of communication and transfer across linguistic and cultural boundaries within the enlightened republic of letters. I shall start with a discussion of intellectual developments on the wider European and the Scottish scene relevant to the shaping of a historical sensibility shared by Robertson with many contemporaries, and then move on to consider some peculiar features of German historical scholarship.

Stages, conjectures, narratives: Scottish history and the science of man

To begin with, it is important to remember that a great deal of historical writing in eighteenth-century Scotland continued to be conceived in terms of the themes of virtue and corruption, familiar from the humanist *historia magistra vitae* tradition. Philosophical history—the exploration of war, politics, and the *arcana imperii* in the style of Machiavelli and Guicciardini, with a view to inculcating the principles of conduct best suited to the preservation of the public good[1]—was alive and well, and formed part of Robertson's own initiation into the profession. It has also been argued forcefully that in regard to its commitment to the teaching of moral precepts and its "obsession" with providential determinism, Enlightenment historical writing owes a great deal to traditions of Scottish scholarship established in the aftermath of the Calvinist reformation, perpetuating much of its humanist principles, vocabulary, and conceptual toolkit.[2]

However, the historical culture that informed Robertson's oeuvre was marked by an attempt to understand these concepts (and make such traditions functional) against the background of new political, sociocultural, and international circumstances that emerged in Europe (which, in a well-known passage, he defined as "one great political system")[3] as the seventeenth century was fading into the eighteenth. The rise of the United Provinces, the Peace of Westphalia, the Glorious Revolution, and—certainly, in a very different way—even the revocation of the Edict of Nantes contributed to the ebbing away of religious and civil strife that had been almost the order of the day in Western European societies for the century and a half that followed the "protestation" of a part of the German estates at the imperial diet of Speyer in 1529. The peace settlement of Utrecht in 1713 seemed to have signaled the ultimate frustration of two centuries of attempts—by Holy Roman Emperors, but also Kings of Spain, and then of France—at reestablishing "universal monarchy" in Europe. Having resisted the dynastic ambition to exercise political and military control over extensive territories, the old continent came to be recognized as an assemblage of medium-sized states. In spite of the diversity of political, religious, and commercial interests that quite often threw them, individually or in coalitions, into armed conflict, they could be understood as constituting a neatly balanced system, even a "commonwealth" or "confederation" knit together by a strange blend of cooperation and emulation. In their conflicts as well as their conflict management practices, "jealousy of state" was being replaced by (or transformed into) "jealousy of trade" and political survival became dependent on success or failure in international markets. This was a development that gave rise to concerns, especially given that it seemed to contradict the enlightened topos about the inherently civilizing and pacifying potential of "sweet commerce" and material improvement.[4] To further complicate the picture, some of these "imperial" (in the ancient sense of "sovereign") states proved, and all of them were anxious to prove, themselves fitting cores of a type of empire well-suited to the times in being not continental and territorial, but overseas and commercial–colonial. All of this served to underline the significance of the economic realm for the social realities behind these historic developments, including the patterns of the production, consumption, circulation, and distribution of goods, and the agents of such processes, together with the cultural practices, habits, beliefs, and lifestyles peculiar to them.

Historical reflection in the eighteenth century could have hardly afforded not taking into account such conditions of emerging modernity. Even among these circumstances, neither history's traditional concern with and for public life nor the consequent endeavor to derive normative judgment and moral purpose from narrative was abandoned. But its horizons became broadened to include, besides politics, a social narrative responding to new interests among the potential readership. In the focus of such interests were the histories of "learning, arts, commerce, and manners," subjects that seemed "most useful and agreeable by themselves, or most suitable to their respective ways of life."[5] These interests indicate a preoccupation with specific modalities of social–civil life among the circumstances of modern refinement that were difficult to integrate into a traditional historical narration chiefly concerned with the chances and the hazards of *vita activa*. What was at stake was the self-image and self-esteem of a society, or rather its intellectually sophisticated and articulate members, who were increasingly aware of its indebtedness to commerce, together with the complex and invisible relations it created on the shifting boundaries between public and private life: relations which on the one hand set various kinds of limitations to the scope of political action, but at the same time also expanded that scope by redefining action deemed capable of generating civil virtue.

With respect to the civic sphere, commerce and the material well-being that it brought about was traditionally regarded as producing one of two dispositions, both of them conceived as forms of "corruption": a decrease of commitment to the public weal and a propensity to expropriate civic institutions for private aggrandizement. Such threats did not cease to haunt public moralists, which historians continued to be throughout the eighteenth century and beyond. They nevertheless keenly realized that as an antidote to its role in the lapse of civic institutions, commerce in both the strict and the metaphorical sense—as the exchange of material goods in the market hall as well as that of ideas and sentiments in the coffee house or the assembly room—performed valuable civilizing functions. By enhancing men's and women's character as sociable and communicative creatures, "commerce" enabled them to promote each other's well-being in a way that was different from, but not at all inferior to, participatory activism, and was better suited to the conditions of the eighteenth century. Given this awareness among some of its most outstanding practitioners, history began to drift away from its ultimately civic foundations, and its gaze began to incorporate the category of the social, a realm in which such interactions occurred. It did so by appropriating the perspective of what has become known as the enlightened "science of man."

At the core of this vast intellectual enterprise was the Augustinian–Epicurean anthropology of Robertson's fellow Edinburgh literati, Hume and Smith in the first place, who portrayed man as an essentially self-regarding and pleasure-seeking creature guided by interests and passions in his conduct and attitudes, and were challenged to ask fundamental questions about the apparent paradoxes of the relatively orderly and peaceful conditions they observed in the ever more complex societies of contemporary Europe.[6] Their explanations for the abatement of the "violent passions" of man, conceived in the terms of moral psychology and political economy, pointed toward a refined understanding of the notion of "unsocial sociability" that seemed to govern the realities of commercial modernity. *Ungesellige Geselligkeit* was, of course, Kant's later succinct formula for a whole paradigm of thought nearly two centuries old by his time.[7] It was first bred by the painful experience of religious and civil strife in the sixteenth and seventeenth centuries, but was eminently capable of application to more stable social situations, the chief regulative mechanism of which was commerce, depending on emulation as well as accommodation.

Methodologically, this inquiry into the human and the social constituted itself as a counterpart of seventeenth-century natural philosophy as cultivated by the members of the Royal Society, in the sense that as "empiricists and experimentalists," its practitioners disavowed the precepts of Aristotelian metaphysics and logic and presumed to arrive at first principles from the observed "facts" of nature—which in the case of the study of politics and society would be human nature. Building on skepticism and stoicism as well as historical and natural jurisprudence, thinkers in the paradigm of "unsocial sociability" conceived of men and women as interest-driven and sensual creatures, motivated by fear and suspicion, vanity or greed, but still—even as a result—inclined to behave in a sociable manner. Hugo Grotius, Thomas Hobbes, and Samuel Pufendorf portrayed humans as refraining from causing "wanton injury" while competing for mere subsistence because this would have authorized others (or the sovereign, instituted precisely for this purpose) to resort even to violent retaliation in order to maintain mutual security.[8] Besides and beyond the safety of life and limb, the Port Royal Jansenist Pierre Nicole also discovered in vanity a fundamental type of self-regarding motivation. Nicole suggested that for the sake of obtaining the recognition of their fellows, self-loving men were inclined to conform to virtuous codes of conduct. Montesquieu molded this idea into a comprehensive theory of monarchical government, the cement or "principle" of which was the quest for "honor" on the part of an ambitious aristocracy, and thus explored a distinctively historical dimension of "unsocial sociability" as an active force in shaping European modernity in a broad comparative perspective. The paradoxical divorce of the selfish motivation of an act from its potentially charitable effects was most openly stated in Bernard Mandeville's formula about "private vices, publick benefits."[9] The notion of the quest for material wealth through satisfying the daily needs of others (an "unintended consequence") then became the cornerstone of Smith's observations on the lack of "benevolence" among the primary motives of the butcher and the baker in serving their customers—but also including the idea of the "impartial spectator," which would evoke the desire, even in the butcher or the baker, not only to *earn* praise, but also to *be* "praiseworthy."[10]

In the sophisticated intellectual stances, summarized in an unduly synoptic fashion above, it is possible to detect a style of thinking that also informed eighteenth-century secularist, stadialist–materialist types of historical causality. For indeed, the theories that they put forward, and the realities that these theories meant to interpret, also called for a spacious analysis of the historical dynamics leading to the emergence of the modern commercial societies they analyzed. The perspective that they offered allowed a notion of the past as a series of continuities from which the present has unfolded, and it was by tracing this unfolding that the study of history could contribute to the science of man. Campaigns and battles, treaties and edicts, transgressions and assassinations, had hitherto been chiefly regarded to be the main substance of history as a chronological succession of events understood as *exempla*, and often also as providing a pedigree or justification for the present. Now they came to be viewed as dependent on and arising from processes of material and cultural progress or decline, as well as the operations of the mind, in which the role of human agency was a far more complicated matter to assess than in essentially political histories of virtue and corruption. On the one hand, the contexts in which action was taking place required an ever more complex effort at exploration and explanation, to the extent that such contexts began to form, to a very great extent, the substance of history itself. On the other hand, even as the constitutive elements of contexts, the histories of agents commonly regarded as lacking the capacity for "action" in the traditional (political) sense—primitive communities, women, and "private persons" in general—became discussed by authors with ever-increasing frequency.

The outcome was twofold. We tend to celebrate conjectural history, the theoretically stringent, materialistic study of the "great movements" of history through "stages," defined in terms of the dominant "mode of subsistence" toward "refinement," as the great contribution of Enlightenment historical thought and the practice of historical writing.[11] At the same time, such macro-sociological pursuits were in permanent dialogue with the quasi-biographical representation of the immediate environment of individual lives and the forces that shaped them. The success of the one enterprise, stadial history, depended on the consistency of methodological principles and their application, which made it possible to develop a distance from the subject of investigation characteristic of the sciences. As regards the other, it was also realized that in order to cultivate narrative history in the new style, with sensibility, empathy, and an appeal to emotion, the properties of creative literary genius as well as the insight of the moral philosopher were indispensable. Political history, and the political relevance assigned to history, underwent thorough changes that reflected these shifting emphases in the study of the past. Let us briefly examine these changes one after the other.

On the one hand, it was an important consequence of the preoccupation with the structural that instead of (or at least besides) the ups and downs, the glories and the scandals, the heroes and the villains of the political histories of individual nations, often represented in strongly partisan terms, there developed an increasing interest in locating such histories on the map of the "commonwealth" of European states and societies. This was described as a balancing system marked by a great deal of complementarity: its composite parts were drawn together by a complex web of ties resulting from political, religious, and commercial cooperation and emulation.[12] In this discourse, "Europe" replaced "Christendom," its history being understood as the progress of commerce and manners, of religious plurality and the rise of the rule of law in strong (predominantly monarchical) states, and it was in such terms that its exploration was set into a comparative framework with its significant, colonial "others." The "Enlightenment narrative" was a narrative of civil governments, more precisely of the processes whereby they emancipated themselves from the real or attempted universal monarchy of popes and emperors, and established their own character as "imperial" (that is, as above, sovereign) entities.[13] The Neapolitan Pietro Giannone provided, in his *Istoria civile del regno di Napoli* (1723), a history of largely unsuccessful resistance to usurpation by the Ecclesiastical State, which intruded into the (Roman) Empire and established one "empire" within another. In *Le Siècle de Louis XIV* (1751), Voltaire showed the significance of the "Ludovican moment" in its search for the foundations of the neoclassical perfection of courtly manners in the commerce and useful arts of the middle classes, as well as the subsequent emergence of a plurality of strong and cultivated states (*états policés*) under the leadership of France—but in emulation of it—resulting in a "confederation of Europe" succeeding the age of religious warfare and the threat of universal empire. Robertson's *History of Charles V* (1769) was an important and influential variation on the same theme. One of the chief messages of Edward Gibbon's six thick volumes exploring *The History of the Decline and Fall of the Roman Empire* (1776–1788) was also the ultimate frustration, in the long run, of the model of universal monarchy represented by Rome through the social and political system introduced by the barbarians.

Empire in the sense of political and military control over a vast territory was thus historically shown to be incompatible with European conditions. At the same time, the small or medium-sized states of the old continent (as "imperial" or sovereign states, in possession of the plenitude of the power of command over their populations and resources, whether monarchies or republics) were regarded as proper core areas of empires established on the principle and the practice that was newly recognized to provide for their unique dynamism as well as precarious equilibrium: the principle and the practice of commerce. The spread of commercial, mercantile, and maritime empires into regions previously unexplored by Europeans naturally stimulated the further deepening and sophistication of an already long-standing interest in the comparative and historical exploration of the patterns of socioeconomic development and cultural–anthropological differences. Accounts of the habitat, customs and manners, beliefs, occupations, and arts and crafts of noble and ignoble savages filled the pages of travelogues from the early eighteenth-century accounts of Baron de Lahontan and Joseph François Lafiteau onward (themselves looking back to eminent predecessors, such as the sixteenth-century Jesuit missionary José de Acosta). In combination with the intellectual patterns provided not only by social scientific inquiry, but also the rival systems of natural historical taxonomy put forward by Buffon and Linnaeus, the accounts of Lahontan and Lafiteau became used as source material in large-scale systematic treatments of "the history of man" ("in rude and cultivated ages," as some of them added in their titles) by Cornelius de Pauw, or indeed the Scots Lords Kames and Monboddo, and James Dunbar.[14] The process of European expansion was usually acknowledged to be compatible with the values of civilization and modernity, now being propagated globally. Yet there were doubters like Abbé Raynal, or Denis Diderot, who seems to have contributed the most polemical portions to the former's *Histoire des deux Indes*, or Edmund Burke. They were concerned that the physical removal of the agents of this process from the cradle of these values might turn them into "tigers" in the colonial jungle, whose depredation of local cultures and brutalization of native populations also threatened to undermine civilized conditions—including not only polite manners and sociable humanity but also civil liberty and security under the law—in their home countries.[15]

The Enlightenment narrative was cosmopolitan in the sense that while it endeavored to promote "patriotic" goals exactly in support of this pursuit—encouraging types of civic attitudes suited to the eighteenth-century realities, hinging upon the commitment to material improvement and to the preservation of sociability amidst competing interests—it could not afford operating in any other than broad European and global contexts. In a well-known comment on his own *History of England*, Hume distinguished between his account of "things," that is, events, processes, institutions, and structures, on the one hand, and "persons," on the other hand, adding that his views on the former were "more conformable to Whig principles" and on the latter to "Tory prejudices."[16] This is a very subtle distinction, in more ways than one. The two Stuart volumes of the *History*, which were the first to appear, seem to present a rather narrowly confined English history. This was a history chiefly preoccupied with the classical Tacitean and Thucydidean theme of prudent or—more often—imprudent statecraft exercised by "persons" for whose predicaments Hume indeed harbors a Toryish sympathy. Even in these volumes, however, a broader scheme of "things" emerges, which is marked by the endeavor of the English people to preserve or obtain constitutional liberty, and is cautiously Whiggish. This scheme, however, can be fully appreciated when the Stuart volumes are read in conjunction with the subsequently published Tudor and medieval parts, in which there is a greater emphasis on "things," and the distinctive, even anomalous character of the English quest for liberty receives its proper perspective from the placement of England within (or, to be more precise, at least partly outside) European developmental patterns. In regard to "things," both the completeness and the impartiality of representation depended on the adoption of a cosmopolitan and comparative perspective.

Besides and in complement to "things," however, it was also essential for the historian to consider "persons," which Hume cultivated mainly but not at all exclusively in the Stuart volumes. The interest in the "personal," the human, even psychological, generated an endeavor to understand character in a dynamic relationship with situation (as against, and beyond the motive and effect of action). In a highly subtle fashion, this also contributed to the neutralization of the themes of vice and virtue, and thus the tone of partisanship, familiar from patriotic renderings of history.[17] Progress, improvement, and public happiness, as well as manners, sympathy, and politeness, emerged as important threads in such histories, now marked by an effort at "impartiality" in this latter sense, too. Robertson's *History of Scotland* was conceived in an attempt to challenge ancient traditions of Scottish liberty and patriotism and to lay the foundations for an alternative one, better adjusted to the realities, imperatives, and opportunities created by the Union of Parliaments in 1707.[18] His history operated likewise at the level of large-scale comparative structural inquiry as well as personal–psychological analysis, with both endeavors arising from the same inspiration and pointing in the same direction. While its backbone was a narrative of statecraft and political action in a century of endemic trouble for Scotland, the character and the dimension of the trouble was impossible to assess fully without the introductory canvas of sociocultural developments in contemporary Europe. The account of these developments showed the public scene of Scotland, presented in the subsequent narrative, almost irredeemably captive to the rude passions of resentment and revenge,[19] and thus to be following a rhythm entirely different from the countries in the vanguard of the progress of civilization. Equally indispensable for the desired effect of a realistic and responsible understanding of the national past was, however, a view of historical figures that, without condoning their frailties or crimes, divested them of the increments of party sentiment and thus their status as political emblems, and focused on their character as necessarily imperfect human beings facing complex, even unsolvable situations.

It has been argued that the claims about the intellectually innovative character of historical scholarship in the Scottish Enlightenment are to a considerable extent based (1) on the self-fashioning (and self-congratulation) of a handful of thinkers who constituted an "inner circle" and (2) on a kind of reading history backward by later thinkers who picked the former as their own predecessors. It has been further pointed out that (3) even this "vanguard" was in fact far more indebted to native traditions of historical inquiry than it cared to acknowledge and (4) inasmuch as it departed from those traditions, it also found itself seriously challenged. In other words, we must appreciate the degree of continuity in several crucial respects. First, no fundamental change is supposed to have occurred in regard of the status which history had held in humanism and Calvinism as an edificatory discourse and a form of knowledge intended to inculcate values of political leadership. History thus preserved its polemical commitment and the desire to articulate moral and social purposes. Second, historical methodology, especially causality, was also of interest, still, for moral and public as much as for purely scientific or philosophical reasons.[20]

In several crucial respects, Robertson was no exception. We have been reminded that his forays into the apparently more avant-garde domains of "theoretical history" have obscured the fact that the bulk of his output is conceived in terms of (a predominantly political) narrative, with "the character of men and manners" at its center. Moreover, even though it is important to observe that "character" for him no longer serves an exemplary function but is historicized, thus becoming a tool for social analysis as well as a literary device, Robertson's "philosophical" discussions (which seem to break up the unity of some of his works) essentially served such newly conceived narrative purposes. At the same time, scholars have also suggested that in his narrative of action Robertson transcended the limitations imposed by stadial forms of history, with which his name is usually associated, and that, in fact, he wrote an enriched and innovative version of narrative history at a time when it was subject to critical pressure. In the process, marked by a quest for "truthful ways of writing" about history, he also realized that the principles of historiography are not immutable and allowed the theoretical assumptions of his work to be modified by the qualities of the subject.[21] It must also be reemphasized that stadialism was by no means incompatible for him as a principle of causality with providentialism.[22] Finally, given his titles and roles as principal of the University of Edinburgh, as Historiographer Royal, and especially as Moderator of the General Assembly of the Scottish *Kirk*, he could have hardly afforded an aloofness vis-à-vis the public–political debates of the times. It is a matter of course that the agendas he pursued in these debates infiltrate the themes he addressed and the arguments he developed as a historian, and while each of these, in general, can be readily associated with "moderatism," on some subjects his position is found close to traditional Presbyterianism.[23]

Robertson's character as an essentially political historian who derived the very topic of his major works from developments and challenges experienced on the scene of contemporary domestic and international politics has also been reemphasized. His own and his fellow Moderates' views were powerfully shaped by the experience of populist evangelical fervor and the atmosphere of theological faction that marred Scotland in the 1740s, not to speak of the civil warfare of 1745, when he joined the Edinburgh Volunteers to defend the city against Charles Stuart and the Jacobite army.[24] It could have been no coincidence that the historical work that first earned him fame as an author addressed a period of the Scottish past notorious on account of its religious and civil turbulence. His second great historical saga explored the first episode in the formation of the system of European balance of power at a time when Britain was emerging from a protracted war, one of the major stakes of which was the preservation of that system after the "diplomatic revolution" of 1756. From this perspective, the masterly sketch of the development of social structures over a whole millennium on a continent-wide scale in the voluminous preface to the *History of Charles V* appears as an anomalous digression, needed to explain the emergence of states with a vastly enhanced capacity to wage war by the beginning of the modern era. Similarly, the philosophical analysis of the "savage character" in the celebrated Book IV of the *History of America* may have been motivated less by the ambition to contribute an innovative piece of anthropology, and more by a realization of the difficulty that civilized Scottish Lowlanders had in accommodating their primitive compatriots of the Highlands, or the disadvantages suffered by British troops in North America because of the superior skills displayed by the French in negotiating with the Iroquois.[25] One might add that Robertson's late masterpiece on the intercourse of Europeans with the Indian subcontinent over the whole of recorded history was written at a time when Britain, having lost one colonial empire, had just gained another—only to be almost immediately confronted with the problem of colonial mismanagement, culminating in the spectacular political case of the times, the parliamentary prosecution of Warren Hastings, governor general of the British East India Company.[26] In this sense, it is undoubtedly tempting to conceive of Robertson's historiography "as counsel to the statesmen of his day."[27]

And yet these perceptive qualifiers tend to confirm rather than undermine the view that we have become accustomed to form about the distinctiveness of Robertson and the historical culture for which his name stands. They do not affect but, on the contrary, serve to put in sharper relief his character as a "cosmopolitan" historian whose patriotism drew inspiration not from the vainglory of the putative medieval liberties of Scotland but from the standards which his comparative explorations identified in Europe's gradual progress toward cultural refinement, socioeconomic well-being, and political stability. He derived these standards not from the narrative of "the character of men," which lacked any explanatory force of its own, but was rather to be explained through generalizations about "the character of manners," allowed by the stadialist approach. Even in cases in which the character and conduct of a people, like the Mexicans or Peruvians, seem to emerge "from outside the typology of philosophical history," they are recorded as anomalies that are strange, but ultimately not as ones that challenge the pattern.[28] The same was also instrumental for Robertson's specific profession of "impartiality": one not (necessarily) based on independence from party (like in the case of Hume), nor on skepticism (like Gibbon), but on the endeavor to grasp and express the unlimited wholeness of history, as far as this was at all possible.[29] At the same time, another key to impartiality is provided by the almost literary sensitivity toward individual character[30]—of Mary Queen of the Scots, Charles V, Maurice of Saxony, Henry the Navigator, Christopher Columbus, Hernán Cortes, and so forth. Similarly to the employing of stadial patterns (but also pointing beyond them), this sensitivity led Robertson to make it an absolute priority to register the fullness of historical phenomena, as against passing judgment over them.

In all these respects he participated in the methodological and theoretical explorations described earlier in this chapter, and departed from the ground occupied by a host of historians with whom he shared in the rightly stressed continuities. An overview of Robertson's making as a historian, in combination with his public roles, will support this claim. In the late 1730s, the lectures of Charles Mackie, the first professor of universal history at the University of Edinburgh, provided Robertson with a great deal of inspiration and a lasting commitment to philosophical history[31] (a version of history whose task was to provide a selective narrative of events with a view to revealing men's moral and political character) and to highlighting "by example" to readers or listeners the principles conducive to the preservation or the subversion of the public good. Adopting this scheme of explanation depended on the historian's willingness to regard past historical agents as his contemporaries whose actions could be judged by timeless standards of morality. Even the kind of relativism introduced by Machiavelli could be accommodated in this scheme: the circumstances that warranted conduct of otherwise questionable morality were themselves entirely contingent in the sense that they might occur with equal probability in any age or society. It was in the late 1740s that Robertson, already having embarked on the research toward his first great work, was confronted with the kind of historical approach that he would embrace and apply consistently in his own narratives. Montesquieu's preoccupation with the effects of the physical environment and the historical principles that animated the laws and customs of an age and determined the spirit of the people made a deep impression on him. So did Hume's alternative to Montesquieu, suggesting that the moral determinants of national character had to do with political, legal, religious, and cultural institutions, rather than geography or climate. Above all, Robertson seems to have become inspired with the system of historical jurisprudence which the young Adam Smith outlined in a series of lectures in Edinburgh in 1748–1750. Smith endeavored to show that the principles of justice and politics depended on sentiments, manners, and customs, which, in turn, were themselves functions of the means of subsistence and the distribution of property; and also combined these observations with a theory of the stadial progress of civilization from rudeness to refinement, or hunting-gathering to shepherding and agriculture to commerce.[32] It is important to reemphasize that, while these were genuinely new intellectual departures, they were heavily indebted to the radical conceptual distinction between the "state of nature" and the "civil state" introduced by modern natural law, to whose temporalization they greatly contributed by introducing ever more historical nuance, and to whose transformation into an empirical inquiry they provided plenty of ammunition.[33]

Needless to say, this approach constituted a challenge for the philosophical historian, especially if that historian was as good a Christian as may be expected from a devoted and ambitious minister and moderator of the established *Kirk* of Scotland. In terms of stadial or "conjectural" history, people who lived in civilizations different from one's own were separated by a cultural chasm to the extent that they not only possessed different manners and opinions, but even different minds and selves. Any attempt to assess their moral, political, or other virtues by standards other than their own was "wrong," not only in the sense of being unfair toward the objects of the investigation, but also methodologically incorrect and therefore inevitably doomed to failure. Most disturbingly, then, it became unclear what lessons the modern reader could learn by studying the past. Especially perplexing was the question of what the knowledge of the progress of civilization could reveal about the eternal and unchanging mind of God.

Robertson's solution to this problem was befitting the man of synthesis he was in his scholarship and the man of compromise he was in his politics. As to the latter, recent convincing demonstrations of his strong and principled commitment to Presbyterianism as the purest form of Christian doctrine and the best form of church government (in particular, vis-à-vis Catholicism and Anglicanism) certainly undermine his image as a champion of universal enlightened tolerance, if our standard of "Enlightenment" is that of an uncompromising movement toward a fully secularized and egalitarian world.[34] But they at best qualify and enrich his image as the leader and most influential voice in a party still styled as "moderate," which during his tenure as moderator of the General Assembly of the Church of Scotland and beyond[35] was willing to make gestures toward Episcopalians and Catholics on a principle of Enlightenment that focused on the chances of human betterment in this world while also mindful of the next (even when such gestures were ill at ease with their theological or ecclesiological views).[36] The case is similar with Robertson's endeavor to understand the history of the Western world—of Scotland in her relations with Europe and of Europe in its relations with the widening overseas spaces—in terms of the ever-increasing access to the full richness of the Gospel *through* material and cultural progress and refinement, in the lack of which any revelation of the primitive Christians could only have been incomplete. Conversely, Robertson was also convinced, and illustrated it with many examples throughout his oeuvre as a historian, that without the necessary foundations in Christian revelation, the morality established upon the grounds of natural progress is incomplete and uncertain; although self-interest is generally compatible with ethical conduct, in some cases vice remains unpunished and virtue remains unrewarded in this world, and hence the need for a belief in the next one.[37] In this sense, Robertson's was a Christian Enlightenment, which he shared with his fellow Moderates (leaving Hume and Smith the outstanding exceptions of the Scottish Enlightenment), and which made a strong imprint on his outlook as a historian.

The nature and extent of the distinctiveness of this outlook is discussed in greater detail in chapter 3, and is further underlined by a comparison between his approach to history and the methodological assumptions, thematic preoccupations, and professional concerns of eighteenth-century German practitioners of the field, which presumably, to some extent at least, also informed the expectations that Robertson's German interpreters and readers harbored toward his texts. In many ways, the historical interest of the Scottish Enlightenment was present-oriented, and from this point of view the situation in contemporary Germany was not substantially different. In both cases, history was cultivated predominantly in order to show how the present arose from the past, and, consequently, how the nature of the present—and the future—can be better understood through the study of the past. What was different was the present, or rather the vision of the present, and its aspects that history was expected to highlight.

Varieties of *Geschichte*, toward *Wissenschaft*

Hume's assertion about Scotland being the "historical nation" (and his age being the historical century)[38] could be equally claimed for Germany, and the deep anchorage of the "historicist" approach to the past in eighteenth-century German culture has received a great deal of scholarly attention in the past few decades.[39] One way of assessing the differences between the historical culture that bred Robertson and the one in which the German transmitters of his texts were raised, is to locate them on the contemporary maps of learned inquiry. The "neighbor disciplines" to which Robertson's historiography was chiefly indebted were clearly the ones which constituted the Edinburgh-style "science of man": historical and natural jurisprudence, combined with political economy and moral philosophy which, with an interest in the social dynamics arising from different "modes of subsistence" as well as the psychological and physiological aspects of the human condition, came close to the commitment of modern anthropology to the study of "culture" as a complex system. A comparable *Wissenschaft vom Menschen* was indeed arising in contemporary Germany as well, in particular at and around the University of Göttingen,[40] with which, as we shall see in the ensuing chapters, not a few of the individuals involved in the reception of Robertson's works were connected. However, even at Göttingen, the consolidation of the psychological and ethnological components of the "anthropological turn" seem to have much preceded the transformation of cameralist science into *Nationalökonomie*, a process which, together with the questioning of academic statistics, also led to a shift within the state sciences (*Staatswissenschaften*) from concern with the state itself to "civil society." The former process, with the appearance of philosophical anthropology (after the earlier rise of physical anthropology and ethnography) was in full gear by the 1760s, but the latter one did not seriously commence until the 1790s, coinciding with and inspired greatly by the "second reception" of Smith's *Wealth of Nations*.[41] In other words, there was a phase displacement, which was of some consequence for the chances and the ways in which history might constitute itself as one of the "sciences of man," and concerned exactly the period when Robertson's four major histories were published in Britain as well as in Germany. Anthropology was acknowledged to have arisen out of moral philosophy and theology in regard to its "philosophical" aspects and out of anatomy and zoology in regard to its "physical" aspects; ethnology, on the other hand, as a comprehensive *Völkerkunde* was a par excellence historical discipline, heavily indebted to geography and linguistics. The strong historicity of the Smithian (and Humean) economic analysis of commercial modernity was also recognized by German commentators. Characteristically, however, the authoritative German reviewer of both the original and the first translation of the *Wealth of Nations*, the Göttingen philosopher Johann Georg Heinrich Feder, failed to point out the continuities between it and the *Theory of Moral Sentiments*[42]—an early manifestation of what later came to be known as *das Adam Smith Problem*. This lopsidedness in Feder's assessment of Smith resembles the perspective of the reviewers of Scottish historical texts in the *Göttingische Anzeigen von gelehrten Sachen*. They were almost invariably enthusiastic about the abandonment by Hume, Robertson, Millar, and others of wars, kings, and dynasties as their principal focus, which August Ludwig Schlözer later on described as suited to the tastes of the "Anno Domini men of the Middle Ages."[43] However, they took very little notice of the Scottish Enlightenment idea of "progress" as dependent on the succession of systems of production and distribution or "modes of subsistence."[44] *Geschichten der Menschheit*—the very name of the genre signaling an endeavor to locate history among the "sciences of man"—flourished to an astonishing extent in Germany in the 1760s to the 1780s, and while the authors of works whose titles included this compound tended to hold chairs in philosophy rather than history, the foremost professional historians also employed the perspective offered by the concept. But the kind of history of cultural forms toward which it points is little concerned with the ways in which these forms are related to needs and the provision for them.[45]

As regards the further traditions of historical inquiry *per se* relevant in the German recipient environment of Robertson's works, they were numerous and diverse. Some of them directly answered the need for history to talk to the present in ways that arose from Germany's recent and current political predicament, and reflected the fact that in this sense the 1648 Osnabrück–Münster Peace Settlement represented for her what 1707 and the Union of Parliaments was for Great Britain, and the Utrecht peace treaty system of 1713 for Europe and its colonial dependencies. The federative character and the religious and institutional pluralism of the Holy Roman Empire, which the Westphalian system preserved in defiance of Habsburg efforts at imperialism, inspired a great deal of *Reichshistorie* or "imperial history," with a focus on the legal and constitutional distinctiveness of the empire.[46] The same outcome of the Thirty Years' War, however, can also be detected in the background of *Landesgeschichte*, the histories of the particular territorial states whose specific internal arrangements constituted the immediate reality in which the *Aufklärer* lived and worked.[47] These genres were instrumental in the formation and expression of identities on local, regional, and national scales.[48] At the same time, it is important to note that while *narratio* and *exemplum*, the long-established means of pursuing such ends through historical representation, continued to characterize especially *Landesgeschichte* into the 1760s, from then on the horizons of both types of inquiry increasingly came to embrace the entirety of the *Verfassung* or constitution of their respective domains, in the comprehensive sense of the interactions between the prevailing governmental–administrative, sociocultural, and geographic–economic systems.

This move, however, together with the emergence of a more genetic and analytical thrust in imperial and regional history, owed a great deal to the rise of *Universalgeschichte* as another relatively recent development in German historical scholarship. Universal history was understood as a systematic but not speculative rendering of the flux of history, weaving together the important threads of national histories in a single narrative after carefully weighing the significance of data and paying due attention to cause and effect. One of its early promoters, the first of the great history professors at Göttingen, Johann Christoph Gatterer,[49] campaigned to have it supplant *Völkergeschichte*, a genre of respectable pedigree, which he considered a mechanical registration of successive events and a mere assemblage of national histories. Gatterer thought that "the well-known work of the English approaches in some particulars the outlines of such a general history of the world"[50]—but he also added that a history like this was yet to be written. The German edition of the encyclopedic English *Universal History* was at that time already under heavy attack by his younger colleague August Ludwig Schlözer.[51] It might be added that Gatterer's own specific recommendations on how to approach the task of writing universal history and his practice as an author of historical texts hardly reflected the principles he enunciated. While he spoke of the necessary "preoccupations" (*Beschäftigungen*) of the historian, implying that the field was still understood by him mainly as a research subject, Schlözer conceived of it in terms of methods specific to it.[52] In Schlözer's rendering, the "mighty glimpse" of universal history "molds the aggregate into a system...and regards the nations merely in terms of their relationship to the great changes in the world"; it "grows out from the particular histories, but as it orders these into a lucid whole it gratefully throws light on each of these parts."[53] In other words, universal history was conceptualized as an epitome of history and a symbiotic system of causal connections that was more than an aggregate of its constituent elements.[54] Thus defined, it became an important vehicle of the overall separation of *Geschichte* as a "collective singular" from *Historien*, which exhibits the pursuit of "the truth" in the line of mere *narratio* or is preoccupied with ethical and political ends, rather than being epistemologically motivated, organized by the inquiring subject himself, or striving to produce new knowledge. In virtue of the features now associated with universal history, it came to be viewed as capable of theorization and generalization, in a word, of operating *as* philosophy: of being elevated from the rank of mere fact-finding to that of a cognitive process in pursuit of regularities or "laws" peculiar to the field.[55]

As another aspect of the German-style "scientization" (*Verwissenschaftlichung*) of history, as the process came to be described in retrospect, each of the above-mentioned kinds of history were cultivated with a heightened philological awareness, inherited from humanism.[56] Thus they were on the way of being developed into the "philological–critical method," and also a refined historical hermeneutics. In terms of the skills required from the expert historian, in the German context perhaps more than any other it was especially these latter two features that were supposed to make history answer the newly conceived, eighteenth-century criteria of "science": the knowledge of causes acquired through the application of strict methodological principles, resulting in critically demonstrated probability, concerning a clearly defined and delimited subject matter, and in the case of history, man and humanity.[57] Under the impact of philology, both as an auxiliary science and as a methodology, the very aim of historical inquiry in Germany became transformed into the reconstruction of historical "facts" through the study and interpretation of original documents.[58] The "critical" character of historical research was to be manifest no longer merely in the criticism of earlier accounts, but in the exercise of the researcher's philological skills in the uncovering and weighing of new evidence as the foundation of historical representation. To be sure, this was a philology, the scope of which was expanded, first, to embrace a broad spectrum of disciplines from Biblical studies and classics to jurisprudence, and, second, to replace a purely linguistic and lexicographical analysis of texts with a hermeneutic approach that saw the source as the manifestation of a culture.[59] This was the sense in which the practitioners of the field sought to establish the "immanence" of history. Against such a background, it is no wonder that Robertson's sometimes cavalier treatment of the sources, while in his own understanding supportive of the cause of "impartiality," met incomprehension or criticism among his German reviewers and editors. In respect to historical taste, synthesis, interpretation, and presentation, Robertson—as well as other Scottish (and in general British and French) Enlightenment historians—were readily acknowledged to represent models for German historical writing. However, they were not found "critical enough" when measured against the standards of the new philological–hermeneutical approach developed and employed by scholars like the Göttingen classical scholar and a philologist par excellence Christian Gottlob Heyne, or historians of the make of Schlözer and his colleague Ludwig Timotheus Spittler.[60]

But this was neither all that different from the kind of commentary Robertson quite often received from Scottish colleagues (a paramount and well-researched example being Gilbert Stuart[61]), nor was it the main feature of, and the main reason for, the anomalies in the reception. It has been suggested that despite the interest which Germans took in contemporary British historical works, the actual "influence" of the latter was limited by a number of factors including the differences in the level of professionalization and the nature of the public. For the Britons, history was a literary genre with a need for greater scholarly accuracy that was keenly recognized, yet it was aimed at an expanding educated public. In Germany, by contrast, the lack or weakness of such a public throughout most of the eighteenth century went together with the concentration of history as a discipline in the universities and its consequent emergence as a highly specialized branch of knowledge cultivated by and for a narrowly defined community of scholars. In this interpretation, these features of the German scene are linked to the weakness of "civil society" and the pettiness of the estates-dominated German *Kleinstaaterei* (system of small states).[62]

While this explanation bears the stamp of the *Sonderweg* theory and therefore deserves to be treated with caution, it does not appear inaccurate. In spite of the demonstrated expansion of the German literary public during the 1760s to the 1780s, it is reasonable to assume that the lack of a "German Robertson" (or Gibbon, or Hume) can be explained in terms of a lack of demand for historical works that combined large-scale structural analysis with literary merit. While Schlözer, in particular, succeeded in amalgamating the philological and critical tradition with a broadly comparative approach and a heightened attention to the ethnographic and material bases of history, the narrative quality of his texts is patently inferior. Spittler did aspire to transform history into a more readable genre, but it was not until the late 1780s, with Johannes von Müller's *Geschichten schweizerischer Eidgenossenschaften* (1786) and Friedrich Schiller's two works, the *Abfall der vereinigten Niederlande von der Spanischen Regierung* (1788) and the *Geschichte des Dreyßigjärigen Krieges* (1792), that a "primarily literary form of historical writing" established itself in Germany.[63] Even then, Schiller's call to "ennoble science into work of art" seems to have remained a minority endeavor, or a largely unsuccessful one if we are to believe August Wilhelm Schlegel's complaint on behalf of the refined German readers concerning the lack of a "grander style" and comprehensive meaning in the works published by contemporary historians; perhaps a pointer to an emerging discrepancy between the concerns of professionals and the interests of the broader public.[64] In other words, a "phase displacement" similar to the one mentioned earlier in regard of the rise of the Göttingen *Wissenschaft vom Menschen* can also be detected in the development of the relationship between a purportedly scientific history and its appropriate narrative form.

Whatever these circumstances may have to do with *Kleinstaaterei*, I would rather draw attention to some of the consequences which derive from Germany's political fragmentation to eighteenth-century historical inquiry in a less socially deterministic fashion, and which arise more directly from the stakes and the appropriate subject matter of such inquiry, in view of its already mentioned "presentism." These stakes were enlightened in the same sense as in Robertson's Enlightenment histories, concerned as they were with the growth and the chances of political stability, denominational peace, legal security, and material improvement. For many eighteenth-century Germans, such chances seemed to be predicated to a considerable extent on the specific structure of the Holy Roman Empire of the German Nation, as it became consolidated, even almost literally enshrined, after the traumas of the Thirty Years' War in the peace settlement of Münster and Osnabrück in 1648. As a counterpart of Robertson's modern Europe on a broader scale, the Westphalian system was conceived as one of the equilibrium of larger and smaller states *within* Germany, characterized by the plurality of political and religious establishments. Germany's fragmentation became consecrated and institutionalized as an internal "balance of powers," the maintenance of which was seen as indispensable for its continent-wide equivalent, too. The immobility secured by the intricate system of checks and balances, already existing before 1648 but further refined then and afterwards, seemed a promoter of stability to be celebrated, at least in the eyes of the more powerful imperial estates of the "Third Germany," which harbored increasing concerns in regard to the rise of Brandenburg and the ensuing Austro-Prussian dualism. A respectable range of external observers, from Montesquieu, and—oddly—Rousseau, to Burke also commended German "federalism" as an ideal type that could be invoked to oppose political centralization in general.[65] On a European scale, one might argue that the key to the balance was the existence of this "dead mass," lacking a unitary political will and situated in the heart of the continent, separating the hostile great powers from one another and possessing enough strength to protect its own independence but not enough to constitute a threat to them. Internally, there also seemed to be advantages that compensated for the political paralysis arising from the territorial fragmentation of the Holy Roman Empire: a "diversity in the forms and policies of governments, in social structures and attitudes, in cultural and educational milieus, in religions, in economic activities and levels of well-being," providing "Germans with choices which citizens of other countries did not have."[66]

For this state of affairs, the existence of an "imperial constitution" that eschewed universal monarchy and vested the composite parts of the assemblage with considerable powers to provide for the civil, spiritual, and material well-being of their subjects was deemed essential. As an early dissenting voice, in 1667, Pufendorf notoriously described the "state of the German Empire" as *monstro simile*: neither a monarchy, an aristocracy, a democracy, nor a federation; it looked to him like an irregular conjunction of its constituent parts, some of them commanded as quasi-sovereign regions by powerful states external to it.[67] Nevertheless, the *Reich* and its constitution was, for figures from Pufendorf's senior contemporary Hermann Conring to Johann Stephan Pütter a century later, a political self-evidence throughout the later seventeenth and eighteenth centuries for scholars interested in the exploration of German *ius publicum* as a system of civil liberty and security. This pursuit was inconceivable without the reconstruction of the history of the emergence of this system, implying attention to factors such as customs and climate besides laws and institutions. The gradual development of the existing structures passed for a strong argument in their favor as the key to their "appropriateness": the proposition that as the imperial constitution had organically evolved over many centuries, it had come to incorporate the character of the nation, and thus there had emerged a correspondence between its political order and its political culture.[68]

Hence, the preoccupation also with *Teutsche Staats-Historie* (German political history), among scholars of diverse disciplines who were both imperial and local patriots, was widespread. The paramount example of this brand of scholar was Johann Jakob Moser (1701–1785), the first to have produced a comprehensive empirical account of German public law in compendia that ran into several dozens of volumes.[69] Moser claimed to have written more history than almost anybody else, even though his avowed aim was to emancipate public law from history. In the given context, however, this meant that the emancipation was to be mutual. Moser called history to the aid of law not as a source of any validating power but as a tool promoting its better understanding, that is, as a means (a better one than logic) for uncovering the meaning of law through showing the context of documentary materials and traditions, the interests and prejudices that framed it, and for sifting these from valid law. As such, history checked rather than established or enhanced the power of the past over the present. It was invested by Moser with a public–political significance, but exactly as a safeguard against false analogy and anachronism.[70]

The role of historical analysis as an indispensable auxiliary science, or indeed an almost independent dimension of any discipline within the university canon that concerned the operation of the state, was far from being confined to the case of law. Besides providing for good government by making and administering law, the state came to be increasingly recognized as committed to performing the same task in the proper management of the resources of the territory where she was sovereign, for the sake of improving the condition of the subjects, this in itself conceived as the ultimate ground for its legitimacy. At its root, this recognition was indebted both to the traditions of urban government, initially aimed to ensure the good morals and the maintenance of order by *Polizey-Ordnungen*, and to the understanding of the political community in the natural jurisprudence of Althusius and Pufendorf. It received further impetus from the cameralist tradition initiated in the seventeenth century by Joachim Becher, Wilhelm von Schröder, and Philipp Wilhelm von Hörnigk. By the eighteenth century, these tendencies coalesced into a cluster of university-based scientific disciplines: *Kameralwissenschaft* (focusing on the economic theory of the state), *Polizeywissenschaft* (concerned with organizational–institutional aspects), and *Staatistik* (the statistical rendering of knowledge about the state in facts and figures). Together, they constituted the science of the pragmatic, target-oriented fathoming, the registering and allocating of resources with a view to their best utilization.[71] Exercising command over such resources, protected under the imperial "ancient constitution," the *Kleinstaat*, however "narrow" or "petty," was confidently believed to be capable of providing for the enlightened goals sought in different contexts across Europe, including Robertson's Edinburgh as well as so many centers of learning in the German Enlightenment. As was the case with jurisprudence, the new state science also developed its historical counterpart: *historische Staatslehre*, a kind of natural history of the state that had the potential of practical application as "the past of the present." It was in the comprehensive sense of the state sciences outlined above that Schlözer conceived of history as the history of the state, and claimed that "according to the novel taste, the history of the state is a continuous state science, just as the latter is history of the state standing still."[72]

It is no wonder that, as we shall see in the chapters that follow, several protagonists in the German reception history of Robertson's works—not only scholars active in the translation and the reviewing of these works, but also those whose academic contributions were quoted as a frame of reference for approaching Robertson—were recruited from the fields of inquiry just listed. One may conclude this bird's-eye overview of the Scottish and German historical discourses that seem relevant to the reception of Robertson with the proposition that similar questions were not only answered in different ways, but that the answers were also gleaned from different intellectual and academic pursuits, similar to many other cases of Europe in the Enlightenment. At least this is what we learn from a survey of the public–political context of the reception of Robertson's histories in Germany. At the same time, as a final remark it must be added that in both the Scottish and the German context the status of history as a scholarly field was enhanced by the important recognition that all scientific "truth" is based on the description and understanding of real phenomena that have occurred and the relations that exist between them; scientific explanation *per se* is essentially historical, which means nevertheless the apprehension of a causal connection, rapport, and "milieu," instead of a mere succession. This conviction, ultimately derived from Buffon's critique of the mathematical method and his general assault on mechanical philosophy, led to a historicization of nature and the naturalization of history.[73] While this development was rather conspicuous among the literati in Robertson's environment, most of the scholars involved in the immediate German response to Robertson were little affected by it. But here comes an ultimate qualifier: the accomplishment of Georg Forster (anglophile, circumnavigator, naturalist, and revolutionary), who played a complex part in the German reception of Robertson's work on America and India, is an ideal subject for studying the infiltration of the historical into the modern scientific imagination. As such, it also serves as a reminder that it is of little value to conceive of the Scottish and the German Enlightenment in terms of simple dichotomies.

2
Time and Progress, Time as Progress: History by Way of Enlightened Preaching

On January 6, 1755, 33-year-old Robertson preached the annual sermon of the Scottish Society for the Propagation of Christian Knowledge upon the invitation of its governors. The society had been established in 1709 shortly after the Union of Parliaments with the goal of inculcating religion and virtue in the Scottish Highlands and other "uncivilized" (including colonial) areas, in part to counter Roman Catholic missionary activity.[1] The pernicious potential that "popery" held to the 1707 settlement became manifest through the active support of Catholics for the Young Pretender in 1745, when Robertson strongly committed himself in favor of the status quo. During the ensuing decade, Robertson emerged as a recognized member of the Edinburgh social, ecclesiastical, and intellectual scene, and a leading figure in the "Moderate Party" of the Scottish Presbyterian church. The Moderates were endeavoring to alleviate doctrinally based zealotry among the popular wing of the clergy through the control of parish appointments by powerful lay patrons, as a means to secure social order, and nevertheless continued to ward off Catholicism.[2] From this perspective, the invitation of Robertson by the governors of the society was a political act, and the sermon itself a political text: in its concluding remarks, Robertson reminded that "in this neglected field [i.e., the Highlands], the enemies of our religion and liberty have sown the seeds of the worst superstition, and the most pernicious principles of government."[3] At the same time, *The Situation of the World at the Time of Christ's Appearance* (his first published text and his only published sermon) is also a concise but sophisticated piece of theoretical reflection on issues central to historical interpretation. It is helpful to introduce the discussion of these aspects of the sermon by recalling the argument of Reinhart Koselleck in the opening essays of his seminal *Futures Past*, where he offers an engaging and succinct illustration of the course of what he calls the "temporalization of history" in European thought during the early modern period.

Koselleck conceives this process in terms of the changes in the perception of the "compression" (or "acceleration") of time that, supposedly, precedes the onset of the future in the thought of these past generations: "For Luther, the compression of time is a visible sign that, according to God's will, the Final Judgment is imminent, that the world is about to end. For Robespierre, the acceleration of time is a task of men leading to an epoch of happiness, the golden future."[4] In the intervening period, experience showed that religious and civil wars did not herald the Final Judgment, at least not in the direct manner previously envisaged: first, the absolutist state suppressed prophecy, while humanists and skeptics revealed its psychology, undermining oracles and associated superstitions; second, as a "counter-concept" of prophecy, rational prognosis marked out new horizons for the future by both remaining within the dimensions of the (political) situation and attempting to change it or "relat[ing] to events whose novelty it releases"; finally, in the eighteenth century the appearance of the philosophy of the historical process, which exploits the notion of progress in order to combine rational prediction with salvational expectation, "inaugurated our modernity with a new future."[5] Koselleck further states: "Acceleration, initially perceived in terms of an apocalyptic expectation of temporal abbreviation heralding the Last Judgment, transformed itself—also from the mid-eighteenth century—into a concept of historical hope."[6]

Agency and event, Christian and other times: "progressive revelation"

Robertson's sermon is an excellent medium to approach what might be described in Koselleck's terms as the very moment of this transformation. However, it also allows us to point to certain limitations in this transformation, ones which existed within the discourse of the Enlightenment; it prompts us to express some reservation and offer correctives to the approach that associates the Enlightenment with "secularization" and "critical spirit." Despite the profoundly nuanced character of Koselleck's presentation, this image is a leitmotif in his work.[7] Despite its sophistication, the Koselleckian typology of conceptualizations of time is still teleological, in the sense that according to its premises, any approach that marries Christian stories (endeavors and expectations) of salvation with those of the improvement of the temporal condition of man is likely to be divested of its intellectual distinctiveness and discussed as a transitional position, at some distance both from pre-modern "origins" and modern "culminations." For the purposes of this chapter, Robertson must be regarded as a Christian historian who was at the same time one of the outstanding masters of enriching the "enlightened narrative" with the perspective of "stadial history," most commonly associated with Adam Smith and the French physiocrats.[8] He understood the history of the western world as the unfolding of the great plan of providence, a gradually increasing accessibility of the divine revelation, a process which in his view crucially depended on, but also furthered, the improvement of the means of subsistence, and the consequent refinement of manners and enlightenment of the human mind. There is reason to believe that Robertson's hardly paralleled contemporary popularity as an author of historical works was to a considerable extent due to his power in representing this synthesis—for which, however, taking account of the problematic relationship between Christian and secular understandings of time was an important theoretical condition. This, I want to suggest, is one of the tasks performed in Robertson's early sermon, published at a time when he was also busy working on the historical narrative that established his literary fame.

Before turning to the sermon, it will be useful to address two questions. The first one concerns the nature of the challenges and dilemmas that the adoption of a stadialist–relativist position implied for a scholar desirous of retaining a Christian framework of interpretation. The second question, and not unrelated to the above, is Robertson's theology—or rather the little that can be known about the theology of an influential minister whose public statements about the church concerned its social role rather than its doctrine, who left no autobiography, whose commonplace books disappeared, and whose surviving correspondence is predominantly businesslike and silent on matters of personal sentiments, convictions, and faith.

As far as the first question is concerned, it was argued above in chapter 1 that Robertson made strenuous efforts to reconcile the stadialist perspective with the Christian one, and it must be added that, perhaps, the difficulty is not so great as it might at first seem. After all, even Augustine stressed the significance of context: he displayed an acute awareness that man could only act in his own age, that humans before and after Christ could not be expected to be the same, and that good and evil ought to be judged in terms of the conditions necessary to the individual at a particular time and place.[9] The point, however, is that this is still possible to explain in terms of a conscience that places the highest priority on personal spiritual progress occurring within a narrative of creation, fall, incarnation, and redemption. While these truly cataclysmic events may certainly be identified with points in time, the succession of particular events between them is not rendered intelligible, nor is any special importance ascribed to time itself as the dimension of that succession. The time-bound experience of individuals is contrasted to a timeless and eternal God, occupying a *nunc-stans*, a standpoint from which he can see every moment in time as simultaneously present. To man, whose intelligence is imprisoned in one moment, the knowledge of another one is neither quite possible, nor quite relevant. Insofar as it is still both possible and relevant, it has to do with providence. It is our awareness of divine foreknowledge that persuades us about the meaning of each apparently insignificant episode in the flow of history from one cataclysm to the other.[10]

It is centrally important for the topic of this chapter that Robertson's own views of providence were heavily influenced by his early acquaintance, through his father's library, with the work of late seventeenth- and early eighteenth-century Arminian authors such as the Huguenot refugee Jean Le Clerc, John Locke's Dutch friend Philippe van Limborch, and the Swiss Samuel Werenfels.[11] Theologically, Arminianism was defined by its opposition to the absolute predestination that Calvin had argued, and by a greater emphasis on man's free will. Philosophically, it was based on a constructive and mitigated skepticism that established a permanent suspension of judgment (rather than doubt) as a means of arriving at truth. For Robertson the minister and church politician, the import of Arminianism was its being instrumental in combating the Calvinist orthodoxy prevailing in the Presbyterian *Kirk*, and to reshape it as a moderate and tolerant establishment. For Robertson the historian, Arminianism was a way to accommodate human agency with God's sovereignty, the central tenet of Calvinist theology. Even for Limborch, it had been possible to acknowledge God's power in ordering the universe while finding in that ordered universe a scope for independent human action: actions by human individuals making free choices, but ones which invariably contribute to the plan of God.[12] God does not coerce or decree absolutely, but orders the interaction of the parts of the universe in accordance with his grand yet varied design, which admits some flexibility regarding how his ends will be accomplished.

From this it is possible to develop a synergetic view of historical agency, according to which human actions may be seen as expressions of divine providence, while at the same time God's providence may be conceived as offering so many opportunities for the exercise of human will. This is what Robertson was doing in the sermon. In fact, it was dramatically differing views that he sought to accommodate within a larger whole, in order to give an account of the sequentiality of events and of the rhythm of historical changes that precede and prepare the cataclysmic events of Christian history and fill the time gaps between them. Just to make the whole scheme even more paradoxical, he also relied on the incipient, essentially materialist interpretations referred to above, which portray human beings as creatures of need. Hume and Smith argued that our needs and our understanding of needs are historically determined and that our minds will only develop insofar as we require them to develop in order to go about the business of seeking the satisfaction of our needs. Robertson's move that aimed to marry these views with his providentialism was to shift the argument from the mind itself to the circumstances in which the mindful human being finds himself or herself. In this argument, our understanding will only develop in proportion to the development of the faculties we possess to improve the world around us. With improvement comes a more acute understanding of the material and the spiritual world, and only then can God be expected to display more of His being and nature to us. To orthodox Presbyterians, with whom Robertson was trying to build bridges, the theological consistency and rigor of this position may have looked shaky. But this was not to upset Robertson who, in fact, took pains to evade the immensely difficult metaphysical and theological issues at stake, and strove instead to provide a pragmatic scheme in which the emphasis was on social progress and on the intended impact of civic harmony—objectives of attainment in which he did not fare poorly.

From the very beginning of the sermon, Robertson leaves no doubt that his preoccupation is with the problem of design in human history, and shortly thereafter it is also made clear that he intends to confront the problem in terms of "before" and "after," that is, before and after one of the epoch-making events of sacred history, the advent of Christ and the preaching of the Gospel.

> There is no employment more delightful to a devout mind than the contemplation of the divine wisdom in the government of the world. The civil history of mankind opens a wide field for this pious exercise. Careful observers may often, by the light of reason, form probable conjectures with regard to the plan of God's providence, and can discover a skilful hand directing the revolutions of human affairs, and compassing the best ends by the most effectual and surprising means: But sacred history, by drawing aside that veil which covers the counsels of the Almighty, lays open his designs to the view of his creatures; and we can there trace the steps which he taketh towards accomplishing them with more certainty, and greater pleasure... The publication and establishment of Christianity in the world is a remarkable event of this kind.[13]

What Robertson sets out to address is the objection by Christ's "adversaries... and modern infidels" that if the Gospel is indeed the truth, why was it "so long concealed from the world?"[14] Robertson's problem, then, becomes a problem of time: Why so late—and not earlier? He seeks to answer the question by reference to the "divine oeconomy" and the "particular juncture to render the discovery of the Christian religion more necessary, or the propagation of it more successful." He is concerned with the urgency of the revelation in a specific historical moment.

His particular explanations befit a conjectural historian who was at the same time a Presbyterian minister with a strong Arminian inspiration. To begin with, Robertson lays down two general principles. First, it is one of the general laws whereby "the Supreme Being conducts all his operations" that "no perfection of any kind can be attained of a sudden. The motion by which his works advance towards their final and complete state is gradual and progressive." He also expresses the same principle in the metaphor of time: "The obscurity of dawn went before the brightness of noon-day." As a consequence, it was "in proportion as the situation of the world made it necessary, [that] the Almighty was pleased farther to open and unfold his scheme."[15] Second, Robertson stresses that although there is a strong and manifest design in human history, direct interventions by God are infrequent, and even then they are organically embedded in a context of processes predominantly triggered by mere human agency: "The Almighty seldom effects, by supernatural means, any thing which could have been accomplished by such as are natural."[16]

The advent of Christ is of course one of these rare supernatural interventions, but the thrust of Robertson's analysis is to demonstrate how it was catalyzed by the confluence of a colorful variety of natural causes that, as it were, increased the density of history or accelerated the flow of time after a long period of stagnation. Providence and human agency are thus assigned complementary roles in bringing about the design in human history; human agency, while "ordained in reality by the wisdom of God," still possesses a sufficient degree of independence to create conditions propitious for the working of providence, should that prove "necessary." In the particular case discussed in the sermon, the advent of Christ is at once a supernatural event and an event in the secular world (domains between which Robertson is moving constantly), an event that has been thoroughly prepared by previous history.

Time, then, itself becomes a dimension not only defined by the rhythm of the "cataclysms" but one also marked by a periodicity emerging from the contemplation of human activity exerted in the intervals between those cataclysms and taking momentum in the period immediately preceding them—and as a result, contributing to the crucial definitions of "before" and "after." It would be tempting to explore the extent, if any, to which Robertson may have relied on then relatively recent philosophical approaches to time, each of which could be easily demonstrated to have been relevant for these perceptions. These include, first, Newton's ideas of "absolute" and "relative" time, the former being an equable flow, in irreversible succession, of a mathematical straight line, independent of matter and motion, the latter being the relation between time and sensible objects, depending very much on motion of variable rates.[17] Second, Leibniz retorted (to Newton) that were time merely absolute, there would be no reason for things (including the Creation!) to exist at one time rather than at another, and therefore all time can only be "relational."[18] Third, there was Locke's attempt to provide this with an empiricist epistemological grounding by explaining time in terms of duration as traced to its source in sensation and reflection.[19] However, while these sources were easily available for Robertson, there is no evidence that he availed himself of them. What he did employ, with a great deal of ingenuity, was the organizing principle of stadial history: the idea that, because of certain natural propensities of the human animal, societies have undergone stages of progress that can be defined in terms of the dominant mode of subsistence, and the degree of refinement expressed in their standards of conduct, as well as their ability to comprehend sophisticated and abstract notions of morality, religion, etc., depending on the stage reached in that process.

To be sure, the argument that the Word had not, and could not have, been revealed to the world until it was ready to receive it is also at least as old as

Augustine.[20] However, the dynamics that Robertson added to this view was of a peculiarly eighteenth-century character in its suggestion that even the world of primitive Christianity had been unrefined and pre-commercial, inhabited by peoples who *therefore* could not possibly have understood the laws whereby God exercised his governance of the natural and moral worlds; and, consequently, that God could have only revealed as much of his Word as the primitive Christians were able to understand. It was also necessary to assume that the rest would be revealed gradually as progress made it appropriate. It must be added, and it does not contradict the argument presented here, that the interdependence of revelation and progress is fully reciprocal for Robertson: he indeed also believed "revelation to be critical for the true refinement of manners and for moral improvement, and that without revelation, human intellectual and cultural development will be limited and inevitably lead to error, delusion, and moral corruption."[21]

Robertson's conjectural history of the propagation of the Gospel starts with the observation that "[t]he world, in the most early ages, was divided into small independent states... Commerce had not hitherto united mankind, and opened the communication of one nation with another. The world may now be considered one vast society... But, in those more simple ages, the intercourse between nations was extremely inconsiderable."[22] Naturally enough, such conditions, in which mankind had languished too long, by themselves constituted an insurmountable obstacle before the propagation of the Gospel across the whole of the western hemisphere. The catalytic role of removing this obstacle was played by "Roman ambition and bravery" that "paved the way, and prepared the world for the reception of the Christian doctrine": union and tranquility, as well as civilization, all corollaries of conquest and enslavement by the Romans, brought about with them as an unintended consequence in the best Smithian fashion the moment auspicious for the spread of Christianity.[23]

Besides the civilizing effects of Roman expansion, there were moral causes too, related to the former in a rather paradoxical way. The Roman Empire imposed itself on the small independent states of earlier times in which public liberty rested on the foundation of the private virtues—in regard to which, however, "the conduct of every citizen was subjected to the eye of the magistrate." The Romans themselves were no exception from this rule; "[but], by subduing the world, [they] lost their own liberty... The alliance between morals and government was now broken... Together with despotic power, entered all those odious vices, which are usually found in its train." The corruption characteristic of empires that succeeds upon the republican purity of manners, however, supplied the occasion for God to "manifest the Christian revelation to the world, not to re-establish virtue upon the same insecure foundation of civil government [mere human agency], but to erect it upon the eternal and immoveable basis of religion."[24] In Robertson's account, Christianity appeared in order to mitigate the pernicious effects of "despotic and unlimited empire" (as well as luxury that inevitably proceeds from safe commerce over a vast territory) and to perpetuate virtue among men by divine causes at a time when human causes were no longer sufficient to effect this.[25]

Robertson then considers the state of the world with respect to religion, domestic affairs, and what might be called social justice, and finds that in these terms, too, it was sufficiently critical—"crisis" in this case denoting a sort of pregnancy with changes—to invite a thoroughgoing "reformation." Religion languished between extreme forms of corruption as represented by the superstition and hypocrisy of the Pharisees and the libertinism of the Sadducees. The theme is developed by Robertson in terms vaguely resembling the version of the Enlightenment discourse on religion as presented in one of the most famous essays of Hume, first published in 1741.[26] This was a discourse which employed the dichotomy of superstition and enthusiasm, as the two archetypical forms of false religion, to account for the social and political turmoil of the preceding two centuries all over Europe, offering itself as an antidote. For some, like Hume, this could be skepticism, but for many others it was "moderation," or the virtuous middle: a sober and reasoned commitment to religious truth without subscribing to either the fanatic conceitedness of those sectarians who claimed immediate divine inspiration or an uncritical submission to authority. Robertson also conceived of two extreme attitudes, between which the force of true religion evaporated. To him as well, the one was superstition; the other, for the time being, he styled as "scandalous libertinism."

It was only shortly thereafter that he, as an ecclesiastical leader, recognized a militant interpretation of Calvinism, as professed by a considerable party within the *Kirk*, to be an even more dangerous disposition.[27] A mere year after the sermon was preached, the famous *Edinburgh Review*, which boasted Robertson among its founders, came under attack by Calvinist enthusiasts who protested against criticisms of their theological works in it; approximately at the same time Robertson and his moderate associates in the church had great difficulty in averting the threat of excommunication from Hume and his cousin Lord Kames as pernicious skeptics. Such struggles occupied Robertson throughout his career as a church politician until shortly after his retirement in 1780, when the lifting of some of the centuries-old sanctions against Catholics, implemented in England in 1778 and initiated in Scotland too, evoked riots that even presented a threat to his personal safety (and caused the Scottish Relief Bill to be shelved). Shocked, in one of his last speeches, Robertson said: "I love to see my countrymen discover that jealous concern for the preservation of their rights which characterizes the spirit of liberty: but I am sorry to behold them wasting their zeal without a cause." He called upon the church to denounce "the principle for conscience sake, as repugnant to the spirit of the gospel, and contrary to the genius of the Protestant faith."[28]

As regards the "regular system of superstition" introduced among the ancient Jews by the Pharisees, this type of "false religion" already stands in full armor before the reader of the sermon: the proliferation of traditions, ceremonial prescriptions, and rites caused the decline of principles. "Superstition never prevailed among any people, but at the expense of morals. The heathen superstition, far from giving any aid to virtue, seems not to have had the least connection with it." As elsewhere, political degradation is also consequent upon the spread of superstition and the moral decay it occasions: "Tyranny and superstition, like those other destroyers of mankind, famine and pestilence, are nearly allied. Superstition breaks the spirit, and prepares it for servitude. Tyranny, for this reason, encourages superstition, and employs it as a useful auxiliary to illegal power."[29]

Further on, Robertson also presents the domestic scene during the times immediately preceding the appearance of Christ in dark tones, as having been marked by polygamy in the East and by the practice of divorce carried to extremes among both the Jews and the heathens of the West, the one conducive to domestic slavery, and the other bringing the idea of the natural bond between man and woman into disrepute. Finally, as in view of "the wants of human society...far the greater part of mankind is condemned to constant toil and labor, in order to supply them," and due to the primitive means of subsistence in ancient times, the majority of people were reduced to slavery—a state that became truly intolerable under the despotic government of the Roman Empire. In other words, needing reformation were the religious attitudes of virtually all—and "the lives of those who are at the head of domestic society"—while "the sufferings of those who were subject to them merited relief."[30]

Time in secular terms was then on all fronts—social and domestic, political and moral—ripe in a peculiar sense for the most important event of sacred time between the Creation and Redemption to occur. And indeed, in the time "after" (the incarnation), the benevolent potential inherent in Christianity on all of these fronts asserted its corrective effect on the very phenomena in the secular domain whose "unintended consequence" was its appearance. Particularly noteworthy is Robertson's unhesitating ascription of the abolition of slavery to the mild and liberal spirit of Christianity: indeed the Book of Isaiah is cited by him in order to draw a parallel between the spiritual salvation prophesied there and the temporal deliverance from personal servitude.[31] The mildness and humanity of modern manners is summarily represented as having been inspired, even awakened, by the Christian religion.[32]

Here, however, there seems to be some confusion about cause and effect, at least if the whole of Robertson's historical thought is taken into consideration. Of the entire "great generation" of the Scottish Enlightenment, he was perhaps the most straightforward "progress-and-refinement" thinker. He came closest to believing that progress was irreversible, that the values and virtues of modernity were ultimately superior, and that man's capacity to absorb and comprehend sophisticated truths and to develop refined perceptions of his moral and physical environment depended on the advance of civilization in more broadly conceived terms. And all of his thinking revolved around the recognition that commerce had a transformative effect on civilization. Market relations and commercial exchange on the one hand functioned as a generic metaphor to describe so many other forms of human intercourse; while on the other hand it was also a very direct communication situation, which, by virtue of its peculiar rules, was especially well-suited for grasping the needs and interests of the one party in terms of and as depending on those of the other. To the extent that commerce comes to prevail in supplying for men's needs, enhanced opportunities of intercourse lead to the growth of sympathy, politeness, and sociability, as well as affluence and knowledge, even among otherwise self-regarding individuals. Emulation, inspired by a self-regard that had once been violent assumes milder forms,[33] until even laws, issued by the civil magistrate to tame such passions and suppress eruptions of violence, cease to be regarded as cumbersome limitations of liberty, but rather come to be valued by polished citizen-subjects as the instruments of the rule of law.

This conspicuously materialist logic could be abundantly documented from the works of Robertson. The following passage, which concerns the awakening of medieval urban communities from their long slumber, is taken from the classic blend between narrative and stadial history:

> The spirit of industry revived: commerce became an object of attention and began to flourish: the population increased: independence was established: and wealth flowed into cities which had long been the seat of poverty and oppression. Wealth was accompanied by its usual attendants, ostentation and luxury; and though the former was formal and cumbersome, and the latter inelegant, they led gradually to greater refinement in manners and in the habits of life. Together with this improvement in manners, a more regular species of government and police was introduced. As cities grew to be more populous, and the occasions for intercourse among men increased, statutes and regulations multiplied of course, and all became sensible that their common safety depended on observing them with exactness, and on punishing such as violated them with promptitude and rigour. Laws and subordination, as well as polished manners, taking their rise in the cities, diffused themselves insensibly through the rest of the society.[34]

From Robertson's views on the formative effect of material progress on manners and the mind, it would not necessarily follow that the truth of the Gospel could at once triumph among the prevailing conditions of civilization, represented by him as rather primitive. And indeed, while on the one hand he thought that cultural progress itself was of doubtful value, with even dangerous consequences in the absence of revelation, on the other hand he also believed that it was in his own century that religion, which at the time of the Reformation and the Counter-Reformation was still rooted in a necessarily imperfect understanding of the Word of God and permeated by superstition and enthusiasm, could at last be understood as it was intended by the Almighty and his messenger. Developments in secular human history, then, have again prepared the world, if not for a further revelation, at least for a fuller and more self-conscious grasp of the one already available.

To underpin this, Robertson's conclusion to the sermon opens with reflections upon Europe's special place in the history of Christianity. It cannot be by way of sheer coincidence that Europe, where Christianity first spread, surpasses other regions of the earth in science and improvements. "Of this superiority the Europeans have availed themselves to the utmost, in every project for extending their empire and commerce...Now, the same attainments in science or policy, might be employed to good purpose, on the side of religion."[35] Europe, or at least a part of it, has been privileged by its running the full cycle of stadial progress at a quicker pace, and reaching the pinnacles of the commercial and civilized stage earlier than the more and less remote corners of the globe that were opening themselves to the gaze of Europeans in Robertson's lifetime. In his experience and interpretation, the progress of commerce also coincided with the growth of politeness and knowledge, and thus advanced the cause of a more moderate and tolerant version of Christianity than the one that had held souls in subjection throughout the Middle Ages, and subsequently inspired the ravages of a whole continent in the age of religious wars. At last, while fulfilling their civilizing mission in bringing commerce and refinement to the barbarous nations of distant regions, in other words, accelerating secular time for them, Europeans should also pay more attention to rendering their souls the service of propagating the Gospel in a more systematic manner, thereby also accelerating sacred time—the progress toward their receiving of the revelation, and ultimately for all concerned, of redemption.

Perhaps I might conclude here by recapitulating that Robertson employs the paradigm of Enlightenment stadial history to present a highly dynamic picture of the intersections of secular and sacred time, and of the mutually supplementary roles of human and divine agency in these dynamics. But there is yet another also very characteristically eighteenth-century dimension to his variations on the theme of time and progress. Underlying the sermon, as indeed virtually all of his works, is the idea that travel in space might easily assume the character of travel in time. In the wilderness of North America, one can obtain a fair idea of the life of Tacitus' barbarians, while the Pacific islands are home to various modifications of Adamite man.

> [T]he characters of nations depend on the state of society in which they live, and on the political institutions established among them; and...the human mind, whenever it is placed in the same situation, will, in ages the most distant, and in countries the most remote, assume the same form, and be distinguished by the same manners...Many of the German tribes were more civilized than the Americans...The resemblance, however, between their conditions, is greater, perhaps, than any that history affords an opportunity of observing between any two races of uncivilized people, and this has produced a surprising similarity of manners.[36]

Or, in even more simple terms, on account of the theory of the population of America from the old continent: "The character and occupations of the hunter in America must be little different from those of an Asiatic, who depends for subsistence on the chase. A tribe of savages on the banks of the Danube must nearly resemble one upon the plains washed by the Mississippi."[37]

The observation of "primitive" peoples in remote continents and the vast work of collecting data about them contributed immensely to the development of early ethnology,[38] while in the eyes of contemporaries fulfilling the mission as referred to above in relation to such peoples also passed for a heroic feat indeed. But does one truly need to cross the oceans in order to collect the same kind of anthropological knowledge and perform the same kind of civilizing service? Far from it, according to the approach adopted in Robertson's texts, but also represented by many others in the eighteenth century. Distance in space and distance in time can be brought to a common denominator, but occasionally the relationship is inverse: crossing just a few hills would sometimes suffice for traversing many centuries. Indeed, Robertson concludes the sermon suggesting that

> the conversion of distant nations is not the chief care of the Society for the propagating of Christian knowledge: An object nearer at hand demands its more immediate attention. The Highlands and Islands of *Scotland* present to us a scene, which we would little expect in a nation where true religion and polished manners have long flourished. There society still appears in a rude and imperfect form: Strangers to industry, averse from labour, inured to rapine; the fierce inhabitants scorned all the arts of peace, and stood ready for every bold and desperate action.[39]

As mentioned at the beginning of this chapter, Robertson blamed it on this primitive state of society, that the "superstition" and "pernicious principles of government" associated with it fell on a fertile soil among the Highlanders and led them to support the Jacobite rebellion of 1745. Human agency is then again enlisted for the advancement of divine purposes: Robertson urges the legislature to enhance its already existing policy of enacting laws "with the most humane spirit, in order to retrieve that part of the kingdom from ignorance and barbarism"—a course of action from which "the members of the Society expect great assistance in the prosecution of their design."[40]

In view of the textual environment, this is fairly revealing. World and time are both "given" for Robertson, in the strictest Christian sense of the word. There is design and ordination in the arrangement of both, but in such a way that motion in the one has inevitable consequences for motion in the other; and the character of that motion, Robertson seems to remind us, depends, as much as on what is "given," on the disposition of the receiving agent who uses the world once given, in the time given, turning the one to the well-being of his body and finding in the other the salvation of his soul. Accordingly,

Robertson's ideas on time and the event, especially events of particularly great importance from the point of view of the divine plan, represent a very interesting shade within the thought of the Enlightenment about these questions. As a parallel case, we might invoke that of the transformation of the meaning of "revolution" simultaneously with his own career. At the time when Robertson was born, *revolutio* was still, as Copernicus had described it in the case of the movement of celestial objects, regarded as a circular movement concluding in reoccupying an initial position (such as, in the political world, the Glorious Revolution in England in 1688), or the sudden and shocking interference of an unpredictable force beyond man's control into human affairs (usually in affairs of government). Around the time when Robertson's sermon was published, a version of the same perspective started to take shape, where such calamities may provide an enlightened people with an opportunity to take their fate into their own hands—without implying that the cataclysmic event is prepared by the people itself, but that using the event as a springboard they thereafter might become sovereign agents.[41] Robertson's logic, in a certain sense, is the very reverse: men engaged in commerce, refining their manners and discovering the natural, social, and moral world around them, further the course of Christian history through these very activities, because doing so they facilitate and abbreviate their own path to the clear understanding of the Gospel, while they do not have any influence on the ultimate outcome of that history.

Both approaches are capable of an interpretation on whose basis the modern terminology and conceptualization of historical change and of the role of human agency in that change emerged. However, it is equally useful and intellectually perhaps more rewarding to regard these conceptual cousins, including Robertson's position, not as yet "imperfect" anticipations of a later more "developed" idea, but rather as mature theoretical experiments representing specific shades of opinion within the Enlightenment, claiming our attention in their own right. Paraphrasing Koselleck, one might suggest that Robertson's early sermon catches for us the very moment in which the notion of the acceleration of history was not yet quite divorced from the apocalyptic hope attached to the ever-shortening periods preceding the Last Judgment, but was already being transformed into a notion of historical hope. But a reformulation of the above sentence that would drop the words "yet" and "already," and replace "moment" with "perspective," might in fact describe the situation far more accurately.

An unnoticed translation

In his account of Robertson's life and writings, Dugald Stewart reported that the sermon "hath long been ranked, in both parts of the island, among the best models of pulpit eloquence in our language," illustrating this by pointing to the five editions which it underwent, and also adding that it "is well known in some parts of the Continent, in the German translation of Mr. Ebeling."[42] Precisely how "well known" it was, is actually difficult to establish. Apart from the availability of the translation mentioned by Stewart in a few German libraries, the only information about it that I have been able to locate is contained in a letter to Robertson by the translator himself. Johann Philipp Ebeling (1753–1795) took a medical degree at Glasgow in 1779 with a dissertation on the quassia tree (a plant indigenous to the West Indies whose medical uses included the treatment of upset stomach and loss of appetite as well as fevers) and the Iceland moss (*lichen islandicus*—also effective against lack of appetite and coughing).[43] Ebeling wrote the letter on November 17, 1779, to express his gratitude to Robertson for the warm reception in Edinburgh on his way back to Lüneburg, and for supplying him with a copy of the sermon—which he found, to his surprise, never to have been translated into German. He proudly reported having accomplished this task[44] (adding that in the meantime a very incompetent rival in Frankfurt did the same—an enterprise whose fruits seem to have been lost). The rest of the letter reads like a series of replies to queries that may have been posed to Ebeling during his visit in Edinburgh by Robertson about the current conditions of Germany:

> The emperor is publicly known to meditate upon a fifth monarchy, but probably his schemes will prove as abortive as those of Louis of France. At any rate we want a war very much; all our regiments are overflocked with volunteers waiting for commissions. Commerce affords with us, some few towns excepted, no prospects of young men of family, and all their views are therefore confined to civil offices and military places, of which however there is not near a sufficient number to provide for all the children of a peace of eighteen years.[45]

These remarks coagulate around issues that are known to have been of central interest to Robertson. While it needs some stretch of one's imagination to style Joseph II's military emulation of Frederick II (in particular its latest and remarkably eventless episode, the War of Bavarian Succession of 1778–1779, also called the "potato war") as an endeavor to build universal monarchy, the topic itself was of lasting concern for the Scottish historian, similar to the issue of the social dynamic generated by commerce (or the lack of it). If it is added that Ebeling's letter also contained comments and information relevant to Robertson's *History of America* (which will be discussed in chapter 5), the young German physician emerges as a quite intimate *Kenner* of the pursuits of the venerable Scottish historian, and the conversation which they had seems to have been as serious in breadth and depth as it was brief.

As Robertson's rise to international recognition was triggered by the publication of the *History of Scotland* in 1759, it should not be surprising that the *Situation of the World* went unnoticed in Germany until the contingent factor of the personal meeting with Ebeling. A copy of the sermon as a gift to commemorate the meeting motivated the latter to translate it at a time when, as we shall see, three major works of Robertson had already been widely commented on and were also available in German translations. However important the sermon is as a testimony to the early development of theoretical convictions that were to exert an impact on each of Robertson's mature historical works, in view of this chronology it is also of little wonder that its appearance on the German book market apparently evoked no critical response at all. Unlike most fellow translators of Robertson, Ebeling moreover refrained from adding a preface or notes of his own to the text.

Nevertheless, there are two issues raised by Ebeling's performance that are worth exploring in the rest of this chapter. One of them, the character and the quality of the translation itself, with an emphasis on the terminological choices of the translator, will be a recurrent theme throughout the pages that follow. Second, Robertson's combination of providence and progress as a framework of historical interpretation, and more broadly his discussion of a Christian theme as a piece of secular narrative, calls for an assessment of compatible perspectives in contemporary German religious thought.

Apart from relatively insignificant instances of imprecision, Ebeling proved to be a competent and confident translator: the text runs smoothly, and in the liberties he occasionally took he departed from Robertson's original only to the extent required to make the German idiomatic. At the same time, he was helpless in regard to a feature of Robertson's compositions that invariably caused problems also for the other German translators whose contributions are discussed in this book. The intellectual discourse of Robertson as a historian of human progress is organized around a basic vocabulary, the coherence of which is difficult to convey by the means of German as a natural language. This must be borne in mind even though he is evidently much more than *just* a historian of human progress: a historian of human progress as interdependent of the accessibility of the Christian revelation, as in the *Situation of the World*, or a historian of human progress as contextualizing political drama and the conflict of characters, as in the *History of Scotland*, and so forth. While none of Robertson's works are outright stadial histories, the semantic possibilities inherent in the stadialist vocabulary are crucial to the texture and the conceptual unity of each, the *Situation of the World* being no exception. Here too, "commerce" and "intercourse" are used to denote the exchange of goods with the potential of generating sociability (an inference prompted by the fact that in English these words are also capable of denoting the exchange of much more than just goods). The refinement or civilization of "manners," the ethical, aesthetic, and custom-based standards of human conduct characteristic of a society is understood as dependent on the proliferation of the opportunities for each type of such exchange. Further, the "political state," or simply the "policy" or "police" of a community, assumes more regular forms in proportion with the advance of its "manners" toward more "polished" or "polite" stages. Etymological confluences, whether real or assumed (as in the case of polished/polite/police), played a major role in cementing this vocabulary as a tool of sociological and historical interpretation.[46]

The success of Ebeling in rendering such consistencies was as meager as it was in the case of any of his colleagues. *Handlung* (for commerce) is trade in goods but hardly anything else, though by extending it to mean "action" it at least preserves the notion of agency; *Gemeinschaft* (for intercourse—as well as communication) is "community," thus an accomplished fact, rather than active engagement.[47] Finding an equivalent for "manners" in German was apparently an easy job: *Sitten* was used in this role as frequently by Ebeling as others. However, as I shall argue in greater detail in chapter 3, this routine was not unproblematic, because in *Sitten* the ethical overtone seems to suppress the others which are present in "manners"—a point that is also illustrated by Ebeling's indiscriminate use of it for "morals" as well as "manners."[48] This imbalance is somewhat redressed by rendering "civilized" with *gesittet*[49]—which, however, does not evoke the connection of the process of refinement with progress toward and within the "civil," that is, political state. To further undermine the status of stadialist terminology as a vocabulary, Ebeling translated "policy" as *Staatsklugheit*,[50] a term used extensively in German reason of state literature to denote the prudence necessary for effective statesmanship, but rather inadequate as a tool to point to the progress—"polishing," that is, refinement—of civil (political) society.

Such difficulties, even blunders, in coping with Scottish stadialist vocabulary were not atypical in the history of the reception of Robertson's texts in German. As direct German responses to the argument presented in the sermon are lacking, for the possible reasons mentioned above, in the rest of this chapter comparison will prevail over the study of reception: I shall explore what parallels for Robertson's reliance on secular causation, applied to themes in sacred history, may have existed in the German "religious Enlightenment." That several strains of thought deserving of such an appellation operated in eighteenth-century Germany is now widely accepted. That these displayed a broad family resemblance with the interpretation of the meaning of the New Testament offered in the *Situation of the World* is a less obvious fact, but one which dovetails well with both the generally amenable atmosphere in which his other works received a great deal of attention and the incomprehension that surrounded some of their aspects.

Baumgarten and Semler: history and the religious Enlightenment in Germany

One possible German counterpart of Robertson's attempt to present the biblical story as one in which human agency and intentions are as manifest as the divine contents of the books, was the historical exegesis encapsulated in the "theological Wolffianism"[51] of the Halle professor Siegmund Jacob Baumgarten (1706–1757) and his disciple Johann Salomo Semler (1725–1791).

The University of Halle was founded in 1694 by Frederick III of Brandenburg-Prussia as a bulwark against the Lutheran orthodoxy prevailing at the nearby universities of Wittenberg and Leipzig in Saxony. Initially, the means to rejuvenate Lutheran belief was Pietism, which countered the strongly speculative–scholastic dogmatizing and intolerance of orthodoxy via a stress on edificatory preaching, devotional experience through Bible-reading and individual access to God, and freedom of conscience.[52] At the same time, Pietism remained just as untouched as orthodoxy by the most important intellectual developments of the age. There soon arose a generation of scholars at Halle and more broadly in German Pietism that acutely felt the need for thorough empirical research, methodological rigor, and a general open-mindedness toward the new scientific–mathematical thinking, if theology was to retain its position on the map of learning. While the Pietists of Halle at first secured the suppression of both of the early representatives of the German "rival Enlightenments," Christian Thomasius and Christian Wolff (constraining the former to the teaching of law in 1696, and expelling the latter from the university in 1723), Wolff's reinvitation in 1733 signaled the changing of the tides. Baumgarten's theology took shape in the context of these contests and was an attempt to reconcile reason and revelation by resorting not only to the Wolffian standards of achieving quasi-mathematical certainty, but also to historical analysis as a field capable both of accommodating such standards and of consolidating faith by mediating between human experience and divine truth.

The endeavor of Baumgarten, and in his wake Semler, to supersede Pietism by resorting to Wolff's philosophy thus arose out of local debates, but had a great deal in common with other forceful statements of a moderate and religious Enlightenment elsewhere in Europe. Affinities between the thought of Baumgarten and figures like William Warburton, Jacob Vernet, or Moses Mendelssohn have been pointed out convincingly.[53] For the present study, the centrality of history as a discipline to Baumgarten's intellectual strategy, and the importance of his contributions to eighteenth-century German historical scholarship, must be stressed. His theological oeuvre was thoroughly imbued with a historical approach, but he also published an influential work on ecclesiastical history in 1743 and edited 17 volumes, between 1744 and 1758, of the German translation of the highly popular and influential English *Universal History*—with commentaries that were later translated into English and published as a supplement to the original.[54] Thus Baumgarten, another "moderate" as well as a highly successful professional historian, also needs to be reckoned with in tracing the local conditions for the reception of Robertson in Germany.

If Robertson's sermon was a formidable effort at developing a historically contextualized understanding of the full import of the account of Christ's suffering as related in the testimonies of the Gospel, the same was true for a considerable portion of Baumgarten's oeuvre. He was fully convinced of the significance of history for theology.[55] Extracting truth from scripture for him depended on the application of a philological and historical method, which consisted of the excavation of the meaning of words among the exact historical conditions in which they had once been used.[56] On the same grounds, Baumgarten stressed that "before we form a Judgment of ancient and foreign Historians, we ought to consider the Opinion and Customs of the Times and Places in which they were written," adding that competence in the source languages was an indispensable qualification of the historian in developing such a contextual understanding.[57] Further, he not only suggested that his "grammatical and dogmatic" method of exegesis was capable of extracting from scripture the "vital knowledge" needed for Christian "union,"[58] but also, as a corollary, that history pursued with this method rendered a service to belief because, whether sacred or secular, it was unitary. The Bible certainly incorporated aspects that were strictly temporal, and thus subject to error,[59] as well as truths central to salvation and therefore incontrovertible. All the same, Baumgarten held these two apparently opposed characters of the holy books to be subject to the same methods, applicable to the sacred as well as the secular, pointing to the soundness of the one and the uncertainty of the other.

He was able to do so on the grounds of his importation of the premises of Wolff into the study of history (and theology). Wolff despised history as a field of inquiry concerned only with particulars (but not, as a proper science ought to, with *generalia*), and where no certainty is feasible.[60] Baumgarten insisted that the widely accepted charge concerning the lack of certainty in historical scholarship is unfounded, and in fact that a "demonstrable certainty" exists based on the same notions of credibility and coherence—the noncontradiction of facts and events to themselves, the laws of nature, or divine attributes—as in any other branch of knowledge. True, Baumgarten's understanding of historical credibility was one that was peculiar to the field. It differed from mathematical certainty and the "demonstrability" of general truths: a "credible" historian may not be "infallible," yet "a Fact is considerably more demonstrable if supported by the Credibility of the Historian" (though it is added that "the bare mention of an Event by a credible Historian, doth not constitute the whole proof of its Certainty").[61] This sounds like a circular argument, but Baumgarten merely points to the fact that it belongs to the nature of certainty and probability in history that "the Demonstrability of Events has different Degrees and Limits," and that it is philosophically wrong just for this reason to deny history the character of a certainty-based science.[62] On the contrary, Baumgarten confidently asserted that it is

> no difficult nor tedious matter to refute the trifling Arguments made to depreciate the Study of History...Every Inquiry into the real Grounds and different Degrees of Probability and Certainty of historical Events and Facts, a Discovery of the Connection of different Events, and their mutual Influence over each other, and a right Judgment and Application of the same, require as much Reflection and Exercise, and sharpen the reflecting Powers as much, as any other Science.[63]

However, Baumgarten championed history not only on account of it possessing a legitimate claim to the status of a science, but also because of its distinct sociocultural uses. He argued that a "thorough insight" in sacred history—which, as pointed out above, had in his view a symbiotic relationship with secular history—was the best "weapon" in defense of the Christian religion against its detractors, thanks to its capacity to promote a middle course between "all the cruelty, deception, sinfulness and dominant passions occasioned by superstition and ignorance under the pretext of worshipping God" and "fanatical enthusiasm."[64] Baumgarten's agenda was chiefly to reclaim history from deists and freethinkers, in whose hands it had become an instrument of undermining the credibility of revelation. But his conviction that this arose precisely from the defectiveness of historical knowledge as cultivated by these rivals, and that its correction would help suppress all the error they stood for, was typical of moderate enlightened Christians across Europe who aimed at keeping an equal distance from all varieties of enthusiasm and superstition through the application of scientific reason. For them, the knowledge of history seemed crucial in order to overcome the erroneous notions that had thrown several generations of Europeans into a terrible cycle of religious and civil warfare.

As a further Enlightenment trademark, Baumgarten moved on in his *Supplement to the English Universal History* to extol the "usefulness" of history, notably associated with the "agreeableness, pleasure, and entertainment" found in it. Thanks to such associations, it is easy to comprehend that the study of history fulfills a social mission, in the eighteenth-century sense, because "it will fill up the longest Life of the idlest Man, the pleasures of it will engage him to relish it; it will insensibly correct his Manners and improve his Understanding; and it may excite him to other useful Employments."[65] The purpose of the study of history is eminently sociable for Baumgarten, and thus congenial to the constitution of humanity in the highest order:

> History is the means of our acquaintance with a much greater and more remote part of the human Race than would be possible without it....Man is of a sociable nature, formed for a social Life, and obliged to it. Now Societies cannot subsist, much less can all the ends of their Institution be answered, without a retrospect to past Events...no one can either be a useful Member of human Society, or even enjoy all its Advantages, who is indifferent to the public Good, and therefore careless of the Concerns, the Prosperity, or Distresses of his Fellow-members....The more we consider the close Connection between all human Societies, which all together make up but one general Society, the more interesting the Events and Actions of our Fellow-members will appears to us, even those that happen in the remotest part of the Universe. And as this connection not only unites all Contemporaries, but likewise extends to different Periods, whence general obligations to our Ancestors and Posterity arise; it follows, that the

Attention must likewise be extended to Events of former times, if we chuse to be the better of our Predecessors, to discharge our Duty to them, and to render their Actions, and the effects they have produced, more useful to Posterity. For it would be an unaccountable Conduct to live in the World as if the human Race had begun and was to perish with us.[66]

Similarly, Hume's metaphor about silkworms versus humans, marked respectively by a discontinuity between generations and the indissoluble ties that bind them together, or Burke's notion of society as a contract among the living, the dead, and those who are not yet born, are widely known formulations of the same sentiments. But more important than the apparent conservative overtones of Baumgarten's statement are its implications for the gift of sensitivity and empathy toward different human situations as they arise across time and space, and the consequences for the anthropology of the Enlightenment. Man cannot subsist outside society; society is by definition a product of history and man's sociable disposition is nurtured by the knowledge of history, which is, therefore, one of the most effective means of securing the perpetuation of the social bond.

In the 1740s and 1750s, Baumgarten thus invested history with an authoritative voice in the matters both of religion and sociability. Both this combination and the agenda that it was intended to promote were strikingly similar to the ones which marked Robertson's 1755 sermon. The topics, though, which Baumgarten addressed in his own historical texts (confined as these were to the history of the church) and the principles of causality applied to them (devoid of the materialistic aspects of stadial history) obviously separated him from the Scottish historian. Baumgarten's initiatives in Halle were taken up with a great deal of commitment and competence by his student Johann Salomo Semler, who not only continued his master's work in editing the German translation of the English *Universal History* (volumes 18 to 31, between 1758 and 1766), but also further refined and broadened the establishment of theological theorizing on the foundations of historical epistemology.

Semler's seminal contributions to the development of academic source criticism, and the particular value of a handbook he published in 1761 on the use of sources for medieval political and ecclesiastical history,[67] were already recognized by contemporaries, including Gatterer, who simply called Semler "a classic."[68] There is neither scope nor need to reproduce here the comprehensive and in-depth analysis of Semler's contribution to the rise of "scientific history" that is now available in the literature.[69] As regards the possible parallels with the position which Robertson took in the *Situation of the World*, the most noteworthy feature of Semler's thought is his conviction that, thanks to providence, he lived and worked in an age that was "better" than all the preceding ones, and that if there ever was an age that enjoyed the advantage of being able to put together a "fruitful history of moral notions and maxims," it was exactly his.[70] This claim has several important implications. First, Semler thought that all ages had their own new histories, which were peculiar to them, because they both needed and deserved them. This was because all forms of consciousness existed in mutual conformity with the surrounding changing sociocultural environment: it is not the sources that constitute history, but the engagement with them and the process of interpretation and reconstruction, inevitably taking place according to principles of selectivity peculiar to the time and place in which the historian is active. Take, for instance, the stories of the life of Jesus and the religion of the early Christians as related in the Gospel: they are not "history proper," which arises out of the judgments [Urtheile] we form about them. "Now, readers make judgments about [such histories] according to their present way of thinking; thus their own history is what they think about that history, according to a mixture of a Christian kind."[71] It is this "mixture" of past events and experiences with present judgments, their evaluation in light of current standards and values that results in a "relation, representation, collection of cases which its author regards as interesting, as useful, and as far as he himself is concerned, truthful."[72]

Thus, according to Semler, different histories of the same object, including the scripture, were possible, even desirable. In a slightly different perspective, he thought that just as history itself was plural and context-dependent, so were all other forms of consciousness, religion not excepted. "[A] theologian...does not do justice to his calling, if he is foreign to history," is how he summed up his relevant convictions early in his career, in a preface to the translation of a popular history of Spain.[73] The idea of religion as a closed, immutable, "perfect" system was no more realistic to him than that of an impeccable social order; on the contrary, religion was a universal force in constant flux, growing together with the human mind, and obliged, as it were, to answer the distinct spiritual needs of all times. As a result, the same hermeneutical principles and patterns of interpretation were applicable to sacred as to profane history.[74] In Semler's view, this approach was indispensable for eighteenth-century men and women to realize that while they could understand the past, it was impossible for them to become first-century Christians—a recognition that seemed to him all-important for the present understanding of the Gospel.

Christianity, for Semler, following Baumgarten, had a crucial temporal dimension, which made it inseparable from developments in the secular environment. He clearly conceived of such developments as "progress," as a result of which his age was better equipped than its predecessors to access the past, including the Christian past. Further enhancing this access was emphatically proposed by him as an instrument of Enlightenment: "As history in general diffuses the most powerful light, and most certainly suppresses ignorance; so do I also hope to achieve through many such historical proofs among all thinking contemporaries that they no longer remain the slaves of human opinions and prejudices."[75] While Semler was apparently rather uninterested in the forces and the working of historical causality, his forceful effort at inscribing historical relativism into the learned account of the Christian religion

Lessing: progressive revelation remastered

"Neology," as the theological stance represented by Baumgarten and Semler came to be referred to, took issue with both the orthodox and Pietist currents of contemporary German Protestantism, while resorting to methods of historical criticism keenly employed already for a century by the deists, whose idea and agenda of natural religion constituted a fundamental challenge for them all.[76] During the 1770s, yet another new voice appeared on the already crowded stage of enlightened debate on religion in Germany. That voice belonged to Gotthold Ephraim Lessing (1729–1781), one of the most famous German *philosophes* of the time, whose earlier views on the matter, to the extent he was concerned with it,[77] could be most closely associated with deism. After about 1773, however, his approach changed. Lessing, librarian of the splendid collections of Duke Ferdinand of Brunswick at Wolfenbüttel from May of 1770, published a sequence of writings displaying a genuine interest in giving a rational account of the Christian revelation while making gestures to revealed religion. The change did not go unnoticed: as his friend, the Berlin writer and publisher Friedrich Nicolai wrote to Lessing on April 24, 1777, "the theologians think that you are a freethinker, and freethinkers, that you have become a theologian."[78]

The first set of publications, which triggered this shift in Lessing's reputation, was seven fragments from 4,000 pages of manuscripts by the Hamburg gymnasium professor of Oriental languages, Hermann Samuel Reimarus (1694–1768). The manuscripts seem to have been entrusted to Lessing by Reimarus's children, whom he had befriended during his stay in Hamburg as literary advisor of the newly founded German National Theater prior to his engagement in Wolfenbüttel. They were collectively titled *Apologie oder Schutzschrift für die vernünftigen Verehrer Gottes* (Apology or Vindication for the Rational Worshippers of God) and contained a radical statement of the deist position. As Lessing promised Reimarus's heirs to never reveal the identity of the author, and the immunity from censorship he received from his employer was conditional on him refraining from any attack on Christianity, he chose a dual strategy in making the manuscripts public. First, pretending to have found them among the holdings of the library, he published them in the series *Zur Geschichte und Literatur: Aus den Schätzen der Herzoglichen Bibliothek zu Wolfenbüttel* (Contributions to Literature and History from the Treasures of the Ducal Library at Wolfenbüttel), which he had just initiated, under the title *Fragmente eines Ungenannten* (Fragments by an Unnamed Author, 1774–1778). Second, he equipped the texts with critical commentary (*Gegensätze*—"counterarguments"). Neither of these strategies was fully successful. As Lessing's correspondence demonstrates, in spite of his precautions, Reimarus was widely suspected of being behind the texts. More importantly, the *Fragments* evoked a torrent of angry refutations. Initially, the main target of these responses was the anonymous author and his highly erudite assaults on the historical roots and historical legitimacy of Christianity—among other things, denying the possibility of universal revelation, undermining the credibility of crucial accounts of the holy books, such as the passage of the Israelites across the Red Sea or the resurrection of Christ, and imputing disingenuous intentions to apostles. While Lessing's own objections to Reimarus advanced in the *Gegensätze*, which aimed to use the opportunity of the debate with the heterodox author to establish Christianity on a firmer footing, were primarily based on methodological grounds, the respondents simply reclaimed the historical truthfulness of the Bible.[79] However, with the involvement of Johann Melchior Goeze (1717–1786), *Hauptpastor* of the Hamburg pastors, the editor and his counter-positions came to be repudiated as even more dangerous than the fragments themselves. Eventually, in 1779, Semler also entered the debate with a wholesale and point-by-point response, especially to the supposedly most provocative of the fragments concerning the purpose of Jesus and his disciples.[80] But even before then, the intervention of civil authority effectively closed the "fragment controversy" (*Fragmentenstreit*): from July 1778 onwards, all of Lessing's publications in the Duchy of Brunswick-Wolfenbüttel were to be censored. Yet he continued addressing the status of revealed religion and the topic of reason and revelation by "finding out whether I am still allowed to preach undisturbed at least from my old pulpit, the theater"[81]—with the result of the famous drama *Nathan the Wise*—and by completing in 1780 a brief piece begun in 1777, titled *Die Erziehung des Menschengeschlechts* (The Education of the Human Race).

In the 11 essays that comprise his *Anti-Goeze*, Lessing vindicated himself against orthodoxy by stressing both that "the ultimate purpose of Christianity is not our salvation, wherever it comes from, but our *salvation by means of our enlightenment*,"[82] and that the publication of texts by someone unnamed who appears to be a genuine adversary of religion served the attainment of this end by facilitating an open discussion of "the question of truth" (*Wahrheitsfrage*). In the pursuit of truth—"salvation by means of enlightenment"—Lessing advanced intellectual and methodological positions that were in the first place directed against Goeze and his orthodox supporters, but were also firm vis-à-vis his other rivals, deists and Neologists. In an apparent fundamental contradiction to the resorting to historical criticism in the interpretation of Christianity, urged by the latter, he proposed that "contingent truths of history can never become the proof for indispensable truths of reason,"[83] and famously employed the metaphor of the "hideous broad ditch" (*der garstige breite Graben*) separating the two from one another. In Lessing's view, there was a problem with the character of historical knowledge—in the given case, the knowledge of miracles and the fulfillment of prophecies—because of the difference between the immediate experience and the indirect mediation and reporting of these past phenomena. Certainty may arise from the former, but never from the latter, which supplies only probable and relatively credible knowledge and is therefore an insufficient ground for true faith. The capacity inherent to truths of "other classes" but, according to Lessing, lacking in historical truth, is demonstrability, perhaps an implicit retort to Baumgarten.[84]

Instead of a detailed exploration of the notion of the "inner truth" of religion introduced by Lessing as the true ground for Christian faith, what is pertinent here is a further discussion of the arguments for eschewing "the historical" in this quest. Somewhat ironically, these arguments are advanced on a basis that might be described as historicist: sensitivity toward cultural–contextual specificity and difference. What Lessing denies is not "that in Christ prophecies were fulfilled" or

> that Christ performed miracles. But since the truth of these miracles has completely ceased to be demonstrated by miracles still occurring in the present, since they are no more than reports of miracles (may these reports be as undisputed and as incontrovertible as possible), I deny that they can and should bind me in the least to faith in the other teachings of Christ.
>
> What does then bind me? Nothing but these teachings themselves. Eighteen hundred years ago they were so new, so foreign to the whole mass of truths recognized in that age, that nothing less than miracles and fulfilled prophecies were required if the multitude were to take heed of them at all.[85]

As Lessing wrote these lines, he was already also working on the 100-paragraph essay on "The Education of the Human Race," to which they read like an introduction. They challenge the assumption that the orthodox and deists shared about the basic character of any religion with a claim to the status of being "revealed," namely, that it must from the very outset contain the rational truths of the unity of God and the immortality of the soul. To highlight the weakness of this assumption, Lessing employs the metaphor of the elementary schoolbook in explaining the role of the books of the Bible in the education of mankind. Just as a good pedagogue considers the abilities of the student in constructing a curriculum, God resorted to a method for the moral education of the Israelites (chosen precisely because they were "the least polished and the most ferocious, so that he could start with them from the very beginning"[86]) that was suited to their condition of "childhood," that is, direct and immediate rewards and punishments. "Thus, the books of the Old Testament, this primer of the rude and in the matters of the mind inexperienced people of Israel, may have lacked the doctrine of the immortality of the soul: but at least it ought not to have contained anything which could have arrested the advance of the people for whom it was written on the path towards these great truths."[87] Human beings do possess the capacity to discover truths on their own, and the role of education consists merely in accelerating and facilitating the process. Similarly, revelation does not provide anything for them which they are incapable of arriving at by themselves; "it only supplies them with the most important of these things sooner."[88]

The analogy between revelation and education was as old as Augustine's *De Civitate Dei*, and its pedigree included statements by further eminent church fathers, Luther and other leading German Protestants like Iohannes Cocceji, the founder of "federal theology," and, more recently, some Pietists. It was also an idea which, for obvious reasons, was congenial to the adherents of a religious Enlightenment. Lessing's contribution was its combination with the idea of the historical development of human reason, and the proposition of a dynamics in which revelation and reason both received stimuli from one another. This is possible because reason also possesses the power of revelation (*offenbarungsmächtig*).[89] In view of the "reciprocal service" and "mutual influence"[90] taking place between revelation and reason, Lessing opposed any rigid demarcation between revealed and rational principles and the tracing of them back to separate sources; as he had already set down in his counter-arguments to Reimarus, "revealed religion does not in the least have rational religion as its prerequisite, but encapsulates it."[91] At all times, the stage of development attained in this process of evolution is decisive for the nature of the truths that can usefully serve the purposes of God and man. The "second, better primer" (*zweite beßre Elementarbuch*) could only be issued to a part of humanity which "was already bound together through language, conduct, government, and other natural and political relations—was ripe for the second great step of education."[92] Thanks to the Greeks and Romans, this part of mankind was already familiar with the "shadows" of the necessary principles and "was so advanced in the exercise of its reason that it needed, and could make use of, nobler and worthier motives for its moral actions than the secular rewards and punishments which had guided it so far."[93] And yet, even in this second, better primer, the doctrine of the immortality of the soul was "*preached* as revelation, not *taught* as a result of human keys."[94] In other words, the truths of revelation were not truths of reason at the time when they were revealed; but Lessing harbors no doubt that they have the capacity of becoming ones, and even that they were revealed with the very purpose of becoming ones. Revelation is not something that occurred at a distinct moment in time ("at once"—*auf einmal*), but progressively (*fortschreitende Offenbarung*). God decided to guide human reason to higher truths "gradually" (*allmählig*), providing "directing impulses" (*Richtungsstoß*) with the Old and then the New Testament, so that humanity may pass through the stages of childhood and youth to full maturity, in which "truths of immediate revelation" (*unmittelbare geoffenbarte Wahrheiten*) are to be transformed into "bare truths of reason" (*bloße Vernunftswahrheiten*).[95] Lessing saw this process as yet unfinished in his own time, but toward the end of the *Erziehung* he gave voice to the conviction that the "highest grade of enlightenment and purity [of heart]" (*höchste Stufe der Aufklärung und Reinigkeit [des Herzens]*) of the human race, will be attained. The "time of perfection" will come, when "man, the more his understanding feels convinced about an ever better future, will nevertheless no longer need to obtain motives for his actions from this future; for he will act right because it is right, and not because there are arbitrary rewards fixed to it."[96]

To the extent that Lessing asserted the fundamental historicity of all truths,[97] it is worth noting that in a sense his approach is not all that distant from a Neologist such as Semler, whose critique of "the Unnamed" was based on the latter's insufficient awareness of the historical relativity of the biblical accounts. Semler spoke of a "dual mode of teaching" (*doppelte Lehrart*) in the gospels, "of which the one, sensual and visual, constitutes the true character of that time and place...rich in images and modes of speech from the circle of the Jews, in order to facilitate the beginning of new notions of their current (greater) significance....However, the other mode of teaching already contains the pure spiritual doctrine of Jesus, and can fully dispense with such images, as the listeners or readers are no longer such sensual and inexperienced Jews."[98] Long before the fragment controversy, Semler had established that "the so-called historical circumstances of any text...belong to the grounds of the satisfactory interpretation of the same," including the "circumstances" of the author as well as the readers; the scholar must therefore also investigate whether a (biblical) text had been developed or revised, and if so, arrange textual versions in a temporal order on the basis of specific groups of addressees.[99] These were to be central points of contention in the polemic against the Unnamed,[100] who in Semler's view neglected to consider such distinctions, and thus lagged behind in recognizing the relevance of a new, dynamic concept of history to biblical exegesis.

And yet, Lessing was separated from Neology not only by his low judgment on its intellectual quality and the consequent hazards it constituted to proper enlightenment in religious matters.[101] With all their emphasis on historicity, the Neologues' perspective was focused on the Bible (thus sharing the *Schriftprinzip* of Orthodoxy, which retained the Bible as the only legitimate source of faith). "Our doctrine is not established upon *auctoritatem patrum* or upon *particularia*; but on the contents of the holy scriptures and their correct interpretation; what *concilia* and *patres* correctly hold thereof, we also hold, but *not because they hold it*,"[102] is what Semler wrote in the preface to a work on theological debates in early Christianity by Baumgarten, which he edited after the death of his master. The last clause seems to be echoed in Lessing's statement in the *Gegensätze* to the effect that "[r]eligion is not true because the evangelists and the apostles propagated it: rather, they propagated it because it is true. The written traditions must be explained from its inner truth, and no written tradition is capable of investing it with inner truth if it has none." Lessing's Christian truth, however, is not fully encapsulated in the Bible, nor even in its interpretation, and the reasons have to do exactly with its historicity. First, even the New Testament itself was the outcome of a historical process:

"There had been religion before there was a Bible. There had been Christianity before the evangelists and the apostles wrote. Some time passed before the first of them wrote; and a considerable amount of time passed until the whole of the canon arose. Thus however much depends on these scriptures, the full truth of religion can still not possibly rest on them."[103] Furthermore, there was the process of "progressive revelation," in which reason was assisted by providence. For, on the final analysis, the progress of human reason is not understood by Lessing as a fully autonomous evolution: the final *dénouement* of the "third age" and the coming of a "new, eternal Gospel" are expected by him to be wrought by "eternal Providence."[104]

Given the combination of historicity and providentialism, and the amalgamation of motives, themes, and *telos* from sacred and profane history, in Lessing's grappling with the difficulties of championing a Christianity that answers the requirements of modern times, it is tempting to speculate about the affinities between his stance and that of Robertson advanced in the *Sermon*. The publication date and place of Ebeling's German translation (Hamburg, 1779) also point to interesting possibilities: the translation could have been intended as a (belated and indirect) contribution to the fragment controversy, and could have served as a potential buttress for the position being developed by Lessing in the *Erziehung*. There is, however, no evidence to corroborate such speculations. Lessing had some correspondence with Ebeling's brother Christoph Daniel (who will be also discussed at some length in chapter 5), but not with Johann Philipp. He was certainly aware of the work of English theologians applying a historical approach. He favorably reviewed a German translation of William Warburton's *Divine Legation of Moses* (1737–1741),[105] and he obtained a copy of William Whiston's heterodox *Primitive Christianity Revived* (1711–1712) from his fellow librarian, Christian Gottlob Heyne of Göttingen;[106] he was apparently also enthusiastic about the thought of Adam Ferguson.[107] There is, however, no trace of any concern with anything Robertson ever wrote in the whole of Lessing's mighty oeuvre. How he would have reacted to the materialist aspects of stadial history that lurk even in the background of the account of the Gospel that Robertson advanced in the *Sermon* remains a tantalizing question. For those aspects certainly created a gulf that separated the two minds, however closely they met on the general ground of historicity as married with providentialism.

Michaelis: Göttingen and the cultural approach to Christianity

Having probed into different estimates of the relevance of historical understanding to religious faith in the milieus of Halle and Wolfenbüttel, a brief glance at how this relationship was dealt with at Göttingen will be interesting. The reason for this is not just the geographic proximity and the level of interaction among these seats of learning, or the general significance of the Georgia

Augusta alone, suggested in the Introduction, for a comparative treatment of the Scottish and German Enlightenments. Recent studies of the transformation of Christianity during the eighteenth century identify a fundamental shift in assigning legitimate grounds to the authority of the Bible.[108] With the Reformation, these studies argue, the Bible became a contested legacy. Competing and incompatible claims, increasingly referring to extra-scriptural concepts, were raised as to its "meaning," so that it ceased to function as scripture, that is, the self-authorizing, unifying document of European culture. Two centuries of philologically and historically based biblical criticism further undermined the prestige of the "scriptural Bible," until biblical scholarship, arising as an academic discipline in the eighteenth century, aimed and finally managed to disengage the study and interpretation of the Bible from confessional paradigms, and to reassert its status not on strictly theological but rather philological, philosophical, literary, and historical grounds, as a common stock of cultural inheritance. To a considerable extent, the advent of the "cultural Bible" was the achievement of university men who understood that "the scriptural Bible embedded as it was in confessional particularities, was inimical to the socio-political project from which Enlightenment universities drew their purpose and support," and that if the theological faculty was to retain an honorable position, new functions were to be invented for it, which were conducive to the creation of "an irenic social order based on reason, morality and the growing power of the state."[109] The revivification of the Bible as a cornerstone of European culture was thus principally a university project, and the product an "academic" as well as a "cultural Bible."

Baumgarten, Semler, and a host of other figures from the eighteenth-century German university scene receive attention in these studies, but none so extensively as the Göttingen orientalist and theologian Johann David Michaelis (1717–1791). Michaelis, who studied with Baumgarten in Halle, arrived in Göttingen at the invitation of Münchhausen as *Privatdozent* in 1745, to live and work there (from 1750 as ordinary professor at the philosophical faculty) for almost half a century. His strategy to assert the value of the Bible for contemporary life (in a way, to restore its "catholicity," i.e., its universal meaning) was facilitated by the atmosphere of academic freedom at the university, which he and his theologian colleagues at Göttingen used to investigate the historical dimensions of the Christian tradition without correlating the results to specific theological positions (while remaining true to a dogma of minimal Protestantism intended less to distinguish among denominations than to separate what was respectably Christian from what was not).[110] What came to be emphasized in the volumes of scholarship that these investigations yielded (including a monumental translation of the Old Testament) was the essential, striking strangeness of the Bible;[111] no longer studied as text but as document, as the archive of a splendid but alien civilization, what the Old Testament conveyed was not theological dogma or religious truth, but the heritage of an ancient Israelite society whose relevance to modern Europe paralleled that of Hellas or Rome. Michaelis thus chose to "decompose" the Bible through philological–historical research in order to recover it as a literary remainder capable of fertilizing modern European culture.

It has been argued that for all the historical character of his method it is unhelpful to regard Michaelis as a middling figure between orthodoxy and historicism, for he was chiefly interested in the philosophical, literary, indeed poetic—"cultural," in the modern sense, which we owe to the Enlightenment—treasures unearthed with that method, and the possible uses to which they could be turned in the present.[112] Thus, Michaelis along with several fellow Göttingen philologists and philosophers, who have been recently collectively styled as "the Göttingen School," are perhaps better understood as neo-humanists interested in reshaping antiquity in the light of contemporary realities, or as "scientists of culture." The latter term refers to university academics engaged in a nonideological mode of inquiry oriented toward "collectivist particularism." They rejected universal principles in favor of particularism in the study of "real" historical and unique nations via an empirical disposition. Whether examining the origin of language, legal collections, or societies in newly discovered lands, they were sensitive to the peculiar genius of such groups and aimed to understand data within its own conditions. The critical analysis to which they subjected received tradition—their own or that of others—was motivated by an interest in what makes societies distinct and resilient, and did not lead them to embrace radical or revolutionary principles; if anything, their political sympathies were gradualist, favoring conservative reform.[113]

Michaelis and the other members of this group seem, then, to stand for another moderate, conservative version of Enlightenment, one where interest in history had little to do with the idea of the discipline of history as temporal progress, and where concern with religion (and the relevance of history to religion) had little to do with the aim of justifying faith in Christian revelation. In this sense, there was also little to connect them with the agenda pursued by Robertson in the *Sermon*, and more generally in his career as a historian-cleric, though perhaps more to share with him as an entrepreneur in academic and ecclesiastical politics. But as with all generalizations, this one is in need of qualifications, and indeed in the literature summarized in the last few pages it is repeatedly emphasized that the nontheological and nonconfessional outlook of these scholars went together with a deep commitment to Christian religious forms, and the eclecticism they applied to the refurbishment of Christianity was compatible for them with engaging in apologetics against atheism and skepticism. Michaelis himself is an interesting case. Most of his formidable oeuvre was devoted to the excavation of ancient Israel as a classical civilization from the Old Testament, as a means of providing a cultural key to social order under the post-confessional state. However, still at the beginning of his career at Göttingen, he also wrote a lengthy introduction to "the divine writings of the New Testament," which was successful enough to merit several revised editions,[114] and in 1783 also served as the basis for his own belated contribution to the *Fragmentenstreit*. These are, to all intents and purposes, apologetic writings, one of their recurrent themes being the "authenticity" of the gospels and the letters of the apostles, besides the question whether they are of immediate divine inspiration. Michaelis's position on authenticity is remarkable. As to the second, he simply dismisses it as not being a question of decisive importance:

> The question whether the books of the New Testament are inspired by God is not at all as important for the Christian religion as the previous one, whether they are authentic....Suppose that God did not inspire any of the books of the New Testament, and that Matthew, Mark, Luke, John, and Paul were left completely to their own resources to write as well as they could. Yet if the writings were merely old, authentic, and credible, the Christian religion would still remain the true one. The miracles which lend support to it would just as well prove its truthfulness if their witnesses were not inspired but merely human witnesses, because in the investigation of these miracles we are anyway not postulating the divine authority of these writers, but regard them as merely human witnesses...Thus it would be fully well possible for someone to doubt, or even deny, the divine inspiration of the complete books of the N. T., and yet wholeheartedly believe in the Christian religion.[115]

The question of inspiration is thus beside the point: there is nothing to lose from acknowledging that "in merely historical matters" the evangelists were not inspired.

As for the other, to his mind, really decisive issue, Michaelis proposes the standard methodological apparatus and procedure of historical philology as the ground for evaluating the genuineness of the books of the New Testament. First of all, he insists that the same criteria should be accepted in establishing the authenticity of these documents as are usually deemed satisfactory vis-à-vis the works of "profane authors": there is no reason why "more explicit witnesses" (*ausdrücklichere Zeugnisse*) should be required and produced to prove the authenticity of the writings of the evangelists or Paul than is the case with Thucydides, Xenophon, Polybius, or any other ancient writer. This basic principle, Michaelis suggests, is often neglected. It follows for him that the "contradictions" within and among the accounts of the four evangelists, which have been instrumentalized in challenging the credibility of the gospels by adversaries of the Christian revelation from ancient Manicheans to modern deists, ought to be assessed by the standards applied to apparently contradictory testimonies about the same set of events by different reporters in secular history. To highlight the point, Michaelis brings examples from ancient and modern history. The accounts of two Prussian officers of the great war of 1756–1763, related from memory, may differ and contradict one another in many more or less important details; but does this call into question the veracity and "reality" of the basic facts and the story as a whole? Almost naturally, there are contradictions among the sources used to construct a scientifically credible history, but it is still possible to establish upon them a coherent and consistent narrative, from which contradictions are eliminated. Michaelis uses the example of his colleague Johann Stephan Pütter's widely acclaimed "Reichsgeschichte" (probably the *Vollständiges Handbuch der deutschen Reichshistorie*, 1762) to illustrate this argument.[116]

Next, Michaelis points out that the suspicion of forgery depends on the assumption of a forger possessing "a superior genius and superhuman circumspection, a near-omniscience in history," because the accounts advanced in this most inspected text of all texts is "in a miraculous way consonant with the history, manners, and opinions of the first century," especially when it comes to minute details.[117] Implicit here is an acute awareness of the paramount importance of contextual understanding for historical interpretation and thus—consistently with the arguments advanced about the identical status of testimonies relevant to sacred and secular history—for biblical exegesis, which in the case of Michaelis's *Einleitung* and *Erklärung* is specifically concerned with buttressing faith in the Gospel. To refute objections leveled against the authenticity of the gospels, he repeatedly refers to the consonance of the manners, customs, and practices as described in them with other testimonies from the same period, but as a philologist, of all usages he is most concerned with linguistic ones. Whether Greek, the language in which the gospels were passed down to posterity, was the language in which they were originally written, was another question often discussed by doubters of their authenticity, who were confirmed in their doubts by the alleged "impurity"—the swarming of "Hebraisms" and other "isms"—in the texts. Michaelis emphatically disagrees with those who regard such objections as mere blasphemy: this is mere "pedantry," which "much too overrates the purity and gracefulness [*Reinigkeit und Zierlichkeit*] of language." Zealous goodwill for the cause of the Christian religion have blinded theologians and philologists to this fact and led them to assert, wrongly, the "cleanness" of the Greek-language gospels. Historically, it could not have been anything but "impure." Once again, Michaelis illustrates his point by recent developments in the history of the German language. In the early eighteenth century, German was a "hideous mixture" of native and foreign words, and as one of the reasons was a "stupid affectation" in aping the French, "the blending of the rich mother tongue with a poor foreign language presented itself in its worst aspect."

Then came the movement for the reforming of the German language, associated with the name of Johann Christoph Gottsched, whose services are warmly commended by Michaelis. But before then, anyone who undertook to write a book or a letter, "wrote in a German as mixed as it was usual at that time; this may have been disliked by posterity in the short run, between 1735 and 1755, but in fact he wrote for his own time, sought and feared its opinions, and did not know what the future would bring; so he judged himself according to the habits of his own time."[118] By the same token, it would have been ridiculous affectation for the evangelists and the apostles to address their highly mixed audience in a Greek as pure as if they had been in Athens or before a Roman court: "One cannot generally regard the purity of language a duty and its opposite a fault, but consider here time, place, purpose, and material. One must write differently when one acts as an author who endeavors at stylistic beauty, and differently in letters, where the intimacy of tone and the language of the addressee take precedence to bookish language. If in a certain discipline or subject a certain style, however mixed, is already habitual, it would be striking to change it all of a sudden."[119] By no means was it, therefore, a fault of the authors of the Gospel to have interspersed their Greek discourse, addressed to a multitude of Jews and heathens including many women, with phrases from a wide array of the languages of the region and even "idiotisms," that is, words from the spoken language of the common folk as distinguished from the literary standard.

If the bulk of Michaelis's investigations of the Old Testament were geared toward one aspect of the program of enlightened university theology (modernizing Christianity by recovering and reappropriating the materials of traditional culture in a new irenic, pragmatic, and academic mode[120]), his engagement with the New Testament demonstrates that he was no less competent in applying his scholarship to the other, apologetic goals of that program. In these writings he evidently aimed at shoring up faith in Christianity as a revealed religion by resort to advanced methods of historical and philological criticism, including a strong awareness of the relevance of historically specific human contexts to biblical exegesis. It is remarkable that he did so by radically denying the legitimacy of any distinction between the standards of interpretation applied in sacred and secular history. This is certainly not the same as Robertson's assimilation or reciprocal insertion of sacred and secular themes in his narrative account of the gradually unfolding meaning of the Gospel; and the Robertsonian–Lessingian idea of "progressive revelation" is also missing from Michaelis's theoretical apparatus. Nevertheless, the family resemblances among all the authors discussed in this chapter are strong enough to construe them as representatives of several varieties of a moderate, conservative, and religious Enlightenment, for whom the vindication of the Christian revelation and of its continuing relevance to their contemporary circumstances was indissolubly wedded to the recognition of the historicity of religion, and strongly depended on the application of methods deriving from the ever more professional and "scientific" historical discipline.

3
A Different *View of the Progress of Society in Europe*

As noted in chapter 1, recent scholarship has introduced a great deal of nuance into our understanding of the overall character of Robertson's achievement, recontextualizing it within the mainstream of eighteenth-century historical studies, which were inspired by narrative as well as political, religious, and educational agendas. However, these valuable correctives to the received image of Robertson as an avant-garde structuralist historian do not seriously affect the status of his admittedly most experimental text on which this image has been largely based (together with Book Four and other portions of the *History of America* and passages from his other works). The *View of the Progress of Society* was written by Robertson as a volume-length introduction to the *History of Charles V*, in an attempt to explore the forces of causality underlying long-term historical processes which led, by the beginning of the sixteenth century, to the rise of states capable of sustaining large-scale and long-standing military efforts. It has been suggested that in his writings Robertson moves rather flexibly between the patterns of "Enlightenment" history (where progress takes place, or at least may take place, as a result of conscious choice, even intervention) and "stadial" or conjectural history (which is dominated by a theory of spontaneous order emerging from a natural succession of various stages in people's mode of subsistence).[1] This is an important distinction in accounting for the variability of perspective within the oeuvre as a whole, but less helpful in approaching the specific case of *A View of the Progress of Society*. In this composition, Robertson's smooth combination of descriptive and narrative history[2] is distinguished by an exceptionally rigorous application of a set of standards derived from the sciences of man in order to reveal the logic of the unfolding of European history and to identify the place of each distinct period in this process. This was necessary, in his own words, "in order to mark the great steps by which [the northern nations] advanced from barbarism to refinement, and to point out those general principles and events which, by their uniform as well as extensive operation, conducted all of them to that degree of improvement in policy and in manners which they had attained at the period when Charles V. began his reign."³

This is also important to stress because it was exactly this logic and these standards that were, for linguistic, cultural, and other reasons, obliterated in the complicated history of the work's German reception, which was already hinted at in the beginning of the Introduction. In this chapter, I shall explore the nature and the causes of these transformations, contextualizing them especially in regard to the ways in which they bear the imprint of the environment, the personality, as well as the limitations of the stature of the translator–editor as "new author." A brief reassessment of Robertson's own argument in *A View of the Progress of Society* will be followed by portraits of the German interlocutors. Then I shall proceed to considering the fortunes of Robertson's "intended meaning" in the translating process through an exploration of the relevant terminology and textual strategies deployed to produce a different kind of meaning: one pursued by the recipients.⁴

Manners and sociocultural dynamics

Robertson's presentation is organized around the concept of manners, the unwritten ethical and aesthetic rules of human intercourse, essential for the eighteenth-century Scottish thinkers as a category of social science inquiry as well as a set of norms to live by.⁵ In *A View of the Progress of Society*, manners function like a seismograph: in their transformation the minor and major tremors in the mode of subsistence and material well-being of society, on the one hand, and in its legal and political framework, on the other, are faithfully registered. Already in the very first sentence of the text, the key word "manners" occupies a central place: "Two great revolutions have happened in the political state and in the manners of the European nations. The first was occasioned by the progress of the Roman Empire, the second by the subversion of it." The latter was especially destructive of earlier structures: "Very faint vestiges of the Roman policy, jurisprudence, arts, or literature remained. New forms of government, new laws, new manners, new dresses, new languages, and new names of men and countries, were every where introduced."⁶

But this represented the last case of dramatic discontinuity in Europe's civilizing process, the proper subject of the voluminous introduction to *The History of Charles V*. From this several centuries' chasm onwards, Robertson's account is that of unbroken—gradual, if uneven—development from rudeness to refinement, resulting from shifts in the mode of subsistence, and giving rise to innovations in the public institutions of Europeans. While paying tribute to some of the virtues of the conquering barbarians, Robertson uses dark colors to depict the medieval stagnation of the human mind, and invokes for the first time one of the characteristic ideas of the Scottish Enlightenment in the book. The cultivation and flourishing of the arts and sciences play a decisive role in the ennoblement—and their neglect, in the degradation—of the forms of human intercourse, with far-reaching consequences on the public domain as a whole. Also, these factors mutually reinforce each of the other's effects.

> If men do not enjoy the protection of regular government, together with the expectation of personal security, which naturally flows from it, they never attempt to make progress in science, nor aim at attaining refinement in taste or manners.... Force of mind, a sense of personal dignity, gallantry in enterprise, invincible perseverance in execution, contempt of danger and of death, are the characteristic virtues of uncivilized nations. But these are the offspring of equality and independence, both which the feudal institutions had destroyed.... Human society is in its most corrupted state, at that period when men have lost their original independence and simplicity of manners, but have not attained that degree of refinement which introduces a sense of decorum and of propriety in conduct, as a restraint on those passions which lead to heinous crimes.[7]

Watching for the key word has led us to the central organizing principle of *A View of the Progress of Society*: the idea in stadial or conjectural history that manners—as we shall see in more detail, in close interplay with the division of labor, mode of subsistence, and institutions—characteristic of European society had undergone several stages of refinement, until, by the advent of the modern period, they came to serve as the foundation of a sophisticated and highly developed civilization. This civilization was not considered flawless, but certainly unparalleled, representing a different quality, and a higher order than either its predecessors or its contemporary counterparts outside Europe. The low level of material culture and intellectual accomplishment (the "mode of subsistence" and primitive stage of "refinement") among the barbarian peoples are linked by Robertson to their warlike virtues, which, however, in turn account for their ethos of personal liberty. Reflecting on the false assumption of historians about their great numbers, he claims

> that some of the most considerable of the barbarous nations subsisted entirely by hunting or pasturage, in both which states of society large tracts of land are required for maintaining a few inhabitants; and...all of them were strangers to the arts and industry without which population cannot increase to any great degree...But the same circumstances that prevented the barbarous nations from becoming populous, contributed to inspire or to strengthen the martial spirit by which they were distinguished.

Later, this is supplemented by the following remark:

> Not only the different nations that issued from the north of Europe, which has always been considered as the seat of liberty, but the Huns and Alans,

who inhabited part of those countries which have been marked out as the peculiar region of servitude, enjoyed freedom and independence in such a high degree as seems to be scarcely compatible with a state of social union, or with the subordination necessary to maintain it.[8]

In a note placed in the section "Proofs and Illustrations," which he contrived in order to avoid the traditional digressions within the text that tended to break the flux of the narrative, Robertson supplies an example of, and methodological advice on, the application of a device peculiar to conjectural history. Comparing the "political state" and material circumstances of the ancient Germans and the North American Indians, he claims that observations on the latter could throw light on the "character and manners" of the former almost as usefully as the works of Caesar or Tacitus. The reason for this was that "the characters of nations depend on the state of society in which they live, and on the political institutions established among them." Robertson called attention to the limits of the applicability of such material of anthropological nature in comparative history: "I do not pretend that the state of society in the two countries was perfectly similar in every respect." But he still asserted that "[t]he resemblance, however, between their condition, is greater, perhaps, than any that history affords an opportunity of observing between any two races of uncivilized people, and this has produced a surprising similarity of manners."[9]

Soon enough, in what are perhaps the most striking passages of *A View of the Progress of Society*, Robertson sets out "to point out those general principles and events" that led the European nations from this barbarous state "to that degree of improvement in policy and in manners which they had attained at the period when Charles V. began his reign." The crucial events were the Crusades, in whose wake Europe gradually emerged from the feudal system, described by Robertson in disparaging terms. Having reduced many from freemen to serfs, it also failed to provide a satisfactory degree of security. In the feudal kingdom, which is "a military establishment rather than a civil institution...[t]he bond of political union was extremely feeble, the sources of anarchy were innumerable. The monarchical and aristocratical parts of the constitution having no intermediate power to balance them, were perpetually at variance, and justling with each other."[10] The Crusades put an end to these miserable conditions not merely by exporting Europe's surplus violence. First, they acquainted Europeans with long-forgotten attainments and standards of civilization:

> Although the attention of the historians of the Crusades was fixed on other objects than the state of society and manners among the nations which they invaded...[i]t was not possible for the crusaders to travel so many countries, and to behold their various customs and institutions, without acquiring information and improvement. Their views enlarged; their prejudices wore off; new ideas crowded into their minds; and they must have

been sensible, on many occasions, of the rusticity of their own manners, when compared with those of a more polished people.... [T]o these wild expeditions, the effect of superstition or folly, we owe the first gleams of light which tended to dispel barbarism and ignorance.[11]

Especially in the light of this last remark, the passage sounds very much like an ingenious application of the Smithian rule of unintended consequences, and somewhat later Robertson indeed takes up a thread, which appears in Book III of *The Wealth of Nations* as an exemplary case of the operation of that rule.[12] For, according to Robertson, a further result of the Crusades was that through the stimulus they gave to commerce they unwittingly contributed to the strengthening of those "intermediate powers," in a rudimentary state under feudalism, which he had earlier lamented. Among such circumstances, the civilizing potential inherent in exchange relationships could also grow to full blossom:

> Wealth [generated by commerce] was accompanied by its usual attendants, ostentation and luxury; and though the former was formal and cumbersome, and the latter inelegant, they led gradually to greater refinement in manners and in the habits of life.... As cities grew to be more populous, and the occasions of intercourse between people increased, statutes and regulations multiplied of course, and all became sensible that their common safety depended on observing them with exactness, and on punishing such as violated them with promptitude and rigour. Laws and subordination, as well as polished manners, taking their rise in the cities, diffused themselves insensibly through the rest of society."[13]

These blessings appeared hand in hand with other progressive developments, such as the loosening of the dependence of serfs here and there, the strengthening of royal authority and the success in restraining baronial feuds, the greater stability of jurisdiction through the revival of Roman law, the renaissance of the arts and sciences, and the softening of martial virtues into chivalric manners.[14] Robertson inserts several further eulogies on commerce and its role in refining the political, moral, and intellectual condition of European society before, and even after, he proceeds to the history of the military organization of the main European states, to be followed by their constitutional arrangements at the beginning of the sixteenth century—both topics being obviously essential in the introduction to a history of the reign of Charles V.[15]

What emerges quite clearly from this summary of Robertson's main argument is that he follows the logic of cause and effect very rigorously, to which in one case he explicitly draws attention. He stresses that "[i]n pointing out and explaining these causes and events [of the improvement of government and manners after the eleventh century], it is not necessary to observe the order of time with a chronological accuracy; it is of more importance to keep in view their mutual connexion and dependence, and to show how the operation of one event or one cause prepared the way for another, and augmented its influence."¹⁶ The reader is constantly reminded how the developments highlighted by the author are organically embedded into one and the same process; how the ever-increasing specialization of functions, and with it the differentiation and mutually counterpoising role of orders, constitute a common background of all of them; and how all of this is attended by the growth of a set of standards in human intercourse, which is already familiar to the citizen of the modern eighteenth-century world. A succession of events—crusades, commerce, refinement, polite manners, rule of law, in this order—whose motive forces are traditional and "superstitious" gives rise to unexpected consequences, which are first felt on the level of the prevailing "mode of subsistence," next, in the norms that regulate interpersonal relationships, and finally in the sphere of the institutions through which civil society is governed. This is not to deny that Robertson, strongly attached to the Scottish civic moralist tradition, struggles to save intentionality, and thus the possibility of moral example in history, and to avoid the deterministic implications of stadial history.¹⁷ The above is an admittedly simplified epitome of an argument that is admirably multifaceted in all of its conciseness. But what matters for the purposes of this chapter is that, if the "meaning" of the progress of society in Europe according to Robertson is the rise of the rule of law under stable monarchy, this is shown by him to have taken place in close interaction with the growth of commerce and manners, the other two distinctive features of modern society. And according to the thrust of Robertson's argument, their succession in the logical–causal sequence should be understood as irreversible.

An "exotic" interlude

Before turning to the versions of the *View of the Progress of Society*, which appeared in the standard German editions of the *History of Charles V*, the independent rendering of the text by Ludwig Heinrich von Nicolay, mentioned in the Introduction, deserves some attention. Nicolay (1737–1820) was born as the son of the local archivist in Strasbourg, where he studied philosophy and law. Already as a student he started publishing his poetry, and after his graduation in 1760 he moved to Paris and soon made the acquaintance of some of the leading lights, including Voltaire, Diderot, d'Alembert, and Melchior Grimm (with whom Nicolay maintained a long-lasting correspondence). These contacts earned him entry in the world of the salons, which was decisive for his future career: one of the *habitués* of the salons, the Russian Prince Dmitry Mikhailovich Golitsin, was so impressed with Nicolay's manners and talents that he hired him as a personal secretary, and also took him to Vienna when he became appointed there as Russian ambassador in 1761. After a subsequent brief spell at the university of his hometown as *Privatdozent*, Nicolay became the tutor of another Russian aristocrat, the young Count Aleksei Rasumovsky (son of the president of the Saint Petersburg Academy of Sciences, a former student of his at Strasbourg). Nicolay accompanied Rasumovsky Jr. and Rasumovsky Sr. on a European Grand Tour, including Italy, Switzerland, southern Germany, France, and England. While still in England, in 1769, he received and accepted an invitation from the influential statesman Count Nikita Panin, who supervised the education of Grand Duke Paul, to serve as one of the tutors of the son and heir of Empress Catherine the Great. While Nicolay continued to publish his literary works in Germany, his rise at the Russian court was steady. He escorted his former student after the death of the grand duke's first wife in 1776 to arrange a new marriage in Berlin (where he made important new acquaintances, including the publisher and *Aufklärer* Friedrich Nicolai), and in 1781–1782 on a European tour highlighting Vienna and Versailles (where he could be an expert guide of the traveling Russian "small court," and earned the esteem of Joseph II, as well as a patent of imperial nobility). He also filled secretarial positions to both Paul's first and second wife. This went together with the acquisition of emoluments, titles, and estates—including Monrepos, a real gem outside the city of Vyborg, the seat of his remarkable collection of books and art objects. The zenith of Nicolay's career was his appointment, after the succession of Paul as Tsar in 1796, as a member of the imperial cabinet council and, in 1798, as president of the Academy of Sciences. After the murder of his patron in 1801, he was discharged from his positions and lived a quiet life of writing while managing his estate at Monrepos.[18]

In the preface to the *History of Charles V*, Robertson wrote: "History claims it as her prerogative to offer instruction to Kings, as well as to their people." Nicolay took this claim in the narrowest literal sense. Whether prompted by the Empress[19] (who was keen on adding erudition in literary and philosophical matters to the curriculum prescribed by Panin, focusing on military administration and statecraft) or on his own initiative (based on his possible familiarity with the work and status of Robertson from his stay to Britain), Nicolay identified in the *View of the Progress of Society* an excellent tool for the education of a future ruler. He must have recognized an object lesson in the "barbarity, disorder, and infertility" (*Barbarei, Verwirrung und Unfruchtbarkeit*) of the Middle Ages, which for a long time discouraged even the best experts (*die geschickteste Männer*) from dealing with them. Montesquieu is praised as the first to have "brought the torch of genius into this obscure cave, [and] showed us among its debris the sources of our present laws. Robertson penetrated with the same deliberation into the still dark pit, identified the elements of scattered rubble, arranged them in order, and demonstrated to us on them the history of human understanding."[20] There was one problem, though, with Robertson's masterpiece: its length, sophistication, and scholarly apparatus were deemed by Nicolay to be forbidding for his 17-year-old pupil. He therefore decided for a free adaptation: "In order to lay such an important canvas before the eyes of a young prince, I have attempted to render the work of the famous Briton in a language and in a style that is familiar to him [Paul], and corresponds with his age, which abhors its length, and to his discernment, for which it is much too detailed."[21]

Accordingly, Nicolay dropped in its entirety Robertson's substantial "Proofs and Illustrations" from the end of the volume, and condensed them into rudimentary explanatory footnotes. The size of the book became reduced by about one-half, and the internal proportions were also subverted: Section I, which occupies less than one-half of the original, takes nearly two-thirds of Nicolay's rendering, in which Sections II and III are little more than *précis* of the English version. The relentless exercise in abbreviation performed by Nicolay did not escape the attention of reviewers. "The style is too affectedly concise," the reviewer of the first edition complained, "not merely compact, but fragmented"; and he thought that it was "modeled after Tacitus" (whose biography of Agricola was also translated for Paul by Nicolay, and was included in the same edition of his poetical and prose works as the *Entwurf*).[22] True, the reviewer of the 1793 edition found merit in Nicolay's translation as one which is "free, but executed with gusto, and it reads like an original."[23] His objections against the style notwithstanding, the first reviewer thought that "as R. is not in every hand, this short excerpt of such an excellent book must be in any case welcome." What the second, 1793 reviewer found odd was the context in which Nicolay's rendering was published, and agreed with the decision to omit it from the previous, second edition: "and it would not have been missed here, either, for hitherto people, not at all unjustly, wanted to see only poetical translations included in the work of a writer."

A few interesting points emerge from these elements of a mosaic, which are worth registering. That Nicolay's work consisted not merely of a condensation of Robertson's text but its concentration as well, is revealed by the first glance at the title: the Scottish historian's "view of the progress of society" becomes an "outline of the political condition" of Europe (*Entwurf des politischen Zustandes in Europa*) in the rendering of the German writer, a lapse which may be fortuitous, but at least in part reflects the real character of the changes of the text itself. While the strongly analytical thrust of Robertson's account is more or less still retained in the first section of Nicolay's rendering, in the radically shortened second and third sections the sociocultural contextualization of political developments and institutions is entirely weeded out, and it is a narrative of events that remains. It is perhaps little wonder that this transformation went unnoticed by the literary critics, who were more interested in matters of style and presentation. More surprisingly, they also failed to comment on the fact that by the time Nicolay took to translating the *View of the Progress of Society*, there was already a full German edition of the *History of Charles V* available on the book market. It is a genuine puzzle that the silence about this alternative edition continued at the time of the reedition of the *Entwurf* in Nicolay's works in 1793, the year when Remer's thoroughly reworked *Abriß des Wachstums und Fortgangs des gesellschaftlichen Lebens in Europa*, published in 1792, was already reviewed in the *Göttingische Anzeigen von gelehrten Sachen*. Still further to complicate the matter, one might ask whether, in 1772, Nicolay, a man of broad erudition and intellectual horizon as well as good connections in the world of letters, could have truly been unaware of the existence of what was to be the standard German edition of the text he was about to translate for his pupil, or whether Remer's similar neglect to mention Nicolay's rival attempt in either the 1778–1779 or the 1792–1795 editions prepared by him arose out of ignorance, contempt, or jealousy. In the lack of documentary evidence, these questions remain unanswered.

Some interlocutors

It is now time to move on to the remarkable history of the versions of the *View of the Progress of Society*, published in the full German editions of the *History of Charles V*, by introducing first the figures of the interpreters. Unlike Robertson, and perhaps even Nicolay, they are relatively obscure figures.[24] Theodor Christoph Mittelstedt (1712–1777), church councilor, and court pastor of the Dukes of Braunschweig, was a successful translator of contemporary English and French works. His first noteworthy translation was *Ophiomaches*, or *Deism Revealed,* Philip Skelton's compilation of texts by Herbert of Cherbury, Hobbes, Shaftesbury, Toland, Tindal, Collins, Mandeville, and others in 1756. His later translations include Gilbert Burnet's *History of the Reformation* (1765–1769) and *A Sentimental Journey* by Laurence Sterne (1769, 2nd ed. 1774). When Mittelstedt undertook to render *The History of Charles V* into German in 1769, he had already been familiar with Robertson as a writer through his translation of the latter's *History of Scotland* (1762).[25] Shortly before his death, he translated Richard Price's *Observations on the Nature of Civil Liberty* and Edmund Burke's *Speech on Conciliation with the Colonies*, published in the first volume of the *Amerikanisches Archiv* (1777), edited by Julius August Remer.

Though also not a particularly shining light of the German *Aufklärung*, Remer (1738–1803) had a more interesting as well as more scholarly career than Mittelstedt. Son of a Protestant pastor in Braunschweig, he studied first at Helmstedt, where the once famous university was on the decline at that time, and later at the vigorously developing new University of Göttingen.[26] At both universities, he enrolled in the theological faculty; nevertheless, his main interest was already history. We can only guess who his mentors may have been. In view of Remer's later intellectual development, it is safe to assume that Gatterer, who joined the Göttingen faculty in the same year as Remer began his studies, made an impact on the latter's scholarly attitudes. Though his great dream of a historical society and a journal only came true several years later, Gatterer's commitment to a fresh brand of universal history, described in chapter 1, was well known from the outset. Another Göttingen professor who might have influenced Remer was Pütter, also mentioned earlier, whose fame as an expert on *Reichsgeschichte* and German *Staatsrecht* and popularity as a lecturer rose sharply during Remer's student years.[27] In view of

Pütter's possible impact on the later editor of Robertson's *History of Charles V*, it is noteworthy that the English translator of his *Historische Entwickelung der heutigen Staatsverfassung des Teutschen Reichs* (1786–1788) seems to have thought, whether rightly or wrongly, this work to be a German counterpart of Scottish "philosophical history."[28]

Having graduated from Göttingen, in 1763 Remer became a tutor, in 1770, a lecturer, and in 1774, professor of *Universal- und Staatengeschichte* at the Collegium Carolinum in Braunschweig, while also editing various local journals. In 1787, he returned to Helmstedt, then as ordinary professor of history and statistics (*Staatistik*, that is, state sciences). Having held an office in the ducal intelligence and press service after 1774, Remer rose to the rank of court councilor in 1796.

Remer seems to have lived the life of the industrious provincial scholar within rather narrow geographic confines, never leaving his native land apart from a short trip to Schleswig. He was a prolific if unoriginal author of compendium-like textbooks of history and state sciences, which went through several editions.[29] While not later than in 1771 he revealed familiarity through quotations (without references) with Robertson's *History of Charles V*, his acknowledged mentor was Gatterer, and he did his best to prevent, as the Göttingen professor warned, the "degeneration" of his history into mere state or imperial history—"which general [in effect, universal] history should never be."[30] His most important work besides his revision of Robertson's *History of Charles V* was *Versuch einer Geschichte der französischen Constitutionen* (1795), an account of the transformation of the French state from the Middle Ages to 1789, also containing thoughtful analyses of the causes of the Revolution. Remer also earned a reputation as one of the main German authorities on America, especially on the 13 colonies' relations with England and the circumstances of the War of Independence.[31] Besides the documents in the three volumes of *Amerikanisches Archiv* (1777–1778) mentioned above, he published a carefully annotated German translation of Charles Stedman's *History of the Origin, Progress, and Termination of the American War*.[32]

Within Remer's own relatively confined circle of operation, these achievements earned him not only titles and honors, but also a considerable amount of respect, a circumstance about which even Robertson was informed. Writing from Braunschweig in November 1780 and recalling his acquaintance with Robertson in their youth, a certain J. Westphalen (about whom I have not been able to find out any more detail) reported to Robertson not only about the "universal Applause" which his works evoked in Germany, but specifically about the revised edition of the *History of Charles V*, "which was undertook & now finished by a Man of great Abilities professor Römer [sic] at the Colledge Carolin at Brunswic well known in the literary world for some able performances." Westphalen added that Remer was even "honoured with the particular esteem of her Royal Highness the Duchess of Brunswic, with whom he reads History twice a Week" (and assured Robertson that at these sessions his works are "not forgot").[33] Though Remer could never have equaled the financial status Robertson attained with his intellectual accomplishments, these labors rewarded the former with comfortable, if not luxurious circumstances. According to his last will in 1800, his fortune exceeded 1,000 thalers in cash and in debts owed to him (though he also incurred a debt of 450); he had a house worth 2,500 thalers.[34] His chief treasure, however, was his library, with a size estimated in the will at 6,000 volumes and its value at 1,500 thalers; but when his son—a doctor who later became a professor of medicine—put the books up for auction, the catalogue revealed that Remer's zeal as a collector was even greater than he thought, the list containing over 7,400 titles and 43 manuscripts.[35]

All of these circumstances taken together, Remer's figure seems to be ideally suited for a study of the significance of the interpreter of foreign intellectual and cultural attainments in the eighteenth century, a role which he undertook enthusiastically. First, while his library in particular testifies to the remarkable breadth of his intellectual horizon and his erudition, as an author Remer was more representative of the accomplished artisan than the artist of genius. He possessed a fine sense of relevance, and a fair ability to summarize and synthesize, but little sensitivity for nuances of meaning, and still less elegance of style. This, however, also meant accessibility: it was precisely on account of his average character or typicality that Remer and his likes could play an immense role in shaping the dominant modes of thinking in the confined universe of the German small town or province. At the same time, in the succession of prefaces and remarks placed in the notes with which he equipped Robertson's text, one may recognize a voice of growing self-confidence, supported by climbing into ever more respectable academic and administrative positions. This was a characteristic combination on the contemporary public scene in Hanover and elsewhere in Germany, where university professors became almost automatically appointed *Hofrat*. By virtue of his own record of scholarly contributions as well as his visible social advance, Remer could well have felt entitled to assert an independence from his source, besides (or, in many cases, precisely because of) the meticulous care he in general devoted to its proper rendering. Performing this exercise on one of the international historical bestsellers of the time was also quite beyond doubt a strategy calculated to further consolidate his own status and credentials in the academic community and his wider social world.

In addition, it must be reemphasized that his critical remarks on Robertson—which are sporadic and relegated to the notes of the 1778–1779 edition, while sweeping and essential in the 1792–1795 revision of *The History of Charles V*—are in full compliance with the established practices of translating foreign texts in eighteenth-century Germany. True, Gatterer himself warned that a translation "may contain neither more nor less than the original. That is, the translator may neither expand nor shorten the original," and this must be applied to content and style as well.[36] But such rigor and self-discipline was

84 Translations, Histories, Enlightenments

by no means a rule among contemporary German translators.[37] The boundaries between faithful translation and adaptation were dim; dropping chapters and inserting prefaces, notes, or appendices in order to explain or challenge the author's meaning was not only common, but even required as a means of making the foreign text more accessible to the German reader. Besides the obviously felt needs of a different cultural environment and the dubious status of translation between piracy and independent achievement, this was due to the fact that publishing a text was considered to enhance the reputation of the publisher in proportion to the element of originality contained in it. Remer, when he expressed his pretensions to surpass his model Robertson—politely and awkwardly in the 1778 preface to the *Geschichte Kaiser Carls des Fünften*, and boldly and uncompromisingly in 1792[38]—could therefore only expect to meet the approval of the audience he addressed.

As a matter of fact, one has to distinguish between intended changes and unintended distortions of the original meaning of a text through translation into a foreign language. Some of the pitfalls of translation set by the insurmountable linguistic and cultural barriers between eighteenth-century Scottish and German thought have been perceptively analyzed in the cases, for instance, of David Hume and Adam Ferguson: we know how, and with what consequences, Humean "belief" became *Glaube*, or the terms of Fergusonian civic activism were translated into a language of spiritual perfectibilism.[39] I shall argue that in the case of Robertson, too, unwittingly committed errors supplemented intentional textual revision in transforming a natural into an idealist history of the rise of modern European society. Due to the combination of deliberate changes arising from the translator's interpretative strategy and shifts of meaning occasioned by the manner of translating the pivotal elements of Robertson's vocabulary mentioned above, the logic these established became gradually overwhelmed in the course of the German publishing history of *A View of the Progress of Society*. It is chiefly not mistranslations but the rendering of those key English words of classical derivation, whose breadth of meaning is difficult to convey by using even their closest German counterparts, that obscure some crucial associations, described above in my summary of Robertson's argument, in the main text of the 1778 version. Let us first look at some examples of this.

Sitten and ethnocultural specifics

"Arts and industry" ("without which population cannot increase to any great degree" among the barbarous peoples) is translated as *erfinderischer Fleiß*.[40] In the case of both of the central terms in this phrase, one of their several connotations is thus selected in the translation—"inventiveness" or "resourcefulness" for art, and "diligence" for industry. As a result, sifted out of the German text is the additional sense of the concrete productive activities that stem from these human qualities, and even the fruits of such activities, which is all undoubtedly implied in the original and essential from the point of view of the meaning of the book. Further on, in a sentence where Robertson writes that "the arts of elegance, which minister to luxury, and are supported by it...were neglected or lost," Mittelstedt chooses to translate "luxury" as *Ueppigkeit*, a solution of which Remer approves.[41] Luxury is, of course, one of the grand topics of moral and political discourse in eighteenth-century Britain and elsewhere in Europe, a phenomenon applauded as often as denounced.[42] But when, as in the given context, it appears unqualified, it is used as a neutral term to describe splendor, or a higher degree of affluence than that ensured by the merely "useful arts, without which life can scarcely be considered as comfortable." *Ueppigkeit*, on the other hand, more than simply meaning opulence, carries the notion of lusciousness, that is, an exorbitant enjoyment of superfluity, and thus some moral disapproval even when it is in no way qualified.

The case of "commerce," when it is translated as *Handel*,[43] is analogous to that of "arts and industry." Whereas the English term automatically anticipates the strong linkage Robertson is about to suggest between the exchange of goods and the refinement of manners by denoting any kind of communication or free intercourse in the affairs of life, the latter is clearly outside the semantic content of *Handel*. The problem of sociability as a function of commercial society, which is central for the thinkers of the Scottish Enlightenment, is thus rendered somewhat difficult to grasp in the German translation.[44]

Finally, one needs to confront the intricate cluster of ideas connected with the terms "police," "polite," "polished," whose etymology is divergent, but whose near homophonous character could prove quite deceiving. Thus, Ferguson—having, of course, the classical *polis* as a civic ideal in mind—thought that

> [t]he term *polished*, if we may judge from its etymology, originally referred to the state of nations in respect to their laws and government. In its later applications, it refers no less to their proficiency in the liberal and mechanical arts, in literature, and in commerce.[45]

Even though throughout his oeuvre, and especially in the *View of the Progress*, Robertson showed himself to be more of a full-blown progress-and-refinement theorist than Ferguson ever was, there is reason to believe that he thought similarly when he wrote in conjunction about "the forming of cities into communities, corporations, or bodies politic" and the introduction of "regular government, police and arts"; or when he claimed that "[l]aws and subordination, as well as polished manners, taking their rise in the cities, diffused themselves insensibly through the rest of society."[46] Indeed, if one considers that the meaning of "police" could be expanded to include not only public policy, organized government, or civil administration but even civilized relationships in general, there was a way to associate it with "polished," that is, elegant, cultured, and refined.

Such associations, however, were rendered extremely difficult to coin by the expressions used in Mittelstedt's translation. Neither *Polizei* (*Polizey*, *Policey*) nor *Politik* carried the general civilizational connotations of "police." The former term referred to the maintenance of internal public order, safety, and moral as well as physical well-being in the commonwealth through laws, administration, and disciplinary action in municipal government and increasingly on the level of the territorial state as well; by the eighteenth century, *Polizei* in this sense became the subject matter of a university discipline.[47] In the seventeenth century, *Politik* in the tradition of the *politica* of Justus Lipsius, and also Johannes Althusius, was understood as the science of men's common life in the state, including the issues of virtue and utility as the motive of association, of power and command, judgment (*prudentia*), obedience and order, and many others. The "political Aristotelianism" built on such foundations was also a university-based field of study, before it gave way to both *Polizeiwissenschaft* and a general state science drawing on jurisprudence, politics, economics, and the historical and statistical disciplines.[48] Thus, on the one hand, both *Polizei* and *Politik* are hardly adequate to recall the qualities of "polite" or "polished." On the other hand, while the latter words are (quite properly) rendered into German by Mittelstedt as *verfeinert* or *geschliffen*, no reader could have supposed them to be etymologically linked with *Polizey* and *Politik*.[49]

Apparently, then, even in the main text of Mittelstedt's translation, Robertson's grand design suffers as a result of the choice of certain terms. Besides weakening the coherence of Robertson's train of thought, these terms seem to reflect a mentality and a milieu that is somewhat different from the one that bred the viewpoints of the "moderate literati." They belong to a morally austere *bürgerlich* world, where respectable middle-class activities, such as trade (*Handel*), are pursued with diligence (*Fleiß*) under the paternal solicitude of *gute Policey*. How all these naturally reinforce each other to constitute a complex web of social relationships governed by good manners and justice can by no means emerge as spontaneously from the German as it does from the English text.

Turning to the notes with which Remer supplemented the translation, they can be classified, first, as methodological objections against Robertson's quasi-anthropological approach and the generalizations he made on its basis, and, second, as comments on his terminology and a number of statements, mainly in regard of the institutions of feudalism and the German and other constitutions. Remer found these insufficient or inaccurate. The first kind of criticism occasionally results in some inconsistencies. In agreement with Robertson, Remer complements his account of the causes of the barbarian invasions of the Roman Empire by stressing the peculiarities of the mode of subsistence they all shared ("they all subsisted from pasturage, hunting, and the booty of war"); at other places, however, Remer emphasizes that their remarkable similarity is mainly due to their ethnic identity, that is, *not* their similar circumstances.[50]

It is also in this spirit that Remer criticizes Robertson for drawing the above-mentioned parallel between the Germanic peoples and the native Americans, a device peculiar to conjectural history. He thought that this comparison, which is "neither particularly necessary, nor particularly well-founded," was only made because "the history of the Americans is one of Mr. Robertson's favorite themes." "The Americans," Remer goes on, "resemble the Germans no more closely than any people [resemble] another one in the state of nature. It might be far more apposite to draw a parallel between the ancient Germans and the Tartars of Asia. For these ultimately belong to the same original tribe [*Stammvolk*]."[51] Remer introduces here a quite different principle of sociohistorical explanation from the one Robertson uses: that of race and ethnicity. Since Robertson himself, while stressing the value of anthropological material for comparison and generalization, also admits its limits—"I do not pretend that the state of society in the two countries was perfectly similar"[52]—Remer's captious remark even seems somewhat unfair. It should probably be conceived as one of the tokens of his attempt at independence and originality, dictated by the contemporary conventions of judging the standard of a translation.

By contrast, the notes with factual criticism usually contain useful additions and corrections of the text, and complement Robertson's intellectual power with careful attention to the minute details of the functioning and transformations of the feudal order, mainly its legal and jurisdictional framework. Such notes concerned, for instance, the rise of urban liberties, some aspects of the administering of laws among the Germanic peoples, and the restoration of royal supremacy as a result of the suppression of baronial jurisdiction. Commenting on Robertson's treatment of certain subjects of German history, Remer could not conceal a sense of patriotic resentment: "Throughout this entire book, Mr. Robertson failed to make a proper use of German writers, which gives rise to a false, confusing, and incomplete presentation of subjects concerning the internal condition of Germany."[53] Remer, on the contrary, as it is explained in the preface, relied in his notes on the advice of "a learned friend" whose contributions he marked with the letter "P." The characteristic topics of such notes are, first, certain concepts pertaining to feudal tenure; and, second, the constitution of the Holy Roman Empire and the role of its peculiar institutions, such as the *Reichstag*, the imperial cities, the *Reichshofrat*, and the *Kammergericht*.[54] As these are all themes which figured very prominently in the oeuvre of Pütter, it is tempting to guess that the great Göttingen jurist might have assisted Remer in compiling his critical apparatus to Robertson, though in the lack of direct evidence this must be treated with caution.

As long as such modifications were limited to the footnotes and were not included in the main text, they served to adjust the book to the expectations of the learned German reader, rather than adding to the confusion of the original argument caused by the unavoidably unfortunate choice of some key terms and the pretentious methodological objections. Remer, however, did not remain content with such alterations. He must have wished to benefit from

Robertson's fame while taking pride in an "original" achievement that could be considered his own. Were it not for this ambition, it would be quite puzzling that in his revision of the book no reference at all is made to the already eventful history of the book in German—a history in which he himself played an important role. In the 1792 preface to the entirely rewritten *Geschichte Kaiser Carls des Fünften* published from 1792 to 1795, Remer explicitly claimed that a mere annotation of the text would not suffice, as if this were not the course he had chosen to follow 14 years earlier. He promised to retain everything that was "true and correct" in the original, but he thought that the confusion stemming from the structure of the book could only be remedied by a full revision—otherwise the reader, instead of obtaining a true picture, would have merely learned where Robertson was wrong. Similarly to Adam Smith, who also preferred the traditional, digressive style,[55] Remer found it a mark of incoherence to include the dominant tendencies in a fairly concise narrative and refer the reader for nearly everything else (sources, authorities, explanations, doubts, contrary opinions) to the section "Proofs and Illustrations" at the end of the main text, as Robertson did. "According to Robertson's plan, the text should have contained only the great outlines [*große Umrisse*], the more detailed exposition taking place in the notes." But so difficult are the "great outlines" objectively to determine, that this is in fact impossible.[56]

However much he may have admired, as he claimed, Robertson's "philosophical overview" of the Middle Ages, such remarks show that Remer had some doubts concerning the very possibility of what others considered the former's main achievement, that is, historical generalization. Indeed, the text resulting from a revision undertaken in this spirit, if not precisely a step back toward *Völkergeschichte* (which Gatterer had in vain wished to supersede), fell short of the criteria established for a true *Universalhistorie*. In the *Abriß* of 1792, twice as long as Robertson's *A View of the Progress of Society*, Remer rearranged and renamed the chapters of the original, and amalgamated the notes, both those of Robertson and his own from the 1778 edition, into the main text. He also supplemented it with a detailed account of the history of the Germanic peoples until the reign of Charlemagne, a more profound analysis of medieval constitutions, and "nearly all particulars" on the origin of towns, the history of the papacy and the monastic orders, and commerce and warfare. True, the work was enriched in data by such additions, but it became rather difficult to discover the argument they served. As a result of the revisions, Robertson's tightly knit logic was thrown into disarray, making it virtually impossible to follow the natural succession of developments that emerged so clearly from the original.

Such changes in the coherence of the work were, in fact, reflected in its contemporary German reviews. The reviewer of the original English edition, the renowned Swiss polymath Albrecht von Haller (who continued to send reviews to the *Göttingische Anzeigen* long after his departure from the Georgia Augusta), found no difficulty in presenting a fairly correct assessment of the main themes and messages of the text: an account of the transformation of primitive Germanic liberties into representative institutions, in conjunction with the growth of commerce and cities in the aftermath of the Crusades; the contribution of cultural attainments, such as the printing press, to these processes; and the simultaneous decline of feudal dominion and the rise of national monarchies.[57] By contrast, in the review of Remer's revision of the *View of the Progress of Society*, while acknowledging that the book had gained a lot in factual accuracy, Spittler complained not only that the additions "should have followed Robertson's style more closely," but also that the text "in more than one passage...lacks the true clarity of expression."[58]

So far, I have not dwelt on how the term I identified as a cornerstone of *A View of the Progress of Society*, that is, "manners," fared in the various German versions of the work. In the 1778 edition, it was more or less consistently rendered as *Sitten*, conventionally and quite sensibly used to translate *mores*, *moeurs*, and manners into German. In the 1792 revision, however, it became the object of the first conspicuous alterations. "View of the Progress of Society in Europe, with respect to interior Government, Laws and Manners" is the title of Section One (out of three) in Robertson's work. Remer's first chapter (out of eight) is entitled "The general revolution of state [*allgemeine Staatsveränderung*] in Europe through the overthrow of the Western Empire"; and where in the first sentence, quoted above, Robertson mentions the revolution in "manners," the German text has "internal constitution" (*innere Verfassung*). Whereas in Robertson's original, the standards of human intercourse, which arise organically as a result of spontaneous communication itself and/or are dictated by the individual moral sense, occupy an emphatic position, Remer simply uses instead a near synonym of the other adverbial phrase in the sentence (i.e., "in the political state"; *in dem politischen System*). A term denoting governance, "the political state," cannot be directly related to the theme of natural sociability. One might describe Remer's procedure by recalling the categories Leonardo Bruni used in *De Interpretatione Recta* (c. 1426), the first systematic Renaissance treatise on translation. The German terminology was far from being intended as a *translatio* of the word "manners"; quite on the contrary, Remer chose it as an exercise of his *vis traducatur*, the "power of transporting" (into the expressive fabric of the recipient language as a *replacement* for it), implying a *transformatio* of meaning appropriate for the mental world of the recipient environment.[59] In the opening passages of the text, which carry an especially heavy weight, the sphere in which events and changes or "revolutions" of historical significance may take place seems to be reduced to those where human activity, particularly in the contemporary German environment, was usually conceived of as organized, which is by no means implied by Robertson's original.

One also looks in vain for *Sitten* in the revision at the place where "manners" next appears in Robertson's original. Referring to the times when the Roman Empire was at the height of its power, it is claimed there that "[a]s a consolation for the loss of liberty, [the Romans] communicated their arts, sciences, language and manners to their new subjects." This sentence was faithfully reproduced in the 1778, and also retained in the 1792 version of the *Abriß*, with the difference that "language and manners," translated in the former as *Sprache und Sitten*, was replaced by *Bildung* in the latter.[60] The common sense meaning of *Bildung*, that is, learning or erudition and the process of its acquisition through education, or alternatively mental frame and cultural accomplishments in general, embraces that of the terms which preceded it ("arts and sciences"; *Künste und Wissenschaften*). In a near contemporary discussion of this concept, Moses Mendelssohn spoke of it as the perfection of material and spiritual culture that is possessed by a nation in proportion with the harmony (attained through art and industry) between its social condition and the calling of man.[61] In Herder's influential texts, from the letters on recent German literature (1767–1768), to the *This Too a Philosophy of History for the Formation of Humanity* (1774—"formation" being *Bildung* in the original), to the *Ideas on the Philosophy of History of Mankind* (1784), the field covered by *Bildung* is successively expanded to embrace the entire historical process of the formation and successive improvement of natural, mental, and spiritual phenomena.[62] Here we have a term that had increasingly "public" overtones in Germany during this period; nevertheless, Robertson's argument is diluted because "manners" loses its distinct and emphatic status, this time through being subsumed in a more comprehensive concept.

In a passage referred to above in connection with "luxury," Remer's solution is analogous to the problem of police/polished/polite. "In less than a century after the barbarous nations settled in their new conquests," Robertson wrote, "almost all the effects of the knowledge and civility which the Romans had spread through Europe disappeared." The topic of manners, this time not as an analytical category, but as a term implying positive value judgment, is lost in the German rendering of the sentence: where Robertson spoke of "civility," that is, *good* or polite manners as well as liberal education and an orderly political state, Remer has *feine[r] Geschmack* (refined taste). Although "taste" was used in this period in Britain, too, to describe manners or social attitudes, it lacks the etymological association with the public sphere which was so essential for the purposes of Robertson.[63]

Sitten later appears[64] quite frequently in the text. But in certain key passages it is juxtaposed with other words or phrases which make it doubtful whether it means the same, both semantically and methodologically, for Remer as "manners" does for Robertson. In reference to the remarkable similarity of the barbarous tribes—explained by Robertson in sociological, and by Remer, here again, in ethnic terms—the 1792 *Abriß* mentions their *Sitten und Gewohnheiten* (manners *and customs*). The fifth chapter, on "The first steps toward amending the faults of the Middle Ages," is introduced by a reflection on the changes in the *Sitten und Denkart* (manners *and mentality/way of thinking*) of the period. Both passages have their approximate counterparts in the original, which only refers to manners.⁶⁵ Even a paragraph that is retained almost word for word (although heaped together from separate passages of the original) may leave the reader perplexed. The paragraph in question is the one already quoted,⁶⁶ depicting the medieval stagnation of the human mind and, while blaming this lamentable state of affairs on the lack of "regular government," makes ample use of the term "manners." In Remer's revision, the passage bears the heading *Wildheit der Sitten* (the savageness of manners). The word *Sitten*, however, is not used in the passage itself, which is, significantly, introduced with the following sentence: "The constitution of the state and religion are the two great progenitors of the moral character of a nation."⁶⁷

To sum up, it seems that the word *Sitten* is felt by Remer in the first two cases to be in need of supplement in order to convey the full meaning of "manners," an impression confirmed by the third case, where it is not supplemented and is apparently subsumed under morality. These examples suggest that for Remer, if he was aware of the crucial role of the term at all, the purely ethical component in the meaning of *Sitten* was predominant. This impression is confirmed in a passage where he censures the warlike *Sitten* of the noblemen of the Dark Ages, and then observes that

> one could expect even less morality [*Sittlichkeit*] from the common man, whose moral improvement [*moralische Bildung*] is neglected in such a period and among such a nation, which in these unhappy times consisted of a crowd of miserable creatures, deprived of all human rights, even a claim to such rights...The students of the moral condition [*sittlichen Zustand*] of nations have observed that in all peoples it is amongst the well-to-do middle class that the greatest amount of morality [*Sittlichkeit*] is to be found.⁶⁸

But this class disappeared along with the towns that the barbarous invasions had destroyed. Almost imperceptibly, what initially looks like a discussion of the totality of the standards of human intercourse—a category in which grace, elegance, and politeness as well as virtue, justice, and chastity are involved—is reduced to include only the second group of these qualities.

Let us now turn to Remer's treatment of Robertson's account of how European society started to emerge from the miserable state of feudal barbarism. On comparing the two texts, the reader's main impression is the further disruption of Robertsonian causality. The most striking passages of *A View of the Progress of Society*, eloquent in all their conciseness, are frequently rephrased in a way that only dimly resemble the original; what is more, their order of succession is often changed, and they are interspersed with long digressions, explanations, and qualifications that verge on pedantry. Conspicuous examples of this is Remer's exhaustive treatment of the customs relating to private war and jurisdiction in the Middle Ages, and his long lamentation on the fact that the first revival of learning failed to go beyond speculative Aristotelianism.⁶⁹

The impact of the Crusades on commerce and through it on the growth of towns and on the rise of the rule of law is a topic crucial for the message of Robertson, and here Remer's narrative unfolds in a rather peculiar way. He also observes that these undertakings, whose chief motivation was superstition, resulted in an unexpected transformation of property relations, for instance. Besides the ever-growing riches of the Church and monarchs, the rise of the middle classes (*Mittelstand*) is duly mentioned. However, the meticulous description of some particulars of this process in Italy, Germany, France, and England is followed not by the vivid Robertsonian summary of the consequences but rather by dozens of pages on the minutiae of the changing status of serfs, of medieval jurisdiction, of the restoration of Roman law, and of the revival of learning.[70] Only then is the reader's attention animated by the following:

> Above, we have already described those salutary effects which the liberation of the townsman and the peasant had on the activities of both. [In fact, this description was far from being as impressive as in Robertson's original.] There was a general fermentation of humors. New crafts arose; the ones already cultivated were improved; sundry kinds of laborers were united in factories and workshops; neighboring peoples were emulating each other; each product became more refined; the peasant found a market for the produce of his land in the populous cities, and paid the money earned on them back to the townsman in exchange for the articles purchased from him. Commerce became more extensive, enriched a considerable part of the nation, forged links between distant peoples, taught men a thousand new ways to please their senses, made them familiar with forms of comfort and diversion they had never known, and while it thus created new demands, it also satisfied them. Thus, it became one of the most important and most efficient means through which the manners and mentality [*die Sitten und die Denkart*] of Europe took on an entirely different shape.[71]

This passage, with the emphasis it puts on the mechanism of exchange, in fact even surpasses Robertson's text as regards its clarity in representing the intercourse between the various partners in the division of labor. However, its value is seriously reduced by its disjunction from the earlier reflections on the same range of problems, and, more importantly, by the fact that in it the Robertsonian logic is turned upside down. In *A View of the Progress of Society* the institutionalization of freedom under the law is consequent upon the refinement of manners through the accelerated pace of social intercourse, itself stemming from a more vigorous commerce. In the 1792 *Abriß*, the freedom of townsmen (and of peasants) is itself the *cause* which produces "salutary effects"; their liberation comes *deus ex machina*, first fertilizing economic relationships, and through them attitudes and norms of behavior.[72]

It is true that in the next chapter, Remer undertakes once more to strike the balance of "the good and evil effects of the first enlightenment [*erste*

Aufklärung]" and begins by establishing that no improvement could take place in the lifestyle and manners of any people

> until they enter into communication with a more refined people. Among the European nations, such a faster improvement was brought about by the Crusades, by the familiarity with the Orient which they caused by the more extensive trade and the increasing welfare it gave rise to. Among the nobleman, the first step of the improvement of manners [*Sittenverbesserung*] was the spirit of chivalry; among the middle classes, gradually a degree of refinement, pliancy, and affability arose, which are facilitated by a more frequent intercourse with various sorts of people and by the prospect of gain or the achievement of goals.[73]

The last remarks hold out the promise of the restoration of Robertson's logic. However, on the subsequent pages it is not the assessment of the impact of commerce on the growth of politeness that occupies the central place. They are dominated by the theme of chivalry, a subject on which Remer follows Robertson's phrases with unusual accuracy, with the significant difference that according to him the germs of chivalric virtues were already inherent in the ancient Germans.

Reading the *Abriß*, one is left with the impression that it was mainly this "mixture of valor, gallantry, and religious sentiment," which "contributed extraordinarily to the improvement of the manners of the great," that account for any "good effects of the first enlightenment."[74] Although Robertson, too, attributes importance to chivalry in his history of manners, he regards its role as rather complementary. He closes his first section by emphasizing that "[i]n proportion as commerce made its way into the different countries of Europe, they successively turned their attention to those objects and adopted those manners which occupy and distinguish polished nations."[75] In Remer's account the acknowledgement of the civilizing role of commerce and townsmen seems rather half-hearted when compared to the emphasis he puts on the spirit of chivalry and the virtuous knight.[76] While geared to flatter *Bürger* morality, then, Remer's overturning of Robertson's logic also results in another sort of "Germanization" as it harks back fondly to "Gothic" ethos.

If Remer represented chivalry as having been more influential in shaping the rudiments of modern polite manners than other factors, it is tempting to draw a parallel between his twist of Robertson's argument and the polemic of Edmund Burke with the "oeconomical politicians" in the *Reflections on the Revolution in France*.[77] There, too, in a discussion that paraphrases much of the thought of the historians of the Scottish school, the driving force of the growth of civilization is the refinement of the spirit and not that of matter.[78] Remer was an admirer of Burke—viewing him as an "English Demosthenes" whose insight into politics, knowledge of commerce and national characters, and, above all, love of freedom was unmatched[79]—at least until he thought, probably under the impact of Burke's later revolutionary writings, that old age had "weakened his understanding."[80] But Remer was not in the habit of citing contemporary authorities; and, according to the catalogue of his books, he only possessed the *Reflections* not in the original edition but in Friedrich Gentz's translation, published a year after the *Abriß*.

On the other hand, Remer possessed a considerable number of books by authors whose thinking in fact showed a greater affinity to his own than with his model Robertson. One such author was Göttingen's prolific historian Christoph Meiners, who himself relied extensively on Robertson's account of, for example, the Crusades and the rise of urban communities, but in a framework where the structural peculiarities of West European societies sprang from the ethnic identity of the Germanic peoples (and their superiority to others).[81] Like Remer, Meiners argued that chivalry was in the nature of the "Celts" well before they started to play a prominent role in shaping the history of Europe.[82] In both respects, Meiners had a Scottish predecessor, Gilbert Stuart, already mentioned in chapter 1 as a rival and a critic of Robertson. In addition to making similar points about the transhistorical significance of ethnicity, Stuart also claimed in an obvious jest on Robertson that, contrary to what "some writers who have no tincture of philosophy" have written, chivalry and the holy wars were not the cause but the effect of refinement.[83] And, perhaps most importantly, unlike in the case of the first translators and editors of the same text around 1770, in the 1790s it was possible for Remer to have recourse to Johann Gottfried Herder's idea of the *Volksgeist* or "national spirit" as enunciated in the *This Too a Philosophy* of 1774 and the *Ideas* of 1784.

The fact that Remer possessed these books, of course, supplies no evidence for his actual reliance on their authors.[84] Nevertheless, textual and structural similarities put him, interestingly enough, in company with writers whose methodological and theoretical approach to history contradicted that of Robertson (in the case of Stuart, directly and explicitly by a self-proclaimed rival), and whose works he must have known quite well. The following conclusion, then, seems reasonable to draw. The expressions Remer used to translate terms, the proper understanding of which is the clue to Robertson's logic, already had a tendency to weaken the strong socioeconomic links Robertson assumed between the various spheres of human existence and progress taking place in them. In addition, as Remer's narrative in the 1792 *Abriß* unfolds, a quite different system of causality gradually emerges. From the outset, historical change seems to occur in and through organized activities and to be motivated by moral–spiritual enlightenment. Both as the medium and as the cause of such transformations, spontaneous intercourse in the socioeconomic realm takes second place. Whatever the motivation and the influences under which Remer thought it appropriate to wrap up a critical reassessment of Robertson in an adaptation of one of the latter's chief works, the German publishing history of *A View of the Progress of Society* represents a parallel to the above-mentioned cases of David Hume's skepticism and Adam Ferguson's civic activism.

4
Scottish Histories and German Identities

In chapter 3, Robertson's *View of the Progress of Society in Europe* was discussed separately on two grounds: first, its inherent character arising from the consistent application of the stadial scheme throughout the text, and second, the rather drastic nature of the transformations it underwent during the process of German reception. There are similarly compelling reasons for a combined treatment of the narrative sections of the *History of Charles V* and the *History of Scotland* in this chapter. While the fundamental sociological assumptions concerning the incentives and structures of material, cultural, and institutional progress, together with the relevant vocabulary, are nowhere suppressed in them, both of these works are fundamentally political narratives of wielding and losing power, of maneuver and stratagem applied to the building or challenging of states, in which personal sentiment and character receive an amount of attention commensurate with their importance. In discussing these topics, both works inevitably address their implications for the wider themes of the chances of civil and religious liberty in the face of ambitious bureaucratic–military establishments (or, paradoxically, the lack of them). In turn, the tackling of such themes generated conceptualizations of political loyalty, commitment, community, and identity. From the angle of the comparisons and transfers that are the central concern of this book, the preoccupation of this chapter should be the uses to which Robertson's relevant views were put among a linguistic and cultural community that was different from his primary audience. These views themselves ought to be briefly examined first.

Scotland and *Charles V*: Robertson's making of modern Europe

The *History of Scotland* and the *History of Charles V* are litmus tests for investigating the benefits and limits of transferring approaches to national history and judgments about it into a foreign linguistic and cultural environment. Both of them are works of a patriotic national historian who has also been identified as one of the quintessential eighteenth-century cosmopolitan historians. In both of them, Robertson focuses on the sixteenth century, which he considered crucial to his vision of the history of the Western world as the unfolding of the great plan of providence: a gradually increasing accessibility of the divine revelation, made possible by the improvement of the means of subsistence, of manners, and of the human mind.[1] The period of chief interest for the Scottish historian represented a crisis in that process (in the sense in which the term has been used in twentieth-century literature on the early modern period, that is, both as a halt in progress and as the catalyst of a future, pregnant with innovation).[2] In the first work, Robertson sought to show how and why Scotland, although already making its appearance on the horizon of European history by the sixteenth century, did not share in developments that were taking place elsewhere, such as the curtailing of feudalism. The country passed "through the valley of the shadow of despotism,"[3] which Scottish Whigs like Robertson—in a fashion resembling Voltaire's *thèse royale*—regarded as a precondition of attaining true civil liberty extending to the commons. The Union of Crowns in 1603 was at best a mixed blessing and an incomplete remedy for the ills of Scottish society, and the purgatory lasted until the revolutionary settlement of the turn of the eighteenth century completely annihilated the power of the nobles. In exploring Scottish history in such terms, he contributed to the further erosion of a mode of patriotic history writing that rested on the legend of the ancient Scottish constitution, its special virtues owing to a unique Gaelic legacy that was heroically preserved against tyrants within the country and foreign invaders by a valiant, public-spirited nobility.

This interpretation of the Scottish past, most notably represented in the humanist George Buchanan's *Rerum Scoticarum historia* (1582), was already being challenged from at least two angles for over half a century by the time Robertson started his career.[4] One important critic of this interpretation was the republican Andrew Fletcher of Saltoun, a father figure for the Scottish Enlightenment at the time of the Union debates as well as an arch patriot. First, Fletcher ridiculed the idea that the nobility had been a disinterested guardian of Scottish liberty, although he retained the notion of liberty as freedom to take an active part in national affairs, and the view that "no monarchy in Europe was more limited, nor any people more jealous of liberty than the Scots."[5] Second, there was also a trend of royalist, even Jacobite inspiration, which suggested that as freedom was incompatible with the lawlessness that generally prevailed in the country, "actual liberty was a stranger here...our Scottish heroes of old savour a little of the Poles at present: they fought for liberty and independency, not to their country, but to the crown and the grandees."[6] The royalist view also undermined the historical basis of the alleged 2,000-year-old *ius regni*.[7] Such trends were all helpful in working out the historical foundations of an anti-aristocratic and civil patriotism in an atmosphere generally critical of the Scottish past, as encapsulated in Alexander Wedderburn's Preface to the *Edinburgh Review* of 1755–1756 (an initiative whose aim was to improve Scottish letters, and in which Robertson was also active): "The memory of our ancient state is not so much obliterated, but that, by comparing the past with the present, we may clearly see the superior advantages we now enjoy, and readily discern from what sources they flow."[8] He meant, of course, the Union and its consequences.

True, Robertson did pay tribute to the robust traditions of independence and martial vigor that so heavily imprinted themselves on the history of Scotland. He was also as willing as Fletcher to explore these themes by using the classical vocabulary of virtue and in a "mood of carefully contained nostalgia."[9] But at the same time he had, and left, no doubt that these aspects of the Scottish past were indissolubly wedded to the "aristocratical genius of the feudal government"[10] which, because of a few peculiar features of the country and its inhabitants, was only accentuated in the case of Scotland: while the *lairds* acknowledged no master, foreign or domestic, they also refused to recognize legal constraints and exercised an oppressive tyranny over their inferiors. "In rude ages, when the science of government was extremely imperfect, among a martial people, unacquainted with the arts of peace, strangers to the talents which make a figure in debate, and despising them, Parliaments were not held in the same estimation as at present; nor did haughty Barons love those courts, in which they appeared with such evident marks of inferiority."[11] And Scotland, alas, seemed to have been marked by the longevity of these structures:

> The feudal aristocracy, which had been subverted in most nations of Europe by the policy of their princes, or had been undermined by the progress of commerce, still subsisted in full force in Scotland. Many causes had contributed gradually to augment the power of the Scottish nobles; and even the Reformation, which, in every other country where it prevailed, added to the authority of the monarch, had increased their wealth and influence.[12]

A remarkable shift in this (im)balance of power was brought about by the accession of James VI to the throne of England and the consequent augmentation of the resources available for the crown. This, however, temporarily created "a political situation, of all others the most singular and the most unhappy; subjected at once to the absolute will of a monarch, and to the oppressive jurisdiction of the aristocracy, it suffered all the miseries peculiar to both these forms of government. Its kings were despotic; its nobles were slaves and tyrants; and the people groaned under the rigorous domination of both."[13] Not least because of these considerations, Robertson did not hesitate to hail the revolution of 1688 and the subsequent constitutional union of 1707, which "introduced other maxims of government in Scotland." After a "survey of the political state of Scotland, in which events and causes have been mentioned rather than developed," he points out that the commons became "admitted to a participation of all the privileges which the English had purchased at the expence of so much blood." Together with the economic benefits of the Union and the potential for social progress and cultural refinement created by it, in his eyes these developments compensated even for the partial loss of political viability in the traditional sense, as embodied in the institution of an independent Scottish parliament.

Recently, some historians have reemphasized the primacy of Robertson's Scottish patriotic commitment and challenged his classification as a "cosmopolitan" historian. After all, not only in the *History of Scotland*, but also in the *History of Charles V*, he consistently raises his voice against foreign dominance and expresses his sympathy with the defenders of local, regional, and national political traditions.[14] Robertson's "cosmopolitanism" is certainly limited if it is taken to mean a preference for territorial homogenization and the creation of supranational structures of authority and governance. Accordingly, while the Union seemed to him as a "junction" by which "Great Britain hath risen to an eminence and authority in Europe, which England and Scotland, while separate, could never have attained,"[15] he also saw the need to stress that during the "famous controversy" that preceded the Union the "imperial and independent" character of both partners was an issue of crucial importance. With the retrospect of five decades, however, Robertson felt that for his contemporaries the same issue was "a matter of mere curiosity" (although precisely because it was "momentous to our ancestors" it "cannot be altogether indifferent or uninstructive to us"—a qualification of rather little weight).[16] With the ebbing away of the "national animosities" of an earlier age, on which the debates focusing on the desirable degree of parity between the partners fed, the very stakes of tackling the Union issue were shifted. Irrespective of the extent to which it preserved or jeopardized national sovereignty, Robertson represented it as the beginning of an authentic history of freedom in Scotland:

> As the nobles were deprived of power, the people acquired liberty. Exempted from the burdens to which they were formerly subject, screened from oppression, to which they had been long exposed, and adopted into a constitution, whose genius and laws were more liberal than their own, they have extended their commerce, refined their manners, made improvements in the elegancies of life, and cultivated the arts and sciences.[17]

By broadening the horizon of writing Scottish history to include the progress of manners and social structures besides political events—in other words, by adopting a comparative perspective and a "cosmopolitanism" of vision and approach, if not of political commitment—Robertson proposed to supersede the shallow ancient constitutionalism (or rather "institutionalized liberty or right of resistance")[18] and the insularity characteristic of former "patriotic" renderings of that history. Thoroughly depending on a systematic criticism of feudalism, he offered a new, enlightened patriotism, one that has been described as Anglo-British rather than Scottish, but whose chief pursuit was the improvement of the sociocultural condition of Scotland, rather than vainglory and partisanship.

This interpretation of the *History of Scotland* rests exclusively on references to Books I and VIII, the portions within which the narrative sections are bracketed and in which, indeed, "events and causes have been mentioned rather than developed." While it has been suggested that Robertson's first historical work lacks the "complicating dimension of social theory,"[19] the references above, which could be infinitely multiplied from Books I and VIII, bear a striking similarity to the spirit and tenor, if not the analytical tightness, of the *View of the Progress*. The proportions are certainly different, but the function of these sections for the argument of the *History of Scotland* also resembles that of the *View of the Progress* for the *History of Charles V*: to provide a structural and analytical framework for the contemplation and comprehension of the human drama related in the narrative parts. In the *History of Scotland*, this drama is one of chaos and barbarity almost natural to a land whose circumstances do not favor the appearance and success of a type of political personality or "character" motivated primarily by the dictates of interest rather than by passion.[20]

The chief, though by no means innocent sufferer of the drama of sixteenth-century Scottish history, was Mary, Queen of Scots, who was the subject of a significant revival of interest during the period preceding the publication of Robertson's *History*.[21] This was a thoroughly partisan interest, with adversaries diabolizing Mary and adherents showing her to have been innocent and victimized. Robertson chose to follow a different strategy. True to his moderate Whig convictions, he believed that anti-Jacobitism, which he certainly embraced, was more effectively served by marginalizing Mary as a political emblem than by railing against her.[22] His main device to divest Mary of her character as a potent symbol of an independent *and Stuart* Scotland was to feminize her in ways that evoke contemporary aesthetic discourse. Robertson could have been relying on the aesthetics of the Scottish philosopher Francis Hutcheson in intimating that Mary's femininity was a source of her moral weakness, simultaneously inviting empathy from female readers and indulgent yet belittling sentiments of chivalry from men; and used this morally incompetent femininity, stemming as it was from her French and Catholic connections, to demonstrate that Scotland's destiny was with England and Protestantism rather than anything represented by Mary.[23] Yet Hutcheson's directly relevant text, the *Inquiry into the Original of our Ideas of Beauty and Virtue* (1725), makes no explicit reference to femininity. Robertson's representation of Mary's case as one of "beauty in distress"—one in which the frailties that lead to the demise of the suffering person are inseparable from qualities that evoke sentiments essential for the perpetuation of the bonds of sociability[24]—seems to be more akin to the Earl of Shaftesbury's virtual conflation of the moral sense and the sense of beauty, and even more to Edmund Burke's observations on "the origin of our ideas of the sublime and beautiful." These were published two years before the *History of Scotland*, and three decades later provided Burke with an analytical framework to discuss the tribulations of Marie Antoinette, Queen of France, in terms strikingly similar to those which Robertson employed in regard to Mary, Queen of Scots.[25]

More important than the provenance of Robertson's treatment of the subject is its substance. He took great pains to point out the positive effects that Mary's feminine character, combined with the values of refinement with which it was associated, wrought, or at least promised, in Scotland after she had returned there from France. "The amusements and gaiety of her court...began to soften and polish the rude manners of the nation....The beauty and gracefulness of her person drew universal admiration, the elegance and politeness of her manners commanded general respect." She displayed "corteous affability...without lessening the dignity of a Prince."[26] The problem was that Scotland was not yet quite ripe for appreciating such refinements and for being receptive to their soothing effects. "The inhabitants, strangers to industry, averse from labour, and unacquainted with the arts of peace, subsisted intirely by spoil and pillage," and "the nature of the Scottish constitution, the impotence of regal authority, the exorbitant power of the nobles, the violence of faction, and the fierce manners of the people, rendered the execution of the laws feeble, irregular, and partial." Therefore, the attempts of the young queen to exercise a moderating influence, by policy as well as example and simply by character, were doomed to failure or could bring about but an apparent and ephemeral alleviation of the endemic habits of licentiousness, insubordination, and disdain for justice.[27] Robertson's portrayal of Mary is not devoid of the idea of physical and moral feebleness, capable of simultaneously evoking disesteem and empathy, by way of the classical rhetorical device of redescription: the reliance on subtle semantic shifts among apparently related but actually distinct terms while intimating that they are quasi-synonymous. The very same feebleness appears at times as fragility, and ultimately as grace and beauty, capable of exerting a moderating effect on sentiments and interpersonal relations. However, this potential could be realized only in a sufficiently improved physical, moral, and intellectual environment. It was no wonder that it failed in sixteenth-century Scotland, and remained unappreciated until the times of commerce, rule of law, and Enlightenment, when Robertson was writing.

In an environment such as Scotland, insensitive toward the merits of refinement and moderation in most walks of life, politics as a realm in which these notions could be translated into self-control and calculation could not have remained an exception. Elsewhere in Europe, initially in Italy, but on her example quickly spreading to the nations that gained firsthand experience of

Italian policy through their invasions whose ferocity astonished their victims (France, Spain, and "Germany"), "the great secret of modern politics" was discovered and pursued. The "perpetual enmity" of Francis I and Charles V, one of the grand themes of Robertson's next great work, "was not owing solely to personal jealousy, or the caprice of private passion, but was founded...in the nature of true policy," which was "more an exercise of judgment, than of the passions of men."[28] Among the circumstances that prevailed in Scotland, it was impossible for such an approach to arise. Isolated instances of promising beginnings in prudence inevitably degenerated into passion, as can be shown by the examples of James V, Cardinal Beatoun, Mary of Guise, the Earl of Murray, and finally Queen Mary herself.[29] The latter case is especially revealing of the forces at work: under the suffocating pressure of an environment fundamentally different from the one in which Mary's sensibilities had been forged, her religious devotion deteriorated into expressions of a bigotry comparable to the zeal of her opponents; her affability of character faded into a romantic passion that undermined her judgment; and her politic control of appearances entangled her in a spiral of transparent scheming. In striking contrast to the violent but still measured stage of the wider European arena explored in Robertson's next work, sixteenth-century Scotland was a scene for the perpetual struggle of antagonistic passions, resulting in a "carnival of resentment."[30]

Moving on to the *History of Charles V*, its chief endeavor was further to refine and arrange into a comprehensive narrative the pointers offered already in the *History of Scotland* on how Europe in the same period experienced the challenges of absolutism, universal monarchy, and religious wars (before high-taxing territorial monarchies maintaining large standing armies could have become internally mitigated by checks and balances and externally by balance of power and the idea of toleration that reconciled people to religious plurality).[31] The account of the life and the deeds of Charles V, especially the grand conflict with Francis I, serves to illustrate the theme of ambition specifically aimed at creating and consolidating monolithic territorial power in near-continental dimensions. The book also explored the failure of this project and explained it by the increased "vigor" of the individual states of Europe as well as their arising awareness of their shared political identity. These were circumstances whose combination in Robertson's vision favored the development of a system of balancing states rather than universal monarchy. The stage is already set in the concluding sections of the *View of the Progress*. There it is claimed that by the beginning of the sixteenth century several causes and events "contributed either to improve internal order and police in [Europe's] various states, or to enlarge the sphere of their activity, by giving them more entire command of the force with which foreign operations are carried on," and although there was "[a] considerable variety in the constitution of the different nations," the same causes and events still "formed the people of Europe to resemble each other."[32] This thread is then resumed in Book XII, the "general review of the whole period," while the "near resemblance and equality in improvement" already described earlier "prevented the reign of Charles V. from being distinguished by such sudden and extensive conquests as occur in some other periods of history" and "among nations whose progress in improvement is unequal." Moreover, under the provocation of the "perpetual efforts to which his enterprizing ambition roused him," the same tendencies became further consolidated. As a result, on the one hand, "the different kingdoms of Europe...came both to feel their own strength, and to know how to render it formidable to others," and, on the other hand, "became so thoroughly acquainted, and so intimately connected with each other, as to form one great political system, in which each took a station, wherein it has remained ever since that time with less variation than could have been expected after the events of two active centuries."[33]

In a slightly different formulation found in the same section of the book, "there was not among [the states of Europe] that wide diversity of character and genius which, in almost every period of history, hath exalted Europeans above the inhabitants of other quarters of the globe." European exceptionalism has often been ascribed to Robertson, chiefly on account of his representation of native society in the *History of America*, which will be discussed in chapter 5. Here this "exceptionalism" is expressed in a statement embedded in a discussion of the rise of the circumstances in which the domestication of armed violence, the conquest of the violent passions became possible due to structural developments unique to European societies. Each nation "made progress in improvement." As we know from the *View of the Progress*, this was thanks in a great extent to commerce, which by itself "tends to wear off those prejudices which maintain distinction and animosity among nations" and "unites [men] by one of the strongest of all ties, the desire of supplying their mutual wants."[34] However, none of the nations of Europe developed "far beyond its neighbours," and while the same improvement was instrumental in the augmentation of their power in the very material sense of raising standing armies, it was the capacity of military build-up for deterrence (rendering oneself "formidable"), not destruction, that in the long run mattered. The idea that the power to intimidate is a restraint on the violent passions and on the propensity of men to cause wanton injury is as old as the attempt of Grotius and Hobbes to establish a modern system of natural law on the limited sociability they diagnosed in human nature.[35] Together with Mandeville's observations on the manner in which commercial societies—uniquely—enable their members to satisfy self-regarding impulses and make them free to compete for tokens of approbation in nonviolent ways,[36] this idea was crucially, if controversially, important to the version of social psychology employed by the Scottish sciences of man in Robertson's immediate environment. In the *History of Charles V*, Robertson relies on a pattern of analysis that combines each of these theoretical insights in describing a set of situations arising among conditions peculiar to Europe in the sixteenth century. He offers an interpretation in which the events of this period were crucial to the long historical process of the conquest of the violent passions, largely through trial and error, and thanks to the growth of pragmatism nourished by experience.

This spacious pattern accommodated a substantial amount of variety, even contradiction of detail in the engagement with intentions, character, actions, and consequences. Tradition, personality, and other circumstances imposed limitations, even among the favorable conditions that had arisen by the beginning of the sixteenth century, on the capacity of ambition to become "transformed from a private spasm of self-aggrandizement into a product of rational interest and calculating policy."[37] Even in the case of the same individual or social group, a consistent application of the principle of policy to the harnessing of passion occasionally proved to be an unbeatable challenge. The conduct of the Cortes of Castile during the conflict with Charles V is characterized by Robertson in this light: "The principles of liberty seem to have been better understood at this period, by the Castilians, than by any other people in Europe...they had formed more bold and generous sentiments concerning government; and discovered an extent of political knowledge to which the English themselves did not attain until more than a century afterwards." And yet, "the spirit of reformation among the Castilians, hitherto unrestrained by authority, and emboldened by success, became too impetuous, and prompted the Junta to propose innovations which, by alarming the other members of the constitution, proved fatal to their cause."[38] With Henry VIII of England, it was the other way round:

> Though Henry, in entering into alliances with Charles or Francis, seldom followed any regular or concerted plan or policy, but was influenced chiefly by the caprice of temporary passions, such occurrences often happened as recalled his attention toward that equal balance of power which it was necessary to keep between the two contending potentates, the preservation of which he always boasted to be his peculiar office.[39]

Overall, Henry and Francis I are both represented by Robertson as slightly odd examples of incapacity for adaptation to the new requirements of the European stage of politics, on which Louis XI of France had been a trendsetter by establishing maxims and introducing practices further refined and pursued with even greater consistency by Charles V. In contrast to the "desultory and irregular sallies" of the former two, pursued "without assuming any disguise," Charles's measures assumed the character of a "regular system," the result of "cool reflection...and carried on upon a concerted plan." They were marked by a comprehensiveness of vision and unfailing dedication: "cautious and considerate" in forming his schemes, "he was accustomed to ponder every subject that demanded his consideration, with a careful and deliberate attention" and "bent the whole force of his mind towards it." This imposition of discipline over passion serves almost as an excuse to the fact, amply illustrated by examples in Robertson's narrative, that "[s]uch as hold the latter course, are apt, in forming, as well as in executing their designs, to employ such refinements as always lead to artifice in conduct, and often degenerate into deceit."[40]

Charles's sustained adherence to the principles of self-control and calculation appears all the more remarkable as Robertson takes several opportunities to remind the reader of the transitional nature of the age. For instance, Luther's weaknesses of character, from impetuosity and rashness to arrogance then obstinacy, "ought to be charged in part on the manners of the age. Among a rude people, unacquainted with those maxims, which by putting continual restraint on the passions of individuals, have polished society, and rendered it agreeable, disputes of every kind were managed with heat, and strong emotions were uttered in their natural language without reserve and delicacy."[41] The ambiguity of the situation was further enhanced by the process of the Reformation itself, which, besides "many beneficial and salutary effects," also had "some consequences of the opposite nature." Religious enthusiasm is not particularly conducive to the political disposition whose development had been advanced by some long-term structural processes in European history. Robertson provides a succinct account of the coalescence of psychological factors and features of human character that led to the escalation of fanaticism in the early Reformation. Referring to the Anabaptists, he writes:

> When the human mind is roused by grand objects, and agitated by strong passions, its operations acquire such force, that they are apt to become irregular and extravagant....The mind...disdains all restraint, and runs into wild notions...As neither of these fanatics wanted the talents requisite in desperate enterprises, great resolution, the appearance of sanctity, bold pretensions to inspiration, and a confident and plausible manner of discoursing, they soon gained many converts.[42]

Fortunately for the *dénouement* of Robertson's narrative, Protestantism also had at least one leader whose opposition to the "formidable progress of Imperial power," although "flowing from the love of liberty, or zeal for religion, was strengthened by political and interested considerations." Maurice of Saxony was certainly not devoid of "passion" and "resentment," but in his case these impulses are described as only adding "new force to the motives of opposing the Emperor, which sound policy suggested."[43] Indeed, his whole conduct, from the moment of allying with Charles to that of betraying him to the ultimate thwarting of the emperor's ambition, is presented by Robertson as a measured course of political prudence and dissimulation, in which Maurice's adeptness becomes ever more refined by "his long and intimate union with the Emperor [which] had afforded him many opportunities of observing narrowly the dangerous tendency of that Monarch's schemes" and, one might add, the methods whereby these were implemented.[44] An emulation in ambition led to an emulation in calculation between the two princes with an inevitability that culminated in Maurice gaining the upper hand over his role model, thereby also fashioning himself as a new role model, that of a political leader reproducing the type established by Charles in order to resist him. This was an achievement that, according to Robertson, earned him the pride of place among all of his contemporaries, including Charles V himself.

> Of all the personages who have appeared in the history of this active age...Maurice may justly be considered as the most remarkable...At an age, when impetuosity of spirit commonly predominates over political wisdom, when the highest effort even of a genius of the first order is to fix on a bold scheme, and to execute it with promptitude and courage, he formed and conducted an intricate plan of policy, which deceived the most artful Monarch in Europe.[45]

The analysis of the stadial patterns of sociocultural and institutional progress and the narrative of events, intentions, and agency are two styles of historical reflection the reconciliation of which was not always unproblematic in Robertson's works, including the *History of Charles V*. In the characterization of Maurice of Saxony they are brought to a common ground in a mutually reinforcing fashion. According to the former, the tendency of European history has been toward a commonwealth of modern civil polities whose mutual relations are marked by complementarities that result in cooperation as well as emulation and conflict. According to the latter, even among the substantially contingent and circuitous processes of the dealings of particular individuals in particular situations within this larger scheme of structural movements, it has been possible for a social type to emerge that is sufficiently equipped to cope with the complex task of keeping this system "running."

At the end of this rudimentary sketch of the argument of the two works, from the point of view of the *Rezeptionsgeschichte* which interests me, their significance can be summarized as follows. In the *History of Scotland*, Robertson provided a pattern to study national history in the context of the continent-wide development of economies, societies, and polities. Placing Scottish history on the map of Europe was to be a means of overcoming the endemic introversion and partisanship that had characterized Scottish historiography, historical and national consciousness, and political culture. In the *History of Charles V*, the perspective was, as it were, the reverse of this: European history was here shown to be different from the sum total of national histories by exploring the birth pangs of Europe as "one great political system." The reason why this is especially noteworthy is that looking at the sixteenth century from this angle renders one of the central themes of national histories in that period, the struggle for and against religious reform, a subtext,[46] needless to say, with particularly important consequences in the case of German history. My central question will be how far these implications of both works were appreciated in the contemporary German reception. When considering this question, it should also be borne in mind that while Robertson was writing not long after Scotland had lost an identity which could be readily discernible through national political institutions (and was himself seriously at work to consolidate a new one), Germany as a unit had hardly ever possessed an identity other than that manifested in the political institutions of the *Reich*.

Rendering "national" history

In addition to translations, editorial prefaces and notes, and reviews of both books, I shall also pay attention to references to Robertson in contemporary German historical literature and items in this literature on topics similar to ones with which he too was preoccupied. Once Robertson's fame as a historian had been established, the appearance of his works seems to have been expected eagerly in Germany. The *History of Charles V* was first borrowed from the library of the University of Göttingen within a few weeks of its publication in London and in six months' time a lengthy review also appeared in the *Göttingische Anzeigen von gelehrten Sachen*.[47] By that time, late in the spring of 1770, the first German translation had also been turned in by Mittelstedt (already familiar from chapter 3) to a publisher in Braunschweig. This was followed by a new edition of the same translation (Braunschweig, 1778–1779) improved through textual changes and notes by Remer (also discussed above), which in turn was expanded with further notes and republished by Johann Martin von Abele at his own printing house in Kempten, in 1781–1783.[48] Finally, as we have also seen, there followed yet another attempt by Remer (Braunschweig, 1792–1796), who now completely revised and significantly expanded the first volume and reissued the 1778–1779 texts of the second and third volumes. The publishing history of the *History of Scotland* is less complicated, but no less interesting. Being the first work of an as yet unknown author, it was not as avidly snatched off the shelves as Robertson's later volumes, but it was also reviewed within a year of its publication, and by the spring of 1762 Mittelstedt as well as Georg Friedrich Seiler had completed translations of the text.

The quality of each of these translations was above the average that was available in the contemporary German market. Although both Remer and Abele thought all readers would agree that Mittelstedt's previous translation of *Charles V* deserves criticism because of its "heavy way of expression, a certain unpleasant stiffness, and too frequently applied punctuation,"[49] their own modifications of it were not very significant. Mittelstedt's rendering of the *History of Scotland* occasionally indeed suffers from exactly such weaknesses when compared to that of Seiler, but on the whole both of them are readable enough. It is important to point out, however, that for each of the translators, just as it has already been demonstrated on the example of the *View of the Progress*, coping with the vocabulary of Scottish stadial history proved to be a tall order in the *History of Scotland* and the narrative portions of the *History of Charles V* as well. No doubt, in these texts, "industry" (manufacturing activity as well as a diligent exertion of productive powers necessary for such activity, both denoted by the same term) and "commerce" (the exchange of commodities thus produced as well as the exchange of sentiments and ideas between the humans brought together in situations of both types of "intercourse") appear less abundantly. A more frequently used term is "manners." Amidst the proliferation of opportunities to exercise one's sociability, "manners" are described as growing ever more "polished" or "polite," in turn resulting in increasingly enlightened and stable forms of "policy." However, it is important to remember that in Robertson's approach the second cluster (manners-polished/polite-policy) is intrinsically associated with the first one (industry-commerce-intercourse), and even in the latter's absence it is capable of evoking the entire etymological chain. Any break or crack in this chain, likely to occur if translators are unable to find equally tightly knit clusters that prompt similar associations, has serious consequences. First, it puts the whole stadial logic at risk, and may even result in its complete demise. Second, it is likely to obliterate the ways (described above) in which this logic underpins the meaning of the narrative, and, by implication, ultimately jeopardizes the full import of the narrative itself.

Sampling the German translations of Robertson's texts, again no translator could have coped with the difficulty that *Sitten* (mainly because of derivatives such as *Sittlichkeit*, purity of morals) has a more pronounced ethical overtone than "manners," in which the element of custom and aesthetic qualities are equally emphatic.[50] This is shown by the instability in the choice of terms to render "manners": the translators were sometimes content with *Sitten*, but they often used *Sitten und Gewohnheiten* or merely *Gewohnheiten* if the context seemed to suggest so, and occasionally even *Manieren*.[51] Particularly illuminating of the confusion is a sentence according to which Charles V established his firm grasp over the Castilians by "assuming their manners...and complying with all their humours and customs," translated as *"er ihre Manieren annahm...und sich alle ihre Sitten und Gewohnheiten gefallen ließ."*[52] As for "polished/polite" and "police/policy," to the eighteenth-century British mind, both expressions were vaguely linked to the idea of the *polis* and were related to the intercourse of citizens in their private and public capacities, respectively, also suggesting that a bridge existed between these two spheres.[53] To achieve the same effect, similar terms of classical derivation would have been needed, but the ones existing in the contemporary German vocabulary were not particularly helpful. "Nations, which hold the first rank in politeness" (and, one like Robertson might add, in which police is *therefore* also the most sophisticated and efficient) become *wohlgesittete Nationen* in Seiler's translation, and *Nationen, die für die artigsten gehalten werden* in Mittelstedt's translation of the *History of Scotland*.[54] "Police," on the other hand, was more or less consistently rendered by each translator as *Policey*. This term had no supposed etymological link with the German equivalents of "politeness." Moreover, its traditional early modern meaning was governance in the sense of control exercised by the magistrate for the sake of improving morals and maintaining order among the citizens. This made it quite impossible for the German reader to establish the spontaneous link between the concept of refined intercourse of ordinary citizens in the private sphere and the imposition of good manners over their own public conduct by political personages in the form of measure, self-control, and calculation.

In spite of such linguistic limitations, the quality of the translations in and by itself was no serious obstacle for Robertson's historical message to be conveyed to the German audience, and the historiographical context was not unfavorable, either. The endeavor of the Göttingen historians to introduce principles into the study of their field, which encouraged the understanding of particular processes against a background of larger patterns of structural progress was outlined in chapter 2. This endeavor must have been familiar to graduates of the Georgia Augusta of Göttingen who ventured to interpret Robertson's texts for a German audience. Yet, the contemporary German reception of his *History of Scotland* and *History of Charles V* illustrates the difficulty for such principles to strike roots or to make a broader impact. They do not seem to have been read, as they certainly could have been, as attempts to supersede the traditional limitations of both national and universal history (partisan spirit and parochialism on the one hand and compartmentalization on the other), by establishing the kind of link between them urged by Gatterer, Schlözer, and their colleagues. According to the testimony of translators' prefaces, reviews, and annotations, one of the main interests of the German readers was the way Robertson took sides in the "grand debates" with which his topics could be associated, whereas, as it has been argued, his own attitude to such debates was one of studied impartiality, sometimes even amounting to a politically selective use of sources to suit his "moderate Whig" position.[55] His quest for objectivity was not ignored and often explicitly praised, but his strategy to shift interest from immediately partisan issues to the *longue durée* problem of emergence from feudalism in the *History of Scotland* and the growth of a "European system" in *Charles V* was far less appreciated, even less recognized, than his pronouncements on the rivalry of Mary, Queen of Scots, and Queen Elizabeth in the first and on the strife of Protestantism and Catholicism in the second.

By all concerned, *The History of Scotland* was acknowledged to have "enriched British history with a well-elaborated piece," even a "masterpiece,"[56] and thus it established the ground for Robertson's renown in Germany. When *Charles V* was published, he could already be referred to as the author of the "universally applauded History of Mary Stuart."[57] But even this reviewer, the famous polymath Albrecht von Haller, almost wholly neglected Robertson's concise summaries of the preceding and succeeding periods which were essential to recognize the context of the turmoil of the sixteenth century, while the translators, in their prefaces, only made the most passing references to these sections. Each of them were mainly interested in highlighting what they thought was the main theme: the character, the conflict, and the responsibility of the two queens—a preoccupation Robertson thought was an affliction of Scottish historiography from which it ought to be cured. What is more, both translators and the reviewer also decided to discuss Robertson's representation of this theme in evaluative terms. Mittelstedt was the most sympathetic to this representation. He also seems to have realized or at least felt that one of Robertson's devices to divest Mary of her character as a political emblem was to feminize her, with the consequences explored above. In Mittelstedt's assessment, Robertson "represents her for what she was, lovable in youth; rash and despicable in mature years; and worthy of admiration and sympathy in her death,"[58] which was meted out to her by the rage of God for falling prey to characteristically female frailties, including the "unbridled passions" (*ungebändigte Leidenschaften*) that push a "lively spirit" into a deep abyss. Nor does he neglect referring to the tensions that arose from Mary's upbringing in an environment that was "the most polite and refined [*artigsten und feinsten*], but also the most sinful" in Europe, where "all French heedlessness became combined with the refined taste of the Italians [*Raffinement der Italiäner zur Schärfung des Geschmacks*] for sensual pleasure." Mittelstedt also suggested that Robertson examined Elizabeth in the same light. Her qualities as a great ruler are acknowledged, but "as the upright historian must describe not only the acts but also their sources and motives; he must distinguish between great qualities and true virtues; so truthfulness certainly obliged Mr. Robertson to separate the queen from the woman, and amidst all the glitter of Elizabeth's throne also to throw light on the dark spots"[59]—and thus, with great moderation and only when necessary, provide evidence of her jealousy, duplicity, and schemes. Finally, it was important for Mittelstedt to point out that while Elizabeth picked her ministers with more consideration than her favorites, her manner of procedure was still far superior to that of her successor James VI/I, who remained a prisoner of his "passions and selfishness" (*Leidenschaften und Eigennutz*). While the central Robertsonian theme of restraining or indulging political passion is not connected to the analysis of the sociocultural environment that allows or curtails its operation, the centrality of this theme is quite acutely recognized by Mittelstedt, and discussed by him in terms compatible with those developed by Robertson.[60]

Compared to this golden mean, Seiler and Haller represented two extreme opinions. The former, while remarking that the book contains an account of the "core" of the older as well as the most important new period of "profane" history in Scotland, also claims that for him its most important aspect was "a confident and reliable report on the movements of the Reformation, and the great transformations which the Church of Scotland underwent at that time, and which at more than one place evokes an admiration and worshipping of the wisdom, the justice, and the mysterious governance of the Lord of the World."[61] To Seiler's mind, these were features which rendered superfluous all further explication about the importance of the undertaking by the translator. As discussed above, providentialism, in the sense of divine foreknowledge facilitating progressively better access for mankind not only to the Word of God but also to a more comprehensive happiness comprising material as well as spiritual well-being, was central to Robertson's historical thought. However, Seiler's approach here is more restrictive and concerns the significance of the *History of Scotland* as a contribution to modern salvation history. Strangely enough from the angle of someone who believed that the Reformation was the accomplishment of God's design, he then goes on to occupy a sharply pro-Marian stand, arguing that Robertson made a mistake in accepting the famous Casket Letters as authentic proof of Mary's complicity in the murder of Darnley, and finds in general that the circumstances—her youth and "fiery" character, the nature of her upbringing, her inevitable dependence on advice, etc.—supply a sufficient excuse for all of her conduct as queen.

While scholarly argument as well as political polemic in the Protestant *Aufklärung* often bore the imprint of anti-Catholicism and anti-clericalism, the partisanship of Mary by Georg Friedrich Seiler (1733–1807), who later became a quite influential representative of Lutheran practical theology, is noteworthy. Seiler studied philosophy and theology, oriental languages, and mathematics and natural sciences at the University of Erlangen, where he returned in 1770 as a professor of theology after a period of pastoral service in Saxony-Coburg. Even apart from his rendering of Robertson, he earned a reputation as a reliable translator,[62] while his extensive correspondence and publications established him within the tradition of German popular philosophy, referring itself to Leibniz and Wolff and aiming to develop a harmony between reason and revelation (perhaps a remote inspiration for him to become interested in Robertson). It was, however, Kant whom Seiler regarded as the "ultimate conversation partner" of contemporary theologians, and the *"philosophus subtilissimus."*[63] He criticizes Robertson's measured judgment of the Earl of Murray in a frame of reference anticipating that employed in speculations of a "Jesuit" conspiracy aimed at subverting the positions of Protestantism as well as lawful governments in contemporary Germany. In Robertson's presentation, Murray, bringing prudence to control passion, reconciled his devotion to the reformed church with his dutiful service to Mary. Seiler, by contrast, suggested that "Murray's zeal for the church was similar to that of the Jesuits in our century; he did not allow his fatherland to be oppressed by France because he wanted to rule it himself; and he served Queen Mary in order to reign in her name over the whole kingdom"[64]—a version of prudence pursued to Machiavellian extreme. Without resulting in physical violence, but with an intellectual fervor as powerful as in the most intense periods of antipopery in Britain, a decade and a half after these lines were written, influential figures of the German intellectual scene launched a full scale campaign to avert, as they conceived of it, a conspiratorial offensive of the Catholic Church against Protestantism and

Enlightenment, described in the same terms of diabolical Machiavellianism.[65] Such sentiments were entirely foreign to Robertson, who as an ecclesiastical leader recognized a militant interpretation of Calvinism, as professed by a considerable party within the *Kirk*, to be a dangerous disposition.[66] He decided to retire from the Assembly in 1780, shortly after the lifting of some of the centuries-old sanctions against Catholics, implemented in England in 1778 and initiated in Scotland too, which evoked riots that even presented a threat to his personal safety. Shocked, in one of his last speeches Robertson said: "I love to see my countrymen discover that jealous concern for the preservation of their rights which characterizes the spirit of liberty: but I am sorry to behold them wasting their zeal without a cause." He called the church to denounce "the principle for conscience sake, as repugnant to the spirit of the gospel, and contrary to the genius of the Protestant faith."[67]

Given Seiler's denominational loyalties, made explicit in several places, his exculpation of Mary Stuart remains an enigma. In any case, the reviewer's opinion is in stark contrast to his evaluation. According to Haller, Robertson was unfair in imputing infidelity and severity to Elizabeth: Mary's reluctance to abandon her claim to the English throne, as well as her awareness of and possible complicity in the conspiracies of Jesuits, the Roman church, and virtually all the Catholic princes of Europe against Elizabeth made the prosecution of Mary the only means to preserve the security of the English throne, and England itself. In the same vein, Robertson is criticized for treating too mildly the impunity of turbulent Catholic lords under James VI, especially in view of the harsh, even despotic measures against his own capital.[68] If Seiler's position is somewhat contradictory, the reviewer unambiguously aligns himself with the cause of the "improved religion" (*verbesserte Religion*), as he refers to it. But whatever the precise motives of either of these commentators were, from the point of view of the present discussion the central issue is that it is on the partisan aspect of the topic that they felt most inclined and inspired to contribute, and not on the theoretically innovative aspects of Robertson's work.

By and large, similar was the case with the *History of Charles V*, with the difference that, since many technical as well as sensitive points of German history were tackled in it, the reaction was more variegated and occasionally also more animated. To begin again with the review in the *Göttingische Anzeigen*, it is a fairly detailed descriptive summary of the contents. The main recurrent theme in the more reflective pieces of assessment is Robertson's failure to take a more partisan stand in favor of Protestantism. To be sure, Robertson was far from displaying Catholic sympathies, but true to the spirit of Edinburgh moderatism, he also refrained from representing Protestantism in heroic terms and explained the Reformation largely as an event in secular history. But this was precisely what Haller missed. Whereas Robertson "acknowledges all the human springs that promoted this great event, in our opinion he did not sufficiently emphasize the strength of conviction which arose from the comparison of revealed truth and the Roman beliefs, and which uniquely gave so many thousands the courage to testify for the truth in their deaths."[69] He also took issue with Robertson who, reflecting on the history of toleration, claimed that in the sixteenth century,

> the right to extirpate error by force, was universally acknowledged the prerogative of such as possessed the knowledge of truth...Luther, Calvin, Cranmer, Knox, the founders of the reformed church in their respective countries, as far as they had power and opportunity, inflicted the same punishments upon such as called in question any article in their creeds, which were denounced against their own disciples by the church of Rome.[70]

Especially in regard to Luther, Haller found this evaluation grossly unfair, claiming that among the great reformers mentioned "no case [of persecution] by Luther is known," and that the only example of it by Calvin afflicted the "blasphemous" Servet, while there was no atrocity against Roman Catholics at all (but here Cranmer and Knox are conveniently forgotten).[71] Technically he may have been closer to the truth, whereas in broader historical terms it was obviously Robertson who had a stronger case. However, the point is again not so much whether the one or the other was "correct," but that both of these criticisms show the reviewer to have mistaken the very character of Robertsonian "impartiality" (which he otherwise quite frequently praised). Several notes that Remer added in the 1778–1779 edition also fall into this category. At one point, for instance, he expresses his dissatisfaction with Robertson's belittling of the difficulties of the process of Reformation (thus, by implication the heroism of the Reformers) and the severity of certain measures taken against them by imperial diets. Elsewhere he sternly reminds that a letter apparently showing an iconic Protestant leader like the Landgrave of Hesse to give in to the emperor's demands may well have been a forgery.[72]

Some of these specific faults, and many others that Robertson's German interlocutors found in his text, were attributed by them to his unfamiliarity with the German language and the sources of German history. In reporting to Robertson on Remer's completion of his annotated edition, Westphalen[73] mentioned that the latter would have been pleased if Robertson had wanted to see it before it was published. But in the same breath he dismissed the value of this, recalling that Robertson did not read German (which was perhaps the reason why the letter was dated long after Remer's edition had emerged from the press).[74] While admitting that the book was "altogether pieced together from good sources," Haller called attention to this gap in Robertson's erudition, too, in his review of the *History of Charles V*.[75] Commenting on Robertson's treatment of certain subjects of German history, Remer also could not conceal a sense of patriotic resentment: "Throughout this entire book, Mr. Robertson failed to make a proper use of German writers, which gives rise to a false, confusing, and incomplete presentation of subjects concerning the internal condition of Germany."[76]

To redress such shortcomings, Remer, as it were, reveled in mobilizing not only his own erudition, but also relied on the advice of "a learned friend," who wanted to preserve his anonymity, and whose contributions he therefore marked with the letter "P." Apart from the ones already referred to, the characteristic topics of the notes with which Remer and "P" equipped Robertson's text are the system (in this period rather the remnants) of vassalage; the dues and services of the peasantry; and the constitution of the Holy Roman Empire. Their overall tendency is a vindication of what has been called the "German idea of liberty." According to views widely held among German "imperial patriots" in the eighteenth century, the authority of territorial princes as it became stabilized after the age of religious wars, was not only reconcilable with freedom, but as it checked the power of the emperor it was in a sense the very guarantee of it.[77] Freedom in this sense was even identified as *the* German "national spirit" by Friedrich Carl von Moser a few years before the German translations of the *History of Charles V* were published. Moser (1723–1798), the eldest son of the outstanding jurist and *Reichspublizist* Johann Jakob Moser, served in administrative, advisory, and ministerial functions at several German princely courts, including the imperial court in Vienna as *Reichshofrat* in the late 1760s, and was also a widely published author on political subjects. He has even been described as "the political classic of the German *Aufklärung*."[78] "Patriotism" was central to the argument of his works. In an early treatise (an eighteenth-century engagement with the "mirror for magistrates" genre, intended not for professionals but for the educated public) he "depicted with patriotic freedom" the cooperative relationship of "the lord and the servant" (in fact, the sovereign and his minister). In the 1780s, he went on to publish, in 12 volumes, a "patriotic archive for Germany": a collection of sources, correspondences, and biographies of German princes and ministers, which can be regarded as a historical retrospective counterpart of Schlözer's present-oriented *Briefwechsel meist historischen und politischen Inhalts* from a slightly earlier period.[79]

Moser's main and most consistent contribution on the subject of German *Nationalgeist*, besides a pamphlet bearing this title, was a collection of "patriotic letters" published in 1765. He thought that freedom was the watchword and the *Leitmotif* of the constitution of the Holy Roman Empire throughout its history, which was preserved as a fundamental "truth" amidst a succession of "revolutions" and dramatic changes. There was equilibrium between the princes and the estates, and the excellence of the constitution could have been only surpassed by that of England.

> Territorial prerogative [*Landes-Hoheit*][80] is a precious and invaluable ornament of the German imperial estates, and to call it into doubt would be tantamount to a violation of the laws themselves. But it is no sovereign power...The German nobleman, burgher, and peasant is a direct subject to his territorial lord, but according to the same laws which invest his electors,

princes, counts, and lords with the most extensive prerogatives over him, he is also the indirect subject and loyal adherent of the Emperor and the Empire. The German common man, who extorted with his blood and wounds the rights of territorial prerogative for his lord in the Peace of Westphalia, was at the same time defending his own, his children's, his grandchildren's, and posterity's freedom. The election contract [*Wahl-Capitulation*] itself refers to all of the previous, and especially those imperial statutes, which mete out, in fair measure, the rights of each; and hopefully these laws will be retained at least during the present century, even though legions of unknowing chatterers should rise, who claim with the impertinence so commonly shared by the ignorant: *La liberté germanique est une liberté chimerique*.[81]

It has been argued that the periodic resurgence of *Reichspatriotismus* in early modern Germany took place at times of crisis, such as the decades of the post-1517 schism, the final phases of the Thirty Years' War following the Peace Treaty of Prague in 1636, the wars of Louis XIV at the end of the seventeenth century, and, finally, in the late eighteenth century before the collapse of the empire.[82] This latter crisis had been introduced by the mid-century wars, the War of Austrian Succession and especially the Seven Years' War, which immediately preceded Moser's "patriotic" effusions. These wars demonstrated the precariousness (and perhaps chimerical character) of the imperial cooperation in the anti-Ludovican wars and the arising ideal of imperial unity between "head and members" as well as among the members themselves. Much dismay was caused among imperial patriots, on the one hand, by Austria's *volte-face* in its international relations (the alliance with Russia and especially France, which re-alarmed old suspicions about Habsburg designs on Germany) and, on the other hand, by the emergence of a German state, Prussia, which had the resources to organize anti-Habsburg opposition on the strength of its own military might, and to frame the strategies of this opposition according to its own political interests, rather than those encapsulated in the idea of "German liberty." The perplexity which this combination of developments caused is amply illustrated by the trajectory of Moser's personal allegiances. While in *Der Herr und der Diener* (1759) he had been favorably inclined to Frederick II as a Protestant counterweight to Austria, the pamphlet of 1765 already marked his conversion to the cause of Joseph II (to a very great extent under the impact of personal experience with the new Roman king and several of his officials during the election and coronation ceremonies of 1764 in Frankfurt). Moser's views on the German national spirit evoked a wide echo, including critical voices. The latter, including the famous Osnabrück official and publicist Justus Möser, were dissatisfied with Moser's preoccupation with the level of courtly politics, his purported equation of the German nation with the empire, and the implication that the "national spirit" was the spirit of the imperial constitution. Such critics were unhappy with the fact that in spite of Moser's appreciation for the positive effects of the territorial fragmentation of Germany, the overarching national spirit which was to provide a moral cement to the nation was to his mind "the Duty of Submissiveness of the German Imperial Estates to Their Emperor."[83]

While this perspective ignores the gestures made by Moser toward the integrity of the imperial estates, it lays a stronger emphasis on the merits of Germany's division as a guarantee against the haunting image of monolithic despotism by an imperial oligarchy led by the emperor himself and issuing uniform laws with reference to the supposedly unitary "national spirit." The elder Moser, instigated by his realization that since the 1740s a "different empire" had arisen, also revisited his earlier work on German imperial law and between 1766 and 1782 published 24 volumes of *Neues Teutsches Staatsrecht*, with the purpose of "offering observations on how the German Empire so far as possible may sustain its present constitution, and show here and there how correctable defects may be overcome."[84] One of the noteworthy aspects of this revision was the clarification that *Landeshoheit* had "two faces," the one outward and the other inward: a capacity of territorial rulers to act independently and even in defiance of imperial authority, and a direct jurisdiction that they possessed over their subjects and estates. Whichever of these two "faces" obtained preponderance, such a development constituted a hazard to the rights of subjects, which was another topic that received extended treatment in Moser's late synthesis.

The revival of imperial patriotism in the aftermath of the Seven Years' War, illustrated here with a mere handful of prominent examples, indicates a broader intellectual ferment which had political, juridical, as well as historical dimensions. At this point, it is interesting to recall the proposition that Robertson's decision in 1760 to prefer the topic of the reign of Charles V to several alternatives (of his own design, or prompted by others) for his next historical work was elicited by its perceived relevance to the contemporary upheaval of the international system of balance of power. Although a "*translatio tyrannae*" had taken place in the intervening centuries, the character of imperial and Spanish military and religious expansionism in the sixteenth century prefigured the same pursued by France with ever greater vigor since the seventeenth century. In Whig orthodoxy, the idea of Britain's "providential custodianship of the scales of balance in Europe against the threat of Popish universal monarchy" was as strongly entrenched as the contrast between her matchless domestic constitution and French despotism.[85] Such broader connections were looming especially large when, with the *renversement des alliances* and the outbreak of the continental war, existing Tory misgivings about the commitment of the House of Hanover to British interests received reinforcement from Britain being drawn into an apparently local German conflict.[86] In Germany itself, too, the Seven Years' War was perceived as marking a major realignment, but indeed one taking place predominantly on the domestic scene: its central feature was Austro-Prussian antagonism and the corresponding lining up of most of the larger and many of the lesser states. Subsequently, similar alarm was caused in the "Third Germany" by the temporary rapprochement between the two rivals, resulting among other things in the first partition of Poland in 1772—a lot which, many feared, might befall some of the lesser German states too. In this perspective, the Seven Years' War and its consequences were understood as an imperial affair, with internal rather than any other stakes, none of these seeming more important than the preservation of the tradition of German liberty and its precarious foundations in the historically evolved equilibrium of forces.

Argument from history was central to the debate about the Holy Roman Empire and its peculiar system of "checks and balances" throughout the seventeenth and eighteenth centuries, and perhaps never more so than in the last decades of the *Reich*. Some, like Justus Möser, located the origins of this system in the medieval autonomy of the separate estates. Others—one might contend, in a more enlightened fashion—attributed it to the legal institutions arising from the end of the fifteenth century, especially the *Reichskammergericht*, to which all citizens could appeal irrespective of their estate.[87] The latter camp included, among many others, Friedrich Carl von Moser as well as the famous Göttingen professor Johann Stephan Pütter (1725–1807). At this point, it is appropriate to resume the history of the translations of Robertson's *History of Charles V*, for it is tempting to believe that the learned "P" was none other than Pütter, whose possible influence on Remer I have already mentioned. Neither the subject matter of the notes nor the ideas just described were alien to him. Although his compendia on public law and imperial history are regarded as "prototypical products of an apolitical specialist scholarship,"[88] his devotion to the existing institutions and arrangements of the *Reich* shines through even the detached tenor of his texts.

Pütter's work has been recognized as "the culmination of German imperial public law," which in his approach meant the study of the state as a legal order to be comprehended in its historical development; an order not "established" by abstract principle but "unfolding" in time with the development of society, and therefore to be interpreted in close relation to its own past. The tradition of *Reichsgeschichte* he cultivated took to history as a source material capable of shedding light on the currently valid system of law, and his historical works aimed to promote a better understanding of the existing constitution and its fundamental laws. He was a firm believer in the excellence of this system, and while he recognized that it was in a permanent state of development, its ultimate dissolution was unthinkable for him.[89] One of the keys to its excellence lay in the composite character of the *Reich*: rejecting the notion of the *translatio imperii*, Pütter appreciated the empire as "a state composed of several states," and explained even the surviving effectiveness of Roman law in terms of its becoming indigenous custom. "Among all the states of Europe the German Empire is the only one in which each of the imperial estates constitute a fully separate state, so that each of them have their own particular history, and yet the general imperial history comprises all of these states as participants of an empire." This state of affairs was consolidated especially as in the high Middle Ages both the secular and the ecclesiastical estates became proper territorial lords of their provinces, thus "Germany gradually acquired the constitution that finally became peculiar to it."[90] Pütter also retained this feature of German history as a red thread in his arguably greatest literary achievement, the *Historische Entwicklung des heutigen Staatsverfassung des Teutschen Reichs* (1786–1787), in which he claimed that "Germany had been for several centuries in such a situation, that it might easily be foreseen, that it would not, like France and other European nations, continue an undivided Empire, which could not upon the whole be considered in any other light than as a single state."[91] The Westphalian settlement, in which this tendency culminated and became consecrated, not only thwarted imperial despotism, but also prevented the abuse of territorial "prerogative" (*Landeshoheit*) by the estates—a carefully balanced set of arrangements resembling the mixed constitutions of the United Provinces, or the new United States.[92]

Returning to the question of the notes in the German edition, as a matter of fact, some of them are merely pedantic. It is also interesting to see how Robertson's text occasioned debates between the individuals who participated in conveying them to the German public. Abele (who wrote his dissertation at Göttingen in 1778 on the German imperial nobility—again, quite possibly but without surviving evidence under the guidance of Pütter) on several occasions commented on and corrected not Robertson, but his German predecessors.[93] Many of the notes usefully correct Robertson's errors, lapses, or inadequate terminology as regards German history, but just as the review in the *Göttingische Anzeigen*, they are not concerned with Robertson's main theme as enunciated in the first half of this chapter: the ambivalent processes of the formation of the modern European states system and the very character of modern politics. In an age of interpretative editorial prefaces, this theme was also ignored in the ones that our translators provided.

German Robertsons?

This did not mean, however, that Robertson's character as a historian went unrecognized by them. To be sure, there were skeptics as well as pedantic critics of Robertson's approach. These included Franz Dominic Häberlin (1720–1787), a very early graduate of the University of Göttingen, who also started a teaching career at his alma mater before taking up in 1746 a professorial position at Helmstedt, at first in history and then in public law (thus, he was a senior colleague of Remer).[94] Already in the preface to his "new imperial history," Häberlin couched quite sarcastic judgments in his apparent appreciation for Robertson.

> But without taking away in the least from the value of Robertson's very precious and worthwhile history, or underrating it with my reproaches,

yet anyone more closely familiar with the authentic sources of our fatherland's history must admit that some things have been advanced not in the most accurate faithfulness to the available sources, the public documents, and contemporary authors, and sometimes, in order to give the narrative a more refined turn or a greater momentum, his own ideas were mixed in it. Not to mention that in tackling the German affairs this famous writer pays attention more to the general than the particular, which, however, may be excused by the plan he designed; therefore as regards these particular internal affairs of the German Empire, the task of a generous gleaning has been bequeathed to me.[95]

Further on in the book, Häberlin abandons all politeness: he flatly claims that Robertson "wrote something between a true history and a novel."[96] We have seen that Remer, too, occasionally expressed his unhappiness with the lacunae in Robertson's familiarity with the sources of German history. Still, in a note to the 1778–1779 edition, he thought that the "minor inaccuracies" of which Robertson was blamable did not justify the heavy charges leveled against him by Häberlin, exclaiming: "If only God willed that Robertson's philosophical discerning spirit rested in half on our students of the history of Germany!"[97]

There were in fact a few candidates for the role of a "German Robertson," one of them promptly suggested by Abele in a note to Remer's remark just mentioned: "On Schmidt rests this discerning spirit completely, and his patriotic history is already meeting the applause of the public."[98] Whether this aside was complimentary or sarcastic is difficult to judge. "Public applause" was not necessarily a primary standard with which to measure the scholarly merits of a historical work in eighteenth-century Germany.[99] If Abele intended this latter judgment to be negative, he also might have been dismissive about the "discerning spirit" responsible for the popular appeal. But he also might have been enthusiastic to welcome this combination in the work of a German historian. Whichever the case, Michael Ignaz Schmidt (1735–1794) deserves careful attention. He served at the court of the Catholic prince-bishop of Würzburg as university librarian, and professor of history from 1773 until 1780, when he moved to Vienna as director of the imperial archives (*Haus-, Hof- und Staatsarchiv*). He started to publish his *Geschichte der Deutschen* in Ulm in 1778, the same year as the first volume of Remer's annotated edition appeared, and reached, with the fifth volume, the age of Charles V in 1783, simultaneously with the publication of the last volume of Abele's edition of Robertson. A new edition in eight volumes in Vienna followed in 1787, while Schmidt was also busy bringing the story to 1657 in a now six-volume *Neuere Geschichte der Deutschen*. The publishing history is evidence for the "applause" mentioned by Abele. Pütter, who also thought highly of Schmidt's work[100]—a very generous opinion on the former's part, as we shall see—had an indirect candidacy for the role of a "German Robertson," too. In 1790, Pütter's *Historische Entwicklung* appeared in the English translation of Josiah Dornford

(1764–1797), another recent Göttingen graduate. With a bachelor's degree from Oxford, Dornford arrived to study law at the Georgia Augusta in late 1786, and was examined, with Pütter on the committee, for his doctorate in January 1789.[101] He later remembered fondly the "many instances of disinterested friendship I experienced in Göttingen [which] have attached me so much to that University, that I feel myself happy in the smallest opportunity of contributing to its welfare."[102] Translating his master's book was no doubt understood by him as such an opportunity. In his preface to Pütter's work, Dornford claimed that in order to acquire the relevant English terminology he studied a number of British texts, including Robertson's *History of Charles V* (besides John Millar's *A Historical View of the English Government*, and Gilbert Stuart's *A View of Society in Europe in its Progress from Rudeness to Refinement*), the implication being that it could be considered as a German counterpart of the combination of stadial and narrative history.[103]

The piquancy of both Pütter and Schmidt being put forward in this context arises from the fact that hardly could two figures have been more at variance on issues they both considered to be crucial for the period of German history on which Robertson focused. Furthermore, whatever their "philosophical discerning spirit," both of them produced rather partisan readings of German history as a whole and particularly regarding the sixteenth century. Let me conclude this chapter by a comparison of Robertson in the original and the putative "German Robertsons" from this point of view.

In Robertson's own approach, true to his "moderatist" principles, a conjectural–stadialist framework and a European perspective on national histories, as well as a studied endeavor to assert impartiality, were employed in order to transcend the traditional limitations of historical understanding. To some extent, Pütter and, more arguably, Schmidt, was a match to Robertson in the first two respects. Pütter frequently reiterated that the histories of the individual German states can only be fruitfully studied by concentrating on those circumstances that are closely related to the whole of Germany[104] (a counterpart of Robertson's vision of the histories of European states as *pars pro toto*). His concerns were mainly with laws and institutions, and thus his aims were not narrative, so he was quite indifferent to some of Robertson's preoccupations, such as the nature of modern politics and its relation with the problem of character. At the same time, he frequently resorted to stadial patterns of history in order to contextualize the development of the German constitution.[105] Schmidt did so quite systematically. The preface to his first volume was a concise engagement with the manners of the ancient Germans in Robertson's style (including some polemics with the Scottish historian),[106] and sections on "the manners, character, and constitution" (*Sitten, Charakter, Verfassung*) of the Germans, examining these issues in mutual reference to one another, regularly appeared in the subsequent parts of the book. In addition, there were overviews of the European status quo introduced in every chapter in order to establish a context for the ensuing discussion of German developments. The most successful one among these overviews was the tableau of European affairs on the eve of the Reformation, in which Schmidt presented a picture closely resembling that depicted by Robertson on the period of Charles V's accession.[107] At this point, it is worth mentioning Schmidt's avowed aspiration "to show how Germany has acquired its present manners, enlightenment, laws, arts and sciences, and above all its excellent political and ecclesiastical constitution; shortly, how it has become what it is."[108] He thus shared Pütter's attempt to sketch a "historical development" of the "present" constitution, and thus the overall ambition of *Aufklärungshistorie* to grasp history as a comprehensive set of causal relationships between the past and the present. But he also stressed that "the conflict of the power of the rulers and the estates," which most historians are content to discuss, can hardly be "the ultimate goal of history." The true subject of history for him was the progress of "national happiness" (*Nationalglückseligkeit*), and it was for this reason that the more spacious horizon described above was adopted by him.[109] Besides the development of German manners and the moral and religious history of the people, this also implied an interest in the rise of territorial states capable of asserting their authority not only in the secular domain but also in religious affairs; as a prominent representative of the German Catholic Enlightenment and its "Gallican longings," Schmidt looked to these secular establishments as potential aids in promoting an enlightened version of Catholicism against the Roman hierarchy and the popular religious practices supported by it.[110] It has been stressed that Montesquieu and Voltaire were important influences on Schmidt in developing his historical approach, but his generous (sometimes polemical) references to Robertson are also important to note.

Where the German historians parted company with their Scottish colleague was the latter's peculiar brand of impartiality. It has been pointed out that Robertson, in order to comply with his own moderatist standards, had recourse to a politic (rather than scholarly) selection of facts in his assessment of Queen Mary's status in Scottish history as a gesture to demonstrate the possibility "to incorporate Jacobitism...within a Whig and cosmopolitan sense of progress."[111] If no deliberate selection of facts was involved in his evaluation of Francis I and Charles V, he did take considerable pains to show even-handedness, and his judgment of his two protagonists was not based on their attitude to the Catholic-Protestant strife, but on their performance as statesmen amidst the challenges of a new status quo in state and church as well as in the international system as a whole. Even so, while he held Charles's superiority in matters of statesmanship beyond doubt, he sought to explain the contradiction that "Francis is one of the Monarchs who occupies a higher rank in the temple of Fame, than either his talents or performances entitle him to hold." He found a complex answer. First, he "was viewed by most of the other powers not only with the partiality which naturally arises for those who gallantly maintain an unequal contest, but with the favour due to one who was resisting a common enemy." In addition, "[c]aptivated with his personal qualities, his subjects forgot his defects as a Monarch, and admiring him as the most accomplished and amiable gentleman in his dominions, they hardly murmured at acts of maladministration." Finally, his patronage for the arts and sciences preserved his reputation beyond his own times, so that not even posterity "judged of his public conduct with its usual impartiality."[112] Among Robertson's German interlocutors, Remer in fact denied Francis a triumph over Charles even in terms of gallantry, in a sense overthrowing the carefully poised balance. In early 1528, at a highly critical juncture in the great conflict, Francis challenged Charles to settle their differences with a duel—in Robertson's rendering an "[absurd custom] more becoming the heroes of romance than the two greatest Monarchs of their age"[113]— and although at first Charles accepted it, finally the idea was laid aside. In a note, Remer not only criticizes Robertson for dwelling too shortly on this "extraordinary duel," but also makes a point out of proving that the challenger was actually Charles, and the fight was cancelled, "if not because of Francis himself, then because of the French."[114]

On a more general level, whereas Robertson obviously wrote "Protestant history," as we have seen above, he took care to point out excesses of "fanaticism" on the Protestant as well as the Catholic side, and religion, however important and omnipresent, remained an undercurrent in his narrative. By contrast, Pütter's sections on the sixteenth century present a thoroughly partisan reading of the history of the Reformation (even earlier, the anti-papal tenor is quite conspicuous). As soon as, in Book V, he proceeds to the theme of religious reform, he does not omit to claim that "[e]very one who was in the least enlightened, and indulged a freedom of thinking, allowed that Luther and those who were united in his common cause, with respect to the doctrines he had hitherto advanced, were right"[115]—an uncompromising value judgment which dominated every aspect of Pütter's treatment of German constitutional development in the age of confessional strife and religious wars. He in fact insists that the religious and political settlements of 1555 and 1648 were the logical consequences, as well as the confirmation, of German "liberty" as defined in terms of the imperial constitution. Viewed from this angle, that is, with the partisan Protestant principles consistently in the background, the attempts of Charles V and Ferdinand III "to reduce Germany, like France, to the dominion of a single sovereign"[116] appear as almost exclusively the affairs of the *Reich*. The situation is the very reverse of Robertson's *History of Charles V*, where the European perspective and the attempt to transcend the limitations of partisan historiography mutually reinforce each other.

If impartiality is one of the standards whereby to measure the historian's achievement, Schmidt's introductory remarks to his fifth volume, focusing on the reign of Charles V, are quite promising. The reader is reminded that this period is particularly susceptible to partisan treatment, and that in regard of it even the learned Häberlin had lost his temper, suggesting that the Reformation was a work of God's omnipotence, and Luther the instrument of eternity. Schmidt himself claims to aim at impartiality, but doubts that his analysis will satisfy all readers. Indeed, even his fairly unbiased account of Luther's appearance and the circumstances in which the Reformation began, caused consternation among a number of otherwise sympathetic Protestant readers.[117] By the time the reader advances to the translation of the Bible, Schmidt's allegiances start to reveal themselves. It was a major error, he claims, to entrust the common man with the interpretation and discussion of matters vital for salvation: however much Luther repudiated the fanatical enthusiasm of the Anabaptists, their excesses can be traced back ultimately to his own program.[118] Nor is it legitimate to claim, Schmidt suggests, that theoretical and practical religion, enlightenment, and toleration or the cause of liberty gained with the Reformation, which but in fact halted Germany's progress toward emerging as a cultured nation, not in the least by pushing Catholics toward adopting extreme positions.[119] Predictably, then, Charles V—who in the eyes of Pütter pursued universal monarchy, and according to the author of the notes by "P" (who may have been Pütter) was an inconsistent and mediocre politician,[120] and according to Robertson also pursued something like universal monarchy[121] but was a refined practitioner of reason of state—seemed to Schmidt not only a particularly able ruler but even one who saved the imperial constitution from ruin. The Emperor's "limitless ambition and conquering spirit" is not denied by Schmidt, but in his view

> so little did Charles reduce Germany to slavery, that he is rather the sustainer and to a certain extent the creator of the present system of the empire. Without the breaking of the all too powerful Schmalkaldic League, either the dissolution of the whole, or at least the annihilation of the Catholic parts, especially the bishoprics, was bound to occur.... It is also certain that if the leaguers had gained the upper hand, they would have dealt with the Catholics in a very different manner from the way Charles dealt with them.[122]

In other words, the casting became the very reverse of what Robertson, with the balance of power in *Europe* and not merely the Empire in mind, presented.

As in so many other instances of explicit or implicit communication within the enlightened republic of letters, the questions here were similar to a great extent, whereas the stakes and the answers were fundamentally different. Robertson and most of those involved in the process of the German reception of his historical works asked what made modern liberty, the rule of law under stable monarchy, possible. For the Scottish historian, the answer lay in the elimination of feudalism by powerful monarchs and their own subsequent inability to wield the plenitude of power for themselves. From the point of view of national historical self-reflection, the understanding of the reasons for this development to him took precedence over partisan arguments that could be drawn from history, and therefore, in an effort to arrive at an impartial interpretation of controversial themes in national histories, he appealed to their continent-wide horizon. By contrast, although European history is not at all absent from the accounts of Robertson's German interlocutors, their German histories are completely intelligible by themselves. The reason for this was that balance of power and social change (however frequently mentioned) seemed irrelevant to the framework that had defined the chances of *Freyheit* since time immemorial: the constitution of the "Holy Roman Empire of the German Nation." In addition, the character of the latest settlement of that constitution, the Peace of Westphalia, rendered it extremely difficult to tackle the issue in any but partisan terms. Therefore, in spite of the demand for true universal history in contemporary German high academia, and the recognition of the merits of impartiality, the problems which from Robertson's Scottish perspective called for a cosmopolitan and nonpartisan treatment, continued to be discussed in precisely the opposite terms in the German reception of his writings relevant to national history.

5
Maps of Mankind

Robertson's "global histories"

Edmund Burke referred to "the Great Map of Mankind" that is "unrolld" for the gaze of contemporaries, not in the least thanks to Robertson's employment of "Philosophy to judge on Manners," in a now famous letter of compliment to Robertson upon the publication of his *History of America* in 1777.[1] While Burke combined this remark with the observation that "[w]e no longer need to go to History to trace [human nature] in all its stages and periods" (perhaps found not so congenial by the addressee of his praises), it illustrates well the contemporary understanding of the distinctiveness of Robertson's combination of historical narrative with theoretical reflection. In recent literature, Burke's eulogy of Robertson has been cited with such frequency that highlighting it here may risk both being impolite and eliciting boredom. There are still several reasons why it is not entirely awkward to start this chapter by referring to it.

First, Burke's remark assumes that the comparative study of European contact with other human groups (and the attempt to make sense for Europeans both of such groups and the influence of the intercourse with them on their own societies) is a study of "mankind," of humanity. This was a concept still tenuous at the time, but one which we certainly owe to the Enlightenment, and one to which Robertson's late masterpieces on America and India both contributed significantly. Second, it also assumes that such study is best carried out with a "philosophical" approach to "manners"—an approach that has been identified as a Scottish Enlightenment trademark associated with the science of man. Having first turned from national to European themes, from *Scotland* to *Charles V*, by an ease secured by the persistent application of this frame of interpretation, Robertson moved on equally smoothly to what today would be styled as global history: the exploration of the encounter and transactions of Europeans with other civilizations in reciprocal though asymmetric relationships, an indispensable tool for assessing the nature and extent of such asymmetries being once again exactly the systematic use of the stadial scheme. Both in the case of the *History of America* and the *Historical Disquisition*, the most striking features—ones which also had highly important moral and political implications—were "stadialist" pieces of analysis: of the progress of European navigation and commercial expansion (Book I, *History of America*, and much of Sections I–III in the *Historical Disquisition*); of "savage" society (Book IV, *History of America*); of the more sophisticated Inca and Aztec cultures (Book VII, *History of America*); of the "political economy" of the Spanish colonial empire (Book VIII, *History of America*); and of the advanced manners and institutions of India (Appendix, *Historical Disquisition*).[2] As I shall show, however, standards of causal explanation and patterns of interpretation dictated by the stadialist logic also permeate the narrative portions of both works, where they are the principal tool for Robertson to give an account of the conduct and manners of individual protagonists and collective personae.

America: savages and "imperfectly civilized"

Similarly to the cases of the *History of Scotland* and the *History of Charles V*, such avant-garde credentials of Robertson's, with reference to at least the *History of America*, have been put in a more relativistic light in recent literature. For instance, the very incentives for him in making this move toward the topic of Europe's colonial dependencies after an inquiry into the birth pangs of the European state system were not strictly scientific-professional, and certainly included ones arising from his own status within the British political establishment, to whose then-current concerns the retention of a recently preserved empire in North America and the proper control of another one emerging in India were integral.[3] These are highly important findings from the point of view of Robertson's plausible motivations, which, however, together with the British policy considerations with which they were associated, mattered less for the German interpreters and interpretations of Robertson, the chief concern of this book. Of more significance is the overall atmosphere of the late 1760s and 1770s, when the recently concluded conflict of colonial powers threw into prominence the conditions of Europe's unfolding global ascendancy. This was an atmosphere in which the stringent criticism of the practices applied in the conquest of overseas territories and the subjugation of native populations by the Abbé Raynal and his team of authors—in particular, Denis Diderot—in the *Histoire philosophique et politique des établissements et du commerce des Européens dans les des deux Indes* attracted vast audiences across Europe,[4] and in which treatments of the same themes by other authors such as Robertson could also count on avid interest.

In each of the sections of the two works highlighted above, Robertson's discussion is informed by the premise, made explicit by him with a striking regularity in diverse but unambiguous formulations, that human communities normally advance through broadly similar stages of development, defined in terms of the dominant "mode of subsistence" (hunting and gathering; pasturing; agriculture; and commerce).[5] There is also a rough correspondence between the complexity of procuring subsistence, the refinement of manners, and the sophistication of institutions, concepts, and beliefs. The accounts of the history of navigation among the leading maritime nations of Europe offered in both the *History of America* and the *Historical Disquisition* (the latter frequently just referring to the former or adopting passages from it verbatim) are possible to read as extensions of the overall thrust of the "View of the Progress" into a particular thematic field. Navigation and shipbuilding are described by Robertson as "nice and complicated" arts, so that "from the raft or canoe, which first served to carry a savage over the river that obstructed him in the chace, to the construction of a vessel capable of conveying a numerous crew with safety to a distant coast, the progress in improvement is immense." In demonstrating this, philosophical conjecture can be resorted to as a helpful tool: "The rude and imperfect state in which navigation is still found among all nations which are not considerably civilized, corresponds with this account of its progress, and demonstrates, that in early times, the art was not so far improved as to enable men to undertake distant voyages, or to attempt remote discoveries."[6] The existence of "mutual interest and mutual wants" among humans who inhabit different regions with differing resources is an important trigger of the said "progress in improvement":

> It is to navigation that men are indebted for the power of transporting the superfluous stock of one part of the earth, to supply the wants of another. The luxuries and blessings of a particular climate are no longer confined to itself alone... [Besides and above conquest and settlement,] the desire of gain became a new incentive to activity, roused adventurers, and sent them forth upon long voyages, in search of countries, whose products or wants might increase that circulation, which nourishes and gives vigour to commerce. Trade proved a great source of discovery, it opened unknown seas, it penetrated into new regions, and contributed more than any other cause, to bring men acquainted with the situation, the nature, and commodities of the different parts of the globe.[7]

Commerce (interest) and curiosity, enterprise and adventure walk hand in hand. Their incremental growth is slow and cumbersome, guided by trial and error, and ridden with setbacks. But whenever the "spirit of commerce" arose in history (whether from the absence of the natural fertility of the soil, as in the case of the ancient Phoenicians, from the policy of empire-building, as in the case of Alexander the Great, or from the multiplication of needs, as among Western Europeans from the thirteenth century on), it was followed by its "usual effects," that is, it "awakened curiosity, enlarged the ideas and desires of men, and incited them to bold enterprises."[8] This was a spirit that might assume an "adventurous" character, in which it resembled—and received reinforcement from—that of pirates and warriors. Robertson develops this theme with reference to the grant of the Canaries by Henry III of Castile to the Norman Baron John de Bethencourt (who possessed the "valour and good fortune which distinguished the adventurers of his country"), and to the heightening of a "martial and adventurous spirit" among the Iberian nations during the *reconquista*, which "called forth men of such active and daring genius, as are fit for bold undertakings." For them the sea presented a "field of enterprise in which they could distinguish themselves."[9]

However, it is worth remembering that in early modern English usage, "adventure" did not necessarily only refer to a rash, extravagant, chivalrous quest of danger and valiant defiance of fortune. The Company of the Merchant Adventurers of London (chartered in 1407 to export wool to the continent and developing its privileges into a monopoly of the cloth trade during most of the sixteenth and seventeenth centuries) was a thoroughly regulated company of capitalist entrepreneurs, under a governor and several deputies, who all sought decent profit through safe investment and reasonable risk-taking. The word also appeared in the name of companies specifically created in the atmosphere of the lure of geographic exploration, such as "The Mystery, Company, and Fellowship of Merchant Adventurers for the Discovery of Regions, Dominions, Islands, and Places Unknown," founded in 1551 by Sebastian Cabot (as governor), Richard Chancellor, Hugh Willoughby, and some 240 associates, and renamed in 1555 as the Muscovy Company. "Adventurer" continued simply to denote a business investor who "ventures" capital well into the seventeenth century, when the 1642 Adventurers' Act invited the public to invest in the suppression of the Irish rebellion in return for the promise of lands to be confiscated from the rebels.[10] In the *History of America*, Robertson's purpose is eminently served by the ambiguity of language, which allows for a permeability of the boundary between the moral psychology of two social types that were to play a paramount role in Europe's global expansion, showing the merchant and the conquistador to be distant relatives. In the history of Spanish America the disposition of the latter would be irresistible. At the auspicious beginning of the process, the most towering figures among "enterprising" men, like Prince Henry the Navigator, also "added all the accomplishments of a more enlightened and polished age" to the martial spirit, as a result of which the first "regular plan of discovery" was conceived in Portugal. In the classic style of the Edinburgh sciences on man, stadial-conjectural pieces of social analysis lead to (and establish the ground for) a discussion of the moral psychology of discovery and the character of the discoverer. According to Robertson's plastic representation, a curiosity feeding on the prospect of material gain, and thus becoming second nature, thanks to the swelling spirit of commerce, was capable of accommodating the attitudes of a warrior elite whose ethos rested on personal valor and glory; and also of resorting to the advances of "enlightenment"—science and technology as well as a culture of self-control and considered calculation—for the sake of giving direction to both sets of dispositions.

The equilibrium in this character was a tenuous one, and, as Robertson's characterizations of the conquistadors would show, could be overwhelmed or degenerated under the unusual exigencies of the process of discovery itself. But Christopher Columbus still represented the ideal type: in him, "the modesty and diffidence of true genius was united with the ardent enthusiasm of a projector"; his "active mind" was applied to the sciences that gave a new and thorough underpinning to navigation; with a "sanguine and enterprising temper," he turned his speculative knowledge directly to action; in addition, "he possessed a thorough knowledge of mankind, an insinuating address, a patient perseverance in executing any plan, the perfect government of his own passions, and the talent of acquiring an ascendant over those of other men."[11] All these amount to ambition geared to purposefulness by conscious deliberation and composure: the figure of the accomplished discoverer is a companion of the resourceful statesman, familiar from portraits drawn by Robertson in the *History of Charles V* in his picture gallery of modernity.

As a matter of fact, the application of the language of stadial history and the related categories of moral psychology to the New World, and for different reasons to India, too, is paradoxical:[12] strictly speaking, it could be difficult to discern the sequence of stages anywhere in America, while one of the remarkable features of Indian society seemed to be precisely the permanence and immutability of manners and institutions. In most of the territories of the former, what remained of the stadial scheme was the "savage" stage of hunters, gatherers, and primitive planters who did not attain to pasturing, and whatever agriculture they developed was insufficient to generate commerce and the accompanying system of legal codes and political institutions. The fact—or assumption, which Creole historians would ardently debate[13]—that even the most sophisticated of American societies failed to reach the stage where the writing of history as an account of civil society could be a relevant pursuit, was also a chief reason why Robertson abandoned his original plan of inserting the discovery and conquest of America into his history of the reign of Charles V. To all intents and purposes, civil history was "brought" to America by Europeans: it was their history in America (as in the case of Columbus, Las Casas, Cortes, and Pizarro), and that of America in Europe (as in the case of the successes and failures in governing the colonial economy by Spain). As for the history of the Americans and of their encounter with the conquerors, it was incapable of rendering by way of a civil narrative, because the unequal relations of power between the two sides deprived it from any dramatic suspense, essential for this type of history. Robertson suggested that civil history as an account of the emulation of human talents and endeavors is close to its "noblest" when representing "men at a juncture when their minds are most violently agitated, and all their powers and passions are called forth," that is, in war. "But in a contest between naked savages, and one of the most warlike of European nations, where science, courage, and discipline on one side, were opposed by ignorance, timidity, and disorder on the other, a particular detail of events would be as unpleasant as uninstructive."[14] Such encounters and the part played by the indigenous in them—the very history of the latter—was to be intelligible only if rendered in terms that were quasi-ethnographical, philosophical, and conjectural, to which the vocabulary and underlying principles, if not the strict sequence, of stages was still indispensable. India was an altogether different case: manufactures were brought to perfection, social differentiation occurred, legal codes and institutions of police emerged, and a literate culture with written philosophies and histories was established there in the remote past. Yet, although the subcontinent proved resistant to change for many centuries and thus any evidence for "progress" was difficult to invoke, the comparative potential of the stadialist vocabulary made it an attractive tool for Robertson, and one widely resorted to by him, to frame his analysis of situations that were essentially static in this case, too.

It is somewhat remarkable that for Robertson the *absence* of stages still invited a plethora of formulations employing the analytical standards and terminological arsenal of stadial history to make sense of non-European societies. In fact, probably his most uncompromising commitment to the methodological tenets of stadial history is contained in Book IV of the *History of America*: "In order to complete the history of the human mind, and attain to a perfect knowledge of its nature and its operations, we must contemplate man in all those various situations wherein he has been placed. We must follow him in his progress through the different stages of society, as he advances from the infant state of civil life towards its maturity and decline." In the same section of the work, substantial space is devoted by him to the discussion of theories about the settlement of the American continent, only to conclude that "the condition and character of the American nations, at the time when they became known to the Europeans, deserve more attentive consideration, than the inquiry concerning their origin. The latter is merely an object of curiosity, the former is one of the most important as well as instructive researches which can occupy the historian."[15] Further on in the text Robertson also gives the reason for this view: nearly two centuries after the discovery of America, philosophers started to appreciate the fact that a better knowledge of "the Americans in their original state...might enable us to fill up a considerable chasm in [the human species'] progress."[16] He then goes on to provide a concise summary of the dominant tone and tenor of the whole of Book IV:

> In America, man appears under the rudest form in which we can conceive him to subsist. We behold communities just beginning to unite, and may examine the sentiments and actions of human beings in the infancy of social life, while they feel but imperfectly the force of its ties, and have scarcely relinquished their native liberty. The state of primaeval simplicity, which was known in our continent only by the fanciful description of poets,

really existed in the other. The greater part of its inhabitants were strangers to industry and labour, ignorant of arts, imperfectly acquainted with the nature of property, and enjoying almost without restriction or controul the blessings which flowed spontaneously from the bounty of nature."[17]

The assumption that similar conditions of sociocultural existence nurture a similarity of lifestyles is a recurrent feature of the text. "A tribe of savages on the banks of the Danube must very nearly resemble one upon the plains washed by the Mississippi. Instead then of presuming from this similarity, that there is an affinity between them, we should only conclude, that the disposition and manners of men are formed by their situation, and arise from the state of society in which they live."[18] The affinity mentioned extends, beyond habits of conduct in peace and war (especially the latter being a pet topic with many authors of scientific travelogues and philosophical histories),[19] to moral and religious beliefs as well. "Were we to trace back the ideas of other nations to that rude state in which history first presents them to our view, we should discover a surprising resemblance in their tenets and practices; and should be convinced that, in similar circumstances, the faculties of the human mind hold nearly the same course in their progress, and arrive at almost the same conclusion."[20] It is striking—and confirming the ubiquitous character of the pattern—to find a counterpart of this proposition, now applied to the opposite end of the developmental scale, in the important Appendix on the "genius, manners and institutions of India" in the *Historical Disquisition*: "we find that as soon as men arrive at that stage in social life, when they can turn their attention to speculative inquiries, the human mind will, in every region of the earth, display nearly the same powers, and proceed in its investigations and discoveries by nearly the same steps."[21]

In order to account for the apparent inability of most native American societies to progress beyond the hunting-gathering stage, Robertson also resorted to further devices. One of them was another widely available discourse about primitive man: the so-called immaturity or degeneracy thesis, whose supporters—Buffon in its milder statement and De Pauw in its less elegant form—held that in the New World, either because it was too young or too ancient, all forms of life were necessarily tiny and feeble.[22] Robertson duly signals the relevance of these theories, as well as of the adulation of "the rude simplicity of savage life" by Rousseau, to the theme of Book IV, while warning against uncritically giving credit to the "superficial remarks of vulgar travellers, of sailors, traders, buccaneers, and missionaries" (upon which, presumably, he deemed each of these types of analysis to be established). "Without indulging conjecture, or betraying a propensity to either system, we must study with equal care to avoid the extremes of extravagant admiration, or of supercilious contempt for those manners which we describe,"[23] he admonished—only to align himself basically with Buffon and De Pauw in his ensuing account of the pervasive bodily and mental "feebleness" of the Americans. While their overall appearance is pleasant, the indigenous people of the New World are "more remarkable for agility than strength" and "not only averse to toil but incapable of it." Their "native indolence" is logically accompanied by "the smallness of their appetite for food," while their "beardless countenance and smooth skin...seems to indicate a defect of vigour"—altogether, leading the philosophical historian "to suspect that there is some natural debility in their frame."[24] It seemed only logical that among such creatures, not only the progress of arts, but also population growth was arrested. Not surprisingly, their mental faculties are described in matching terms: in this state, the intellectual powers of the human mind are "extremely limited," and "its emotions and efforts are few and languid." Following one of his most cherished sources, Antonio de Herrera y Tordesillas, Robertson's overall judgment is formulated in vivid terms: "Their vacant countenance, their staring unexpressive eye, their listless inattention, and total ignorance of subjects, which seem to be the first which should occupy the thoughts of rational beings, made such impression upon the Spaniards, when they first beheld those rude people, that they considered them as animals of an inferior order, and could not believe that they belonged to the human species."[25] Even the virtues which Americans may boast, such as their independence of spirit, fortitude in the face of indigence, danger, and torture, or satisfaction with their condition, are shown to arise to a very considerable extent from the primitiveness of their social ties, from their insensitivity, and overall lack of motivation. (It must be added that earlier in the text Robertson also described the conquerors as inadequately prepared for the experience of encounter with indigenous populations: they were "mostly illiterate adventurers, destitute of all ideas which should have directed them in contemplating objects, so extremely different from those with which they had been acquainted." What is more, a disparaging estimate of native populations also eminently served their interest.[26])

Robertson viewed the Americans to be averse to labor and indifferent to both "the hope of future good" and "the apprehension of future evil" that might alleviate this aversion, having little prospect of emerging from the savage state out of their own effort. In taking stock of their social conditions, the natural history of the sort cultivated by Buffon and De Pauw still informs Robertson's anthropology, but he predominantly reverts to the analytical frame offered by stadial history. It is "mode of subsistence" that determines relations in the family including the important theme of the status of women, as well as military and civil "establishments," and laws and customs in general. Robertson's indebtedness to the stadial scheme is also the key to his preference for Buffon's view about the New World as being "of a recent original...[whose] inhabitants...still at the beginning of their career, were unworthy to be compared to a people of a more ancient and improved continent" over De Pauw's thesis that because of climatic and other factors "man never attained in America the perfection that belongs to his nature, but remained an animal of an inferior order."[27] Both Buffon's and Robertson's frameworks of explanation allowed for a great deal of diversity within humanity, while unequivocally considering it to be unitary as a species: the former on the ground that the offspring of any male and female specimen was capable of further procreation, and the latter on the ground that mankind everywhere possessed the same "capacity for improvement." It is no wonder that both of them were committed adherents of the monogenetic account of the Creation, which was being called into question in their time, among others, by Robertson's fellow Edinburgh philosopher Henry Home, Lord Kames.[28] Robertson wrote, "We know, with infallible certainty, that all the human race spring from the same source, and that the descendants of one man, under the protection, as well as in obedience to the command of Heaven, multiplied and replenished the earth."[29] And while the "infallible source" for a leading ecclesiastic like him was undoubtedly the Bible, he also sought further underpinnings for his conviction, available from the theory of stages: "The disposition and manners of men are formed by their situation, and arise from the state of society in which they live.... In every part of the earth the progress of man hath been nearly the same, and we can trace him in his career from the rude simplicity of savage life, until he attains the industry, the arts, and the elegance of polished society"[30]—a potential realized to differing degrees and at different paces because of contingent factors. This was the sole reason why Europeans had become "exalted...above the inhabitants of the other quarters of the globe,"[31] and whatever entitlement to domination over these "quarters" they had was inseparable from their calling to help trigger a development among them which would yield similar achievements. Nonetheless, certain stages in it might prove painful through an improper understanding of the requirements of socioeconomic progress, as in the case of the Spanish colonists, and could be disadvantageous both for the conquerors and the conquered.

In any case, Europeans became masters in America not only over the "savage nations," but also over those which "may be considered polished states" when compared to the former, though they "can hardly be considered as having advanced beyond the infancy of civil life."[32] From this cautious formulation it might appear that the Mexican and the Peruvian "empires" were recognized by Robertson to have a place in the civilizational scale of the Edinburgh science of man. There

> we find countries of great extent subjected to the dominion of one sovereign, the inhabitants collected together in cities, the wisdom and foresight of rulers employed in providing for the maintenance and security of the people, the empire of laws in some measure established, the authority of religion recognized, many of the arts essential to life brought to some degree of maturity, and the dawn of such as are ornamental beginning to appear.[33]

The reason why the claim of these societies to civilization was at best imperfect is that they lacked several essential triggers of large-scale stadial progress, including the smelting and forging of "useful metals" and an extensive "dominion over animal creation."

> In our continent, long after men had attained both, society continued in that state which is denominated barbarous. Even with all that command over nature which these confer, many ages elapse, before industry becomes so regular as to render subsistence secure, before the arts which supply the wants and furnish the accommodations of life are brought to any considerable degree of perfection, and before any idea is conceived of various institutions requisite in a well-ordered society.[34]

To shortcomings on these counts, one may add the failure even of the Mexicans and the Peruvians to develop alphabetic writing (an indispensable tool of expressing abstract ideas, as against devices such as the *quipu* and other types of pictograms and ideograms, described as mere mnemonic techniques), money (together with letters, a means of communicating wants to a distance), and wheeled traffic (together with money, a means of multiplying and satisfying such wants). Among such circumstances the excellent system of roads in the Inca Empire is the symbolic expression of a paradox: rather than prosperous merchants, they are trodden by athlete-messengers needed to make up for the lack of written script.[35]

It has been suggested that these explanations for the imperfections of the state of civilization even among the most advanced American societies lie outside the succession of stages and are necessary for Robertson because of the general difficulty of the theorists of the Scottish Enlightenment in accounting for movement from one stage to the next.[36] This observation is helpful if it is taken to refer to the fact that the argument from technology (just as we have seen in the case of the argument from natural history) was complementary and not contradictory to the argument from stages in Robertson's system of causality, which was employed to illustrate and explain the ultimate universality of the savage character in America, despite, however, the "nice discrimination of those shades that mingle so perceptibly in so many different gradations of savage life."[37] Mexico may certainly boast significant refinements in the building of cities, in the splendor of monarchs, in the improved state of police, in the delicate workmanship of artistic products. To these, even the gentle spirit of religion, mitigating the excesses of despotism, may be added, in the case of Peru. Nevertheless, such accomplishments are all described as those of men "just emerging from barbarity," occurring *in spite of* a primitive mode of subsistence, lack of technological improvement, unfortunate geophysical conditions, and their physiological consequences. The gradations "from infancy to adolescence" (but not to "the rest" of the process of growth toward maturity, supplied by "our continent") mentioned by Burke can still be comfortably accommodated within the "savage" state. Whether descending to war with a ferocity animated by the spirit of vengeance, like the Tlascalans or the Mexicans, or marked by an unwarlike feebleness, like the Caribs and the Peruvians, they are a poor match in the encounter with the calculating determination, technological ascendancy, and physical and psychological stamina of the conquerors.

Historians have pointed to the discrepancies between the philosophical and the narrative parts of the *History of America* and suggested that the latter were designed by Robertson as an antidote to the perceived limitations of stadial theory as a self-contained pattern of analysis, and to create room for the "unique" and "particular" as against the "typical."[38] It has even been claimed that the philosophical sections are to be understood mainly as a polite gesture to the fashion of the time and that the stadial discourse that is prominent in them has a negligible function in the rest of the work, in which it is not a theoretical stage of savagery but "real" native Americans that are presented, and in which "barbarism" is not a stadial division but a moral condition—of Spaniards, rather than Americans.[39] This point is valuable as a reminder that Robertson's enthusiasm for empire-building was not unqualified (as it would also be evident in the *Historical Disquisition*), and that especially in instances when empire was pursued through violent armed conquest by a Catholic power that also aspired at universal monarchy in Europe, he found it all the more unpalatable. It also illustrates the fact that even a committed "modern" like Robertson believed that it was possible for Europeans to divest themselves of their civilized habits and fall back to practices associated with savagery and barbarism, such as cannibalism or the violation of the rights of war.

All of this, however, does nothing to prevent Robertson from retaining the stadial vocabulary and its corollary arguments from technological development and natural history as the chief underlying pattern of interpreting individual and collective agency in the narrative portions of the *History of America* as well, most characteristically stressing the anomalous character of actions, events, or other phenomena whenever they seem to contradict the logic dictated by the "typicalities" described in the "philosophical" books. The manners of the natives whom Columbus encountered at the site of his first discoveries in San Salvador and Hispaniola correspond to the model presented in Book IV to an extent that the relevant passages could be inserted in that section of the work without disrupting its argument. In contrast to the "enlightened and ambitious" Spaniards, they are "simple and undiscerning," "unacquainted with all the arts which appear most necessary in polished societies, but...gentle, credulous and timid."[40] Above all, they proved to be at a loss when they realized that the Spaniards had come

> not to visit the country, but to settle in it. Though the number of those strangers was inconsiderable, the state of cultivation among this rude people was so imperfect, and in such exact proportion to their own consumption, that it was with difficulty they could afford subsistence to their new guests.

Their own mode of life was so indolent and inactive, the warmth of the climate so enervating, the constitution of their bodies naturally so feeble, and so unaccustomed to the laborious exertions of industry, that they were satisfied with a proportion of food amazingly small...Self-preservation prompted them to wish for the departure of guests who wasted so fast their slender stock of provisions.

In the subsequent conflict—the first "war" between Europeans and native Americans—a long-lasting pattern was established: especially as the Spaniards were decimated by diseases, "the vast superiority of the natives in number, compensated for many defects," but superiority in weapons, discipline, and strategy in the end almost inevitably prevailed.[41] The only "scheme" the native Americans were capable of attempting was finely in tune with their aversion to "a regular and persevering exertion of their industry": it was starving the oppressors, whose "voracious appetite" seemed to make them vulnerable, by "suspend[ing] all the operations of agriculture." This time they were defeated by the civilizational ascendancy of the Old World, expressed in terms of both greater economic productive capacity and the concomitant human qualities: initiative and adaptability. "The Spaniards were reduced to extreme want; but they received such seasonable supplies of provisions from Europe, and found so many resources in their own ingenuity and industry, that they suffered no great loss of men. The wretched Indians were the victims of their own ill-concerted policy." Famine, diseases, and death ensued among them on a massive scale.[42]

Recognizing the human cost of introducing modern discipline among a population both socially backward and physically "feeble" (the Buffonian/Pauwian term used in Book IV features regularly in Books II and III as well), there were some on the Spanish side who, driven by a charitable disposition, proposed and implemented a more gentle policy in the settlements. But Queen Isabella's solicitude "retarded...the progress of improvement," just as the later experiment of Rodrigo de Figueroa, chief judge of Hispaniola, with "the system of Las Casas" was doomed to failure: "He collected in Hispaniola a good number of the natives, and settled them in two villages, leaving them at perfect liberty, and with the uncontrolled direction of their own actions. But that people, accustomed to a mode of life extremely different from that which takes place wherever civilization has made considerable progress, were incapable of assuming new habits at once." The miserable outcome of the experiment had the result that the Spaniards "pronounced them incapable of being formed to live like men in social life, and considered them as children, who should be kept under the perpetual tutelage of persons superior to themselves in wisdom and sagacity."[43] Robertson knew all too well that arriving at this conclusion and proclaiming it was fully in the interest of the Spanish, and did not hesitate to label the alternative policy, fatal to the indigenous people, as "barbarous." At the same time, he was willing to acknowledge that it not only succeeded in "calling forth the force of a whole nation, and exerting it in one direction," that is, the working of the mines, "with amazing rapidity and success," but also paved the way to the establishment by Nicholas de Ovando at Hispaniola of a government "with wisdom and justice, not inferior to the rigour with which he treated the Indians." Besides equal laws and their impartial execution, this also implied the encouragement of cultivation, manufactures, and commerce, to the extent that Ovando's "prudent endeavours" finally awakened King Ferdinand's interest in the discoveries hitherto neglected by him and prompted him to introduce "many of those regulations which gradually formed that system of profound, but jealous policy by which [Spain] governs her dominions in the New World."[44]

The actions of Ovando, while triggering some consolidation in the emerging colonial establishment, already represent a deterioration from the standard of a public, ordered, and systematic endeavor[45] still represented by Henry the Navigator and Columbus. The brand of adventurism represented especially by the latter, in whom the "enterprising spirit" and "curiosity" awakened by the recent improvement of navigation and commerce was visibly fueled by personal ambition, too, received a lamentable impetus from two forces that disfigured its originally progressive face: "religious enthusiasm always mingled with the spirit of adventure in the New World, and, by a combination still more strange, united with avarice."[46] The fanaticism of religion and the fanaticism of gold had mutually reinforcing effects even on Cortes, whose initial characterization by Robertson still resembled that of Columbus. At first, Cortes's youthful turbulence "settled into a habit of regular indefatigable activity," and "[t]he impetuosity of his temper...abated, by being kept under restraint, and mellowed into a cordial soldierly frankness. These qualities were accompanied with calm prudence in concerting his schemes, and with what is peculiar to superior genius, the art of gaining the confidence and governing the minds of men." By the time, however, he established the first "form of civil government" in Mexico, "[t]he two principles of avarice and enthusiasm, which prompted the Spaniards in all their enterprises in the New World, seem to have concurred in suggesting the name which Cortes bestowed on his infant settlement. He called it *The rich town of the true Cross* [Villa rica de la vera Cruz]."[47] Though sometimes "prudence overruled his zeal," on other occasions "a new effusion of that intemperate religious zeal with which Cortes was animated, no less than other adventurers of the age," put recently forged alliances with local peoples at risk: "astonished and enraged" by the obstinacy of the Tlascalans to embrace Christianity, he "prepared to execute by force, what he could not accomplish by persuasion." His "inconsiderate impetuosity" was only checked thanks to the intervention of father Olmedo, which was another paradox for Robertson: "at a time when the rights of conscience were little understood in the Christian world, and the idea of toleration unknown, one is astonished to find a Spanish monk of the sixteenth century among the first advocates against persecution, and in behalf of religious liberty."[48]

In most situations, however, there was no benign influence to restrain the despicable violence ignited by the combination of material greed and religious zeal. Disappointed by the "smallness of the booty" that "their rapaciousness could collect" after the fall of Mexico and believing that the bulk of the treasure was hidden, the Spaniards decided to torture Guatimozin (Montezuma's nephew and son-in-law, who valiantly defended the city during the final assault) with a "refined cruelty"—"a deed which stains the glory of all [Cortes'] great actions."[49] The subsequent insurrections of the Mexicans were put down and retaliated with a "shocking barbarity": "In almost every district of the Mexican empire, the progress of Spanish arms is marked with blood, and with deeds so atrocious, as disgrace the enterprising valour that conducted them to success."[50] The progress of Pizarro—also characterized as a man of uncommon "patience" and "fortitude," but in every other talent much inferior to Cortes—and his associates in Peru is then related in Book VI as a succession of acts of "unrelenting barbarity" occasioned by the "strange alliance of fanaticism with avarice."[51]

Since in most instances Robertson establishes a direct causal link between greed and zeal as the impulses that undermine the orderly and progressive character of modern enterprise, and the violence of the conquistadors, his is a somewhat different perspective from that of Diderot in the *Histoire des deux Indes*, where European colonists, removed from the polite societies and well-regulated polities that the historical progress of their home countries has bred, throw off the reins of civility and debase themselves, as "domestic tigers returning to the forest," to the level of their new domiciles—also developing a threat to the integrity of metropolitan civilization.[52] According to Robertson, they are not infected by their savage environment: the fault is to be found within themselves, more precisely, in the precariousness and vulnerability of the system of enterprise and adventure that arose through the growth of navigation and commerce as described in Book I. In their case, barbarism is an anomaly that contradicts the normal course of civilization: they engage in it in spite of what they are, could or ought to be—or, have become over the two and half centuries that separates their time from Robertson's own, during which Europe itself has better learned how to preserve faith without proselytization and persecution, and to obtain wealth without plunder. The blemishes which Robertson deplored from the perspective of enlightened civic moralism, which he shared with his fellow Edinburgh moderate literati, "stained the glory" and "disgraced the enterprising valour" of the conquerors. But glory and valor they did possess, and they were of a kind based on the values and dispositions that had been nurtured by the process that also bred Henry the Navigator and Columbus. It was not just through the rare examples of "persons who retained some tincture of the Castilian generosity"[53] that the violence of the conquest could be expected to assume restraints. Pizarro himself, soon after the infamous "trial" and execution of the Inca and the indiscriminate slaughter that followed, is found to be apply[ing] himself with that persevering ardour, which distinguishes his character, to introduce a form of regular government...He distributed the country into various districts; he appointed proper magistrates to preside in each; and established regulations concerning the administration of justice, the collection of the royal revenue, the working of the mines, and the treatment of the Indians, extremely simple, but well calculated to promote the public prosperity.[54]

Even the villain, whose trajectory illustrates the darkest aspects of the corruption of which the "spirit of enterprise and adventure" is capable, preserves the capacity for assiduous application for the sake of stability and well-being, part and parcel of the frame of mind in the role model, when enjoying "an interval of tranquillity, undisturbed by any enemy."[55]

By stark contrast, at every instance when some American achievement that appears to surpass the standard associated with savagery is mentioned, it is described by Robertson in a tone of puzzlement, as an anomaly that occurs in spite of the "nature of things" defined by the stadial pattern. Sometimes such anomalies are illusory, and shown to be based merely on error or delusion. Such was the case with the "sanguine hopes" of the Spaniards about the amount of treasure—in Hispaniola, Mexico, as well as Peru—they could take as booty, which, however, could not be met. Given that "[t]o penetrate into the bowels of the earth, and to refine the rude ore, were operations too complicated and laborious for their talents and industry,"[56] the natives had amassed gold in much smaller quantity than it was assumed. The paradoxical nature of the "refinement in police, unknown, at that time, in Europe," illustrated by the example of conveying intelligence by means of well-trained couriers, has already been mentioned. The Tlascalans are recognized by Robertson to have "advanced in improvement far beyond the rude nations of America," yet "their degree of civilization was incomplete," which also had as its corollary an archaic manner of warfare, doomed to failure in the encounter with the Spaniards: they "were, like all unpolished nations, strangers to military order and discipline," not to speak of their primitive weapons and their "barbarous generosity" in sending forewarnings and even provisions to the enemy.[57] When it comes to character, Montezuma, the only ruler except Atahualpa in the New World who may have had it in his power to resist the tide, turns out to be a disappointingly poor match to the task: "though his talents might be suited to the transactions of a state so imperfectly polished as the Mexican empire, and sufficient to conduct them while in their accustomed course, they were inadequate to a conjuncture so extraordinary, and did not qualify him either to judge with discernment, or to act with decision, requisite to such a trying emergence."[58] The fact that he shared the universally superstitious disposition of his people, profoundly affecting their attitude to the Spanish, only made things worse. The city of Mexico is recognized to have been "the pride of the New World, and the noblest monument of the industry and art of man." But the added clause, "while unacquainted with the use of iron, and destitute of aid from any domestic animal," both enhances the sense of admiration and wonderment, and distracts from it; it is a splendor achieved in defiance of the level attained in stadial progress, and therefore in a realistic estimate is hardly tenable.[59]

The opulence and civilization of Peru is described, if anything, in even more striking terms than is the case with Mexico. It was "a country fully peopled, and cultivated with an appearance of regular industry." Already long before the arrival of the conquistadors, the half-legendary founders Manco Capac and Mama Ocollo had "formed that social union, which, by multiplying the desires, and uniting the efforts of the human species, excites industry, and leads to improvement." They introduced "such laws and policy as might perpetuate their happiness" and "various relations in private life were established, and the duties resulting from them prescribed with such propriety, as gradually formed a barbarous people to decency of manners." The country "soon assumed the aspect of a regular and well-governed state." Although in narrow precincts, the Incas "exercised absolute and uncontrolled authority" and they endeavored to extend their dominions not out of "the rage of conquest" but "the desire of diffusing the blessings of civilization."[60] Robertson's appreciation of Peruvian civilization, expressed with a great deal of lucidity by employing the established categories of stadial history, in the narrative sections of the *History of America* seems almost unqualified (we have seen, however, the qualifications advanced in the philosophical Book VII). It is only logical that subverting it by force depended on the most extreme violation of the principles of civilized humanity by Pizarro and his associates.

Robertson was sometimes criticized by his contemporaries for painting an all too homogeneous picture of the native American "character" in Book IV.[61] This criticism is not entirely unfair. However, if the whole of the work is taken into consideration, an interesting ambiguity strikes the eye: from the variegated account of so many tribes and peoples in the New World, the homogeneity of the character depicted in Book IV appears to allow for a great deal of diversity—"gradations," as Burke put it—while still, by and large, remaining within the confines of that picture. The standard which in varying degrees New World societies fell short of satisfying was the independent ability to employ advanced methods of cultivation, to pursue industry and to maintain commercial intercourse, and to erect on these foundations a sophisticated division of labor, social hierarchy, and a culture of social action based not on unfettered passion but on rational calculation.

India: civilization subdued

In Robertson's assessment, there was only one exception to this near-universal underdevelopment of the non-European world: India, where "the distinction of ranks and separation of professions were completely established" already in ancient times (one of "the most undoubted proofs of a society considerably advanced in progress"), and which, at the time it was discovered by modern Europeans, was "possessed by nations highly civilized, which had made considerable progress in elegant as well as useful arts, which were accustomed to intercourse with strangers, and well acquainted with all the advantages of commerce."[62] All the recognition the savage seemed to have been entitled to receive was that while his rude manners were disparaged, they were allowed to stem not from inherent moral blemish but from his primitive mode of subsistence, and thus in a certain sense were judged according to their own merit. But the same attitude toward a system of civilization—which was different from that of Europe, but could be considered one by the standards derived from the science of man—implied a positive cultural tolerance and empathy, and warranted a considerably lesser degree of political intervention by Westerners to make the relationship mutually profitable.[63]

In spite of the above-mentioned immutability of many centuries that Robertson diagnosed in Indian civilization, the uses of the stadial frame of analysis for this thrust of argument are obvious, and they loomed even larger in view of the fact that unlike in the case of all his other historical works, political narrative was completely missing from the *Historical Disquisition*.

> [I]t is a cruel mortification, in searching for what is instructive in the history of past times, to find that the exploits of conquerors who have desolated the earth, and the freaks of tyrants who have rendered nations unhappy, are recorded with minute and often disgusting accuracy, while the discovery of useful arts, and the progress of the most beneficial branches of commerce, are passed over in silence, and suffered to sink into oblivion.[64]

He decided to redress this omission in advancing his plea on behalf of Indian civilization, with the consequence that the stadial vocabulary, once again, permeates the whole of the text and operates as its primary unifying force. Concise reformulations of, and supplements to, the history of the progress of European navigation and commerce—again characterized as a "vigilant and enterprizing activity"—are interspersed with reports on the stage of civility attained both in Europe and in India. The latter's exceptionally high level of "cultivation" at an unusually early time is emphasized repeatedly, and is illustrated by the fact that the cause of interest in commerce with India has always been its superior improvement and the resulting sophistication of its manufactures. According to the stadial logic, however, these could be fully appreciated only at times when Europeans themselves attained to similar refinement. "In every age, it has been a commerce of luxury, rather than of necessity, which has been carried on between Europe and India. Its elegant manufactures, spices and precious stones, are neither objects of desire to nations of simple manners, nor are such nations possessed of wealth sufficient to purchase them." This was the case with the Romans, who "were not only...in that stage of society when men are eager to obtain every thing that can render the enjoyment of life more exquisite, or add to its splendour, but they had acquired all the fantastic tastes formed by the caprice and extravagance of wealth."[65] After the subversion of their empire, "the state of society, as well as the condition of individuals, became so extremely different, that the wants and desires of men were no longer the same. Barbarians...had little relish for those accommodations, and that elegance, which are so alluring to polished nations." However, thanks to an advance "from rudeness to refinement in the usual course of progression which nations are destined to hold," Europeans "began to acquire a relish for some of the luxuries of India."[66]

The relation of these developments is an occasion for Robertson to burst into another eulogy of "the commercial genius of Europe, which has given it a visible ascendant over the other three divisions of the earth, by discerning their respective wants and resources, and by rendering them reciprocally subservient to one another, has established a union among them." But, as he reiterates, the enormous difference in the "degree of improvement" of the societies of the West and the East made a profound impact on the spirit and character of trade with them. While the Portuguese who, because of a coincidence of circumstances in European power relations, retained a virtual monopoly of intercourse with India for about a century after the discovery of the maritime route around the Cape of Good Hope, could immediately engage in an "alluring trade" in "manufactures which had long been known and admired in Europe," for the Spaniards it took over half a century to reap any benefit from their bloody conquests. The reason was that their new possessions had to be rendered "beneficial by cultivation and industry"; "they found it necessary to establish colonies in every country which they wished to improve...Every article of commerce imported from the New World...is the produce of the industry of Europeans settled there." By contrast, "[t]rade with the East was a simple mercantile transaction, confined to the purchase either of the natural productions of the country...or of the manufactures which abounded among an industrious race of men."[67] Europe and India are aligned together on this side of the civilizational barrier, America helplessly looking to the tutelage received from Old World patrons.

In the remarkable Appendix of the *Historical Disquisition*, Robertson goes on to assess the "genius, the manners, and institutions" that the people of India have established upon such economic foundations. His fundamental assumption is that "the natives of India were not only more early civilized, but had made a greater progress in civilization than any other people."[68] He acknowledges that the peculiar form of social hierarchy (always a reliable indicator of an advanced state), the caste system, may be an obstacle of mobility for the talented among the inferior orders. Nevertheless, he points not only to the economic advantages that derive from early training in the professions assigned to respective castes, but also to the resulting attitudes that promote acquiescence in one's allotted "station" and thus social stability (congenial to Robertson's taste), and even to the restrictions that the existence of castes imposes on the political authority of monarchs. In the absence of "institutions destined to assert and guard the rights belonging to men in the social state," that "never formed a part of the political constitution in any great Asiatic kingdom," the fact that the monarchs are recruited from the second of the four castes and "behold among their subjects an order of men far superior to themselves in dignity" is a substantial check on despotic power.[69] As a further bulwark against the encroachments of sovereign power, the kingdoms of India were too extensive for direct governance by the monarchs, and the "members of the cast next in rank to that which religion rendered sacred" were invested with the "superintendence of the cities and provinces," so that they formed "an intermediate order between the sovereign and his subjects." According to Robertson, not oriental despotism but monarchy, described in recognizably Montesquieuian terms, is the characteristic form of the Indian polity, distinguished by "equity, humanity and mildness" and institutions found "only among men in the most improved state of society, and under the best forms of government."[70] The Indians even had their Justinian in the sixteenth-century Mughal emperor Akbar, who compiled a full code of Hindu laws (thereby setting a precedent for the more recent undertaking of Warren Hastings as governor general of the British settlements in India). "Men must have been long united in the social state, their transactions must have been numerous and complex, and judges must have determined an immense variety of controversies to which these give rise, before the system of law becomes so voluminous and comprehensive as to direct the judicial proceedings of a nation far advanced in improvement." The *Ayeen Akbery* is an eminent proof to Robertson's mind that this was exactly the case with India: it contains "the jurisprudence of an enlightened and commercial people."[71]

Not surprisingly, Indian material culture and artistic achievement is also interpreted according to the standards of stadial progress. Their "stupendous" buildings "could not have been formed in that stage of social life when men continue divided into small tribes, unaccustomed to the efforts of persevering industry. It is only in States of considerable extent, and among people long habituated to subordination, and to act in concert, that the idea of such magnificent works is conceived, or the power of accomplishing them can be found." Turning to the "fine arts," Robertson's focus is on the spectacular output of ancient Indian epic and dramatic poetry, not omitting to mention the recent English translations of the *Bhagavad-gītā* and *Śakuntalā* by Charles Wilkins and William Jones, respectively. In Robertson's judgment, especially from the latter, "we must form an advantageous idea of the state of improvement in that society to whose taste it was suited."[72] Finally, in evaluating the Indian achievement in the realm of science and philosophy—abstract thought, of which native Americans seemed to him altogether incapable—Robertson again takes the opportunity to formulate the already cited generalization about the interdependence of socioeconomic progress and intellectual refinement, and the conditioning of the latter by the former. To name the features most conspicuous in Robertson's survey—all or most of them "stored" in the city of Benares, "from time immemorial the Athens of India"—one finds the neat distinction between matter and spirit, a dignified account of the human soul, doctrines of the Stoic school before the birth of Zeno, "Arabic" numerals, extraordinary methods, and discoveries in astronomy. The retention of these cultural treasures of great value and antiquity also prescribes a respectable intellectual agenda and imposes a responsibility on those who have access to it.

> In an enlightened age and nation, and during a reign distinguished by a succession of the most splendid and successful undertakings to extend the knowledge of nature, it is an object worthy of public attention, to take measures for obtaining possession of all that time has spared of the philosophy and inventions of the most early and most highly civilized people of the East. It is with peculiar advantages Great Britain may engage in this laudable undertaking...[she] may have the glory of exploring fully that extensive field of unknown science, which the Academicians of France had the merit of first opening to the people of Europe.[73]

Robertson's admiration of Indian civilization is only qualified in the concluding section of the book, in which he provides an analysis of religious beliefs and practices. His account is not confined to Indian religion but is intended as "a sketch and outline of the history and progress of superstition and false religion in every region of the earth," and while it reproduces some of the thoughts advanced on the subject in Book IV of the *History of America*, it also reveals the influence of Hume's views expressed in his 1757 essay on "The Natural History of Religion." Particularly noteworthy is the consistent endeavor to trace parallel developments "among the Greeks in Europe, and the Indians in Asia, the two people in those great divisions of the earth, who were most early civilized."[74] Both were polytheistic, for the same reason: in the early stages of civilization, people invented deities to preside "over every function in civil or domestic life," to suit their own fears and desires, and mirroring their own manners. Monotheism arose with the advance of civilization, when, as a result of the diffusion of science and philosophy, "the system of superstition is subjected to scrutiny from which it was formerly exempt." On the authority of "the most intelligent Europeans who have visited India," Robertson asserts that the learned Brahmins themselves are theists: the "principal design of the Bhagvat-Geeta...seems to have been to establish the unity of the Godhead, and...amidst much obscure metaphysical discussion...we find descriptions of the Supreme Being entitled to equal praise with those of the Greek philosophers."[75] In view of the early rise of rationalist, philosophical monotheism among the religious leaders of the subcontinent, however, Robertson was puzzled by the long survival of popular religious practices that included superstitious worship, obscure and even cruel rites, and—what particularly embarrassed his Presbyterian sensibilities—the "connection between the gratification of sensual desire and the rites of public religion, displayed with...avowed indecency." The solution to the puzzle was found by him with reference to that typical Enlightenment scapegoat: "priestcraft," that is, the propensity of sophisticated clerical elites to manipulate false religion as a system of rewards and punishments whereby to retain social control over the "vulgar." They regard it dangerous to disseminate their wisdom to an uncomprehending, "gross multitude" that would revolt against any attempt to overthrow their established opinions. Quoting from Strabo, Robertson stresses that "[t]hese ideas of the philosophers of Europe were precisely the same which the Brahmins had adopted in India, and according to which they regulated their conduct with respect to the great body of the people...They knew and approved what was true, but among the rest of mankind they laboured to perpetuate what is false."[76]

In Robertson's representation, India is distinguished from the rest of the non-European world by its capacity of being comprehended in comparable terms of stadial progress—of material culture, of legal provisions and political arrangements, of cultural, intellectual, and spiritual pursuits—with the old continent. Even the fallacious, truncated, or deformed aspects of this development can be meaningfully portrayed by way of a historical parallel between Europe and India. In the final passages of his last work, these convictions are couched in a highly self-reflexive conclusion to his lifelong engagement with the problem of human cultural diversity:

> Unfortunately for the human species, in whatever quarter of the globe the people of Europe have acquired dominion, they have found the inhabitants not only in a state of society and improvement far inferior to their own, but different in their complexion, and in all their habits of life. Men in every stage of their career are so satisfied with the progress made by the community of which they are members, that it becomes to them a standard of perfection, and are apt to regard people, whose condition is not similar, with contempt, and even aversion. In Africa and America, the dissimilitude is so conspicuous, that, in the pride of their superiority, Europeans thought themselves entitled to reduce the natives of the former to slavery, and to exterminate those of the latter. Even in India, though far advanced beyond the two other quarters of the globe in improvement, the colour of inhabitants, their effeminate appearance, their unwarlike spirit, the wild extravagance of their religious tenets and ceremonies, and many other circumstances, confirmed Europeans in such an opinion of their own pre-eminence, that they have always viewed and treated them as an inferior race of men. Happy would it be if any of the four European nations, who have, successively, acquired extensive territories and power in India, could altogether vindicate itself from having acted in this manner.[77]

Translating the history of mankind: terminologies and interlocutors

Having provided a survey of the aspects of Robertson's two works on the encounter between Europeans and other civilizations that seem relevant to the German reception of his historical thought, there are three loosely interrelated facets of the *Rezeptionsgeschichte*, which I propose to discuss below. The study of each of them might enrich our understanding of the relationship between the patriotic and the cosmopolitan, and the local and the universal in the Enlightenment. First, besides the pitfalls of translation—sometimes inevitably resulting from the nature of the languages concerned—I shall focus on the statures, outlooks, and intentions of the individuals involved in the process of transmission, and hope to shed light on the ambiguous role such factors played in that process. Second, I shall offer insights into some of the sentiments that Robertson's Atlantic and Mediterranean predilection evoked in his German interpreters during this period in Germany of growing consciousness of national identity, and also of Germano–Celtic unity. Finally, the fact that the most faithful interpreter and the most discerning admirer of the moderatist conservative Robertson was the later radical of the Mainz Jacobin republic, Georg Forster, makes the "Robertson in Germany" question truly a test case in the debate over the Enlightenment *in* versus *above* national context. It is a testimony to the permeability of ideological boundaries and the pervasive nature of some fundamental concerns generally shared by protagonists of the Enlightenment until the French Revolution which made the differences between them look more pronounced.

As far as the chronology of the German reception of the *History of America* and the *Historical Disquisition* is concerned, after the stellar success of Robertson's previous works it is little wonder that the publication of both of them evoked eager expectations in Germany. Göttingen led the way again. The historian Christoph Meiners first borrowed the *History of America* from the university library on November 21, 1777.[78] However, by this time, the librarian himself, Meiners's colleague, the classical scholar Christian Gottlob Heyne, had already published a two-part review of the book in the *Göttingische Anzeigen* (18 October and 1 November), and as Meiners was reading Robertson's original, the German translation by Johann Friedrich Schiller was already in press in Leipzig. The first borrower of the *Historical Disquisition*, on May 8, 1792, was Arnold Ludwig Heeren,[79] another relatively young but distinguished member of the Göttingen historical school, who soon published one of the three German reviews of the *Historical Disquisition*. Simultaneously, an anonymous review was also published, while by then the polymath and circumnavigator Georg Forster had also brought out yet another review (in the *Göttingische Anzeigen*, on December 3, 1791) and was busy working on the German translation of the book.

Let us now consider how the translatorial practices adopted in the German rendering of Robertson's last two works affected his presentation of the

Transatlantic and Eastern worlds and Europe's encounters with them. As I have endeavored to show, the vocabulary of stadial history, ingeniously supported from some other sources, provided the conceptual cement of the argument presented in them just as well as it did in the case of the texts that I explored in chapters 3 and 4. The *History of America* and the *Historical Disquisition* largely escaped the fate of those texts (which they suffered because of unhappily chosen and incoherently used equivalents of certain key terms, as well as in particular Remer's ambition to be "original"), though especially the former demonstrates a few cases of—largely unwittingly—inadequate terminology and inconclusive usage, which are of some significance.

Among the key elements of the relevant terminology, it is again unrealistic to expect translators to have coped with the difficulty that the semantic content of *Handel/Handlung* and *Sitten* caused: these closest equivalents of "commerce" and "manners," respectively, available in the German language had a limited capacity to convey the same meanings and evoke the same associations. The case of "industry" became more complicated. Although the German word *Industrie* in this period, to some extent, still retained its early modern ambiguity and continued to denote the propensity to assiduous application as well as actual manufacturing activity, this was precisely the age when its meaning became increasingly confined to the latter, and the former sense was usually rendered by *Fleiß*, *gewerbsamer Fleiß*, or *erfinderischer Fleiß*.[80] Johann Friedrich Schiller in his translation of the *History of America* certainly chose this usage.[81] As with *Handel/Handlung*, the Robertsonian unity of inclinations crucial for the theme of sociability and economic pursuits was again broken, albeit now it was the other way around: the former aspect dominated at the expense of the latter. However, Georg Forster's consistent use of *Industrie* as the equivalent of "industry," in whichever meaning it occurs in the English text, and his decision to reserve *erfinderischer Fleiß* for "ingenuity" in his translation of the *Historical Disquisition*, must have seemed somewhat archaic.[82]

It is interesting and instructive to examine the cluster of terms Robertson used to supplement the stadialist vocabulary in the *History of America* and the *Historical Disquisition*. These included "enterprise/enterprising" and "adventure/adventurous/adventurer" as a means to suggest a transparency between the ethos of the merchant and the conquistador, both possessing a mindset conducive to discovery; and they also included "barbarity" to highlight the paradox that the manners of representatives of a presumably superior civilization had lapsed in America to the level of a more primitive stage. "Enterprise" and "enterprising" was rendered relatively consistently by both Schiller and Forster as *Unternehmung* and *unternehmend*, respectively. "Adventure" and its derivatives, however, posed a problem for them. In German, *Abenteuer*, *abenteuerlich*, and *Abenteurer* cannot be construed to evoke the mercantile connotations of "adventure," summarized above: they denote extravagant situations and exploits during travel or war, and agents acting in such situations.

Consequently, Robertson's German translators do not hesitate referring to the conquistadors as *Abentheurer*,[83] but refrain from using the word when in the original "adventurous" is the adjective of "enterprise" or its "spirit." In such cases they are content to use *kühn* (bold), or—in this case too—*unternehmend* (and are forced to complicate the clause in order to avoid repetition).[84] The fascinating ambiguity of language in Robertson's texts is thereby greatly diminished, if not lost altogether. As regards "barbarity," Schiller reserves *Barbarey* for describing the state of the two "imperfectly civilized" nations of the New World, Aztecs and Incas, which were just emerging from it but still retained some of its remainders. When it comes to the monstrous acts committed by the Spaniards, Schiller invariably chooses a term that is appropriate to condemn those acts, but has no reference within the stadial scheme: "cruelty" or "inhumanity" (*Grausamkeit, Unmenschlichkeit*).[85]

Even more serious was the embarrassment which the terms "polished/polite" and "police/policy" caused the German translators. As a translation of "polished," Schiller experimented just once with the rather infrequently used word *polizirt*,[86] imported from French in the sixteenth century, but he as well as Forster mainly used *geschliffen, gebildet*, or *gesittet*. These terms revolve around the notions of *Sitten*, a concept fundamentally belonging to ethics, and *Bildung*, one in which culture and enlightenment, the practical and the theoretical perfection of man are combined, and which is possessed by a nation in proportion with the harmony between its social condition and the calling of man.[87] Neither of these are suitable for establishing the etymological link supposed in contemporary English between the standards of spontaneous human interaction (politeness) and the organized forms to which such interaction gives rise (policy/the polity). As for *Polizey*, both translators must have realized that its traditional early modern meaning of administration, regimentation, and control by the magistrate in general (which was anyway not quite the same as "policy") was during their lifetime undergoing a change and became increasingly confined to the maintenance of the internal security of the state.[88] Though Schiller—to confuse matters even more, not only for "police," but also for "policy"—used it occasionally, both he and Forster preferred to render these English words with a wide variety of terms as they thought suited to the particular context: *Regierung* (government), *Einrichtung* (institution), *Staatskunst* (statecraft), *Staatsverfassung* (constitution), even *Staatswirtschaft* (national/state economy).

Such anomalies notwithstanding, both translators made a valiant effort to remain faithful to the original within the limits set by the linguistic possibilities, and especially in the case of Forster, who was the more consistent of the two men in his terminology, this effort was largely successful. Also, the fact that during our period the meaning of *Verkehr*—contrary to some of the examples mentioned—was extended to include intellectual and sentimental as well as commercial intercourse, saved quite a lot of Robertson's associations. Finally, both Schiller and Forster refrained from the kind of intentional revision, which, in many cases of the practice of eighteenth-century translation, resulted in effectively new books.

This was due to a peculiar attitude to the original text, stemming in different ways from the status and character of these figures. At this point, as a bridge between the issues confined to language and the more substantive problems of reception, it might be instructive to establish a typology of the translators involved in the process. Among the translators of Robertson's texts, the following models can be isolated.

At one extreme, Julius August Remer represented the type of the ambitious and learned, but pedantic and somewhat unimaginative provincial scholar who, having established a reputation through a number of solid if unoriginal works on history and government, conceived of his rendering of Robertson as a further occasion to assert and enhance his own independent scholarly authority (while obviously benefiting from the fame of the text he used as his raw material). Mittelstedt, Seiler, and Abele, who also approached Robertson's *History of Scotland* and *History of Charles V* with a greater or lesser degree of scholarly and literary interest, but without the ambition of Remer, were much more concerned with preserving the integrity of the original. The attitude of the translators of the *History of America* and the *Historical Disquisition* was also a more "modern" mixture of respect for and detachment from the text, but this can be traced back to different motivations in each case. Before establishing himself as a bookseller in Mainz in 1784, Johann Friedrich Schiller had lived for several years in London, where he did some professional translation, in the sense of merely or mainly doing it for money. Besides the *History of America*, he produced a translation of Adam Smith's *Wealth of Nations* (later overshadowed by that of Christian Garve) and the work of William Robertson's namesake, the deputy keeper of the records of Scotland, on ancient Greece.[89] To be sure, the professional attitude for him also implied, as explained in the Preface to his rendering of Smith's work, becoming thoroughly acquainted with the particular discipline and its terminology.[90] Nevertheless, he was aware that he could not be considered a true expert scholar. For this reason, and because in his case the intellectual adventure and pleasure to be drawn from the work of a translator came second to financial gain, he simply did not care to amend actual or supposed lapses or errors. Moreover, as mentioned above, he was also not strictly scrupulous in his care for authenticity when he encountered difficulties. Finally, the renowned natural and social philosopher and revolutionary Georg Forster (1754–1794) did conceive of Robertson's original as an intellectual challenge, but—true *Weltbürger* as he was with a strikingly cosmopolitan intellectual outlook—in a way quite differently from Remer. He did not consider the book flawless, but he thought that its merits made it deserving of careful attention and committed himself to preserving the argument in all of its shades as accurately as possible. He thought that Robertson's character as a writer, his "calm and philosophical procedure in research, his diligence which connects him with Germans models and his taste which connects him with French ones, his serious but perspicuous and pleasant delivery, his clear and fluent but not flowery manner of writing," made it all the easier to perform the task of the translator: "It is sufficient if he is able to express what is presented."[91] Criticism and independence could and should be asserted in other pursuits—which he did, as we shall see, to a considerable extent.

Before turning to the theme of the unlikely affinity between the moderate Robertson and the restless Forster, I wish to examine a few learned German reactions to Robertson's two works on European encounters with the colonial world. An outlook on the wider world and academic traditions peculiar to Germany as well as discernible marks of incipient nationalist sentiments colored purely scholarly commitments in these reactions, which produced an interesting overall picture.

Landlocked gazes at the new worlds and Oriental lures

Shortly after the publication of the original, and before the German translation came out (but in a vocabulary not very different from the one employed by Schiller), Heyne's extensive two-part review of the *History of America* appeared in the *Göttingische Anzeigen*. Three observations on this review seem to be worth making here. First, the reviewer's main regret was that Robertson postponed the discussion of British colonies in North America until after the current disturbances were over; at the same time, he forecast that the portion of the work that would prove most popular would be Book VIII, the analysis of Spanish policies in the New World.[92] It would be interesting to know whether Heyne would have shared the position of Robertson, who was profoundly interested in the unfolding crisis between Britain and the colonists, and expressed his pro-government opinions both in private correspondence and in the General Assemblies of 1776 and 1777.[93] Heyne's own views on the subject are not enunciated, nevertheless, the remark in general seems to confirm that the main interest of the German reading public in American history was contemporary and Europe-centered.[94]

At the same time, contrary to this assumption, the reviewer himself thought that the most important feature of the work was the description of "the rude and savage state of the Americans, thus their way of life, manners, constitution of society, etc." (*der rohe und wilde Zustand der Amerikaner, und also ihre Lebensart, Sitten, gesellschaftliche Verfassung s. w.*), as developed in Book IV. To Heyne, this most thorough application of the stadialist approach in the entire work seemed as a masterpiece of "philosophical" history.[95] Dugald Stewart was yet to coin "conjectural history," and "stadial history" is a still more recent neologism, so for the time being any systematic application of broad theoretical models (like the one based on the "four stages" of social progress) to historical subject matter was not infrequently and appropriately described as a "philosophical" pursuit. Heyne echoes the admiration of Burke's better known but identical sentiments: "The part which I read with the greatest pleasure, is the discussion of the manners and character of the inhabitants of that New World.... You have employed philosophy to judge on the manners, and from the manners you have drawn new resources for philosophy."[96] Viewed from this angle, the assessment of Robertson's contribution and its significance by the German reviewer does not seem fundamentally different from the main thrust of contemporary British appreciation.

The third point already takes us from the issue of mere transmission to that of direct engagement with the original text and argument in the form of expressing doubt, disagreement, or rebuff. If we disregard the remark that Robertson's method of annotation fails to serve the convenience of the reader, the only actual piece of criticism leveled against the *History of America* by its German reviewer is apparently a fairly pedantic one. It is, however, a recurrent motif in German responses to the work, and fits into the larger pattern of unhappiness with his Atlantic and Mediterranean focus. Nearly at the same time as this review was published, Remer complained that Robertson did not take German history and German historians sufficiently into consideration when writing the *History of Charles V*.[97] With the same sense of patriotic resentment, Heyne wrote in his review of the *History of America*: "It seems that Mr. R. wants to deny the mere existence of Martin Beheimb [sic] to the Germans, imputing him to be Martin de Boemia of Portugal, and here Mr. R. is incorrectly informed."[98]

We are familiar with the meticulous care Robertson took to establish his works on the reliable foundation of archival and other sources and the ways in which he capitalized on his fame and influence for this end by obtaining the necessary information. While at work on the *History of America*, he devised a questionnaire of over 50 items, most of them of an anthropological kind—some relating to the physiological properties of the natives, but many more to their customs, manners, and institutions—and even apart from the questionnaire relied on a host of correspondents far and wide to supply him with comparative material from the frontiers between European and non-European civilizations. He received a huge volume of replies from figures as diverse as Robert Waddilove, chaplain of the British Embassy in Madrid (who translated his queries into Spanish and circulated them in the colonies); Luis de Pinto, the Portuguese Minister in London (who had a respectable amount of experience in Brazil); the celebrated French travellers Bougainville and Godin le Jeune (enlisted by Robertson's French translator, the encyclopedist Jean-Baptiste Suard); Thomas Hutchinson, the Governor of Massachusetts Bay; and missionaries such as Gideon Hawley, not counting the lengthy letters sent by John Rogerson, the physician of Empress Catherine the Great from St. Petersburg.[99] But he also often relied on established prejudices, instead of the fruits of his own labor; and even apart from this, he made mistakes. In the first edition of the *History of America*, he was indeed in error concerning the identity of the Nürnberger Martin Behaim (1459–1507), renowned traveler and cartographer who was held in great honor and attained high dignity in

Portuguese service. He was knighted by King John II in 1485 and took part in several expeditions to West Africa, though he certainly had not "discovered" America before Columbus, as several authors in his native land claimed from the mid-seventeenth century onward.[100]

In the eighteenth century, as Europe's ascendancy in economic, cultural, and military terms over the rest of the globe started to become part and parcel of the identity and self-image of the old continent, lands without actual colonial stakes also felt the need to assert the claim to have contributed to the shaping of this identity. It is a mere coincidence, but hardly a fortuitous one, that the first scholarly biography of Behaim, vindicating his status as the discoverer of the New World, was published by the Nürnberger polyhistor Christoph Gottlieb von Murr (1733–1811) nearly at the same time as Robertson's *History of America*. But even before Murr's *Diplomatische Geschichte des portugiesischen berühmten Ritters Martin Behaim* (1778) came out of the press, Robertson received a letter—by way of an unknown intermediary—which raised the same issue. Its writer stressed that whereas "[h]is lately published History of America very deservedly confirm[ed]" that Robertson was an "incomparable historian," precisely for this reason it was important to point out and correct his errors. Robertson "represents Martin Behaim or de Bohemie as a Portuguese & denies him to be a German, & lastly excludes him entirely from the honour of discovering America." In the correspondent's view, the first two assertions were simply wrong, and the last one was still undecided and would remain so until the papers of the Behaim family became accessible to the public. Robertson's main source Antonio de Herrera y Tordesillas is then severely criticized and refuted by the writer of the letter on the basis of German chroniclers, such as Wagenseil and Doppelmeyer, neglected in the *History of America*.[101]

The letter came from Georg Forster's father, the famous German scholar Johann Reinhold Forster (1729–1798). "The first polyhistor of our century, worthy of comparison with a *Conring* or a *Hugo Grotius*," as one contemporary described him,[102] Forster was already renowned as a naturalist, antiquarian, linguist, and geographer by the time he resettled with his similarly multitalented eldest son from his native Danzig to Britain in 1766. There he embarked on a course of conscious self-promotion on the scientific scene. Despite his notoriously whimsical character and financial extravagance, through involvement in the famous dissenting academy of Warrington and membership in the Royal Society, he earned a position on board the ship *Resolution* as the assistant naturalist of James Cook on the latter's second voyage around the world between 1772 and 1775. The appointment resulted in mutual jealousies and resentments with some colleagues, notably Joseph Banks, Forster's predecessor on Cook's first voyage, but at the same time made his status as a leading natural historian of the South Seas unassailable (and he might have been *the* most outstanding one, had he been as successful in publishing the truly immense material he and his son collected as he had planned). Nevertheless, according to his later account, Forster saw his own role mainly as an anthropologist, his son and another assistant being responsible for other branches of the encyclopedic project he conceived: "It was my particular province...to investigate closely the habits, rites, ceremonies, religious beliefs, way of life, clothing, agriculture, commerce, arts, weapons, modes of warfare, political organization, and the language of the people we met."[103]

There is reason to believe that his interest in and approach to these subjects was influenced by varieties of eighteenth-century stadial history. His vast library contained a wealth of accounts of primitive and civilized man and his political and material culture. Between the summer of 1771 and his departure with Cook, Forster contributed columns of "foreign literary intelligence" to the *Critical Review*, reporting, among many other works, on *Über die Geschichte der Menschheit* (1768, "History of the Human Species," according to the review) by the Swiss philosopher Isaak Iselin, the closest contemporary equivalent in German of Scottish conjectural history. Forster praised it as "one of the most interesting performances of the present century" concerning "the progress of mankind from the state of brutes to that of savages; and lastly, to that of civilization."[104] He was thus certainly well equipped to appreciate Robertson's work, especially the aspect also highlighted in the review of the *History of America* by Heyne (who was his close friend, and later also his brother-in-law), namely, the account of the "rude and savage state of the Americans," which earned his lavish praise in his letter to Robertson. Most of Part 6 of Forster's own *Observations Made during a Voyage Round the World, on Physical Geography, Natural History, and Ethic Philosophy* (in 1778 in English, and in 1783 in German)[105]—over half of the whole book—was an analysis of the progress of the "races" of the Pacific from rudeness to civilization, their customs, manners, and institutions relating to peace and war, and household and religious worship, proceeded along similar lines to Book IV of the *History of America*.[106] Especially striking, and very much in the fashion of stadial history, are the passages in which the empirical material collected about the peoples of the South Seas is compared to accounts of the classics on the manners, religious and social customs, and institutions of ancient and primitive Europeans. Forster, too, ascribed whatever differences existing within a single human species to a combination of climatic factors and ones arising from the "mode of living." Like Buffon, he chose procreation, the capacity to produce fertile offspring with one another, as the criterion of taxonomical identity, also following the French *savant* in referring to temperature and topography as crucial for skin color, physical strength, etc.; and he thought, together with the Scottish students of the science of man, that the rudeness or the refinement of manners was dependent on the prevailing system of satisfying an ever expanding range of needs.[107]

However, the affinity of Forster to Robertson, and, as I shall argue, the use of the latter by the former, goes beyond this. A few years later, Forster wrote a *History of the Voyages and the Discoveries made in the North*, which was translated and published in English in 1786.[108] The book seems to have been intended as a stadial history of European navigation in the northern hemisphere examined in terms of growing commerce and ever more polished standards of civilization. Forster's introduction very lucidly lays out his guiding principles:

> Voyages made for the gratification of curiosity, and for the extension of commerce, seem to have greatly contributed to the promotion of knowledge, and to the introduction of milder manners and customs into society. For it is highly cultivated nations only, that explore distant countries and nations for the sake of commerce, in like manner as the seeking them for the gratification of curiosity, pre-supposes a still higher degree of cultivation and refinement.[109]

This is then contrasted to the motivation of conquest, more characteristic of "rude and uncivilized" nations in extending their horizons. There is an element of providentialism, too: "All these are the varied means which an infinitely wise Being has appointed for the purpose of humanizing mankind, of drawing them, if I may so express myself, out of their native state of barbarism, and of diffusing amongst them the liberal arts and the gentler courtesies of life."[110] Finally, in Forster's Introduction there is an interesting echo of Adam Smith's claim that man, unlike all other creatures, has constant occasion to seek the assistance of his fellows even in his natural state for his mere subsistence, here specifically applied to the circumstances of "long and distant voyages" where "the bands of society and friendship...are cemented by our wants...Our mutual necessities give rise to mutual favours and reciprocal benefits, till the gentle spirit of humanity and kindness, thus kindled from a spark of laudable self-interest, and gradually encreasing by repeated exertions, bursts forth at last into a glorious blaze of habitual benevolence and universal philanthropy."[111]

This already resembles closely enough the project carried out by Robertson in Book I of the *History of America*. Forster then sets out on his narrative, found by its reviewer a "commendable and accurate compilation," which, however, "fails both in profundity of reflection, and philosophical investigation."[112] By and large, this is a fair assessment of the bulk of the work, divided into three books discussing the voyages of ancient, medieval, and modern times, respectively. However, its intellectually most exciting part is a remarkable exception from the rule. At the same time as regards this portion of the text, it is also doubtful whether the reviewer was correct in claiming that Forster's book is based on "authors who are now scarcely read, or can seldom be found." Book II concludes with a section titled "General View of the State of Affairs at this Period" (namely, the Middle Ages), an extremely skillful digest of one of the best known texts by one of the best known contemporary historians. Without literally reproducing any part of it, Forster is actually writing his lesson from Robertson's "View of the Progress of Society in Europe" (and also from Smith, if we are to believe the charges of Robertson plagiarizing Smith). The argument of Robertson is all there, in a magisterial ten-page abstract. As the "barbarous nations from the North" undermined the Roman Empire, the provinces raised by them "to the dignity of kingdoms" were marked by "great debility," fertile lands being turned into wilderness; especially

> cities, once the seats of industry, arts, and commerce, were pillaged and destroyed, and the few remaining inhabitants...became the vassals of their insolent victors....These petty tyrants (of which there were many) sat in their castles and paid casual homage to a sovereign almost without power and authority...Popery, and its superstitious rites, effectually banished religion and its sacred influences...all freedom of thought was totally suppressed by the influence of legions of Monks, and the frowns of a haughty and jealous Hierarchy. There was no longer the least spark of knowledge or information to be found in all Christendom....Taste, the arts, decency, and decorum, were not to be expected in the desolation, the gloomy obscurity, and depth of barbarity in which the whole of Europe was involved....The Philosopher–the Philanthropist–is struck with horror, in contemplating the depth of misery and humiliation to which, from the want of information, and in consequence of moral as well as political corruption, mankind is capable of sinking.[113]

Then, however, unintended consequences, assisted by almighty Providence, came to the rescue of Europeans, who had approached the state of near-universal corruption.

> But, in contemplating this picture, he will naturally be led, on the other hand, to consider the means which an all-wise Providence has, with more than parental kindness, made use of to bring men back to that happiness in social life, for which they were originally destined. In fact, it is these inordinate desires, these insatiable passions, this wild enthusiasm, and this fanatical superstition, by which the Author of our existence conducts us again into the paths of virtue and knowledge, and to a state of exalted felicity.[114]

Forster, of course, hints at the Crusades, in terms that make his tacit reliance on Robertson unmistakable.

> These great peregrinations, however, of Christians, frantic with superstitious zeal, who frequently marked the whole course of their expedition by the most atrocious crimes, and the most infamous actions, and were for the greater part, the very scum of the earth, these peregrinations were the cause of a revolution throughout all Europe, which, in fact, was attended with too great consequences to pass unnoticed by an inquisitive mind.[115]

The nobles "wanted money to equip them as well as to maintain them on these long expeditions" and "to thousands of people they gave liberty in exchange for money; and bestowed on innumerable cities great privileges." The ferocity of Western knights was tamed by acquaintance with the "magnanimity, courage, and gallantry" of their Saracen counterparts. Eastern trade became more intensive, and along with the refined commodities long-forgotten achievements of science and philosophy arrived. Civil peace was established, and the confident burgher not only improved arts and trades, but also ventured "to trust his life and property to the mercy of the winds and the waves." These developments not only "contributed to liberate the human mind from those fetters of superstition, ignorance, and slothful indolence, by which it had hitherto been shackled," but also increased the power of the "Kings and Princes, and their endeavours to annihilate the influence of the higher order of vassals, and of the Nobility, in matters of government... [A]ll these circumstances have produced a great alteration in the forms of Government in Europe. The thoughts of all the European Princes were bent on aggrandizement, and that either by new conquests or by the augmentation of their power in their own states." With the Ottoman occupation of Constantinople, the stage was set for the great Transatlantic voyages of discovery in which Forster does not omit to underline the role of Martin Behaim.[116]

This perhaps overlong abstract of Forster's argument is intended to illustrate his indebtedness to Robertson. Unfortunately, it remains an unacknowledged debt. During his career, Forster and his son were occasionally accused by fellow naturalists, if not of plagiarism, at least of relying on the achievements of others in ways which were not in strict conformity with academic honesty. According to the most recent scholarship, these charges seem to be unfounded.[117] On the other hand, there seems to be little doubt that on this occasion Forster was at least liable to suspicion.

To return to Forster's explicit engagement with Robertson, the ultimate reason he gave as to why he deemed it especially important to redress Robertson's unfairness to the Germans[118] was that "the Discovery of America ought to be considered as an Epocha in the History of mankind, which remarkably influenced all human transactions & opinions, so that it is to me no matter of indifference, who should for the future claim the honour of having discovered the new world & in a manner should originally have occasioned these great revolutions in the History of Man." The discovery of America, therefore, assumed the status of a heroic exploit and thus a source of national glory. What is more, Forster's tone here is one of mild censure: after all, the glory of Germany, due to ancient ethnic and spiritual community, is the glory of the British, so by neglecting the German achievement Robertson was in a sense acting in an unpatriotic way. "I should perhaps seem partial to the Germans; but I protest that nothing can biass my mind in the investigation of truth," Forster wrote, and added that he had special reasons for being even-handed: "I am descended from an antient family, that lived in the North of Britain, &

which in the time of the civil commotions in the last century retired into Prussia. I therefore consider myself as appertaining equally to the British & the German nation & have always preserved a predilection for these two Nations, who have from time immemorial been famous for men of free & liberal sentiments."[119] George Forster, a royalist of Yorkshire dispossessed by Parliament, left England in 1642; his later descendant Johann Reinhold, indeed preserved a strong double identity, with English sometimes even gaining the upper hand.[120]

Nearly two years later another German correspondent reported to Robertson that "Mr Murr has published since my return some other pamphlets about Martin Behaim, in which he seems to retreat a little from his former opinions."[121] The remark shows that, once reminded, Robertson was not at all indifferent to German sources, and took the opportunity of double-checking the information passed on to him by Forster. The writer of this letter was Johann Philipp Ebeling, who was already introduced above as the translator of Robertson's 1755 sermon. He later collaborated with his brother Christoph Daniel Ebeling (1741–1817; a student of theology at Göttingen in 1762–1767), one of the important German authorities on America in his time, in editing and publishing the travels of the Hungarian explorer-adventurer Count Móric Benyovszky and other miscellaneous travel accounts. As such, he belongs to the second tier of figures who, besides the outstanding ones—the two Forsters, August Ludwig Schlözer, Matthias Christian Sprengel, and Anton Friedrich Büsching—contributed immensely to opening the horizon of the late eighteenth-century German audience to the wider world. Also, in highly romanticized terms he keenly emphasized the "special relation" that existed between Scotland and Germany: besides the intellectual achievement of contemporary Scotland, it is the supposedly close and deeply rooted cultural and ethnic ties that make it an object of special interest for German readers—as it were, reversing the case Forster made to Robertson. "The circumstance that their Fingals, as our Herrmanns set limits to the power-thirsty Romans, ought to make [the Scots] dear to all Germans…As regards their manners, the Scots have preserved a lot of old Germanic ways."[122]

Such sentiments were, as a matter of fact, expressed in the expectation that they would be mutual. Indeed, the late eighteenth century saw in Scotland the rise, as a powerful alternative to Gaelicism, of a robust tendency asserting the supposed Teutonic identity of the Picts whose libertarian and industrious characteristics were set against the vice, indolence, and slavishness of Celts.[123] But even if this Teutonist awakening had commenced by the time Forster or Ebeling were writing (*A Dissertation on the Origin and Progress of the Scythians or Goths* was published by John Pinkerton, a pioneer of the tradition, in 1787), it would hardly have influenced Robertson, the moderate conservative, whose patriotism was of an enlightened and cosmopolitan kind, and who thought of civilization in terms of conjectural history rather than racialist theory. Learned engagement with Robertson's *Historical Disquisition on India* in Germany was even more extensive than in the case of the *History of America*. Besides Georg Forster's review and translation, two other detailed reviews were published, both of them after Forster had first reported about the book. Still, before turning to Forster it will be useful to look at these reviews.

The unknown reviewer of the *Annalen der Geographie und Statistik* seasoned his fair account of the content and structure of the book with the general acknowledgement that the book was a "clear and enlightening" account of the ways in which Europeans had established communication with India, making as well highly critical remarks on some specific details. No historian "with a tincture of taste and philosophy," he suggested, would challenge the general thrust of the book, but the author had failed to bring new facts to light or even find new solutions to important questions. Robertson was found to have neglected a number of important sources (not all, but some of them German, again); especially noteworthy is the claim that as a doctor of divinity and a great historian he ought not to display an "almost Voltairean unfamiliarity with the Old Testament."[124] Strikingly enough—yet another proof that religious conformity thus expressed was more than reconcilable with Enlightenment—the same reviewer found Robertson's praise for the law codes of India, which the Scottish historian claimed to have been worthy of "an enlightened and commercial people" (*einem aufgeklärten und handelnden Volk*), rather groundless, citing the barbarous penalties for adultery.[125] The review concludes with a faithful summary and endorsement of Robertson's closing passages.[126]

The other reviewer was Arnold Herrmann Ludwig Heeren (1760–1842), who belonged to the youngest generation of the great Göttingen historians. Heeren was relatively unknown as yet, but the horizons and preoccupations of his future contributions were already taking shape. In his greatest work, Heeren enunciated his "ideas about the politics and commerce of the greatest peoples of the ancient world,"[127] a topic far from being of merely antiquarian interest to him. In this work he suggested that the problem of the peaceful coexistence of a large variety of republican and autocratic polities within the same state system could be examined, not at all without relevance to the European status quo of 1793 when Volume One of the first edition was published. But he also devoted a separate work to the rise of the modern European states system, with balance of power and liberty as ensuring a unity of principle within diversity as its chief characteristics.[128] If this singles out Heeren as an outstanding author within the tradition of *Universalhistorie* as championed by Gatterer and Schlözer, it must also be mentioned that he owed a great deal to the urge to study the *Geschichte der Menschheit*, the history of mankind, as conceived by another elder contemporary, Christoph Meiners: to investigate not "what man in the various ages did or suffered, but what he was" by adopting a quasi-anthropological approach. Heeren is also noted as the first lecturer on *Allgemeine Länder- und Völkerkunde* in German university history in 1802—as it were, formally lifting into the curriculum the discipline whose beginnings are ascribed to the publication of the Forsters' travel accounts a quarter century earlier.[129]

There was thus enough to separate Heeren from and enough to unite him with Robertson in order to make his engagement with the Scottish historian an interesting case, especially when it is added that Heeren, too, considered Europe's intercourse with the broader world as an integral part of her identity and the history of ancient geography a part of the history of the geographic discoveries made by European man. It was thus no wonder that the publication of James Rennell's 1788 map of Hindostan, providing a reliable representation of the territories that because of Alexander's campaign were of the utmost interest to historians of antiquity, thrilled Heeren with the same inspiration as it did Robertson, which was a parallel that the German historian hastened to point out in his review. In 1790 and 1791, no doubt unaware of Robertson's forthcoming work, Heeren delivered two lectures (and a third one in 1792) for the Göttingen Society of Sciences, under almost literally the same titles as that of Robertson's *Disquisition*: of the "knowledge and commerce" of the Greeks and Romans with India.[130] Armed with the confidence drawn from his own erudition on the subject, Heeren criticized Robertson in his review on account of several imprecise or not sufficiently substantiated claims, and on one occasion even concluded that he explored only "what is general and has an interest for everyone, but much, or rather all, is missed by the learned researcher."[131] We have already seen several German commentators pronouncing similar judgments on Robertson's manner of procedure as a professional historian. Heeren also complained that the aspects of the work that have a bearing on natural history are superficially elaborated. Nevertheless, whatever the shortcomings of the work in terms of antiquarian accuracy (the difference of opinion concerning the location of the ancient capital Palibothara is set out by Heeren in cumbersome detail over a full page), the reviewer was in fundamental agreement with the author concerning the significance of the enterprise: whereas all nations that had ever attained a degree of civilization maintained intercourse with India and used the articles she produced, neither India itself nor these relations had been sufficiently well known. He also stressed that the main results of Robertson's research coincided with his own in a far greater degree than is usually the case in similar circumstances, which to him seemed a proof of all the greater reliability of the achievement of both of them.[132] Finally, Heeren was keen to acknowledge Robertson's innovative reliance on the few products of Indian literature already available in Europe, and to commend the appendix about the constitution, laws, arts, and religion of the Indians as answering a newly awakened but well justified interest of Europeans.

Let us now turn to the younger Forster, Georg (or George, a spelling he used with almost equal frequency). He lived with his father in England during his formative years (from 1766 to 1772, and then for another three years after their return from the Cook expedition), and took an increasing interest in non-European, including Oriental cultures. This interest was further stimulated by another important stay in London, the main intersection of European intercourse with the colonial world, in early 1790, when the impeachment of Warren Hastings kept attention to Indian affairs in general wide-awake. To be sure, Forster's more general fascination with ethnology was awakened during the three years on board the *Resolution*, writing in 1789: "Natural history in its broadest sense and particularly anthropology has been my pre-occupation hitherto. What I have written since my voyage is for the most part closely related to it."[133] The exploration of non-European cultures was a permanent commitment for Forster throughout his erratic career after his return to Germany in 1778, first as a professor of natural history in Kassel and Wilno (Vilnius), then as university librarian and revolutionary in Mainz and finally in Paris. Between 1778 and 1788 he also spent shorter or longer periods of time (from September 1787, a full year) in Göttingen, where he took his *magister* degree at the end of 1778, and remained in close contact with the university and its professors to the end of his career in Mainz. He was a regular reviewer for the *Göttingische Anzeigen*, with four-fifths of his over 120 reviews written on travel literature and descriptions of remote lands.[134] Translations, many of them works in the same field, also figured very prominently among the products of Forster's "Mainz writer's workshop" (*Schriftstellerwerkstatt*), though it has also been suggested that the combination of illness, financial distress, and translator's work increasingly "wore him out."[135]

Besides the *Voyage Round the World* and a few anthropological texts that will be discussed below, mention must be made of two outstanding fruits of this interest that do not strictly conform to the genre of travelogue. One of them is a long essay on "Cook, the discoverer," published in 1787 as the preface to Forster's translation of the account of Cook's third Pacific voyage. Here he elaborated a point made in an earlier article on "New Holland and the British colony in Botany Bay" that Cook, whose expeditions lay the ground for the establishment of these promising colonial initiatives, was a second Columbus, inaugurating another glorious epoch in the spread of civilization.[136] Generously acknowledging the superior merits of the recent account of the life of Cook by his friend, the Göttingen polymath Georg Christoph Lichtenberg,[137] Forster intended to offer not so much a biography of the "hero" (an epithet used throughout *Cook, der Entdecker*), but a typological discussion of the explorer as a torchbearer of global Enlightenment. Already in his inaugural speech at the Société des Antiquités de Cassel after his appointment at the university there, he expressed his conviction that the whole of mankind shares a common destiny in civilization, which "is approached by the same degrees in every land, it is just the epochs that are different."[138] This is a concise formulation of a belief congenial to Robertson, too. Just as the latter was convinced that in spite of all the anomalies of European penetration into America, colonial tutelage assisted native societies in accelerating the civilizing process, Forster also thought that the establishment of colonies in the Pacific by the foremost nations of Europe would advance this cause.[139] The portrait and "character" of Cook as the quintessential eighteenth-century explorer and thus an agent of such advances is thoroughly embedded in a discourse of Forster's about humanity and progress, in a way that is akin with the representation of Columbus by Robertson as a discoverer suited to his own times. Whereas a determination to fight the prejudices of his times had been indispensable for Columbus, and the spirit of "enterprise and adventure" mingled with composure and calculation were qualities that distinguished both explorers, according to Forster, Cook went beyond all of his predecessors in introducing into the practice of discovery a methodical empiricism, which was an Enlightenment trademark and a disposition unknown and unthinkable in earlier times when

> former Pacific travelers dreaded the very sight of land; when they stumbled upon a shore, they hastened to move on, without even setting a foot on it, and without investigating the size, the form, and the relationships of their discoveries. If they did land somewhere, they rarely took the time to attain the goal of such landing, and to take advantage of the products that were found. Their behavior toward the natives usually made necessary a speedy retreat, before they could have studied the land and its manufactures, and familiarized themselves with the peculiarities of the human species there. Therefore their reports are often devoid of any interest.[140]

By contrast, Cook "collected for his contemporaries and posterity, with devotion and indefatigable diligence" information on all of these features of newly discovered lands, and many more. Besides and beyond contributing to the general stock of knowledge, this was also understood and commended by Forster as the proof of a practical capacity to absorb new knowledge (such as on how to fight scurvy, how to preserve meat by salting even in the tropics, and so forth) and of the perfectibility of a microcosmic individual in whom it was possible to detect the sum of the "general enlightenment" that may trigger "the joint advance of our whole kind toward a certain goal of perfection...the prospect of a higher social happiness than has been known to the world."[141] Forster's Cook was a consummation of the spirit of an age, just as Columbus was one in Robertson's *History of America*. "Only in the present century could Cook's burning ambition be equipped with all the means whereby he became a discoverer; and only he could do justice to this age" in which the limits of progressive enlightenment are still beyond our horizon—but "human infallibility vanishes at the sight of the dawn of sciences."[142] Cook, enlightened knowledge practices, and colonial (though not necessarily imperial) build-up are conjoined by Forster as essentially progressive, positive phenomena, similarly to the case of "enterprise, adventure and ambition" in the case of Robertson's Columbus.

Forster's other major accomplishment, which does not, strictly speaking, fit into his directly ethnological and travel related output, is his translation of

Śakuntalā, the ancient Indian drama of Kālidāsa. As we have seen, *Śakuntalā* was also invoked by Robertson as a proof of delicate "taste" among the ancient Indians. Forster used his own translation, published in 1791, to render the passages quoted from that work in the *Historical Disquisition* by Robertson in William Jones's 1785 English translation (which was the basis for that of Forster).[143] Forster's translation which, together with Jones's, has been described to have inaugurated the "*Śakuntalā* Era" in Europe's rediscovery of India,[144] was a major impact on Herder's image of India and the *"Morgenland"* more generally, which in turn was of central importance for the latter's highly influential thinking on history, culture, and humanity.[145] Forster reported about Robertson's *Historical Disquisition* on two occasions before his translation was published, and he also evaluated the work in a preface to his rendering of it, all in the tone of general admiration. Most of the very few negative remarks in his case, too, have to do with Robertson's neglect of German sources. Forster's short account of the *Historical Disquisition* in his history of English literature in 1791 contains perhaps the most concise contemporary assessment of Robertson's character as a historian and also recalls the themes of modern scholarship on him: the Scottish historian is praised for his successful combination of stadial and philosophical history (without, of course, using the former of these two labels).[146] While also acknowledging the same merits, the review published in the *Göttingische Anzeigen* has a tincture of criticism. True, Robertson's goal was not to write "a piece of detailed antiquarian criticism," but "a popular work" and "to set the greater moments of history in a clearer light through philosophical reasoning, and to make them more attractive through interweaving them with the most important objects of human application." Forster immediately added that "this explains and excuses what, especially in Germany, needs to be excused," and that "unfamiliarity with our language and literature has naturally separated the author from sources that would have earned him the honor of greater accuracy and perfection."[147] Forster took up the same thread in the preface to his translation of the *Historical Disquisition*. Unfortunately, he suggested, it was "the fate of our literature to be destitute of the sympathetic attention which our own public so heartily pays to the products of foreign learning." This was all the more regrettable to him because German scholarship had produced valuable works that could have facilitated the research and enriched the results of Robertson.[148] The slightly resentful tone of an ever more self-conscious national culture, though polite, is quite unmistakable again. To redress the shortcomings of Robertson's book, Forster even entertained the idea of writing a more comprehensive and up-to-date one, and swiftly sent the outline of a 24-chapter volume on the "history, constitution, religion, literature, and manners" of India to his publisher.[149]

For the time being, the work Forster mentioned in particular as one whose neglect was unfortunate on the part of Robertson was a history of the most important geographic discoveries prior the arrival of the Portuguese in Japan in 1542, written by Matthias Christian Sprengel and first published in 1783.

Another key figure in exploring the wider world for the German reading public, Sprengel (1746–1803) was a favorite student of Schlözer at Göttingen before becoming a professor of history and political science at Halle. His main interest shifted toward geography and colonial history, and he became an immensely prolific author in these fields. Having joined the "Forster clan" by marrying one of Georg's sisters, he wrote original works on the history of Europeans in North America, on British expansion in India and other subjects, and collaborated with the Forsters in editing multivolume series of travel literature and ethnography.[150]

In the preface to the second, enlarged edition of his work, mentioned by Forster, Sprengel regretted that Robertson's "masterpiece" had reached him too late to have been taken into account in the revision of his own work. At the same time, he admitted that he found the *Historical Disquisition* deficient in some particulars, and that he might in the future write another work "which could serve as an appendix to Robertson's disquisition" (a plan that was never realized). As regards his own approach, Sprengel was also trying to provide a stadialist account of the discoveries. Barbarians and savages, he wrote, having no idea of geography, believed that their own immediate environment constituted the whole world. "It is only after long and repeated travels, and often after several fruitless efforts, that a newly discovered land adds to the geographical knowledge of polished nations." Centuries might pass before "a nation acquires about its own habitat and that of their neighbors such knowledge as polished nations now possess about the interior of remote continents."[151] Here, however, Sprengel seems to part company with Scottish stadialist logic, in which the driving force of history is material progress. According to him, the successive additions to geography are

> owing exclusively to those enlightened nations which did not sacrifice the sciences and the progress of human knowledge to commercial policy. Hunger and feuds, the hunt and storms, the fear from foreign oppressors has certainly chased savages or barbarian nations far enough from their homelands. But the world and its most hidden corners have been explored only by such nations that sent out conquerors and missionaries, argonauts and merchants.[152]

This is an ambivalent passage. Commerce, which was the principal motivation of the adventure of geographical exploration in Robertson's account and a spur to curiosity and the accumulation of knowledge, is represented by Sprengel as compromising to true science. "Argonauts and merchants" then reappear among the agents of discovery, but only at the end of a list in which they are preceded by representatives of the spirit of conquest and proselytism. Less explicitly and evidently than with Remer and the "View of the Progress," but in the work of the author recommended as a basis for redressing Robertson's omissions in the *Historical Disquisition*, too, the "civilizing process" seems to be ascribed to growing political vigor, intellectual–spiritual refinement, and the stimuli they give to material progress. The remarkable similarity of vocabulary and discursive tools were deceptive enough to lead even a perceptive reader, such as Forster certainly was, to believe and propose that two authors like Robertson and Sprengel could be viewed as counterparts.

Robertson and Forster: strange bedfellows?

So far, this chapter has attempted to show how the peculiarities of the languages involved in the transmission of Robertson's ideas into German thought, as well as factors of national sentiment and attitudes in contemporary German scholarship, affected the way his historical works on Europe's encounter with the Transatlantic and Oriental worlds were understood in Germany. It remains to assess the significance of the rather different characters of Robertson and his keenest and most sympathetic reader in Germany, Georg Forster, who also surpassed most of the other German figures mentioned so far (with the possible exception of his own father and Heeren) in overall intellectual stature. This also implies an analysis of Forster's own texts relevant to European encounter with non-European peoples, in the context of large-scale transformations in German social philosophy in the period, and holds out the promise of some more general conclusions.

A full assessment of Forster's place and importance on the contemporary German intellectual scene is beyond the scope of the present investigation.[153] What is worth pointing out here is that hardly could two characters and their careers and outlook have been more divergent than those of Robertson and Forster. Embedded in the intellectual, religious, and political establishment, Robertson had a natural predilection toward authority, hierarchy, and subordination, never losing the faith that authority and hierarchy could in all circumstances be infused with sobriety and enlightenment, in which case subordination to it was the only sober and enlightened—therefore, acceptable—kind of conduct. This could also be translated into the terms of intercourse and relationship between different cultures. Convinced about the ultimate community of the human kind, he did not judge the natives of America in racial terms. Nevertheless, his stadial logic and its combination with providentialism also suggested to Robertson that natural right only entitled them to compassion and instruction by their superiors.[154] On the other hand, in the case of the inhabitants of India it was a sort of prescriptive right, accruing to them from the fact that they possessed a civilization that earned them Robertson's respect. He certainly acknowledged "the natural rights of man,"[155] but in most circumstances the civilizational context significantly colored his interpretation of these rights, and the sort of cultural tolerance he urged Western powers to display was in the first place due to *civilized* man. This is how two important routes to and perceptions of Enlightenment were amalgamated in Robertson's hand. There was, first, the recovery of European self-confidence after the "crisis of the European mind,"[156] that is, the consciousness that eighteenth-century Europe was, after all, "superior" to its predecessors in the old continent and its contemporary alternatives. This was not meant, as the Christian paradigm would have it, in moral terms, but in terms of material civilization and the superstructure of manners, sensibilities, and institutions, as both the outcome of the *querelle* of the ancients and the moderns, and stadial history and political economy suggested. Second, there was the notion of universal toleration, generally accepted as a "smallest common denominator" by all the makers of enlightened opinion. All of this, of course, also corresponded to the emphasis on "manner as well as matter" in the attitudes of Robertsonian Moderatism.[157]

The earlier glimpses into Forster's itinerant life may have already created the impression that he was a person ill at ease with establishment and authority; and while Robertson, initially puzzled by the ire of Burke's *Reflections on the Revolution in France*, soon changed his mind and turned against the revolution, Forster's initial enthusiasm for what appeared to be a peaceful triumph of reason over tyranny—which many German writers shared with him—was strong enough to remain a lasting commitment. As he explained to Heyne in a dramatic letter in June 1792, no party in revolutionary France was "faultless," but as the situation had come to a breaking point, one was under the obligation to declare either for or against the Jacobins. Not for a moment did he hesitate: "Without them [the Jacobins] the counter-revolution would have already broken out in Paris, inevitably restoring the situation of 1789."[158] He became vice-president of the Mainz Jacobin Club and member of the city's revolutionary government in 1792, and the "for or against" mentality just described still kept him an adherent of the revolution into its terrorist phase and until his death in Paris in the beginning of 1794. This was because, in spite of all of the anomalies of the Revolution, in Forster's view the Enlightenment reached its apotheosis in it. Forster used the notions of public spirit and public opinion as the expressions of a force overruling individual agency—in spite of his reservations concerning Rousseau on other topics, resembling the *volonté générale*—to make sense of the whole of the revolutionary phenomenon as one whose significance was not confined to the momentary and local context. An analysis of Forster's account of its course in his "Parisian sketches" (*Parisische Umrisse*, 1793) and other writings apparently confirms the vision of the all-pervasive significance of Paris for the entire process. However, while public opinion as it underlies the French Revolution occupies the status of a universal explanatory category of the progress of modernity, it is also a means for Forster to arrive at a realistic estimate of the chances for the transmission of the revolution, and thus to assign a significance to the revolution that is strongly local in its practical consequences. The proposition that the revolutionary idea could be exported from France to the whole of Germany is rejected by him in view of the rather different prevailing conditions in both countries, which are, again, explained by reference to the notion of public opinion; Forster argues that, in the lack of it, even anti-French propaganda will fail to evoke any substantial resonance in Germany.[159]

Georg Forster's reflections on public opinion at the end of the period concern one of the fundamental questions raised by the supposed universalism of the values hailed by the Enlightenment: whether those values and the related practices can indeed be made universal, or, whatever the effort, they must remain heavily context-dependent and of limited "translatability." Given his status as a world traveler, natural philosopher, and ethnologist, it is small wonder that Forster struggled hard with the problem of the local and the universal even apart from his revolutionary experience. Pronouncements in a short fragment on Indian poetry in 1791, around the time when he was also busy working on his translation and review of the *Historical Disquisition*, provide a good starting point for reemphasizing the kindred nature of the intellectual positions of these two diverging characters—and perhaps an indication that Forster took inspiration and reinforcement for his own positions from Robertson's old-age expression of self-critical cosmopolitanism.

> The local, the specific, the peculiar must vanish into the universal, if the prejudices of partiality are to be vanquished. Universality has taken the place of the particular European character, and we are on the way of becoming an idealized people, abstracted from the whole of the human kind, which on account of its knowledge and, may I add, its aesthetic as well as moral perfection, can be styled as the representative of the entire species.[160]

This passage is as elegant an adjustment of Eurocentrism to the requirements of cultural tolerance as the statement of Robertson at the end of the Appendix of the *Historical Disquisition*, quoted earlier. It captures in a strikingly concise formula the thinking of an open, critical mind, at that time one of the most committed German adherents of the ideas of *liberté-égalité-fraternité*, about the processes of the consolidation of Europe's global hegemony and the structural transformation of a Eurocentric approach. In Forster's view, European man was obliged to accept his own universality because his "character" was the most successful accomplishment of the potentials inherent in human nature. Universality in this sense, however, also implied for him responsibility, even humility: abandoning prejudice and "vanishing" into the universal was an imperative precisely on account of his excellence.[161]

This was the overall attitude that informed Forster's contributions to the debate on "humanity" and "race(s)" with Immanuel Kant and Christoph Meiners[162] in the mid-1780s and the early 1790s. At the same time, this was an attitude and a generalization, which Forster, unlike the vast majority of his philosophical contemporaries,[163] was in a privileged position to anchor in three years of experience from personal observation of minute detail, related in his *Voyage Round the World in His Britannic Majesty's Sloop, the Resolution* (1777) and also published in German the following year. Throughout this book, Forster makes consistent efforts to give observed and observer, or rather their civilizational contexts, their due. One might easily construct a eulogy of both rudeness and refinement from diverse passages in the two volumes, and the balance is made perfect by recurrent reflections on what Forster considered as universal properties of the human kind, regardless of the specific circumstances in which men found themselves. This was made possible by his methodological choices. He was an empiricist who rejected both mere fact-finding and system-building for its own sake, while he firmly believed that experience would lead to a sufficiently abstract grasp of human nature—provided that all cultural phenomena are studied "in their own right," that is, in the context of their specific developmental stage. While he did not share the assumption of the *a priori* or "given" unity of mankind, he believed that such unity was demonstrated with his methods. In the given case, his main interest was the status of a "natural" condition of life from the vantage point of civilization—without assigning a normative function to the prejudices of the "refined world."[164]

Forster frequently aserts the moral excellence of the natives, and such assertions are almost invariably formulated in comparative terms. One might observe "the most generous and exalted sentiments among them, that do honour to the human race in general...for one villain in these isles, we can shew at least fifty in England, or in any civilized country."[165] Because of this upright and unaffected character, whereas "we are too often taught to be ashamed of [our emotions, and] we unhappily conquer them by custom," "the simple child of nature, who inhabits these islands, gives free course to all his feelings, and glories in his affection towards his fellow-creature."[166] The failure of the savage to apply reason to the conquest of passion, acknowledged as a marker of humanity since at least Aristotle and, as we shall see, also adopted as such by Forster in his discussion of other subjects, does not at all appear to be a shortcoming in this representation. Forster also expressed his surprise at the natives' "hospitality in so poor a country, especially when we compare it to the custom of civilized nations, who have almost entirely laid aside all tender feelings for the wants of their fellow creatures."[167] In light of such contrasts, it is no wonder that Forster sometimes lamented the impact of European civilization on "the little uncivilized communities." "[T]he loss of a number of innocent lives" which they suffered "is trifling when compared to the irretrievable harm entailed upon them by corrupting their morals." He concluded that "hitherto our intercourse has been wholly disadvantageous to the nations of the South Seas,"[168] and claimed that

> it were indeed sincerely to be wished, that the intercourse which has lately subsisted between the Europeans and the natives of the South Sea islands may be broken off in time, before the corruption of manners which unhappily characterizes civilized regions, may reach that innocent race of men, who live here fortunate in their ignorance and simplicity.

He ended on a pessimistic note: "But it is a melancholy truth, that the dictates of philanthropy do not harmonize with the political systems of Europe."[169]

Nevertheless, one might just as easily reconstruct a straight "progress-and-refinement" narrative by highlighting passages of Forster's work that stress the superior merits of the civilized state. He wrote about Dusky Bay in New Zealand:

> The superiority of a state of civilization over that of barbarism could not be more clearly stated, than by the alterations and improvements we had made in this place...this spot, we had converted into an active scene, where a hundred and twenty men pursued various branches of employment with unremitting ardour...all around us we perceived the rise of arts, and the dawn of science, in a country which had hitherto lain plunged in one long night of ignorance and barbarism![170]

But Forster immediately added a note of skepticism: he was sure that the natives would soon abandon cultivating the land which had been cleared, so that in a few years "it must return to its original chaotic state." He was equally certain that the domesticated animals left behind by the voyagers would not long survive their departure, "as their [the natives'] inconsiderate and barbarous temper would not suffer to make any reflection on the advantages which future ages might reap from the propagation of such a valuable race of animals."[171] New Zealanders seemed to Forster to live "in a state of barbarism...which generally hearkens to no other voice than that of the strongest"; this "warlike disposition" and "irascible temper" caused that "[a]ll the disputes of savage people commonly terminate in the destruction of one of their parties."[172] Forster returns to this feature of rude nations on several occasions and explains it in terms of "self-preservation [which] is doubtless the first law of nature": "among savages every man rights himself, and anger and revenge are implanted in his breast, to repress the injuries and oppressions of others." It is from the account of "civilized communities [where] we have tacitly consented to laws and regulations" that it is clear that Forster attributes the violence of savages to the prevailing circumstances of scarcity and a rudimentary mode of subsistence: the "rule of law" emerges in "a nation, which...by applying to agriculture, has arrived to a degree of opulence, luxury, and civilization, and acquired new and refined ideas of philanthropy, [and therefore] is unaccustomed to the sudden overflowings of the bile, and slow to resent an affront."[173]

The idea that in modern times the "private vice" of selfishness may be reconciled with "public benefit," because the enlarged opportunities of consumption have accelerated the domestication of violent passions, was already central to Mandeville's analysis of commercial society in *The Fable of the Bees* in the 1720s, and it subsequently inspired much of eighteenth-century Scottish moral philosophy and political economy, too. Almost immediately after the passage just quoted, another cherished idea of contemporary social theory, thrown to prominence by the Glasgow civil law professor John Millar's *Observations Concerning the Distinction of Ranks in Society*[174] in the year preceding the embarkation of the *Resolution*, also appears in Forster's text: the idea that the state of society is accurately reflected in the treatment and status of women.

> It is the practice of all uncivilized nations to deny their women the common privileges of human beings, and to treat them as creatures inferior to themselves. The ideas of finding happiness and comfort in the bosom of a companion, only arise with a higher degree of culture. Where the mind is continually occupied with the means of self-preservation, there can be but little refined sentiment in the commerce of the sexes and nothing but brutal enjoyment is known.[175]

Both in regard of barbarity in war and rudeness of manners in peace that characterize the savage man in contrast to his civilized counterpart, textual parallels of these passages abound in Book IV of Robertson's *History of America*, published in the same year as Forster's account of the circumnavigation. "That women are indebted to the refinements of polished manners for a happy change in their state, is a point which can admit of no doubt. To despise and degrade the female sex, is the characteristic of the savage state in every part of the globe," Robertson emphasized in addressing the familiar subject of the commerce of the sexes; he went as far as claiming that "servitude is a name too mild to describe their [women's] wretched state."[176] As regards martial habits, for him the dichotomous contrast of refinement and savageness could not be more striking:

> War, which between extensive kingdoms is carried on with little animosity, is prosecuted by small tribes with all the rancour of a private quarrel.... When polished nations have obtained the glory of victory, or have acquired an addition of territory, they may terminate war with honour. But savages are not satisfied until they extirpate the community which is the object of their hatred.[177]

While it is impossible to demonstrate any direct reliance of either the elder or the younger Forster on Robertson's *History of America*, hot off the press while they were both busy working on the final draft of their accounts of the voyage around the world, the atmospheric similitude between their views on the above topics would be difficult to overlook. They were also in agreement in associating with the "savage" state of society an often astonishing degree of primitiveness of mind. "Surrounded continually with danger, or struggling with hardships, they had little leisure, and less capacity, for any speculative enquiry," Robertson wrote of the native Americans.[178] Languishing as they are "in an unthinking situation...it is hardly to be expected that these savages will attend to the domestication of animals," Forster reported about the natives of Queen Charlotte Sound (something that, as we have seen, was also a decisive element for Robertson in emerging from the savage state). But their condition was still quite blessed when compared to that of the inhabitants of the Tierra del Fuego, who only had on their faces "that vacant stare which is the characteristic of the most consummate stupidity."[179] Forster described the latter as "dull, hungry, deformed savages...having their mental faculties reduced to that miserable situation which places them next to brutes,"[180] and concluded that

> if ever the pre-eminence of a civilized life over that of the savage could have reasonably been disputed, we might, from the bare contemplation of these miserable people, draw the most striking conclusions in favour of our superior happiness. Till it can be proved, that a man in continual pain, from the rigour of the climate, is happy, I shall not give credit to the philosophers, who have either had no opportunity of contemplating human nature under all its modifications, or who have not felt what they have seen.[181]

One of the closing remarks of the whole book is indeed that "[f]rom the contemplation of these different characters [of the peoples observed], the advantages and blessings which civilization and revealed religion have diffused over our part of the globe, will become more and more obvious to the impartial inquirer."[182]

It is important to remind ourselves that these sentiments were to Forster not only fully compatible with the peculiar criteria of "participant observation" (placing the observer both into and outside the situation), but to a certain extent stemmed from it and were confirmed by it.[183] The efforts made in order to dispel the suspicion of the inhabitants of Tanna are described in some detail: it was "[o]ur cool deliberate conduct, our moderation, and the constant uniformity in all our proceedings" that "conquered their jealous fears."[184] It took some time for the natives to realize that "inoffensiveness" was not necessarily "despicable" because of being cowardly, but then "they who had been used to see in every stranger a base and treacherous enemy, now learnt from us to think more nobly of their fellow-creatures." This experience "taught them to relish the sweets of society...In a few days they began to feel a pleasure in our conversation, and a new disinterested sentiment, of more than earthly mould, even friendship, filled their heart." In other words, a type of conduct initially designed to remove the obstacles of studying the characteristics of native society triggers a process whereby the natives start to adopt attitudes characteristic of civilized society, thereby giving occasion for Forster to fall "in a reverie on [its] pre-eminence."[185]

To Forster, "civilized society" seems to have been a broad concept, which embraced not only the contemporary European West, but also, for instance, "the happier tribes of the Society Islands, beautifully formed, in a delightful climate, which supplies all their wants; sensible of the advantages of a well-ordered society, affectionate towards each other, and accustomed to gratify the senses, even to the excesses." But these criteria should be met by any society that was to earn Forster's praise: there is no virtuous middle way between lawless barbarism and civilization. There are certainly different levels of development, but the superior virtue of the stage between brutish rudeness and corrupt refinement is a "pleasing fancy" in which one cannot but be ultimately disappointed.[186]

It is not a distinct stage in the progress from rudeness to refinement that bridges the distance between the two extremes, but a number of sociological phenomena that seem to Forster, the ethnographic empiricist, to be universally shared by humans. For instance, the white color does not possess any intrinsic qualities that relate it to the notion of peace, yet it is universally adopted as symbolizing peaceful intentions.[187] Even though "the ideas of ornament of different nations agree" to a very little extent, the fact that they have generally adopted "such aids to personal perfection" gives occasion to contemplate the unity of mankind amidst the wide diversity,[188] and the same can be legitimately claimed about "the taste for music...so general around the world, when the ideas of harmony among different nations are so distant."[189] Finally, perhaps most importantly, a "simple and only just conception of the Deity, has been familiar to mankind in all ages and in all countries" (similarly to the abuse of such a conception, which has led to idolatry and superstition).[190]

A very complex picture is emerging from Forster's presentation and commentary of his experience of human communities, one in which there is an unmistakable developmental element: it is in terms of progress that the sometimes dramatically different character of the peoples he had the occasion to observe are pointed out, and yet many features seem to indicate the ultimate identity of the human kind. Forster wrote in his Introduction:

> Accustomed to look on all the various tribes of men, as entitled to an equal share of my good will, and conscious, at the same time, of the rights which I possess in common with every individual among them, I have endeavoured to make my remarks with a retrospect to our general improvement and welfare; and neither attachment nor aversion to particular nations have influenced my praise or censure. [191]

This is a rather peculiar vindication of the unitary character of mankind. What Forster claims is not, strictly speaking, the equality of all races of men, but their equal worth or dignity: neither of them is inherently either superior or inferior, but their essentially different character is taken for granted precisely as a condition of an unbiased look at the features that are specific and unique to them.

This subtle position obtained a new dimension in Forster's polemic with Kant and Meiners several years after the *Voyage Round the World* had been published, but obviously with the decisive experience of the Pacific explorations in mind. This engagement started with Forster's response in the journal *Teutscher Merkur* in 1786 to Kant's two essays on the "concept of a human race" and on "conjectures on the beginnings of human history";[192] it continued with a review of several 1789–1790 issues of the *Göttingisches historisches Magazin*, coedited (and largely written) by Meiners and devoted to the same question, in the *Allgemeine Litteraturzeitung* in 1791.[193] In these articles, Forster occupied a precarious middle ground between the two other authors. Kant, whose role in the rise of the modern concept of race has received considerable attention in recent literature,[194] argued that while four human races can indeed be distinguished according to the color of the skin, they can all be traced back to a common origin, and the differences between them are the products of several millennia of separation, during which certain properties (*Keime*: "seeds"), initially possessed in equal proportions by each of them, became dominant among some peoples, and others among other peoples. In Kant's essays, this classification was adopted as an apparently value-free heuristic device, answering his own reminder that "one finds what one needs in experience only when one first knows what to look for";[195] and "whiteness" itself appeared in them as both a race and beyond race, a summation and circumvention of race on the ground that it was "only the development of one of the original predispositions (*einer der ursprünglichen Anlagen*)," that one which disposed men to make the entire globe their home. This has led some scholars to recognize a detachment of Kant's theory of race from his judgments on particular races, which described the peoples of Africa and India as lacking a "drive for activity" and thus the mental capacities to be self-motivated and successful, and those of America as "incapable of any culture." Yet, these judgments clearly bespoke a conviction of a racial hierarchy with European whites at its top. This looked disturbing to Forster, to whom it served also as a reminder that monogenism as professed by Kant does not necessarily imply a benign universalism or egalitarianism.

At this point it will be helpful to recall Forster's relationship with Herder, already hinted at briefly. The two men were friends, and their intellectual stances were very similar on most of the fundamental questions of the emerging field of anthropology or *Wissenschaft vom Menschen*.[196] While it would be false to attribute to them an adherence to any notion of the incommensurability of cultures, they share a methodological relativism and the ideal of impartiality: the requirement of an awareness of one's prejudices and the resulting imperative of developing a "non-partisan" vision when treating human subjects. Armed with such convictions, Forster's attitude to non-European cultures and his stress on the supreme responsibility of Europeans in the development of relations with them (like in the case of Robertson) still had a tincture of paternalism, whereas for Herder the principal benefit of studying such relations was their potential to critically question and improve one's own system of values. Yet, they both understood intercultural communication as a fundamental means of (re)building modern European identities. Neither of them idealized "primitive societies," but both of them (Herder less hesitantly than Forster) thought that "civilization" did not necessarily bring about an improvement of moral character and, especially, happiness. For both of them, the science of man as cultivated in the Scottish Enlightenment was a major stimulus, though Herder at least valued the stadial model not as a tool to trace trajectories of progress, but to distinguish between variants of human excellence.[197]

In this relation it should be mentioned that the mid-1780s were not only the years of the Forster–Kant confrontation on the subject of race, but also the time when Kant pronounced his criticism of Herder's philosophy of history. As is well known, Herder's first statement on the subject, *This Too a Philosophy of History for the Formation of Humanity* (1774), was a response to the prize essay question of the Prussian Academy of Sciences, "Which were the happiest peoples in history?" While Herder's mocking reply cast doubt on the very belief in universal standards to measure happiness, asserting the need for explanations "from within" the entity being studied, Kant altogether questioned "happiness" as the *telos* of the human condition in his reviews of Herder's 1784 *Ideas on the Philosophy of History of Mankind* (published in the *Allgemeine Literaturzeitung* in 1785), his near-simultaneous *Idea for a Universal History with a Cosmopolitan Purpose*, and in the 1785 *Conjectures on the Beginnings of Human History*. He claimed instead that the purpose of human existence and history was progressive self-improvement through the application of reason: the achievement of "autonomy" or mastery of oneself through rational control over natural desires and interests. Kant, already deep into his "critical turn," also dismissed the methodological assumptions he associated with Herder and Forster, who both seemed to him to lack philosophical rigor. While the latter attitude required a preoccupation with lawful regularity as arising from the condition of having been caused or intended, the tradition of German "popular philosophy"—of which Kant was a great innovator in his precritical phase, and which persisted in figures like Herder and Forster after his "turn"—suffered from a descriptive contingency that merely identified objects and events as having taken place.[198] This is certainly not the place to analyze in any detail the debates of the 1770s and 1780s that changed the character and stakes of philosophical discourse in Germany. What must be stressed, and the reason why it was necessary to highlight these debates, is that by inscribing himself into them and associating himself with the side which long seemed to be losing but is being rehabilitated today,[199] Forster had far better opportunities to appreciate the achievements of the "science of man" and develop a more nuanced understanding of Robertson, too, than all of the other interlocutors discussed in this book.

As for Meiners, having published in 1772 a successful restatement of German "popular philosophy," which earned him both a professorial chair at Göttingen and the early antipathy of Kant,[200] and having contributed several works to the then much discussed issue of "rise and decline" (mainly in ancient history), he also turned to developing, in the 1780s, an anthropology, which he styled *Geschichte der Menschheit*, "history of mankind." Building on academic antecedents available in the work of eighteenth-century Göttingen philologists and classical scholars, this was to be a discipline which differed from universal history (*Universalgeschichte*) in going beyond the study of acts and events and their causal relationships in "great nations," and which also transcended philosophical conjecture in regard to analytical rigor by investigating scientific evidence for the uniqueness of all peoples around the globe.[201]

> The history of mankind teaches not what man in different ages did or suffered, but what it was or still is…[It] considers its main preoccupation exactly the savages and the barbarians of all continents…because a single small horde of savages and barbarians may contribute more to the knowledge of human nature than the most illustrious nations that have subjugated and devastated whole continents.[202]

The main objects of this "new science" were the bodies, the spirits, and the cultures of peoples around the world, an inquiry which had been made possible only recently by the proliferation of travel literature—earlier regarded mainly as material for pleasant diversion, but now also discovered by the reading public as a source of knowledge.[203] Meiners spoke reverently about the "more or less valuable contributions" to developing the field by some of his Scottish contemporaries (Millar, Ferguson, and Kames, besides James Dunbar), as well as Iselin and William Falconer. However, he found all of them liable to the charge of still relying too much on "conjecture" (*Muthmaßung*). Robertson's *History of America* was often cited, too. But Meiners's real heroes were Antoine-Yves Goguet, who in his *De l'Origine des Loix, des Arts, et des Sciences* (1758) offered an analysis of savagery and civilization which also influenced Gibbon,[204] and de Pauw, whose ideas pointing toward "enlightened racism" were briefly mentioned above. Inherent differences between human groups were indeed essential to Meiners's own engagement with the topic of human "bodies, spirits, and cultures." In contrast to Kant, he was a polygenist,[205] claiming that "Caucasians" (further subdivided into Celts and Slavs—the latter being "not only much weaker of body and mind, but also more poorly formed and destitute of virtues") and the "Altaic" Mongols were distinguished from one another by innate character marks, which became further accentuated by cultural development, and thus could be directly translated into permanent relations of superiority and inferiority among them.[206] Although he did not become "fully committed" to polygenism until late in life,[207] the binary classification adopted in his 1785 *Grundriß der Geschichte der Menschheit* already annoyed Forster to such an extent that in a letter to

Herder he described the work as "Göttinger erudition applied to an untenable hypothesis."[208]

Forster thought that neither Kant's nor Meiners's position was capable of proof beyond doubt. He did not exclude the possibility of polygenesis, which, however, threw him into the—to him—embarrassing company of Meiners. Although racial superiority was an idea difficult to reconcile with both Christianity and natural law, in the light of contemporary empirical sciences it was far less obviously fallacious. The idea of polygenesis, with which it became combined in Meiners's works, was not antithetical to Linnaeus's very influential system, which realigned the accents of the approach of the Great Chain of Being (once man and ape were classified in the same order on the basis of anatomical similarities, there could be no reason to dismiss the idea that different races of man could be classified there, too). Henry Home, Lord Kames relied on the idea very ingeniously in his Preliminary Discourse to the *Sketches on the History of Man*,[209] published in 1774, when Forster was literally making "sketches" of all sorts of natural phenomena in the South Seas. Forster was from the outset fully aware of the risks involved in embracing the theory of polygenesis, and did his best to erect proper bulwarks in order to avoid the charge of antihumanism. Experience was the only basis he was willing to adopt for his reasoning, although it must be added that he employed a notion of experience that was very different from Kant's. Being an ethnologist who observed and described phenomena, he understood empirical science as a process of abstraction from data and subsequent synthesis, and the ordering of observation results within a nominalistic system. For Kant, on the other hand, empiricism meant the discovery of the causal regularities of scientific cognition, not to be derived from experience but, conversely, constituting the preconditions of (proper) experience.[210] Forster therefore was compelled (or so he felt) to acknowledge that mankind is conspicuously divided into the black and the white races, so that they may have emerged in an autochthonous manner, whereas by making, in the footsteps of Buffon, the ability to produce fertile offspring, rather than origin, the criterion of community between these races, he still maintained a bridge between them.[211] More importantly, he insisted that even though genetically separate, by virtue of the "spark of reason" common (in varying degrees) to all men, they still are of equal "worth." It was beyond any controversy that in Europe "the sciences and the arts have been raised to a level of perfection unattained anywhere else...and [we Europeans] rule over other continents and embrace the whole of the globe with our superior knowledge."[212] But this was hardly owing to superiority in genetic terms, and Meiners should have attempted to be equitable to his own race without applying arbitrary premises to others. Forster claims that superiority is not innate but is brought by improvement: "The ability to make more refined distinctions between the perceptions of the senses is no peculiar property which is lacking in rude men, as Mr. M. generally claims, but an aesthetic sentiment transformed into a mechanism, which is very closely related to enlightenment and the accuracy of notions."[213]

Forster in his critique of Kant, equipped as he was with an incomparable amount of knowledge from firsthand observation about the subject, felt entitled to make the cautious distinction that while he was unable to "unambiguously answer in the affirmative the question whether there are several original human races [*ursprüngliche Menschenstämme*]," it was "at least not improbable or inconceivable" that this was the case. Also thanks to his vast experience, he found himself in an intellectually and morally far more challenging predicament than Kant in his seclusion at Königsberg or Meiners at Göttingen. His background laid a greater amount of responsibility on his shoulders, and he did not fare poorly. He felt the moral imperative involved in the whole issue and decided to shift the very ground of the discussion:

> But in separating the Negro from the white man as an originally distinct race, are we not severing the last bond that tied this much abused people to ourselves, and which still provided for it some protection and mercy in the face of European cruelty? Let me rather ask the question whether the thought that Blacks are our brothers has anywhere even once led a slave driver to put down the whip he had raised?"

Forster implied that whether or not mankind is a single species may not even be the central issue. For him, polygenesis and the theory of innate racial differences was not an academic but a moral, even political matter: Meiners's remarks about the "hideousness" (*Abscheulichkeit*) of blacks are inseparable from his excuses for the cruelties of slaveholders.[214] Echoing the position famously enunciated by Diderot in Raynal's *Histoire des deux Indes*, Forster also points to the potentially destabilizing consequences of racial discrimination and colonial oppression on European morals and political liberty: "Where is the bond that could prevent the degenerate European from dominating over his white fellow men in as despotic a fashion as over the Negroes?"[215] These are remarkable questions, especially if one recalls some of the quotations above which show Forster, the "civilized" European occupying the vantage point of the unbiased observer, discovering very little community between himself and the natives of the Tierra del Fuego.

Behind these questions there lay a profound dilemma and an implicit embracing of an egalitarian and universalist position dictated by moral considerations; a position which, however, was permanently challenged by the indelible memory of the immensely "various modifications of mankind," which he had personally experienced. For the sake of adopting this position, Forster was willing to surmount the experiential evidences (a decision whose significance in his case can hardly be overemphasized). This is the background to the fact that he could claim within the same breath that "both in regard of internal and external constitution, the Negro has much more in common with the race of apes than the white man does," and that "[t]he most ape-like Negro is so akin to the white man that when the two races are mixed, the distinguishing features of both are combined and melt into one another in the hybrid...An ape-like man is not an ape."[216]

Because of Forster choosing procreation as the criterion whereby to assess relatedness, which suits the older, descriptive–comparative study of nature and ethnography, it has been suggested that he failed to take the step, as Kant did according to the testimony of his concentration on common origin, toward a more dynamic, true natural *history*.[217] I should like to conclude this chapter with two remarks on this suggestion.

First, Forster's amalgamation of the viewpoints of a civilizing process and those of race[218] should be sufficient to demonstrate his commitment to study "the natural history of man" in the strictest contemporary sense. In this regard it is again important to stress the "family resemblance" between the approach adopted by him and that of the Scottish science of man. This is a subject that has received some attention by scholars in generic terms, both with an affirmative and a more skeptical attitude. Ludwig Uhlig has emphasized the need to understand Forster's travelogue and his whole anthropology in the context of Scottish "theoretical or conjectural history," focusing mainly on Ferguson's observations on "art itself [being] natural to man" and on the Smithian theory of stages (together with the implicit as well as explicit polemic of both with Rousseau), while Annette Meyer has reminded us that "conjectural history" is a posterior construct of Dugald Stewart which obscures more than it explains. She has also attempted to explore Forster's indebtedness to Scottish theoretical models of scientific reflection *in spite of* his reservations vis-à-vis philosophical conjecture (made explicit at several points in the *Voyage* as well as in his response to Kant's "*Muthmaßlicher Anfang*," and recorded by Uhlig, too).[219] What is noteworthy in these valuable studies, as well as the entire corpus of Forster scholarship, is their near-complete neglect of Forster's relationship with the single figure among the Edinburgh literati whose work he engaged directly and in depth by translation and commentary: William Robertson.[220] The two men shared an intellectual–moral stance whose peculiar composition was rather unique within their respective environments: a deep perplexity caused by the recognition of the challenge that evident empirical facts of human diversity constituted for a universalism formulated in terms of a theory of sociocultural progress; a perplexity, however, which was resolved in the personal conviction of self-reflexive cosmopolitanism and cultural tolerance still built, in the final analysis, on the foundations of their scholarly investigations. The distinctive flavor of Forster's position in the German context, just as that of Robertson in his own, arises exactly from the features of their thought, which demonstrate an elective affinity.

A second point arises from this observation. From the purely philosophical point of view, Forster may have been incoherent, and in spite of his adventurous general and intellectual disposition, a captive of the limits of contemporary paradigms. Yet he stretched the limits of the scientific paradigm to their extremity, and had the courage to transcend them morally. From one angle, in view of this latter step, Forster's "politics of ethnology" is rightly described as "radically partisan" in contrast to Meiners, whose views may have been "ugly," but were founded in the socially conservative but realistic assumption that culture is "greater" than morality.[221] Yet the community between the future *citoyen* Forster and the establishment conservative Robertson seems to introduce a puzzle into this cleavage. As hinted above, recently a distinct identity has been claimed by Michael Carhart for a "science of culture" emerging in Germany in the 1770s and 1780s, referring to a shift of the basis for understanding humanity and society from nature to culture, a rejection of philosophical conjecture as not sufficiently rigorous, and a preference for anthropological empiricism based on ancient philology and on the scientific use of travel literature. Meiners and other members of the "Göttingen School" are identified as the chief agents in this development. Forster was an empiricist whose contributions to philology as well as to the scientific use of travel literature are indisputable, but who—in spite of rhetorical dismissiveness about "conjecture"—admired the theoretical history of the Scottish conservative Robertson and broadly shared his perspective on humanity, while clashing with the Göttingen conservative empiricist Meiners on the same issue. Contemplating these complexities introduces further distinctions into our understanding of the Enlightenment "science of man" and *Wissenschaft vom Menschen*.

Conclusion

This book has investigated Robertson's five historical texts of varying length and style that saw a total of 11 German translations and editions between 1760 and 1795. Both these and the English originals (with the exception of his virgin publication, the *Situation of the World*) were promptly reviewed in sufficient detail in the *Göttingische Anzeigen*, perhaps the most respectable venue of scholarly criticism in the German periodical press, and in other journals as well. A respectable amount of indigenous German scholarship on themes of central concern to Robertson was recognized—rightly or wrongly—to have employed a *modus operandi* similar to his. An impressively broad array of men of letters participated in producing the several thousands of pages of written text in the German language that can be associated with the name and work of Robertson. The interlocutors included: humble artisans of the book business; professionals from the theological, legal, and medical fields who took to Robertson's histories out of interests outside their own profession; real bores and pedants, as well as leading lights and astonishing eccentrics, holding professorial chairs in history, philology, philosophy, jurisprudence, political science, and natural history at lesser and greater German universities; and finally sedentary scholars and intellectual vagabonds.

Thus, without doubt, "reception" took place intensively and extensively. The extent to which there was also "impact" could be a different matter. The "Robertsonian" histories planned by Abbt on Braunschweig, by Remer on post-Reformation times, or by Schiller on universal history, were, after all, never written. As historians threatened with perishing rather than publishing know all too well, the insufficiency of inspiration from the Scottish master may have been but one of the reasons, not even, perhaps, the most powerful, that these histories failed to come about. But there could be further reasons for the apparent discrepancy between reception and impact to be discovered in the nature of Enlightenment print communication and the fact that questions shared across linguistic and cultural frontiers in enlightened Europe called for answers suited to the local environments in which they were diversely posed.

Thanks to the logic inherent in the activity of collecting books and reporting on them at the Georgia Augusta in Göttingen, there was an inevitability in the level and breadth of attention Robertson's works received in Germany, irrespective of any scholarly or literary merit in Robertson's historical works. This activity has been aptly characterized as quasi-encyclopedic by virtue of its aiming at comprehensiveness and order. The teaching and, significantly, research of all academic subjects represented in the curriculum of the university were supported with the full range of up-to-date international literature, and the items appearing on the library's shelves were promptly reviewed by the professorial staff in the *Göttingische Anzeigen*. While reviewing works was almost a part of their job description, it was also a matter of academic ethos for them. The Swiss polymath Albrecht von Haller, who reviewed both the *History of Scotland* in 1760 and the *History of Charles V* in 1770, remained a devoted and highly prolific reviewer for the journal long after his departure from Göttingen. Besides Haller, Robertson was fortunate to have further emblematic scholars of the university as his German commentators in the persons of Heyne and Heeren (and we may well add Forster, too, as an "honorary Göttinger").

What is more, the reviews that Robertson received were distinctive on account of the amount of substance and detail. This is where the reception of Robertson through the pages of the *Göttingische Anzeigen* moves beyond the "inevitable," mentioned above. The encyclopedism of the endeavor embodied in the journal made it an uphill battle for the relatively small academic staff of the Georgia Augusta: the sheer bulk of the material often took the better of them, and the ideal of full coverage could only be pursued more or less consistently if the ideal of critical depth was occasionally compromised. Hollow praise for and even evident signs of a mere browsing of the reviewed works are recurrent and symptomatic features of the "critical" pieces published in the journal. The fact that, as we have seen, the reviews of Robertson's works tended to be serious pieces of sometimes minute criticism, points beyond the above-mentioned mechanism inscribed in the nature of the production and communication of enlightened academic knowledge. It points toward the specific merits that the learned German public found in Robertson, that is, toward the question of what he "was" and what he had to "say" from their perspective.

To German as well as to other European readers of the time, Robertson was a respectable, moderate Protestant ("Arminian"), "philosophical" historian of some of the most important challenges of emerging modernity to his nation and their own, in a European and global context. Such challenges seemed to include: (1) the problem of the integrity and safety of political societies that were increasingly pluralistic in their values, mainly, but not exclusively, from the religious point of view; (2) the international aspect of the same development, namely, the processes of European state formation and the coagulation of those states into a system of dynamic emulation, ever balancing on the thin ridge between cooperation and conflict; and (3) finally, Europe's geographic expansion, the rise of the commercial–colonial system, the confrontation with other, "exotic" peoples and civilizations, and the mutual influences through which the idea of "mankind" emerged and became immediately historicized. From the Göttingen and indeed the larger German point of view, it may not be insignificant that Hanover-Braunschweig was, like Scotland in the period inaugurated by the one explored in Robertson's history, both a partner of England in a personal union, and an electorate of the German *Reich*. Its character as a "state" had long been known to be largely fictitious, but its "constitution" was a subject of avid investigation and much veneration as a system of religious and political "liberty" during a time, with the benefit of hindsight, we now recognize as its swan song. Germany, of course, could also easily be conceptualized as Europe writ small, with its kaleidoscope of smaller and larger sovereignties, with differing denominational and political allegiances and internal arrangements, in a precarious balance always threatened with and often brought down in armed conflict. Germany's landlocked geographic character and lack of actual colonial stakes, in regard to the subject of contact with the non-European world, did not deprive it of an ambition to contribute to "appropriating" that world epistemologically by participation in "scientific travel"; on the contrary (paradoxically and yet understandably) it was encouraged in the processing of the harvest of specimens and other collected empirical data, and in confronting the heritage of literate civilizations philologically and philosophically. Reading and contemplating Robertson assisted them in doing so.

For these reasons and more, Robertson's questions sounded congenial and his endeavors seemed sympathetic to his German audience, which, however, was occasionally uneasy with some of the authorial and intellectual strategies he employed in pursuing them. The depiction of character and the weaving of a plot were paramount to the literary merit justly ascribed to Robertson's histories, and in order to arrive at historical generalization from the representation of such particularities, as a pattern of contextualization he relied on a system of historical causality assembled out of a Christian providentialism and a sociocultural analysis of "stages" in the progress of mankind. At this point, it is important to remember, first, that the moral psychology crucial for Robertsonian characterization, and thus his narrative techniques, and the historical materialism which supported his analytical rigor, were both heavily indebted to one and the same vast intellectual project: the contemporary Scottish "science of man." Therefore, the often mentioned distinction, even discrepancy, between the "narrative" and the "stadial" or "conjectural" sections of Robertson's texts is hardly as dramatic as it may seem; it is of some relevance from the formal–technical point of view, but as a tool for better understanding those texts it obscures more than it explains. Second, while none of the composite parts of this assemblage were theoretically novel, their combination proved highly effective, and could not but exert a magnetic influence on contemporary German—and for that matter any—readers and interlocutors. However, it was foreign to the indigenous practices of historical research, imagination, and composition in Germany. There the most fundamental and lasting legacy of humanist historical inquiry was not its preoccupation with the intricacies of political action and the way they affected human frailty or dignity, which is a recurrent though a highly contextualized theme in Robertson's texts, but its tendency to seek a prestigious (national) pedigree in the past as the vindication of a distinctive status in the present, and a concern with philological accuracy in exploring (predominantly legal, but also other) documents that shed light on this history of distinctiveness. The refinement of philological criticism in mid-eighteenth-century German historical scholarship was as "modern" and as crucial to the rise of a "scientific" historiography as Robertson's endeavor to refresh the discipline with the approaches of up-to-date social science. In confronting the sensitive issues of the national past, highlighted by the recent developments in Anglo–Scottish relations as well as transformations on the broader European scene, Robertson turned these approaches to cautiously questioning a tradition of constitutional nostalgia. However, many of his "moderate" counterpart historians in Germany like Pütter or Schmidt, prompted by the similarly far-reaching transformations in intra-German relations taking place before their eyes, relied on the methodological advances in their own historical culture in order to formulate a discourse about the constitution of the *Reich* and its latest entrenchment in the settlement of Westphalia, which, while certainly not nostalgic, was strongly vindictive. The differences in the civic functions of history, for Robertson on the one hand and for his German interlocutors on the other, thus also mutually translate themselves into differences of the theoretical–methodological apparatus and expressive features of the texts emanating from their hands.

Close to the end of the seventeenth century, Samuel Pufendorf had both written about the past and the present of the imperial constitution in a highly critical spirit, and penned works that proved to be foundational for the Scottish students of the science of man as well as for the eighteenth-century German debate between "civil" and "metaphysical" philosophy. But even when both Pufendorfian threads were first taken up by professional historians like Schlözer and to some extent Heeren a good century later, the narrative flair that distinguished Robertson's texts was still highly unusual among the German practitioners of the craft. Here it is helpful to recall the chronological gap, proposed in chapter 1, between the Scottish and the German intellectual scene both in regard to the rise of a more or less integrated science of man anchored in a philosophical anthropology as well as political economy, and in regard to the rise of an appetite for literary merit in historical works. As I attempted to show in chapter 5, the involvement of Georg Forster in the reception of Robertson in Germany made a significant difference in the former regard; as far as Robertson's credentials as a fine writer are concerned, whenever they were praised, this was accompanied by mild censures of his "accuracy."

If history is a branch of learning which owes much of its modern identity to the Enlightenment, this identity was obviously highly complex. In turn, this very complexity should serve as a reminder of the multiple character of the Enlightenment as a whole, and a study of the reception of Robertson's historical works in late-eighteenth-century Germany has furnished a great deal of evidence on the ways in which this became manifest in the reality of contemporary texts. The sheer volume of response to these works in German illustrates the strong sense of the respondents themselves belonging to a shared intellectual and discursive universe that we are justified in styling enlightened, according to the criteria put forward in the Introduction, even though several readers may well call into question the classification of at least some of the figures mentioned on the pages of this book. At the same time, equally obviously, there were fissures in this universe, in whose perpetuation the barrier constituted by the difference of the natural languages involved in the process of transmission was one, but only one, important factor. Besides the historians, most of the jurists, philosophers, philologists, political scientists, and others whose names became connected with the history of the German reception of Robertson during the last third of the eighteenth century, could plausibly be categorized as "moderate Arminians" (after Pocock, with a degree of inaccuracy), who were, however, kept at a respectful distance from the Scottish master by the linguistic, cultural, professional, and other features of the environment in which they were raised and were active. But just as their "conservatism" did not by itself ensure a smooth translation in the comprehensive sense of Robertson's meaning, neither was a disparity in ideological and political outlook necessarily an obstacle to the development of a strong empathy between enlightened intellects, who were indebted both to a generally shared system of values concerning humanity and to criteria concerning useful knowledge. The unlikely affinity between Robertson, the establishment moderate, and Forster, the restless radical, places the issue of unity versus diversity in the Enlightenment into yet another angle, and suggests that the differences which separated such figures did not inexorably divide enlightened opinion until the French Revolution proceeded beyond the stage of benign constitutional improvement. Before then, Edmund Burke—one of the borderline characters whose case speaks so strongly in favor of the open-ended concept of the Enlightenment adopted in this book—had seemed eccentric in his desperate admonitions that the "rights of man" tended to undermine the rights of civilized man, even to Robertson.

Notes

Introduction

1. *Herrn Dr. Wilhelm Robertsons Geschichte der Regierung Kaiser Carls des Fünften. Nebst einem Abrisse des Wachstums und Fortgangs des gesellschaftlichen Leben in Europa bis auf den Anfang des sechszehnten Jahrhundert*, 3 vols., trans. Theodor Christoph Mittelstedt, notes by Julius August Remer, 2nd ed. (Braunschweig: Waisenhaus, 1778–1779), III: "Vorrede," by Julius August Remer. The first edition was published without Remer's collaboration in 1770–1771.
2. Ibid., I: "Vorrede."
3. Cf. Paul Ricoeur, *Sur la traduction* (Paris: Bayard, 2004), 23–4, 43–4; also Franz Rosenzweig, "The Impossibility and Necessity of Translation," in *Translating Literature: The German Tradition*, ed. André Lefevere (Assen: Van Gorcum, 1977), 110–12.
4. A full-scale modern biography is still missing. As other Scottish literati, Robertson received his due from Dugald Stewart, *Biographical Memoirs of Adam Smith, L.L.D., of William Robertson, D.D, and of Thomas Reid, D.D.* (Edinburgh: George Ramsay, 1811). Robertson as the life and soul of the Moderate Party has been discussed by Jeremy J. Carter, "The Making of Principal Robertson in 1762: Politics and the University of Edinburgh in the Second Half of the Eighteenth Century," *Scottish Historical Review* 49 (1) (1970): 60–84; and Richard B. Sher, *Church and University in the Scottish Enlightenment: The Moderate Literati of Edinburgh* (Princeton: Princeton University Press, 1985). For an excellent, concise overview of Robertson's career, see Stuart J. Brown, "William Robertson and the Scottish Enlightenment," in *William Robertson and the Expansion of Empire*, ed. Stuart J. Brown (Cambridge: Cambridge University Press, 1997), 7–35.
5. Stewart, *Biographical Memoirs*, 265. The phrase refers to Robertson's authority resting on skills in organization and management. Thanks to such skills, his was a dominant voice in the General Assembly of the church even without holding the important position of its "moderator" (elected annually) on a permanent basis.
6. See further the thoughts below on the recent historiography of the Enlightenment, 15–17.
7. The character of Robertson as a historian is explored in the context of eighteenth-century Scottish and European (naturally enough, mainly German) historical writing in chapter 1; his individual works are assessed in more detail in the first sections of chapters 2–5.
8. John Renwick, "The Reception of William Robertson's Historical Writings in Eighteenth-Century France," in *Robertson and the Expansion of Empire*, ed. Brown, 145–63.
9. Gianfranco Tarabuzzi, "Le traduzioni italiani settecentesche delle opere di William Robertson," *Rivista storica italiana* 91 (2–3) (1979): 486–509.

186 *Notes to Pages 5–7*

10. Robin A. Humphreys, "William Robertson and His History of America" [1954], in Humphreys, *Tradition and Revolt in Latin America and Other Essays* (New York: Columbia University Press, 1969), 34–6.
11. Stewart, *Life of Robertson*, 306.
12. The *View of the Progress* seems to have been Catherine's absolute favorite: "[The *History of Charles V*] C'est le compagnon constant de tous mes voyages; je ne me lasse jamais à le lire, et particulièrement le premier volume"; ibid., 306. Cf. Edmund Heier, "William Robertson and Ludwig Heinrich Nicolay, His German Translator at the Court of Catherine II," *Scottish Historical Review* 41 (1962): 135–40.
13. While my study does not belong to the genre of the "history of the book," this point will be illustrated below in the case of Robertson's individual works with reference to the borrowing lists of the library of the University of Göttingen. As for private collections, see a very thorough study on an emblematic eighteenth-century book collector, who possessed the full range of Robertson's histories, some of them in English as well as German (though the author of this monograph wrongly attributes the *History of Ancient Greece*, published by a namesake of Robertson's, also to the historiographer royal). Gabriele Crusius, *Aufklärung und Bibliophilie. Der Hannoveraner Sammler Georg Friedrich Brandes und seine Bibliothek* (Heidelberg: Universitätsverlag Winter, 2008), 95–7, 170–2, 183.
14. See Ludwig Wachler, *Geschichte der Kunst und Wissenschaften seit Wiederherstellung derselben bis an Ende des 18. Jahrhunderts*, vol. 2 (Göttingen: Vandenhoeck & Ruprecht, 1818), 642; Bernhard Pier, *William Robertson als Historiker und Geschichtsphilosoph* (Radbod: Weitfeld, 1929), 100–3.
15. Franz X. Wegele, *Geschichte des deutschen Historiographie seit dem Auftreten des Humanismus* (Munich and Leipzig: Oldenbourg, 1885), 786.
16. *Herrn Dr Wilhelm Robertsons Geschichte der Regierung des Kaiser Carls des Fünften. Nebst einem Abrisse des Wachstums und Fortgangs des Gesellschaftlichen Lebens in Europa bis auf den Anfang des 16. Jhs.*, trans. and rev. by Julius August Remer, 5 vols. (Vienna: Härter, 1819 [based on the edition at Braunschweig: Schulbuchhandlung/Waisenhaus, 1792–1796]), I: "Vorrede."
17. Pier, *William Robertson als Historiker*, 109. See also John A. McCarthy, "Disciplining History: Schiller als Historiograph," *Goethe Yearbook* 12 (Goethe Society of North America, Boydell & Brewer, 2004), 214–5. The reference to Schiller here raises the issue of a literary reception of Robertson in Germany, the study of which, however, is beyond the scope of the present book.
18. László Kontler, "Translation and Comparison: Early-Modern and Current Perspectives," *Contributions to the History of Concepts* 3 (1) (2007): 71–103; idem, "Translation and Comparison II: A Methodological Inquiry into Reception in the History of Ideas," *Contributions to the History of Concepts* 4 (1) (2008): 27–56. See also idem, "Concepts, Contests and Contexts: Conceptual History and the Problem of Translatability," in *Rethinking Conceptual History*, ed. Willibald Steinmetz and Michael Freeden (Oxford and New York: Berghahn, forthcoming, 2014). In these articles, I refer to a vast amount of relevant literature, omitted here for the sake of the economy of size; and outline a commitment to an approach that combines "linguistic contextualism," conceptual history (*Begriffsgeschichte*), and *Rezeptionsgeschichte*.
19. For instance, in an excellent study that has provided much inspiration for this book. See Fania Oz-Salzberger, *Translating the Enlightenment: Scottish Civic Discourse in Eighteenth-Century Germany* (Oxford: Clarendon Press, 1995).
20. Friedrich Schleiermacher, "On the Different Methods of Translating" [Über die verschiedenen Methoden des Übersetzens (1813)], in *Translating Literature: Practice and Theory in a Comparative Literature Context*, ed. André Lefevere (New York: Modern Language Association of America, 1992), 88.

21. See chapter 1.
22. For an introductory overview of the emerging field of study of the interconnections between urban space and practices of knowledge formation, see Antonella Romano and Stéphane Van Damme, "Sciences et villes-mondes: penser les savoirs au large (XVIe–XVIIIe siècle)," *Revue d'Histoire Moderne et Contemporaine* 55 (2) (2008): 7–18; English version idem, "Science and World Cities: Thinking Urban Knowledge and Science at Large (16th–18th century)," *Itinerario* 33 (1) (2009): 79–95.
23. Cf. Roger Emerson, "The Enlightenment and Social Structures," in *City and Society in the 18th Century*, ed. Paul Fritz and David Williams (Toronto: Hakkert, 1973), 99–124; Stéphane Van Damme, "La grandeur d'Édimbourg. Savoirs et mobilization identitaire au XVIIIe siècle," *Revue d'Histoire Moderne et Contemporaine* 55/2 (2008): 152–81; Luigi Marino, *Praeceptores Germaniae. Göttingen 1770–1820* (Göttingen: Vandenhoeck & Ruprecht, 1995), 1–89 [Italian original: Torino: Einaudi, 1975].
24. For a comprehensive account, see David Bayne Horn, *A Short History of the University of Edinburgh, 1556–1889* (Edinburgh: Edinburgh University Press, 1967); Roger Emerson, "Scottish Universities in the Eighteenth Century," in *Studies on Voltaire and the Eighteenth Century*, vol. 167, ed. James A. Leith (Oxford: Voltaire Foundation, 1977), 453–74. On the university in the context of the Edinburgh urban community, and its transformations during the eighteenth century, see Nicholas Phillipson, "Commerce and Culture: Edinburgh, Edinburgh University, and the Scottish Enlightenment," in *The University and the City: From Medieval Origins to the Present*, ed. Thomas Bender (Oxford: Oxford University Press, 1988), 100–16.
25. Sher, *Church and University*, chs. 2 and 3.
26. Ibid., 324.
27. William Clark, *Academic Charisma and the Origins of the Research University* (Chicago: Univ. of Chicago Press, 2008), 238 ff.
28. Ian Hunter, "Multiple Enlightenments: Rival *Aufklärer* at the University of Halle, 1690–1730," in *The Enlightenment World*, ed. Martin Fitzpatrick, Peter Jones, Christa Knellwolf, and Iain McCalman (London: Routledge, 2007), 576–95.
29. Ibid.
30. Götz von Selle, *Die Georg-August Universität zu Göttingen 1737–1937* (Göttingen: Vandenhoeck & Ruprecht, 1937), 24.
31. The tension between Christoph Gatterer and August Ludwig Schlözer, who both "claimed" universal history by launching parallel courses after 1770, is a well-known case. As the conflict was not only an existential one but went together with different understandings of the epistemological grounds of inquiry into world history, it is also somewhat relevant to the subject of this book. See below, 33–4.
32. The survival of "charisma" in the form of institutional self-regard and the resulting esprit de corps as a constitutive factor of Göttingen as a modern research university is emphasized in Clark, *Academic Charisma*, 245–7 and 377–80.
33. Von Selle, *Die Georg-August Universität*, 43.
34. Thomas Albert Howard, *Protestant Theology and the Making of the Modern German University* (Oxford: Oxford University Press, 2006), 11–15 and ch. 5.
35. This is an admittedly awkward phrase, but in the present case the standard "nationalization" would obscure more than it would explain. *Verstaatlichung* is, roughly, "becoming an aspect of the state" or "moving under the sway of the state."
36. Karl Julius Hartmann and Hans Füchsel, eds., *Geschichte der Göttinger Universitäts-Bibliothek* (Göttingen: Vandenhoeck & Ruprecht, 1937), 19, 33; Marino, *Praeceptores Germaniae*, 9; Bernhard Fabian, "Die Göttinger Universitätsbibliothek im achtzehnten Jahrhundert," in *Göttinger Jahrbuch* (Göttingen: Heinz Reise Verlag, 1980), 115; Graham Jefcoate, Karen Kloth, and Bernhard Fabian, eds., *A Catalogue of English Books Printed Before 1801 Held by the University Library at Göttingen* (Hildesheim: Olms-Weidmann, 1988).

37. William Clark, "On the Bureaucratic Plots of the Research Library," in *Books and the Sciences in History*, ed. Marina Frasca-Spada and Nick Jardine (Cambridge: Cambridge University Press, 2000), 201. Cf. Martin Gierl, "Compilation and the Production of Knowledge in the Early German Enlightenment," in *Wissenschaft als kulturelle Praxis 1750–1900*, ed. Hans Erich Bödeker, Peter Hanns Reill, and Jürgen Schlumbohm (Göttingen: Vandenhoeck & Ruprecht, 1999), 100–1.
38. I surveyed such developments in "Introduction: What Is the (Historians') Enlightenment Today?," in "Enlightenment and Communication: Regional Experiences and Global Consequences," ed. László Kontler, special issue, *European Review of History / Revue d'histoire européenne* 13/3 (2006): 337–55. See also John Robertson, *The Case for the Enlightenment: Scotland and Naples, 1680–1750* (Cambridge: Cambridge University Press, 2005), ch. 1; and more recently Karen O'Brien, "The Return of the Enlightenment," *The American Historical Review* 115/5 (2010): 1426–35.
39. For a concise but evocative statement of this perspective, see Lorraine Daston, "Afterword: The Ethos of Enlightenment," in *The Sciences in Enlightened Europe*, ed. William Clark, Jan Golinski, and Simon Schaffer (Chicago: Univ. of Chicago Press, 1999), 495–504.
40. Originally and emblematically in Roy Porter and Mikuláš Teich, eds., *The Enlightenment in National Context* (Cambridge: Cambridge University Press, 1981); cf. Siegfried Jüttner and Jochen Schlobach, eds., *Europäische Aufklärung(en): Einheit und nationale Vielfalt* (Hamburg: Felix Meiner, 1992).
41. See several studies by John Pocock, including "Clergy and Commerce: The Conservative Enlightenment in England," in *L'età dei lumi: studi storici in onore di Franco Venturi*, vol. 1, ed. Raffaele Ajello et al. (Naples: Iovene Editore, 1985), 523–62; "Conservative Enlightenment and Democratic Revolutions: The American and French Cases in British Perspective," *Government and Opposition* 24 (1989): 82–101; "Enthusiasm: The Antiself of Enlightenment," *Huntington Library Quarterly* 60/1–2 (1997): 7–28; "Enlightenment and Counter-Enlightenment, Revolution and Counter-Revolution: A Eurosceptical Enquiry," *History of Political Thought* 20 (1999): 125–39; *Barbarism and Religion*, 5 vols. (Cambridge: Cambridge University Press, 1999–2011); "Historiography and Enlightenment: A View of Their History," *Modern Intellectual History* 5/1 (2008): 83–95. In the German context, cf. Ian Hunter, *Rival Enlightenments: Civil and Metaphysical Philosophy in Early-Modern Germany* (Cambridge: Cambridge University Press, 2001).
42. Jonathan Israel, *Radical Enlightenment: Philosophy and the Making of the Modern World* (Oxford: Oxford University Press, 2001); idem, *Enlightenment Contested: Philosophy, Modernity and the Emancipation of Man, 1670–1752* (Oxford: Oxford University Press, 2006); idem, *A Revolution of the Mind: Radical Enlightenment and the Intellectual Origins of Modern Democracy* (Princeton: Princeton University Press, 2009); idem, *Democratic Enlightenment: Philosophy, Revolution and Human Rights, 1750–1790* (Oxford: Oxford University Press, 2011). Cf. earlier work on "the radical Enlightenment" by Margaret C. Jacob; and Anthony LaVopa, "A New Intellectual History? Jonathan Israel's Enlightenment," *The Historical Journal* 52/3 (2009): 717–38.
43. John Robertson, "The Enlightenment above National Context," *The Historical Journal* 40 (1997): 667–97; idem, *The Case for the Enlightenment*.
44. Dorinda Outram, *The Enlightenment* (Cambridge: Cambridge University Press, 1995); Thomas Munck, *The Enlightenment: A Comparative Social History, 1721–1794* (London: Edward Arnold, 2000); Alan Charles Kors, ed., *Encyclopedia of the Enlightenment*, 4 vols. (Oxford: Oxford University Press, 2002); Martin Fitzpatrick, Peter Jones, Christa Knellwolf, and Iain McCalman, eds., *The Enlightenment World* (London and New York: Routledge, 2004); Anthony Pagden, *The Enlightenment: And Why It Still Matters* (Oxford: Oxford University Press, 2013).

45. David A. Hollinger, "The Enlightenment and the Genealogy of Cultural Conflict in the United States," in *What's Left of Enlightenment? A Postmodern Question*, ed. Keith Michael Baker and Peter Hanns Reill (Stanford: Stanford University Press, 2001), 7–18, here 17–18.
46. Jeremy Black, "The Enlightenment Historian at Work: The Researches of William Robertson," *Bulletin of Hispanic Studies* 65 (1988), 251–60; Mark Duckworth, "An Eighteenth-Century Questionnaire: William Robertson on the Indians," *Eighteenth-Century Life* 11 (1987): 36–49; Jeffrey Smitten, "Robertson's Letters and the Life of Writing," in *William Robertson and the Expansion of Empire*, ed. Brown, 36–54; Bruce Lenman, "'From Savage to Scot' via the French and the Spaniards: Principal Robertson's Spanish sources," in ibid., 196–209.
47. Renwick, "The Reception of Robertson in France"; Richard B. Sher, "Charles V and the Book Trade: An Episode in Enlightenment Print Culture," in *Robertson and the Expansion of Empire*, ed. Brown, 164–95, here 181–3.

1 Politics, Literature, and Science: William Robertson and Historical Discourses in Eighteenth-Century Scotland and Germany

1. The classic statements on Machiavelli and Guicciardini as "philosophical historians" are by Felix Gilbert, *Machiavelli and Guicciardini: Politics and History in Sixteenth-Century Florence* (Princeton: Princeton University Press, 1965); and John G. A. Pocock, *The Machiavellian Moment: Florentine Political Thought and the Atlantic Republican Tradition* (Princeton: Princeton University Press, 1975), chs. 7–8.
2. David Allan, *Virtue, Learning, and the Scottish Enlightenment: Ideas of Scholarship in Early Modern History* (Edinburgh: Edinburgh University Press, 1993); see also Allan, "Protestantism, Presbyterianism and National Identity in Eighteenth-Century Scottish History," in *Protestantism and National Identity: Britain and Ireland, c. 1650–1850*, ed. Tony Claydon and Ian McBride (Cambridge: Cambridge University Press, 1998), 182–205.
3. William Robertson, *The History of the Reign of the Emperor Charles V: With a View of the Progress of Society in Europe, From the Subversion of the Roman Empire to the Beginning of the Sixteenth Century*, 4 vols. (London: Routledge/Thoemmes Press, 1996 [reprint of the 1792 ed.]), I: x.
4. See Sheila Mason, "Montesquieu's Vision of Europe and Its European Context," in *Studies on Voltaire and the Eighteenth Century*, vol. 341 (Oxford: Voltaire Foundation, 1996), 61–87; and especially Istvan Hont, *Jealousy of Trade: International Competition and the Nation-State in Historical Perspective* (Cambridge: Belknap Press of Harvard University Press, 2005).
5. Robert Henry to Horace Walpole, March 3, 1783, *The Yale Edition of Horace Walpole's Correspondence*, 48 vols., ed. W. S. Lewis et al. (New Haven: Yale University Press, 1937–1983), 15: 169 (1952). Cited in Mark Salber Phillips, *Society and Sentiment: Genres of Historical Writing in Britain, 1740–1820* (Princeton: Princeton University Press, 2000), 5.
6. The "Augustinian–Epicurean understanding of man" is indeed the most prominent set of ideas inherited from the seventeenth and early eighteenth centuries in the portrait of the Enlightenment as unfolding from John Robertson, *The Case for the Enlightenment: Scotland and Naples, 1680–1750* (Cambridge: Cambridge University Press, 2005). For a classic genealogy of the central notions of self-interest and self-love in the seventeenth and eighteenth centuries, see Albert Hirschman, *The Passions and the Interests: Political Arguments for Capitalism before its Triumph* (Princeton: Princeton University Press, 1977); for a more recent one, Pierre

190 *Notes to Pages 22–25*

Force, *Self-Interest before Adam Smith: A Genealogy of Economic Science* (Cambridge: Cambridge University Press, 2003).

7. For important reconstructions, see Richard Tuck, *Philosophy and Government, 1572–1651* (Cambridge: Cambridge University Press, 1993); Knud Haakonssen, *Natural Law and Moral Philosophy: From Grotius to the Scottish Enlightenment* (Cambridge: Cambridge University Press, 1996).

8. On Grotius and Hobbes, see Tuck, *Philosophy and Government*; and Haakonssen, *Natural Law and Moral Philosophy*; on Pufendorf, see Istvan Hont, "The Language of Sociability and Commerce: Samuel Pufendorf and the Theoretical Foundations of the 'Four-Stages Theory,'" in *The Languages of Political Theory in Early-Modern Europe*, ed. Anthony Pagden (Cambridge: Cambridge University Press, 1987), 253–76; Fiammetta Palladini, *Samuel Pufendorf discepolo di Hobbes* (Bologna: Il Mulino, 1996); and Ian Hunter, *Rival Enlightenments: Civil and Metaphysical Philosophy in Early Modern Germany* (Cambridge: Cambridge University Press, 2001), esp. chs. 2 and 4.

9. Mandeville's thought is contextualized within this trend in Edward Hundert, *The Enlightenment's 'Fable': Bernard Mandeville and the Discovery of Society* (Cambridge: Cambridge University Press, 1994). See also the same author's edition, including texts by Nicole and Pierre Bayle, of Bernard Mandeville, *The Fable of the Bees and Other Writings*, ed. E. J. Hundert (Indianapolis: Hackett, 1997).

10. Adam Smith, *An Inquiry into the Nature and Causes of the Wealth of Nations*, ed. Roy H. Campbell and Andrew S. Skinner (Indianapolis: Liberty Classics, 1981), I: 26–7; Smith, *The Theory of Moral Sentiments*, ed. David D. Raphael and Alec L. Macfie (Indianapolis: Liberty Fund, 1982), III: 1–2, esp. 112, 117. Cf. Knud Haakonssen, *The Science of a Legislator: The Natural Jurisprudence of David Hume and Adam Smith* (Cambridge: Cambridge University Press, 1981).

11. The academic study of the social scientific embeddedness of eighteenth-century Scottish historiography began seriously with Roy Pascal, "Property and Society: The Scottish Historical School of the Eighteenth Century," *Modern Quarterly* 2 (1938): 167–79; it became more pronounced in Gladys Bryson, *Man and Society: The Scottish Inquiry of the Eighteenth Century* (Princeton: Princeton University Press, 1945); it grew into a torrent with (and included critical assessments of) Ronald L. Meek, *Social Science and the Ignoble Savage* (Cambridge: Cambridge University Press, 1976). "Conjectural history," famously coined by Dugald Stewart in his retrospect to the golden age of the *literati* of Edinburgh, first appeared in the title of an article in Harro M. Höpfl, "From Savage to Scotsman: Conjectural History in the Scottish Enlightenment," *Journal of British Studies* 17 (1978): 19–40. The literature on the subject since then is endless.

12. Cf., also with a view to Robertson's contribution, Frederick G. Whelan, "Robertson, Hume, and the Balance of Power," *Hume Studies* 21/2 (1995): 315–32.

13. Karen O'Brien, *Narratives of Enlightenment: Cosmopolitan History from Voltaire to Gibbon* (Cambridge: Cambridge University Press, 1997); J. G. A. Pocock, *Barbarism and Religion*, especially vol. II: *Narratives of Civil Government* (Cambridge: Cambridge University Press, 1999).

14. In a vast literature, see especially Michèle Duchet, *Anthropologie et histoire au siècle des lumières* (Paris: Albin Michel, 1971); Antonello Gerbi, *The Dispute of the New World: The History of a Polemic 1750–1900* (Pittsburgh: University of Pittsburgh Press, 1973); Gerbi, *The Great Map of Mankind: Perceptions of New Worlds in the Age of Enlightenment*, ed. Peter J. Marshall and Glyndwr Williams (Cambridge: Harvard University Press, 1982); Anthony Pagden, *The Fall of Natural Man: The American Indian and the Origins of Comparative Ethnology* (Cambridge: Cambridge University Press, 1986); Pagden, *European Encounters with the New World* (New Haven: Yale University Press, 1993); Roxann Wheeler, *The Complexion of Race: Categories of*

Difference in Eighteenth-Century British Culture (Philadelphia: Univ. of Pennsylvania Press, 2000); and Silvia Sebastiani, *I limiti del progresso. Razza e genere nell'Illuminismo scozzese* (Bologna: Il Mulino, 2008), rev. Eng. ed., *The Scottish Enlightenment: Race, Gender and the Limits of Progress* (Houndmills, Basingstoke: Palgrave Macmillan, 2013).

15. Frederick G. Whelan, *Edmund Burke and India: Political Morality and Empire* (Pittsburgh: Univ. of Pittsburgh Press, 1996); Sankar Muthu, *Enlightenment against Empire* (Princeton: Princeton University Press 2003); Jennifer Pitts, *A Turn to Empire: The Rise of Imperial Liberalism in Britain and France* (Princeton: Princeton University Press, 2005); Guido Abbattista, "Empire, Liberty and the Rule of Difference: European Debates on British Colonialism in Asia at the End of the Eighteenth Century," *European Review of History/Revue européenne d'histoire* 13/3 (2006): 473–98.
16. Hume to John Clephane, 1756?, *The Letters of David Hume*, ed. John Young Thomson Greig (Oxford: Clarendon Press, 1932), I: 237.
17. Nicholas Phillipson, "Providence and Progress: An Introduction to the Historical Thought of William Robertson," in *Robertson and the Expansion of Empire*, ed. Stuart J. Brown, 55–73; Phillipson, *Hume* (London: Weidenfeld & Nicolson, 1989), chs. 2–3; O'Brien, *Narratives of Enlightenment*, chs. 3–4; Colin Kidd, "The Ideological Significance of Robertson's *History of Scotland*," in *Robertson and the Expansion of Empire*, ed. Brown, 92–121; Phillips, *Society and Sentiment*, esp. chs. 2, 5–6.
18. The standard account of the conflicting historical identity discourses in post-Union Scotland is Colin Kidd, *Subverting Scotland's Past: Scottish Whig Historians and the Creation of an Anglo-British Identity, 1689–c. 1830* (Cambridge: Cambridge University Press, 1993).
19. Neal Hargraves, "Resentment and History in the Scottish Enlightenment," *Cromohs* 14 (2009): 1–21, accessed July 14, 2010, www.cromohs.unifi.it/14_2009 /hargraves_resentment.html.
20. Allan, *Virtue, Learning and the Scottish Enlightenment*. See also, for a fine monographic study of a figure of the "outer circle" and the challenge he and his likes constituted to the new mainstream in William Zachs, *Without Regard to Good Manners: A Biography of Gilbert Stuart 1743–1786* (Edinburgh: Edinburgh University Press, 1992).
21. D. J. Womersley, "The Historical Writings of William Robertson," *Journal of the History of Ideas* 47 (1986): 497–506; Neal Hargraves, "National History and 'Philosophical' History: Character and Narrative in William Robertson's *History of Scotland*," *History of European Ideas* 26 (2000): 19–33; Hargraves, "The 'Progress of Ambition': Character, Narrative, and Philosophy in the Works of William Robertson," *Journal of the History of Ideas* 63 (2002): 261–82; Hargraves, "Enterprise, Adventure and Industry: The Formation of 'Commercial Character' in William Robertson's *History of America*," *History of European Ideas* 29 (2003): 33–54; Hargraves, "Beyond the Savage Character: Mexicans, Peruvians, and the 'Imperfectly Civilized' in William Robertson's *History of America*," in *The Anthropology of the Enlightenment*, ed. Larry Wolff and Marco Cipollini (Stanford: Stanford University Press, 2007), 103–18.
22. Phillipson, "Providence and Progress," esp. 68 ff.; see also in greater detail below in chapter 2. Besides providentialism, but closely related to the paradigm of stadialism, the centrality of "unintended consequences" to Robertson's causal explanations has been argued in Daniele Francesconi, "William Robertson on Historical Causation and Unintended Consequences," *Storia della Storiografia* 36 (1999): 55–80.
23. Mary Fearnley-Sander, "Philosophical History and the Scottish Reformation: William Robertson and the Knoxian Tradition," *Historical Journal* 33 (1990): 323–38; Alexander Du Toit, "God Before Mammon? William Robertson, Episcopacy and the Church of England," *Journal of Ecclesiastical History* 54 (2003): 671–90; Colin

Kidd, "Subscription, the Scottish Enlightenment and the Moderate Interpretation of History," *Journal of Ecclesiastical History* 55 (2004): 502–19.
24. Stuart J. Brown, "William Robertson and the Scottish Enlightenment," in *William Robertson and the Expansion of Empire*, ed. Brown, 9.
25. Geoff Grundy, *The Emulation of Nations: William Robertson and the International Order* (PhD diss., University of Edinburgh, 2005), 272–6. Cf. Troy Bickham, *Savages within the Empire: Representations of American Indians in Eighteenth-Century Britain* (Oxford: Clarendon Press, 2005), ch. 5, especially pp. 195–8.
26. While the Judicial Plan of 1772, which decided that India would be governed by Indian (not British) law, made it imperative for British East India Company officials to understand Indian law and the cultural traditions behind it, and triggered a remarkable range of relevant scholarship by a group of British "orientalists," Hastings and his circle went too far in portraying themselves as "the inheritors of the Indian polity as refounded by Emperor Akbar" in the sixteenth century. For the relevance of these developments to Robertson's work, see Stuart J. Brown, "William Robertson, Early Orientalism and the *Historical Disquisition* on India of 1791," *The Scottish Historical Review* 88/2 (2009): 296. For the background: Peter J. Marshall, *The British Discovery of Hinduism in the Eighteenth Century* (Cambridge: Cambridge University Press, 1970), 1–44; John L. Brockington, "Warren Hastings and Orientalism," in *The Impeachment of Warren Hastings*, ed. Geoffrey Carnall and Colin Nicholson (Edinburgh: Edinburgh University Press, 1989), 91–108.
27. Grundy, "The Emulation of Nations," 132.
28. Cf. Hargraves, "Beyond the Savage Character."
29. Jeffrey Smitten, "Impartiality in Robertson's *History of America*," *Eighteenth-Century Studies* 19 (1985): 56–77. It must be added that his own contemporaries appreciated Robertson's impartiality in a less sophisticated sense, one in which Hume's version of it was conceived. "[Y]ou have shewn that you can write on ticklish subjects with the utmost discretion, and on subjects of religious party with temper and impartiality," wrote Horace Walpole upon reading the *History of Scotland*. Quoting Walpole, while also expressing his own admiration, Dugald Stewart somewhat toned it down with a simple explanation: "at this distance of time, it is difficult to conceive how prejudice and passion should enter into the discussion." Dugald Stewart, *Biographical Memoirs of Adam Smith, L.L.D., of William Robertson, D.D, and of Thomas Reid, D.D.* (Edinburgh: George Ramsay, 1811) 183, 195.
30. Noted by Stewart, *Biographical Memoirs*, 181.
31. On the relationship between Robertson and Mackie, see Phillipson, "Providence and Progress," 57–8. On Mackie, L. W. Sharp, "Charles Mackie, the First Professor of History at Edinburgh University," *Scottish Historical Review* 41 (1962): 23–45.
32. Montesquieu's *The Spirit of the Laws* was published in 1748, while Hume's *Essays Moral and Political* from 1741, in several, continually re-wrought editions (the third, "improved and expanded" edition also exactly in 1748). "Of National Characters" is one of these essays. As for Smith, he never published a text on jurisprudence in his lifetime: his lectures held on this subject ("on the third and fourth part of moral philosophy," i.e., on justice and expediency) after his appointment as professor of logics and moral philosophy at the University of Glasgow in 1751, have been reconstructed on the basis of lecture notes of his students by modern scholarship. See *Lectures on Jurisprudence*, ed. R. L. Meek, D. D. Raphael, and P. G. Stein (Oxford: Clarendon Press, 1978). Previously, however, between 1748 and 1750, the young Smith also held a few public lectures in Edinburgh, allowing Robertson to borrow some of his views, perhaps literally so: Smith is said to have accused Robertson of having plagiarized the backbone of *A View of the Progress of Society in*

Europe. Ian Simpson Ross, *The Life of Adam Smith* (Oxford: Oxford University Press, 1995), 105–6.
33. Locke's claim that "in the beginning all the World was America" is sometimes quoted to demonstrate the propensity inherent in seventeenth-century natural law to think in stadial terms, but the most articulate early statement of the "stages" theory (and the one that is regarded to have had the strongest impact on eighteenth-century social science) is associated with Pufendorf. John Locke, *Two Treatises of Government*, ed. Pater Laslett (Cambridge: Cambridge University Press, 1988), 301; Hont, "The Language of Sociability and Commerce."
34. Cf. Du Toit, "God Before Mammon?"; and Du Toit, "'A Species of False Religion': William Robertson, Catholic Relief and the Myth of Moderate Tolerance," *The Innes Review* 52/2 (2001): 167–88.
35. Cf. Introduction, endnote 5.
36. For Robertson as the central figure in the "Moderate Party" within the *Kirk* and the moderates' place in the Edinburgh Enlightenment, see Richard B. Sher, *Church and University in the Scottish Enlightenment: The Moderate Literati of Edinburgh* (Princeton: Princeton University Press, 1985). See also Ian D. L. Clark, "From Protest to Reaction: The Moderate Regime in the Church of Scotland, 1752–1805," in *Scotland in the Age of Improvement: Essays in Scottish History in the Eighteenth Century*, ed. Rosalind Mitchison and Nicholas T. Phillipson (Edinburgh: Edinburgh University Press, 1996), 200–24.
37. Cf. Thomas Ahnert, "Fortschrittsgeschichte und religiöse Aufklärung. William Robertson und die Deutung außereuropäischer Kulturen," in *Die Aufklärung und ihre Weltwirkung*, ed. Wolfgang Hardtwig (Göttingen: Vandenhoeck & Ruprecht, 2009), 101–22.
38. Hume, *Letters*, II: 230.
39. Peter Hanns Reill, *The German Enlightenment and the Rise of Historicism* (Berkeley: Univ. of California Press, 1975); Frederick C. Beiser, *The German Historicist Tradition* (Oxford: Oxford University Press, 2011), chs. 1–3.
40. *Die Wissenschaft vom Menschen in Göttingen um 1800*, ed. Hans Erich Bödeker, Philippe Büttgen, and Michel Espagne (Göttingen: Vandenhoeck & Ruprecht, 2008). For another comprehensive treatment of the subject within the extensive literature, see also Luigi Marino, *Praeceptores Germaniae. Göttingen 1770–1820* (Göttingen: Vandenhoeck & Ruprecht, 1995).
41. Han F. Vermeulen, "Göttingen und die Völkerkunde. Ethnologie und Ethnographie in der deutschen Aufklärung, 1710–1815"; and Guillaume Garner, "Politische Ökonomie und Statistik an der Universität Göttingen (1760–1820)," in *Die Wissenschaft vom Menschen*, ed. Bödeker, Büttgen, and Espagne, 199–230, 371–92. On the latter subject, cf. also Keith Tribe, *Governing Economy: The Transformation of German Economic Discourse, 1750–1840* (Cambridge: Cambridge University Press, 1988).
42. *Göttingische Anzeigen von gelehrten Sachen* (hereafter *GAgS*) 30 (10 March 1777): 234–40, *Zugabe*, 213–20, 240.
43. August Ludwig Schlözer, *Stats-Gelartheit. Zweiter Theil: Theorie der Statistik nebst Ideen über das Studium der Politik überhaupt* (Göttingen: Vandenhoeck & Ruprecht, 1804), 92.
44. Norbert Waszek, "Die Schottische Aufklärung in der Göttinger Wissenschaft vom Menschen," in *Die Wissenschaft vom Menschen*, ed. Bödeker, Büttgen, and Espagne, 141. For a highly sophisticated study of the Scottish "natural history of mankind" and the German *Menschheitsgeschichte* within the context of the science of man and the *Wissenschaft vom Menschen*—and therefore, emphatically, not as a part of the history of historiography in the narrower sense but as a critical phase in the reconstruction of the entire contemporary landscape of knowledge—see Annette

Meyer, *Von der Wahrheit zur Wahrscheinlichkeit. Die Wissenschaft vom Menschen in der schottischen und deutschen Aufklärung* (Tübingen: Niemeyer, 2008).

45. Jörn Garber, "Von der Menschengeschichte zur Kulturgeschichte. Zum geschichtstheoretischen Kulturbegriff der deutschen Spätaufklärung," in *Spätabsolutismus und bürgerliche Gesellschaft. Studien zur deutschen Staats- und Gesellschaftstheorie im Übergang zur Moderne* (Frankfurt: Keip Verlag, 1992), 409–33; Gérard Laudin, "Histoire de la civilization et histoire anthropologique. Adelung et la *Culturgeschichte*," *Le Texte et l'Idée* 17 (2002): 59–78; Laudin, "Gatterer und Schlözer: Geschichte als 'Wissenschaft vom Menschen'?," in *Die Wissenschaft vom Menschen*, ed. Bödeker, Büttgen, and Espagne, 393–418. See also Johan van der Zande, "Popular Philosophy and the History of Mankind in Eighteenth-Century Germany," *Storia della Storiografia* 22 (1992): 37–56. *Geschichte der Menschheit* is also a central theme in Michael Carhart, *The Science of Culture in Enlightenment Germany* (Cambridge: Harvard University Press, 2007); most recently, see André de Melo Araújo, *Weltgeschichte in Göttingen. Eine Studie über das spätaufklärerische universalhistorische Denken, 1756–1815* (Bielefeld: Transcript Verlag, 2012), 9–14, 97–138. For a further discussion, see chapter 5.

46. Notker Hammerstein, *Ius und Historie. Ein Beitrag zur Geschichte des historischen Denkens an deutschen Universitäten im späten 17. und im 18. Jahrhundert* (Göttingen: Vandenhoeck & Ruprecht, 1973); Hammerstein, "Reichshistorie," in *Aufklärung und Geschichte. Studien zur deutschen Geschichtswissenschaft im 18. Jahrhundert*, ed. Hans Erich Bödeker, Georg G. Iggers, and Jonathan B. Knudsen (Göttingen: Vandenhoeck & Ruprecht, 1986), 82–104.

47. Hans Erich Bödeker, "Landesgeschichtliche Erkenntnisinteressen der nordwestdeutschen Aufklärungshistorie," *Niedersächsisches Jahrbuch für Landesgeschichte* 69 (1997): 247–79.

48. See Leonard Krieger, "Germany," in *National Consciousness, History, and Political Culture in Early-Modern Europe*, ed. Orest Ranum (Baltimore: Johns Hopkins University Press, 1975), 67–97.

49. The latest—magisterial—treatment of Gatterer as an embodiment of the endeavor of mid-eighteenth century historical science to establish itself as a worthy counterpart of the natural sciences by accommodating the standards of precision, system, method, and a holistic aura, is Martin Gierl, *Geschichte als präzisierte Wissenschaft. Johann Christoph Gatterer und die Historiographie des 18. Jahrhunderts im ganzen Umfang* (Stuttgart-Bad Cannstatt: Fromann-Holzboog, 2012).

50. J. C. Gatterer, "vom historischen Plan, und der darauf sich gründenden Zusammenfügung der Erzählungen," in *Allgemeine historische Bibliothek vom Mitglieder der königlichen Instituts des historischen Wissenschaften zu Göttingen* 1/1 (1767), 26.

51. *GAgS* (January 27, 1766): 90–3, and (April 10–12, 1766): 340–8. Cf. Johan van der Zande, "August Ludwig Schlözer and the English Universal History," in *Historikerdialoge. Geschichte, Mythos und Gedächtnis im deutsch-britischen kulturellen Austausch 1750–2000*, ed. Peter Schuman, Stefan Berger, and Peter Lambert (Göttingen: Vandenhoeck & Ruprecht, 2003), 137–56.

52. Gatterer's "preoccupations" included the "most helpful historians," the "description of the earth," the "account of historical events according to synchronic and chronological methods," and "peoples and states according to their constitution," while the methods listed in Schlözer's scheme were source criticism, and the geographic, chronographic, ethnographic, and "technographic" methods. The transparencies and differences are discussed in further detail in de Melo Araújo, *Weltgeschichte in Göttingen*, 71–95.

53. August Ludwig Schlözer, *Vorstellung seiner Universal-Historie* (1772/73), ed. Horst Walter Blanke (Hagen: Margit Rottmann Medienverlag, 1990), 19, 34.

54. On the relevance of the "part versus whole" problem to historical thought and universal history, see Peter Hanns Reill, "Das Problem des Allgemeinen und des Besonderen im geschichtlichen Denken und in in den historiographischen Darstellungen des späten 18. Jahrhunderts," in *Teil und Ganzes: Zum Verhältnis von Einzel- und Gesamtanalyse in Geschichts- und Sozialwissenschaften*, ed. Karl Acham and Winfried Schulze (Munich: DTV, 1990), 141–68; Jörn Garber, "Selbstreferenz und Objektivität: Organisationsmodelle von Mensch- und Weltgeschichte in der deutschen Spätaufklärung," in *Wissenschaft als kulturelle Praxis*, ed. Bödeker, Reill, and Schlumbohm, 137–85. On universal history, see further Hans Erich Bödeker, "The Debates about Universal History and National History around 1800: A Problem-Oriented Historical Attempt," in *Unity and Diversity in European Culture c. 1800*, Proceedings of the British Academy, 134, ed. Tim Blanning and Hagen Schulze (Oxford: Oxford University Press/British Academy, 2006), 135–70.

55. The theoretical work of Martin Chladenius, in particular his *Allgemeine Geschichtswissenschaft, worinnen der Grund zu einer neuen Einsicht in allen Arten der Gelahrtheit geleget wird* (Leipzig, 1752) broke much new ground for Gatterer and Schlözer. For concise explorations of the theme, see Reinhart Koselleck, "Geschichte, Historie," section V, in *Gescichtliche Grundbegriffe. Historisches Lexicon zur politisch-sozialen Sprache in Deutschland*, ed. Otto Brunner, Werner Conze, and Reinhart Koselleck (Stuttgart: Klett-Cotta, 1975), II: 647–78; Michael Gottlob, *Geschichtsschreibung zwischen Aufklärung und Historismus. Johannes von Müller und Friedrich Christoph Schlosser* (Frankfurt: Peter Lang, 1989), 27–48; Wolfgang Hardtwig, "Die Verwissenschaftlichung der Geschichtsschreibung zwischen Aufklärung und Historismus," in *Geschichtskultur und Wissenschaft* (Munich: DTV, 1990), 58–91.

56. For humanism and Enlightenment as both belonging to the "prehistory of historicism," see Ulrich Muhlack, *Geschichtswissenschaft im Humanismus und Aufklärung. Die Vorgeschichte des Historismus* (Munich: C. H. Beck, 1991).

57. Horst Dreitzel, "Die Entwicklung der Historie zur Wissenschaft," *Zeitschrift für Historische Forschung* 8/3 (1981): 257–84.

58. Ulrich Muhlack, "Historie und Philologie," in *Aufklärung und Geschichte*, ed. Bödeker, Iggers, and Knudsen, 49–81.

59. Michael Ermarth, "Hermeneutics and History: The Fork in Hermes' Path through the 18th Century," in *Aufklärung und Geschichte*, ed. Bödeker, Iggers, and Knudsen, 193–221.

60. In general terms, see Georg G. Iggers, "The European Context of Eighteenth-Century German Historiography," in *Aufklärung und Geschichte*, ed. Bödeker, Iggers, and Knudsen, 237; for details of similar assessments of, for example, Gibbon, see Wilfried Nippel, "Gibbon and German Historiography," in *British and German Historiography 1750–1950: Traditions, Perceptions, and Transfers*, ed. Benedikt Stuchtey and Peter Wende (Oxford: Oxford University Press, 2000), 67–81.

61. On Stuart as an opponent of Robertson in regard of his historical approach and performance as well as his politics, see Zachs, *Without Regard to Good Manners*.

62. Iggers, "The European Context of Eighteenth-Century German Historiography," 232–7.

63. Daniel Fulda, *Wissenschaft aus Kunst. Die Entstehung der modernen deutschen Geschichtsschreibung 1760–1860* (Berlin and New York: Walter de Gruyter, 1996), esp. pt. 2.D; Thomas Prüfer, *Die Bildung der Geschichte. Friedrich Schiller und die Anfänge der modernen Geschichtswissenschaft* (Cologne: Böhlau, 2002)

64. Rudolf Vierhaus, "Historisches Interesse im 18. Jahrhundert," in *Aufklärung und Geschichte*, ed. Bödeker, Iggers, and Knudsen, 264–5.

65. Maiken Umbach, *Federalism and Enlightenment in Germany, 1740–1806* (London: Hambledon Press, 2000), 130–1.

66. For an evaluation of the Westphalian settlement and its long-term consequences in this sense, see John Gagliardo, *Germany under the Old Regime 1600–1790* (London: Longman, 1991), chs. 7–8 and 22, here p. 363.
67. Severinus de Monzambano [Samuel von Pufendorf], *De statu imperii Germanici* (The Hague, 1667), bk. 6, pts. 1 and 9. Modern German edition: *Die Verfassung des deutschen Reiches*, ed. Horst Denzer (Stuttgart: Reclam, 1976).
68. Umbach, *Federalism and Enlightenment*, 133–4.
69. *Teutsches Staatsrecht* (1739–1747), 53 vols.; *Neues Teutsches Staatsrecht* (1766–1782), 24 vols. Moser's entire oeuvre amounts to over 500 published volumes.
70. On Moser's historical contribution, see Mack Walker, "Johann Jakob Moser," in *Aufklärung und Geschichte*, ed. Bödeker, Iggers, and Knudsen, 105–18; more extensively, Walker, *Johann Jakob Moser and the Holy Roman Empire of the German Nation* (Chapel Hill: North Carolina University Press, 1981), esp. chs. 13–15, 29–31.
71. The standard treatment of *Polizey* in the German context is Hans Maier, *Die ältere deutsche Staats- und Verwaltungslehre (Polizeiwissenschaft). Ein Beitrag zur Geschichte der politischen Wissenschaft in Deutschland* (Neuwied and Berlin: Luchterhand, 1966). A research project at the Max-Planck-Institut für Europäische Rechtsgeschichte in Frankfurt has yielded many local and regional studies as well as a few more comprehensive volumes, including *Policey im Europa der Frühen Neuzeit*, ed. Michael Stolleis, with Karl Härter and Lothar Schilling (Frankfurt: Vittorio Klostermann, 1996); Karl Härter, ed., *Policey und Frühneuzeitlicher Gesellschaft* (Frankfurt: Vittorio Klostermann, 2000); Thomas Simon, *"Gute Policey." Ordnungsleitbilder und Zielvorstellungen politischen Handelns in der Frühen Neuzeit* (Frankfurt: Vittorio Klostermann, 2004). For wider implications of "police" and the problem of governmentality in the early modern period, see Michel Foucault, "Governmentality," in *Power*, ed. James D. Faubion (New York: New Press, 2000), 201–22; Gerhard Oestreich, "'Police' and Prudentia Civilis in the Seventeenth Century," in *Neostoicism and the Early Modern State* (Cambridge: Cambridge University Press, 1982), 155–86. On the same issue and the relevance of natural jurisprudence, Robert von Friedeburg and Michael Seidler, "The Holy Roman Empire of the German Nation," in *European Political Thought 1450–1700: Religion, Law and Philosophy*, ed. Howell Lloyd, Glenn Burgess, and Simon Hodson (New Haven: Yale University Press, 2007), 120–6, 133–41, 167–72. On eighteenth-century state sciences, Keith Tribe, *Strategies of Economic Order: German Economic Discourse, 1750–1950* (Cambridge: Cambridge University Press, 1995), 8–31; Tribe, "Cameralism and the Sciences of the State," in *The Cambridge History of Eighteenth-Century Political Thought*, ed. Mark Goldie and Robert Wokler (Cambridge: Cambridge University Press, 2006), 525–46.
72. Gabriella Valera, "Statistik, Staatengeschichte, Geschichte im 18. Jahrhundert," in *Aufklärung und Geschichte*, ed. Bödeker, Iggers, and Knudsen, 119–43; Pasquale Pasquino, "Politisches und historisches Interesse. Statistik und historische Staatslehre bei Gottfried Achenwall (1719–1772)," in ibid., 144–68; Hans Erich Bödeker, "... wer ächte freie Politik hören will, muss nach Göttingen gehen," in *Die Wissenschaft vom Menschen*, ed. Bödeker, Büttgen, and Espagne, 325–69, esp. 343, 354; Johan van der Zande, "Statistik and History in the German Enlightenment," *Journal of the History of Ideas* 71/3 (2010): 411–32.
73. Paul Wood, "The Natural History of Man in the Scottish Enlightenment," *History of Science* 28 (1990): 89–123; Peter Hanns Reill, "Science and the Science of History in the Spätaufklärung," in *Aufklärung und Geschichte*, ed. Bödeker, Iggers, and Knudsen, 430–50; Reill, "Das Problem des Allgemeinen und des Besonderen," esp. 146–57; see also Reill, "Anthropology, Nature and History in the Late Enlightenment," in *Schiller als Historiker*, ed. Otto Dann, Norbert Oellers, and Ernst Osterkamp (Stuttgart and Weimar: J. B. Metzler, 1995), 243–65; Reill, *Vitalizing Nature in the Enlightenment* (Berkeley, Los Angeles and London: University of California Press, 2006).

2 Time and Progress, Time as Progress: History by Way of Enlightened Preaching

1. See Margaret Cornell Szasz, *Scottish Highlanders and Native Americans: Indigenous Education in the Eighteenth-Century Atlantic World* (Norman: University of Oklahoma Press, 2007).
2. For the circumstances and the grounds of Robertson's rise to recognition and a concise account of the rise of "moderatism," see Stuart J. Brown, "William Robertson and the Scottish Enlightenment," in *Robertson and the Expansion of Empire*, ed. Stuart J. Brown (Cambridge: Cambridge University Press, 1997), 10–15. The standard, full account of the Moderates is in Richard B. Sher, *Church and University in the Scottish Enlightenment: The Moderate Literati of Edinburgh* (Princeton: Princeton University Press, 1985)
3. William Robertson, *The Situation of the World at the Time of Christ's Appearance, and its Connection with the Success of His Religion*, in *The Works of William Robertson* (London: Routledge/Thoemmes Press, 1996), XI: 54.
4. Reinhart Koselleck, *Futures Past: On the Semantics of Historical Time* (Cambridge: MIT Press, 1985), 7.
5. Ibid., 14, 16
6. Ibid., 36.
7. See also Reinhart Koselleck, *Critique and Crisis: Enlightenment and the Pathogenesis of Modern Society* (Oxford: Oxford University Press, 1988)—the German original was published in 1959.
8. Smith and Turgot have also received special emphasis in the literature devoted to the idea of progress, and by implication to the concepts of time and history. See, for instance, John B. Bury, *The Idea of Progress: An Inquiry into Its Growth and Origin* (New York: Dover, 1955); Leslie Sklair, *The Sociology of Progress* (London: Routledge, 1998), ch. 1; Robert Nisbet, *The History of the Idea of Progress* (New York: Basic Books, 1980), ch. 4; David Spadafora, *The Idea of Progress in Eighteenth-Century Britain* (New Haven: Yale University Press, 1990).
9. Cf. Robert F. Nisbet, *Social Change and History: Aspects of the Western Theory of Development* (Oxford: Oxford University Press, 1965), 85 ff. For Augustine on the paradoxes of time, see *Confessions*, trans. R. S. Pine-Coffin (Chicago: Encyclopaedia Britannica, 1990), bk. 11, especially sections 10–27, 116 ff.
10. Cf. J. G. A. Pocock, *The Machiavellian Moment: Florentine Political Thought and the Atlantic Republican Tradition* (Princeton: Princeton University Press, 1975), ch. 1. It must be added that, from patristic times on, the idea of progress asserted itself in various ways in the Christian apocalyptic-cataclysmic conception of history, the more so as both of these approaches also regarded time as not merely an exact chronological standard, but the framework of change, which becomes intelligible through understanding the relationship between separate events. A more thorough investigation of this problem is beyond the confines of this study, but for the intersections of apocalyptic and progress-based approaches to time, see the pioneering and still relevant work of Ernest Lee Tuveson, *Millennium and Utopia: A Study in the Background of the Idea of Progress* (New York: Harper & Row, 1946). See also Chester G. Starr, "Historical and Philosophical Time," *History and Theory* 6/6 (1966): 24–35; Elizabeth Eisenstein, "Clio and Chronos: An Essay on the Making and Breaking of History-Book Time," *History and Theory* 5/6 (1966), 36–64.
11. Jeffrey Smitten, "The Shaping of Moderatism: William Robertson and Arminianism," *Studies in Eighteenth-Century Culture* 22 (1992): 281–300.
12. Philippe van Limborch, *A Compleat System or Body of Divinity* (1713), quoted in Smitten, "The Shaping of Moderatism," 287.
13. Robertson, *Situation*, 6–7.

14. Ibid., 8–9.
15. Ibid., 9–10.
16. Ibid.
17. Isaac Newton, *Mathematical Principles of Natural Philosophy* (Chicago: Univ. of Chicago Press, 1952), 8.
18. The increasingly bitter dispute that started between Newton and Leibniz over the "copyright" of differential calculus later also concerned other scientific as well as philosophical and theological questions, and involved Newton's disciples, above all Samuel Clarke, the translator of the *Optics*. The problem of time and space is abundantly discussed in the Leibniz-Clarke correspondence, published in 1717. On the idea mentioned above, see *The Leibniz-Clarke Correspondence*, ed. H. G. Alexander (Manchester: Manchester University Press, 1956), 27–8. For a comparison of the relevant views of Newton, Locke, and Leibniz, see Philip Turetzky, *Time* (London: Routledge, 1998), 71–83; and Julius Thomas Fraser, *Of Time, Passion, and Knowledge: Reflections on the Strategy of Existence* (Princeton: Princeton University Press, 1990), 33–34.
19. John Locke, *An Essay Concerning Human Understanding*, ed. Peter H. Nidditch (Oxford: Clarendon Press, 1975), bk. 2, ch. 14, "Of Duration, and Its Simple Modes," 181–96. Cf. W. Von Leyden, "History and the Concept of Relative Time," *History and Theory* 2 (1963): 263–85.
20. Nisbet, *Social Change and History*, 85–91.
21. On this basis, it is further argued by Thomas Ahnert that "Moderatism was not characterized by 'reasonable religion', but by a (theologically inspired) epistemological skepticism, which emphasizes the limitations of human, natural reason in theological questions"—a case for a "pious Enlightenment," not characterized by religious indifference, but integrating the cultivation of "polite" manners with emphasis on religious reform. Ahnert, "Religion and the Moderates' Enlightenment: the Historiography of William Robertson," manuscript (paper read at the conference "Empire, Philosophy and Religion: Scotland and Central/Eastern Europe in the Eighteenth Century," Central European University, Budapest, 23–26 June 2005), also Ahnert, "Fortschrittsgeschichte und religiöse Aufklärung. William Robertson und die Deutung außereuropäischer Kulturen," in *Die Aufklärung und ihre Weltwirkung*, ed. Wolfgang Hardtwig (Göttingen: Vandenhoeck & Ruprecht, 2009).
22. Robertson, *Situation*, 14–15.
23. Ibid., 15–19.
24. Ibid., 20–4
25. Ibid.
26. David Hume, "Of Superstition and Enthusiasm," in *Essays Moral, Political and Literary*, ed. Eugene F. Miller (Indianapolis: Liberty Press, 1985), 74–9.
27. See Sher, *Church and University*, 67–70, 277–97; Brown, "Robertson and the Scottish Enlightenment."
28. *A Narrative of the Debate in the General Assembly of the Church of Scotland, May 25, 1779*, ed. [John Erskine] (Edinburgh: n.p., 1780), 49, 61. It has, however, also been argued that Robertson's approach to the issue of relief was at best "lukewarm," his part in the crisis was ambivalent, and there was a contradiction between his "own views and his public support for relief." Du Toit, "'A Species of False Religion': William Robertson, Catholic Relief and the Myth of Moderate Tolerance," *Innes Review* 52/2 (2001).'" But Robertson's obvious antipathy toward popery is one thing; his decision to put on it the rein of civil discipline is quite another.
29. Robertson, *Situation*, 25–31.
30. Ibid., 39.
31. Ibid., 44. The obvious objection that slavery did not prove to be incompatible with Christianity in his own times is dismissed by Robertson by claiming that "[t]he

genius and tendency of any religion are known by the operation of its vigorous, not of its declining age."
32. Ibid., 47.
33. The Mandevillean formula of "public vices—private benefits" and his extreme statement of the paradigm of unsocial sociability might have been universally rejected as a "system" by eighteenth-century theorists, but its implications were hard to escape.
34. William Robertson, *A View of the Progress of Society in Europe from the Subversion of the Roman Empire to the Beginning of the Sixteenth Century*, in *The History of the Reign of the Emperor Charles V* (London: Routledge/Thoemmes Press, 1996), I: 42–3.
35. Robertson, *Situation*, 51.
36. Robertson, *View of the Progress*, 62.
37. William Robertson, *The History of America* (London: Routledge/Thoemmes Press, 1996), II: 30.
38. See Hans Erich Bödeker, "Aufklärerische ethnologische Praxis: Johann Reinhold Forster und Georg Forster," in *Wissenschaft als kulturelle Praxis, 1750–1900*, ed. Hans-Erich Bödeker, Peter Hanns Reill, and Jürgen Schlumbohm (Göttingen: Vandenhoeck & Ruprecht, 1999), and the literature quoted there.
39. Robertson, *Situation*, 53.
40. Ibid., 54–5.
41. Cf. Keith Michael Baker, "Inventing the French Revolution," in *Inventing the French Revolution*, 203–23. See also Neithard Bulst, Jörg Fisch, and Reinhart Koselleck, "Revolution," in *Geschichtliche Grundbegriffe. Historisches Lexikon zur politisch-sozialen Sprache in Deutschland*, 8 vols., ed. Otto Brunner, Werner Conze, and Reinhart Koselleck (Stuttgart, 1972–1997), V: esp. 714–24 (1984).
42. Dugald Stewart, *Biographical Memoirs of Adam Smith, L.L.D., of William Robertson, D.D., and of Thomas Reid, D.D.* (Edinburgh: George Ramsay, 1811), 160.
43. *Dissertatio medica iauguralis de Quassia et lichene islandico...pro gradu doctoratus...in comitiis Universitati Glasquensis. Eruditorum examini subjicit Joh. Theod. Phil. Christ. Ebeling, Luneburgensis....Glasquae*, 1779.
44. William Robertson, *Der Zustand der Welt bey der Erscheinung Christi und sein Einfluß auf den Fortgang der Religion*, trans. Johann Philipp Ebeling (Hamburg: Herold, 1779).
45. Robertson-MacDonald papers, National Library of Scotland, MS. 3943. ff. 106–107. Ebeling then complained that the shrinking job market affected him as well, and requested Robertson to mobilize his aristocratic contacts to find him a position as a travelling tutor. Ebeling ended up pursuing a career as a physician in Germany, but he remained devoted to Scotland and its culture, and also translated the account of Thomas Pennant on his travels across that country. See further below, chapter 5, 315.
46. This theme is developed in greater detail in chapter 3, where one of Robertson's most consistently "stadialist" texts and its German reception is discussed. See below, 212 ff.; cf. chapter 4, 240 ff., and chapter 5, 299 ff.
47. Robertson, *Zustand der Welt*, 10, 42.
48. For instance, ibid., 16. To confuse matters even more, at one instance *Sitten* is also employed to render "custom"; ibid., 45.
49. Ibid., 11, 39.
50. Ibid., 11, 43.
51. On this concept, see Horst Stephan, *Realencyklopädie für protestantische Theologie und Kirche*, vol. XXI, ed. Albert Hauck (Leipzig: Hinrichs, 1908), 452–64; cf. David Sorkin, "Reclaiming Theology for the Enlightenment: The Case of Siegmund Jacob Baumgarten (1706–1757)," *Central European History* 36/4 (2003): 505. It must be added, however, that Wolffianism was found increasingly unsatisfactory by the Halle professors exactly because of its hostility to history. See below.

52. The standard monograph is Klaus Deppermann, *Der hallesche Pietismus und der preußische Staat unter Friedrich III./I.* (Göttingen: Vandenhoeck & Ruprecht, 1961). See further Carl Hinrichs, *Preußentum und Pietismus. Der Pietismus in Brandenburg-Preußen als religiössoziale Reformbewegung* (Göttingen: Vandenhoeck & Ruprecht 1971); Richard L. Gawthrop, *Pietism and the Making of Eighteenth Century Prussia* (Cambridge: Cambridge University Press, 1993).
53. David Sorkin, *The Religious Enlightenment: Protestants, Jews, and Catholics from London to Vienna* (Princeton: Princeton University Press, 2008)
54. Cf. below, endnote 55 ff. For modern commentary, see Martin Schloemann, *Siegmund Jacob Baumgarten. System und Geschichte in der Theologie des Überganges zum Neuprotestantismus* (Göttingen: Vandenhoeck & Ruprecht, 1974), ch. 3; Lutz Danneberg, "Siegmund Jakob Baumgartens biblische Hermeneutik," in *Unzeitgemäße Hermeneutik. Verstehen und Interpretation im Denken der Aufklärung*, ed. Axel Bühler (Frankfurt: Klostermann, 1994), 88–157.
55. This conviction became especially strong from the late 1730s. It has been emphasized that Baumgarten saw the task of the confrontation with and the refutation of "freethinking" increasingly as a historical one. See Schloemann, *Siegmund Jacob Baumgarten*, 109 ff. and 170.
56. Siegmund Jacob Baumgarten, *Auszug der Kirchengeschichte, von der Geburt Jesu an* (Halle: J. A. Bauer, 1743), "Vorrede," 8. Cf. Baumgarten, *Unterricht von Auslegung der heiligen Schrift* (Halle: J. A. Bauer, 1759), cited by Sorkin, "Reclaiming Theology," 511.
57. Siegmund Jacob Baumgarten, *A Supplement to the English Universal History, Lately published in London* (London: Dilly, 1760), vii, xiv; translation of the *Übersetzung der Allgemeinen Welthistorie die in England durch eine Gesellschaft der Gelehrten ausgefertiget worden...Genau durchgesehen und mit häufigen Anmerkungen vermeret von Siegmund Jacob Baumgarten* (Halle: Gebauer, 1744), "Vorrede," 7, 13.
58. Sorkin, "Reclaiming Theology," 512.
59. This was because God's universal benevolence led him to "accommodate" to contexts and contingencies when dealing with mankind and its frailties. For "accommodation" in providential histories throughout the Middle Ages and beyond, see Amos Funkenstein, *Theology and the Scientific Imagination from the Middle Ages to the Seventeenth Century* (Princeton: Princeton University Press, 1986), ch. 4., esp. 243–70.
60. For Baumgarten's departure from Wolff, especially in regard of the appreciation of history, see Schloemann, *Siegmund Jacob Baumgarten*, 129–56.
61. Baumgarten, *Supplement*, xxv–xxvi. Cf. *Übersetzung*, 19–20.
62. It has been suggested that with these insights Baumgarten "anticipated the efforts of such later eighteenth-century historians as Johann Martin Chladenius, Johann Christoph Gatterer and Jacob Wegelin." Sorkin, "Reclaiming Theology," 515 (fn. 58). Cf. Petr Hanns Reill, *The German Enlightenment and the Rise of Historicism* (Berkeley: Univ. of California Press, 1975), ch. 5; and above, chapter 1, 126 ff.
63. Baumgarten, *Supplement*, li. Cf. *Übersetzung*, 36.
64. Baumgarten, *Auszug der Kirchengeschichte*, 10–11.
65. Baumgarten, *Supplement*, xxxii. Cf. *Übersetzung*, 24.
66. Baumgarten, *Supplement*, xxxii–xxxiv. Cf. *Übersetzung*, 24–5.
67. Johann Salomo Semler, *Versuch den Gebrauch der Quellen in den Staats- und Kirchengeschichte der mittleren Zeiten zu erleichtern* (Halle, 1761), ed. Dirk Fleischer (Waltrop: Hartmut Spenner, 1996).
68. Johann Christoph Gatterer, "Nähere Nachricht voin der neuen Ausgabe der gleichzeitigen Schriftsteller über die teutsche Geschichte," *AhB* 8 (1768): 17.
69. Semler's importance in the development of eighteenth-century German historical thought has received a more extensive echo in modern scholarship than that of Baumgarten. Unlike the latter, Semler is discussed at some length in Reill, *The German Enlightenment*, 166 ff. Substantial monographic studies and articles also address his

contributions. See Gottfried Hornig, *Die Anfänge der historisch-kritischen Theologie. Johann Salomo Semlers Schriftverständnis und seine Stellung zu Luther* (Göttingen: Vandenhoeck & Ruprecht, 1961); Eric Wilhelm Carlsson, *Johann Salomo Semler, the German Enlightenment, and Protestant Theology's Historical Turn* (PhD diss., Univ. of Wisconsin, Madison, 2006); Dirk Fleischer, *Zwischen Tradition und Fortschritt: Der Strukturwandel der protestantischen Kinchengeschichtsschreibung im deutschsprachigen Diskurs der Aufklärung* (Waltrop: Hartmut Spenner, 2006), 517–768; Fleischer, "Geschichte und Sinn. Johann Salomo Semler als Geschichtstheoretiker," *Zeitschrift für Geschichtswissenschaft* 56/5 (2008): 397–417; Marianne Schröter, *Aufklärung durch Historisierung: Johann Salomo Semlers Hermeneutik des Christentums* (Berlin: De Gruyter, 2012).
70. Johann Salomo Semler, "Vorrede," in Johann Moritz Schwager, *Beytrag zur Geschichte der Intoleranz* (Leipzig, 1780), xiv, cited in Fleischer, "Geschichte und Sinn," 399.
71. Johann Salomo Semler, "Vorrede," in *Hugh Farmer's Briefe an D. Worthington über die Dämonischen in den Evangelien* (Halle, 1783), cited in Fleischer, "Geschichte und Sinn," 403.
72. Johann Samolo Semler, *Neue Versuche die Kirchenhistorie der ersten Jahrhunderte mehr aufzuklären* (Leipzig: Weygand, 1788), 3–4.
73. Johann Samolo Semler, "Vorrede," in Johann von Ferreras, *Algemeine Historie von Spanien mit den Zusätzen der französischen Uebersetzung nebst Fortsetzung bis auf gegenwärtige Zeit*, vol. VIII (Halle: Gebauer, 1757), 5.
74. Reill, *The German Enlightenment*, 166–7.
75. Johann Salomo Semler, "Vorrede," in *Sammlungen von Briefen und Aufsätzen über die Gaßnerischen und Schröpferischen Geisterbeschwörungen* (Halle: Gebauer, 1776), cited in Fleischer, "Geschichte und Sinn," 416.
76. For the deists as a much neglected radical undercurrent in the early German Enlightenment, see Israel, *Radical Enlightenment*, ch. 29, esp. 552–8; ch. 34. Also, Winfried Schröder, "Natürliche Religion und Religionskritik in der deutschen Frühaufklärung," in *Strukturen der deutschen Frühaufklärung 1680–1720*, ed. Hans Erich Bödeker (Göttingen: Vandenhoeck & Ruprecht, 2008), 146–64.
77. Lessing refused to be considered a theologian but acknowledged being "a lover of theology" (*Liebhaber der Theologie*). Gotthold Ephraim Lessing, *Axiomata*, in *Werke und Briefe in zwölf Bänden*, ed. Wilfried Barner et al., vol. IX: *Werke 1778–1780*, ed. Klaus Bohnen and Arno Schilson (Frankfurt: Deutscher Klassiker Verlag, 1993), 57. He did not publish anything specifically addressing theology before the 1770s, but there is evidence for his engagement with it throughout his career. See Arno Schilson, *Geschichte im Horizont der Vorsehung. G. E. Lessings Beitrag zu einer Theologie der Geschichte* (Mainz: Matthias-Grünewald-Verlag, 1974), ch. 1; Toshimasa Yasumata, *Lessing's Philosophy of Religion and the German Enlightenment: Lessing on Christianity and Reason* (Oxford: Oxford University Press, 2002), ch. 1.
78. Nicolai to Lessing, 24 April 1777. In *Werke und Briefe*, vol. XII: *Briefe von und an Lessing 1776–1781*, ed. Helmuth Kiesel et al. (Frankfurt: Deutscher Klassiker Verlag, 1994), 69. In his reply, Lessing rejected being either a theologian or a freethinker; *Briefe von und an Lessing 1776–1781*, 78.
79. For an excellent concise account of the contents of the *Fragments*, together with the thrust of Lessing's criticism and the responses, see Arno Schilson, "Lessing and Theology," in *A Companion to the Works of Gotthold Ephraim Lessing*, ed. Barbara Fischer and Thomas C. Fox (Woodbridge: Camden House, 2005), 163–70.
80. Johann Salomo Semler, *Beantwortung der Fragmente eines Ungenanten insbesondere vom Zweck Jesu und seiner Jünger*, ed. Dirk Fleischer (Waltrop: Hartmut Spenner, 2003 [Halle, 1779]). Semler's lengthy contribution focused overwhelmingly on Reimarus, and Lessing was chiefly criticized because of the foolish decision to publish the *Fragments*. It is interesting that just a decade earlier, Semler and Goeze (both

of them former students of Baumgarten) were engaged in a fierce debate on the source value of an early sixteenth-century Spanish edition of the New Testament, with implications for textual criticism as well as dogmatics. See Gottfried Hornig, "Orthodoxie und Textkritik. Die Kontroverse Zwischen Johann Melchior Goeze und Johann Salomo Semler," in *Verspätete Orthodoxie. Über D. Johann Melchior Goeze (1717–1786)*, ed. Heimo Reinitzer and Walter Sparn (Wiesbaden: Harrassowitz, 1989), 159–77.

81. Lessing to Elise Reimarus, 6 September 1778, *Briefe 1776–1781*, 193.
82. Gotthold Ephraim Lessing, *4. Anti-Goeze*, in *Werke 1778–1780*, 196.
83. Gotthold Ephraim Lessing, *Über den Beweis des Geistes und der Kraft*, in *Werke und Briefe*, vol. VIII: *Werke 1774–1778*, ed. Arno Schilson (Frankfurt: Deutscher Klassiker Verlag, 1989), 441. Lessing wrote this short polemical essay in response to Johann Daniel Schumann, *Über die Evidenz der Beweise für die Wahrheit der christlichen Religion* [On the Evidence of the Proofs for the Truth of the Christian Religion, 1777]. In fact, in regard to the imperfect demonstrability of historical truths the opinion of the two authors was quite similar. On the differences of Lessing and Goeze about the relevance of history to Christian faith, see Arno Schilson, "Offenbarung und Geschichte bei J. M. Goeze und G. E. Lessing. Hinweise zu einer offenbarungstheologischen Neuorientierung," in *Verspätete Orthodoxie*, ed. Reinitzer and Sparn, 87–120.
84. For a detailed discussion of these views and their genealogy from Leibniz and Spinoza, see Yasukata, *Lessing's Philosophy of Religion*, ch. 4; Martin Bollacher, *Lessing: Vernunft und Geschichte. Untersuchungen zum Problem religiöser Aufklärung in der Spätschriften* (Tübingen: Niemeyer, 1978), 109–29.
85. Lessing, *Über den Beweis*, 444.
86. Gotthold Ephraim Lessing, *Die Erziehung des Menschengeschlechts*, §8, in *Werke und Briefe*, vol. X: *Werke 1778–1781*, ed. Arno Schilson and Axel Schmitt (Frankfurt: Deutscher Klassiker Verlag, 2001), 76.
87. Ibid., § 27. 82.
88. Ibid., § 4. 75.
89. Gotthold Ephraim Lessing, *Axiomata*, in *Werke 1778–1780*, 82.
90. Lessing, *Erziehung des Menschengeschlechts*, §§ 36, 37. 84.
91. Gotthold Ephraim Lessing, *Gegensätze des Herausgebers*, pt. 1, in *Werke und Briefe*, vol. VIII: *Werke 1774–1778*, ed. Arno Schilson (Frankfurt: Deutscher Klassiker Verlag, 1989), 319.
92. Lessing, *Erziehung des Menschengeschlechts*, § 54. 89.
93. Ibid., § 55. 90.
94. Ibid., § 71. 92.
95. Ibid., §§ 13, 63, 70–72. 77, 90, 92.
96. Ibid., § 85. 96.
97. For an in-depth exploration, see Wilm Peters, *Lessings Standort: Sinndeutung der Geschichte als Kern seines Denkens* (Heidelberg: Stiehm, 1972).
98. Semler, *Beantwortung*, "Vorrede," b1.
99. Siegmund Jacob Baumgarten, *Untersuchung Theologischer Streitigkeiten. Mit einigen Anmerkungen, Vorrede und fortgesetzten Geschichte der christlichen Glaubenslehre*, 3 vols., ed. Johann Salomo Semler (Halle: Gebauer, 1762–1764), I: 16, II: 7 (Semler's prefaces to both volumes).
100. Semler, *Beantwortung*, 23.
101. He despised the "new-fangled" theology even more than orthodoxy: its representatives seemed to him "far too weightless as theologians, and not nearly weighty enough as philosophers," who may become more tyrannical than the orthodox had ever been. Letter to Karl Lessing, 8 April 1773. *Werke und Briefe XI/2: Briefe von und an Lessing 1770–1776*, ed. Helmuth Kiesel et al. (Frankfurt: Deutscher Klassiker Verlag, 1988), 540.

102. Baumgarten, *Untersuchung*, III: 13 (Semler's preface).
103. *Werke 1774–1784*, 312–13.
104. Lessing, *Erziehung des Menschengeschlechts*, §§ 86–91, 97–8.
105. The translation, by Johann Christian Schmidt, was published in Frankfurt in 1751, and Lessing's review appeared in the same year in the *Berlinische Privilegierte Zeitung*. *Werke und Briefe*, vol. II: *Werke 1751–1753*, ed. Jürgen Stenzel (Frankfurt: Deutscher Klassiker Verlag, 1998), 263. There are further references to Warburton in the fourth fragment of Reimarus (see *Werke 1774–1778*, 247 f.) and in the *Erziehung*, § 24 (see *Werke 1778–1781*, 81.)
106. Lessing to Heyne, 23 October 1778, *Briefe 1776–1780*, 203.
107. The possibility of Lessing's reliance on Ferguson for the "historical and evolutionary dimension" of his thought is discussed at length in Oz-Salzberger, *Translating the Enlightenment*, ch. 7, concluding that the German scholar "neither accepted nor attacked Ferguson's model of civilization" and that the "absence of a political dimension" distances the *Erziehung* from Ferguson's *Essay*.
108. Jonathan Sheehan, *The Enlightenment Bible. Translation, Scholarship, Culture* (Princeton: Princeton University Press, 2005); Michael C. Legaspi, *The Death of Scripture and the Rise of Biblical Studies* (Oxford: Oxford University Press, 2010).
109. Legaspi, *The Death of Scripture*, viii, x.
110. Ibid., 48–9.
111. Sheehan, *The Enlightenment Bible*, 185–6.
112. Legaspi, *The Death of Scripture*, 50.
113. Michael Carhart, *The Science of Culture in Enlightenment Germany* (Cambridge: Harvard University Press, 2007), *passim*. Carhart's "Göttingen School" includes many greater and lesser figures, not all of them necessarily associated with the Georgia Augusta: principally, besides Michaelis, his disciple Johann Gottfried Eichhorn; the legal scholar Johann Jakob Moser; another philologist, Christian Gottlob Heyne; and the eccentric polymath Christoph Meiners. Some of them will reappear in the pages below.
114. Johann David Michaelis, *Einleitung in die göttlichen Schriften des Neuen Testaments*, 2 vols. (Göttingen: Vandenhoeck, 1750). By 1788, the fourth edition came out; the book was also popular in Britain as *An Introduction to the New Testament, by John David Michaelis, late Professor in the University of Göttingen. Translated from the fourth edition of the German, by Herbert Marsh, D.D.*, 6 vols. (Cambridge, 1793–1802).
115. Johann David Michaelis, *Einleitung in die göttliche Schriften des Neuen Bundes. Dritte und vermehrte Ausgabe* (Göttingen: Vandenhoeck, 1777), I: 73. A part of this passage is copied, and the argument is reproduced in order to support Michaelis' argument against Reimarus, in Johann David Michaelis, *Erklärung der Begräbnis und Auferstehungsssgeschichte Christi nach der vier Evangelisten. Mit Rücksicht auf die in den Fragmenten gemachten Einwürfe und deren Beantwortung* (Halle: Waisenhaus, 1783), xxxx.
116. Michaelis, *Erklärung*, xvii–xxi.
117. Michaelis, *Einleitung*, I: 24–5, 48–9.
118. Ibid., 115.
119. Ibid., 117.
120. Cf. Legaspi, *The Death of Scripture*, 50, 55.

3 A Different *View of the Progress of Society in Europe*

1. Karen O'Brien, "Between Enlightenment and Stadial History: William Robertson on the History of Europe," *British Journal for Eighteenth-Century Studies* 16/1 (1993): 53–64.

2. "Descriptive history is the detail of coexistent circumstances and qualities. Narrative history is the detail of successive events." Adam Ferguson, *Institutes of Moral Philosophy* (Edinburgh: Kincaid and Bell, 1769), 61. Cf. O'Brien, "Between Enlightenment and Stadial History," 54.
3. William Robertson, *The History of the Reign of the Emperor Charles V. With a View of the progress of society in Europe, from the subversion of the Roman Empire to the beginning of the sixteenth century* (Routledge/Thoemmes Press: London, 1996), I: 13–14.
4. Cf. Quentin Skinner, "Retrospect: Studying Rhetoric and Conceptual Change," in *Visions of Politics*, vol. I: *Regarding Method* (Cambridge: Cambridge University Press, 2002), 180. Skinner distinguishes between three kinds of meaning: (1) that of the words or sentences in a text, (2) what the text means to "me," that is, the reader, and (3) what a writer means by what is said in a text. For an application of these distinctions to translation processes, see Kontler, "Translation and Comparison II: A Methodological Inquiry into Reception in the History of Ideas," *Contributions to the History of Concepts* 4/1 (2008); 31 ff.
5. For a particularly perceptive analysis of how politeness, progress, and patriotism were part and parcel of one and the same program in Robertson's immediate environment, that of the "moderate literati" in Edinburgh, see Richard B. Sher, *Church and University in the Scottish Enlightenment: The Moderate Literati of Edinburgh* (Princeton: Princeton University Press, 1985).
6. Robertson, *History of Charles V*, I: 1, 12.
7. Ibid., I: 21, 23, 24.
8. Ibid., I: 5, 14.
9. Ibid., I: 253.
10. Ibid., I: 17.
11. Ibid., I: 31.
12. In Smith's account, the magnetism of luxury articles offered at the market by greedy merchants tamed the lust for domination of noblemen into mere vanity and drained their wealth; and thus, as a result of two selfish social actors who in fact neglected the public good, urban liberties, the core privileges of later safety under the law, arose in the high Middle Ages. Adam Smith, *An Inquiry into the Nature and Causes of the Wealth of Nations*, ed. Roy H. Campbell and Andrew S. Skinner (Indianapolis: Liberty Classics, 1981), I: 422; cf. Adam Smith, *Lectures on Jurisprudence*, ed. R. L. Meek, D. D. Raphael, and P. G. Stein (Oxford: Clarendon Press, 1978), 420. Cf. also endnote 34 in chapter 1 for charges on Robertson's unacknowledged reliance on Smith in the *View of the Progress of Society*.
13. Robertson, *History of Charles V*, I: 42–3.
14. Ibid., I: 46–51.
15. See for instance ibid., I: 91–8, 162, 399–408.
16. Ibid., I: 25. See the contrast drawn by David J. Womersley between *The History of Charles V* and Robertson's other historical works on account of his strict adherence to the principle of causality in it, "The Historical Writings of William Robertson," esp. 503–4.
17. O'Brien, "Between Enlightenment and Stadial History," 57–8.
18. On Nicolay's life, career, and European contacts, see Edmund Heier, *L. H. Nicolay (1737–1820) and His Contemporaries* (The Hague: Martinus Nijhoff, 1965).
19. Relations between the imperial mother and son tended to be loveless and tense, even hostile, but the early 1770s were a period of temporary reconciliation.
20. *Entwurf des politischen Zustandes in Europa, vom Verfall der römischen Macht an bis auf das sechzehnte Jahrhundert. Aus Robertsons Einleitung in die Geschichte Karls des Fünften gezogen*, in *Vermischte Gedichte und prosaische Schriften von Herrn Ludwig Heinrich von Nicolay* (Berlin and Stettin: Friedrich Nicolai, 1793), III: 98. Nicolay's

rendering of the *View of the Progress of Society*, was first published in his *Verse und Prose* (Basel: Schweighäuser, 1773), II: 5–155.
21. *Entwurf des politischen Zustandes in Europa*, 98.
22. *Allgemeine deutsche Bibliothek* 24/1 (1775): 108.
23. *Neue allgemeine deutsche Bibliothek* 7/1 (1793): 293.
24. The following biographical sketches of Mittelstedt and Remer are mainly based on Johann Georg Meusel, *Lexikon der vom Jahr 1750 bis 1800 verstorbenen teutschen Schriftsteller*, 15 vols. (Leipzig, 1802–1816, repr. Hildesheim: Olms, 1967), IX: 190–2; Georg Christoph Hamberger and Johann Georg Meusel, *Das gelehrte Teutschland oder Lexikon der jetzt lebenden teutschen Schriftsteller*, 23 vols. (Lemgo, 1796–1834, repr. Hildesheim: Olms, 1965), VI: 305–8; *Allgemeine Deutsche Biographie*, vol. XXVIII (Leipzig, 1889), 198–200.
25. To be considered later in chapter 4.
26. See the October 3, 1757, entry in *Die Matrikel der Universität Helmstedt 1685–1810*, ed. Herbert Mundhenke (Hildesheim: Lax, 1979), 187; and the October 17, 1759 entry in *Die Matrikel der Georg-August Universität zu Göttingen*, ed. Götz von Selle (Hildesheim: Lax, 1937), I: 132.
27. On Pütter in general, see Wilhelm Ebel, *Der göttinger Professor Johann Stephan Pütter aus Iserlohn* (Göttingen: Vandenhoeck & Ruprecht, 1975); Christoph Link, "Johann Stephan Pütter (1725–1807). Staatsrecht am Ende des alten Reiches," in *Rechtswissenschaft in Göttingen. Göttinger Juristen aus 250 Jahren*, ed. Fritz Loos (Göttingen: Vandenhoeck & Ruprecht, 1987), 75–99.
28. See the "Preface" by Josiah Dornford (a British disciple of Pütter's) in *An Historical Development of the Present Political Constitution of the Germanic Empire*, vol. I (London: Payne and Son, 1790). For more details, see below, chapter 4, 259.
29. *Handbuch der Geschichte neurerer Zeiten, von der grossen Völkerwanderung bis zum Hubertusburgischen Frieden* (1771); *Ausführliches Handbuch der ältern allgemeinen Geschichte; nebst einer Vorstellung der politischen, geistlichen, gelehrten und bürgerlichen Verfassung der Nationen in jedem Zeitpunkte* (1775); *Handbuch der allgemeinen Geschichte I-III* (1783–1784); *Lehrbuch der Staatskunde der vornehmsten europäischen Staaten* (1785); *Tabellarische Uebersicht der wichtigsten statistischen Veränderungen in der vornehmsten Europäischen Staaten* (1786–1794).
30. Julius August Remer, *Handbuch der Geschichte neurerer Zeiten*, "Vorrede." Shortly later in the text, on p. 5, one finds the first of several word-by-word quotes from Robertson, referring to the rise of "new forms of government, new laws, new manners, new dresses, new languages," etc., cited above (endnote 8).
31. See Horst Dippel, *Germany and the American Revolution, 1770–1800* (Chapel Hill: University of North Carolina Press, 1977), 57–8.
32. *Geschichte des Ursprungs, des Fortgangs und der Beendigung des Amerikanischen Krieges*, 2 vols. (1774–1796).
33. J. Westphalen to Robertson, November 12, 1780. National Library of Scotland, Robertson-MacDonald papers, MS. 3943. ff. 128–129. Remer's local reputation is also clear from a published obituary, J. P. Bruns, "Etwas von dem Leben und den Verdiensten des de 26sten August 1803 zu Helmstedt verstorbenen Professors und Hofraths Julius August Remer," *Braunschweigisches Magazin* 37 (September 10, 1803).
34. Niedersachsisches Staatsarchiv in Wolfenbüttel, 37 Alt 3643. The will is dated August 6, 1800, and was opened on August 27, 1803.
35. *Julius August Remers weil. Herzogl. Braunschw. Lüneb. Hofraths und Professors der Geschichte und Statistik auf der Julius Karls Universität zu Helmstedt hinterlassene Büchersammlung, welche den 1sten November 1804 und folgende Tage zu Helmstedt öffentlich verkauft warden soll* (Braunschweig, 1804). The titles in the catalogue are arranged into 18 classes according to subject matter. As it might be expected,

nearly half of the books in the collection (c. 3,500 titles) were about the various branches of history, politics, and related subjects, with most of the important eighteenth-century German, British, and French authors being represented. Literature and literary history, travelogues, theology, geography, philosophy, jurisprudence, art, and art history followed (roughly in this order), while the few books on the natural sciences which Remer possessed are found dispersed in several of these subdivisions.

36. Johann Christoph Gatterer "von der Kunst zu übersetzen, besonders in Absicht auf historische Schriften," *AhB* 1/2 (1767): 11–12.
37. See Bernhard Fabian, "English Books and their Eighteenth Century German Readers," in *The Widening Circle: Essays on the Circulation of Literature in Eighteenth Century Europe*, ed. Paul Korshin (Philadelphia: University of Pennsylvania Press, 1976), 117–96; and especially Kenneth E. Carpenter, *Dialogue in Political Economy: Translations from and into German in the Eighteenth Century* (Boston: Kress Library Publications, 1977), ch. 1.
38. "I hope the readers will not consider it as a mark of arrogance or cavil that in the attached notes I have endeavored to improve the accuracy of this excellent book." Remer, "Vorrede," in *Herrn Dr. Wilhelm Robertsons Geschichte der Regierung Kaiser Carls des Fünften. Nebst einem Abrisse des Wachstums und Fortgangs des gesellschaftlichen Leben in Europa bis auf den Anfang des sechszehnten Jahrhundert*, 3 vols., trans. Theodor Christoph Mittelstedt, notes by Julius August Remer, 2nd ed. (Braunschweig: Waisenhaus, 1778–1779), I: iii. "In certain subjects Robertson follows completely false principles, others he touches very superficially, and fully neglects many highly important ones, although they significantly contributed to the shaping of the character and mentality of the Middle Ages." Therefore the only remedy is a full revision of the text. Remer, "Vorrede," in *Herrn Dr Wilhelm Robertsons Geschichte der Regirerung des Kaiser Carls des Fünften. Nebst einem Abrisse des Wachstums und Fortgangs des gesellschaftlichen Lebens in Europa bis auf den Anfang des 16. Jhs.*, trans. and rev. by Julius August Remer, 5 vols. (Vienna: Härter, 1819, based on the edition at Braunschweig: Schulbuchhandlung/Waisenhaus, 1792–1796), I: v.
39. Isaiah Berlin, "Hume and the Sources of German Anti-Rationalism," in *Against the Current: Essays in the History of Ideas* (London: Hogarth Press, 1979), 162–87; Oz-Salzberger, *Translating the Enlightenment*, ch. 6.
40. Robertson, *History of Charles V*, I: 5; *Geschichte Carls des Fünften* (1778), I: 7. Cf. *History of Charles V*, I: 42 and *Geschichte Carls des Fünften* (1778), 53, where the "spirit of industry" is rendered as *Geist der Emsigkeit* (a close synonym of *Fleiß*, also lacking the comprehensiveness implied by "industry").
41. Robertson, *History of Charles V*, I: 21; *Geschichte Carls des Fünften* (1778), I: 30. See also p. 42 of the former and p. 53 of the latter.
42. See, e.g., Maurice M. Goldsmith, "Liberty, Luxury and the Pursuit of Happiness," in *The Languages of Political Theory*, ed. Pagden, 225–51; John Dwyer, *Virtuous Discourse: Sensibility and Community in Late Eighteenth-Century Scotland* (Edinburgh: John Donald, 1987), esp. ch. 2; Istvan Hont, "The Early Enlightenment Debate on Commerce and Luxury," in *The Cambridge History of Eighteenth-Century Political Thought*, ed. Mark Goldie and Robert Wokler (Cambridge: Cambridge University Press., 2008), 379–418.
43. Robertson, *Geschichte Carls des Fünften* (1778), I: 53 ff.
44. A similar point is made about the German translation of the same term in the case of Ferguson by Oz-Salzberger, *Translating the Enlightenment*, 151.
45. Adam Ferguson, *An Essay on the History of Civil Society*, ed. Fania Oz-Salzberger (Cambridge: Cambridge University Press, 1995), 195.
46. Robertson, *History of Charles V*, I: 36, 42–3.

47. From the extensive literature on the early modern German theory and concept of *Polizey*, I have used Maier, *Die ältere deutsche Staats- und Verwaltungslehre*, pt. 3; Jutta Brückner, *Staatswissenschaften, Kameralismus und Naturrecht. Ein Beitrag zur Geschichte der politischen Wissenschaft im Deutschland des späten 17. und frühen 18. Jahrhunderts* (Munich: C. H. Beck, 1976); Franz-Ludwig Knemeyer, "Polizei," in *Geschichtliche Grundbegriffe*, ed. Brunner, Conze, and Koselleck, IV: 875–98; Michael Stolleis, *Geschichte des öffentlichen Rechts in Deutschland. Erster Band: Reichspublizistik und Policeywissenschaft 1600–1800* (Munich: C. H. Beck, 1988), ch. 8.
48. Volker Sellin, "Politik," in *Geschichtliche Grundbegriffe*, ed. Brunner, Conze, and Koselleck (1978), IV: esp. 814–30; Friedeburg and Seidler, "The Holy Roman Empire of the German Nation," 134–66.
49. Cf. the passages quoted above from Robertson, *History of Charles V*, I: 36–43 with *Geschichte Carls des Fünften* (1778), I: 45–54.
50. Robertson, *Geschichte Carls des Fünften* (1778), I: 9, 23.
51. Ibid., I: 290.
52. Robertson, *History of Charles V*, I. 253. Cf. above, n. 9.
53. Robertson, *Geschichte Carls des Fünften* (1778), I: 56–7, 84, 90, 243.
54. Ibid., I: 243, 247, 297, 483; 247, 354, 417.
55. Dugald Stewart, *Biographical Memoirs of Adam Smith, L.L.D., of William Robertson, D.D, and of Thomas Reid, D.D.* (Edinburgh: George Ramsay, 1811), 173.
56. Robertson, *Geschichte Carls des Fünften* (1792/1819), I: vii.
57. [Albrecht von Haller], review of William Robertson's *History of Charles V*, GAgS 18 (1770): I: 571.
58. [Ludwig Timotheus Spittler], review of Julius August Remer's *Abriß des gesellschaftlichen Lebens in Europa…Nach dem ertsen Theile von Robertsons Leben Carl V. bearbeitet*, GAgS 41/2 (1793): 787–8.
59. Cf. László Kontler, "Translation and Comparison: Early-Modern and Current Perspectives," *Contributions to the History of Concepts* 3/1 (2007): 74, and the literature cited there.
60. Robertson, *History of Charles V*, I: 2; *Geschichte Carls des Fünften* (1778), I: 4; *Geschichte Carls des Fünften* (1792/1819), 3, 4.
61. Moses Mendelssohn, "Über die Frage: was heißt aufklären?," [*Berlinische Monatsschrift*, 1784], in *Was ist Aufklärung? Thesen und Definitionen*, ed. Ehrhard Bahr (Stuttgart: Reclam, 1974), 4.
62. Rudolf Vierhaus, "Bildung," in *Geschichtliche Grundbegriffe*, ed. Brunner, Conze, and Koselleck, I: 508–51, for Herder specifically 515–17.
63. Robertson, *History of Charles V*, I: 21; *Geschichte Carls des Fünften* (1792/1819), I: 288.
64. First, in the passage about the introduction of "new forms of government, new laws, new manners," etc., as a result of the Germanic invasions throughout Europe. Cf. *History of Charles V*, I: 12; and *Geschichte Carls des Fünften* (1792/1819), I: 27–8.
65. Cf. *Geschichte Carls des Fünften* (1792/1819), I: 64 and II: 4, with *History of Charles V*, I: 17, 24.
66. See above, 129.
67. *Geschichte Carls des Fünften* (1792/1819), I: 316.
68. Ibid., II: 318.
69. Ibid., II: 75–119, 170–8.
70. Ibid., II: 21–178.
71. Ibid., II: 179.
72. Cf. ibid., II: 253, where "welfare and freedom" are mentioned as parallel causes whose effect is the improvement of manners.
73. Ibid., II: 246.

74. Ibid., II: 247–51. Cf. Robertson, *History of Charles V*, I: 329.
75. Ibid., I: 333.
76. See, e.g., *Geschichte Carls des Fünften* (1792/1819), II: 251 ff., 337.
77. Edmund Burke, *Reflections on the Revolution in France*, in *The Writings and Speeches of Edmund Burke*, vol. VIII: *The French Revolution 1790–1794*, ed. Leslie Mitchell (Oxford: Clarendon Press, 1989), 130.
78. See J. G. A. Pocock, "The Political Economy of Burke's Analysis of the French Revolution," *The Historical Journal* 25 (1982): 331–49, repr. in Pocock, *Virtue, Commerce, and History: Essays on Political Thought and History, Chiefly in the Eighteenth Century* (Cambridge: Cambridge University Press, 1985), 198–9.
79. Julius August Remer, ed., *Amerikanisches Archiv* (Braunschweig: Waisenhaus, 1777–1778) I: 6–7.
80. Remer's note in Charles Stedman, *Geschichte des Ursprungs, des Fortgangs und der Beendigung des Amerikanischen Krieges*, 2 vols., trans. Julius August Remer (Berlin: Voß, 1795), I: 117. Robertson actually thought in a similar fashion upon the publication of the *Reflections*, referring to Burke's "ravings" (to change his mind about the French Revolution soon afterwards). See Richard B. Sher, "1688 and 1788: William Robertson on Revolution in Britain and France," in *Culture and Revolution*, ed. Paul Dukes and John Dunkley (London and New York: Pinter Publishers, 1990), 103. As for Remer's own views on the French Revolution, the only source to assess them is a series of tantalizingly incomplete remarks in his *Geschichte der französischen Constitutionen* (in which the revolutionary constitutions are not discussed). These show him to have been by and large in agreement with Burke's Hanoverian followers, Ernst Brandes and August Wilhelm Rehberg, without referring to either of them.
81. See Christoph Meiners, *Geschichte der Ungleichheit der Stände unter den vornehmsten Europäischen Staaten*, vol. II (Hannover: Helwing, 1792), chs. 5 and 7. Meiners' preoccupation with race as a decisive factor in history had been well known since the publication of his *Grundriß der Geschichte der Menschheit* (Lemgo: Meyer, 1785). On Meiners, see Friedrich Lotter, "Christoph Meiners und die Lehre von der unterschiedlichen Wertigkeit der Menschenrassen," in *Geschichtswissenschaft in Göttingen*, ed. Hartmut Boockmann and Hermann Wellenreuther (Göttingen: Vandenhoeck & Ruprecht, 1987), 30–75.
82. Christoph Meiners, *Geschichte des weiblichen Geschlechts*, vol. I (Hannover: Helwing, 1788), ch. 6.
83. Gilbert Stuart, *A View of Society in Europe in its Progress from Rudeness to Refinement: Or, Inquiries Concerning the History of Law, Government, and Manners* [1778] (Basel: Tourneisen, 1797), 59.
84. Remer had Christoph Friedrich Blankenburg's 1779 German translation of the *View of Society* by Stuart. For reference to this book and the ones by Meiners and Herder, see *Remers hinterlassene Büchersammlung*, 8, 56, 59, 79, 93.

4 Scottish Histories and German Identities

1. Nicholas Phillipson, "Providence and Progress: An Introduction to the Historical Thought of William Robertson," in *Robertson and the Expansion of Empire*, ed. Stuart J. Brown; cf. chapter 2 above.
2. This use of "crisis," perhaps introduced by Jakob Burckhardt in ch. 4 of the *Reflections on History*, was applied to the birth pangs giving rise to the Enlightenment in Paul Hazard, *La crise de la conscience européenne*, in 1935. This book in turn was to some extent responsible for the fashionableness of the term in the 1950s and thereafter among historians studying the "general crisis" of the seventeenth century which marked the advent of capitalism.

3. Cf. Colin Kidd, *Subverting Scotland's Past: Scottish Whig Historians and the Creation of an Anglo-British Identity, 1689–c. 1830* (Cambridge: Cambridge University Press, 1993), 182.
4. On Buchanan's relevant views, see Hugh Trevor-Roper, "George Buchanan and the Ancient Scottish Constitution," *English Historical Review*, supp. 3 (1966); Roger A. Mason, "Scotching the Brut: Politics, History and National Myth in Sixteenth-Century Britain," in *Scotland and England 1286–1815*, ed. Roger A. Mason (Edinburgh: Edinburgh University Press, 1987), 60–84.
5. Andrew Fletcher, "Speeches by a Member of the Parliament which Began at Edinburgh on the 6th of May, 1703," in Andrew Fletcher, *Political Works*, ed. John Robertson (Cambridge: Cambridge University Press, 1997), 135.
6. From a 1735 article by the jurist James Erskine of Grange, quoted in Colin Kidd, "The Ideological Significance of Robertson's *History of Scotland*," in *Robertson and the Expansion of Empire*, ed. Brown, 126–7.
7. By the Jacobite antiquary Thomas Innes. Ibid.
8. *Edinburgh Review* (1755–1756), ii. For the general context, see Nicholas Phillipson, "Scottish Public Opinion and the Union in the Age of Association," in *Scotland in the Age of Improvement*, ed. Nicholas Phillipson and Rosalind Mitchison (Edinburgh: Edinburgh University Press, 1970), 125–47.
9. The expression of Karen O'Brien, *Narratives of Enlightenment: Cosmopolitan History from Voltaire to Gibbon* (Cambridge: Cambridge University Press, 1997), 108.
10. William Robertson, *The History of Scotland during the Reigns of Queen Mary and of King James VI, till His Accession to the Crown of England*, 2 vols. (London: Routledge/Thoemmes Press, 1996), I: 25.
11. Ibid., I: 82–83.
12. Ibid., II: 300.
13. Ibid., II: 302.
14. Alex du Toit, "Cosmopolitanism, Despotism and Patriotic Resistance: William Robertson on the Spanish Revolts against Charles V," *Bulletin of Spanish Studies* 86/1 (2009): 19–43.
15. Robertson, *History of Scotland*, II: 299.
16. Ibid., I: 7.
17. Ibid., II: 305.
18. J. G. A. Pocock, *Barbarism and Religion*, vol. II: *Narratives of Civil Government* (Cambridge: Cambridge University Press, 1999–2011), 263.
19. O'Brien, *Narratives of Enlightenment*, 95.
20. Cf. Neal Hargraves, "National History and 'Philosophical' History: Character and Narrative in William Robertson's *History of Scotland*," *History of European Ideas* 26 (2000): 22.
21. See O'Brien, *Narratives of Enlightenment*, 114 ff.
22. Dugald Stewart makes the point that such is Robertson's "skillful contrast of light and shade, aided by the irresistible charm of his narration, that the story of the beautiful and unfortunate Queen, as related by him, excites on the whole a deeper interest in her fortunes, and a more lively sympathy with her fate, than have been produced by all the attempts to canonize her memory, whether inspired by the sympathetic zeal of the Romish church, or by the enthusiasm of Scottish chivalry." Stewart, *Biographical Memoirs of Adam Smith, L.L.D., of William Robertson, D.D, and of Thomas Reid, D.D.* (Edinburgh: George Ramsay, 1811), 181.
23. Ibid., 118–19.
24. As Robertson wrote on account of Mary's final tribulations: "A woman, young and beautiful, and in distress, is naturally the object of compassion. The comparison of their present misery with the former splendour, usually softens us in favour of illustrious sufferers" – irrespective of our moral or political judgment on the

sufferer's character. "But the people," he adds, "beheld the deplorable situation of their sovereign with insensibility." *History of Scotland*, I: 445–6. As a matter of fact, the question why tragedy pleases was a hotly debated one in Edinburgh at the time of the writing of Robertson's *History of Scotland*, with virtually all of the literati contributing something on it. For the broader context see Richard B. Sher, *Church and University in the Scottish Enlightenment: The Moderate Literati of Edinburgh* (Princeton: Princeton University Press, 1985), 65–92.

25. Among many references in Anthony Earl of Shaftesbury, *Characteristics of Men, Manners, Opinions, Times, etc.* [1900], ed. John M. Robertson (Bristol: Thoemmes Press, 1997), see II: 137; Edmund Burke, *A Philosophical Enquiry into the Origin of our Ideas of the Sublime and the Beautiful*, ed. James T. Boulton (Oxford: Blackwell, 1987), 38–65; Edmund Burke, *Reflections on the Revolution in France*, in *The Writings and Speeches of Edmund Burke*, 127 ff. I have discussed this in more detail in László Kontler, "Beauty or Beast or Monstrous Regiments? Robertson and Burke on Women and the Public Scene," *Modern Intellectual History* 1/3 (2004): 305–30.
26. Robertson, *History of Scotland*, I: 274–5.
27. Ibid., I: 283, 292.
28. Ibid., I: 90.
29. Cf. Hargraves, "National History and 'Philosophical History,'" 25–6.
30. Cf. Hargraves, "Resentment and History," 20.
31. Cf. O'Brien, *Narratives of Enlightenment*, 130 ff.
32. Robertson, *History of Charles V*, I: 146–7.
33. Ibid., IV: 302, 304–5.
34. Ibid., I: 97.
35. Richard Tuck, *Philosophy and Government, 1572–1651* (Cambridge: Cambridge University Press, 1993), chs. 5 and 7.
36. Edward Hundert, *The Enlightenment's 'Fable': Bernard Mandeville and the Discovery of Society* (Cambridge: Cambridge University Press, 1994), esp. ch. 4; Hundert, "Introduction," in Mandeville, *The Fable of the Bees and Other Writings*, ed. E. J. Hundert (Indianapolis: Hackett, 1997), esp. xx–xxxii.
37. Neal Hargraves, "The 'Progress of Ambition': Character, Narrative, and Philosophy in the Works of William Robertson," *Journal of the History of Ideas* 63 (2002): 270.
38. Robertson, *History of Charles V*, II: 220–1.
39. Ibid., 301.
40. Ibid., IV: 286, 289. Cf. Hargraves, "The 'Progress of Ambition,'" 275.
41. Robertson, *History of Charles V*, III: 311–12.
42. Ibid., III: 71–2, 74.
43. Ibid., IV: 11–13.
44. Ibid., III: 352 ff.; IV: 10–11.
45. Ibid., IV: 121.
46. Cf. Pocock, *Barbarism and Religion*, II: 294.
47. Niedersächsische Staats- und Universitätsbibliothek, Göttingen. Bibliotheksarchiv, Ausleiheregister A, Mich. 1769. f. 37. The borrower was, on October 14, 1769, the historian Christoph Gatterer. Borrowal registers of the library of the Georgia Augusta are extant from 1769 onward; from that time till the end of Robertson's life (1793), the *History of Charles V* was the most frequently borrowed work of his—with 45 records, vs. the *History of Scotland* with 19 (which is respectable, in comparison with Hume's *History of England*, scoring 15 during the same period), the *History of America* with 20, and the *Historical Disquisition* with 5 records. To be sure, these latter two titles had a shorter time to "compete with" the *History of Charles V*. The review published in the *GAgS*, no. 65 (May 31, 1770), was written by the Swiss polymath Albrecht von Haller, who had also written the review of the *History of Scotland* ten years earlier (*GAgS*, no. 107 [September 6, 1760]).

48. Abele (1753–1805) graduated with a degree in law from Göttingen in 1778. He soon moved to Kempten as a syndic of the town, also running a journal on "recent world events, by a citizen of the world" (*Neueste Weltbegebenheiten, von einem Weltbürger*), publishing works of his own on various aspects of German public law, and contributing to an edition of Raynal's *Histoire des deux Indes* (1784–1788).
49. See Robertson, *Geschichte Carls des Fünften* (1778–1779), II: "Vorrede"; cf. *Dr. Wilhelm Robertsons, Vorstehers der Universität Edinburg, und königlichen Großbritannischen Geschichtsschreibers, Geschichte der Regierung Kaiser Carls des V*, trans. Johann Martin von Abele, notes Julius August Remer et al. (Kempten, 1781–1783), I: "Vorrede."
50. Cf. above, 89–91.
51. Each of the first three options appears, for instance, in the same passage in both *Herrn William Robertsons Geschichte von Schottland unter den Regierungen der Königinn Maria, und des Königes Jacobs VI. bis auf dessen Erhebung auf den englischen Thron*, trans. Theodor Christoph Mittelstedt (Braunschweig: Meyer; Leipzig: Breitkopf, 1762), I: 135; and *Wilhelm Robertsons Geschichte von Schottland unter den Regierungen der Königinn Maria und des Königs Jacobs VI. bis auf die Zeit, da der Letztere den englischen Thron bestieg*, trans. Georg Friedrich Seiler (Leipzig and Ulm: Gaum, 1762), 69. Cf. Robertson, *History of Scotland*, I: 134; for manners as *Manieren*, see below.
52. Robertson, *History of Charles V*, II: 245; and *Geschichte Carls des Fünften* (1778–1779), II: 267.
53. It is instructive to see that such associations were relevant even for figures committed to a tradition of active civic virtue, such as Adam Ferguson. See, for instance, Ferguson, *Essay on the History of Civil Society*, 195. Cf. above, 206.
54. Again in the passage referred to in endnote 51 above.
55. For the idea and practice of "impartiality" in Robertson's works, see Jeffrey Smitten, "Impartiality in Robertson's *History of America*," *Eighteenth-Century Studies* 19 (1985); Jeffrey Smitten, "The Shaping of Moderatism: William Robertson and Arminianism," *Studies in Eighteenth-Century Culture* 22 (1992)"; O'Brien, *Narratives of Enlightenment*, 104 ff.
56. [Albrecht von Haller], review of William Robertson's *History of Scotland*, GAgS, 8 no. 107 (September 6, 1760): 913; *Geschichte von Schottland* (Abele), "Vorrede."
57. [Albrecht von Haller], review of William Robertson's *History of Charles V*, GAgS 18 (1770), 571.
58. *Geschichte von Schottland* (Mittelstedt), I: "Vorrede."
59. Ibid.
60. To lend further support to his own "revisionist" position, Mittelstedt quotes at length from the *Moral and Political Dialogues* (1759) of the Anglican divine Richard Hurd (1720–1808). The future bishop of Lichfield and Coventry, Hurd was a staunch supporter of William Warburton's political theology of the "alliance of Church and State," and the editor of Warburton's works (1772).
61. *Geschichte von Schottland* (Abele), "Vorrede."
62. The classical philologist Christian Gottlob Heyne praised Seiler's translation of Demosthenes and Lysias as a proof of his "diligence, erudition, and his study of the language and genius of his orators." *GAgS*, no. 145 (December 3, 1768): 1209.
63. On Seiler, see Ottfried Jordahn, *Georg Friedrich Seilers Beitrag zur praktischen Theologie der kirchlichen Aufklärung* (Nuremberg: Selbstverlag des Vereins für bayerische Kirchengeschichte, 1970). Cf. also the references to "theological Wolffianism" above, chapter 2, 159 f.
64. *Geschichte von Schottland* (Abele), "Vorrede."
65. The causes of the initiative, and especially of its bitterness, have not been sufficiently explored. General explanations as the crisis of Protestant rationalism, or the relatively weak self-confidence of the *Aufklärung*, are hardly satisfactory. For an overview, see Johannes Rogalla von Bieberstein, *Die These von der Verschwörung*

1776–1945 (Frankfurt: Peter Lang, 1976), ch. 1. Aspects of this episode relevant to the present subject are summarized in Wolfgang Schieder and Christoph Dipper, "Propaganda," in *Geschichtliche Grundbegriffe*, ed. Brunner, Conze, Koselleck, V: 71–6. See also László Kontler, "Superstitition, Enthusiasm and Propagandism: Burke and Gentz on the French Revolution," in *Propaganda. Political Rhetoric and Identity 1300–2000*, ed. Bertrand Taithe and Tim Thornton (Phoenix Mill: Sutton Publishing, 1999), 97–114.

66. See Sher, *Church and University*, 67–70, 277–97; Stuart J. Brown, "William Robertson and the Scottish Enlightenment," in *William Robertson and the Expansion of Empire*, ed. Brown.
67. *A Narrative of the Debate in the General Assembly of the Church of Scotland, May 25, 1779*, ed. [John Erskine] (Edinburgh: n.p., 1780), 49, 61.
68. [Haller], review of *History of Scotland*, 914, 917.
69. [Haller], review of *History of Charles V*, 932.
70. Robertson, *History of Charles V*, IV: 185–6.
71. [Haller], review of *History of Charles V*, 998.
72. Robertson, *Geschichte Carl des Fünften* (1778–1789), I: 302, 402, III: 234.
73. Cf. above, 201.
74. Westphalen to Robertson. I have not found evidence that Robertson ever cared to respond.
75. [Haller], review of *History of Charles V*, 931, 996.
76. *Geschichte Carls des Fünften* (1778–1789), I: 243.
77. See Leonard Krieger, *The German Idea of Freedom: History of a Political Idea* (Chicago: University of Chicago Press, 1957). But cf. also the view that apparently "absolute" monarchies were in fact moderate, with a generally constructive relationship between crown and estates, and the system of *Landstände* and imperial *Kreistage* perceived by several Germans as representative bodies comparable to the British parliament. Rudolf Vierhaus, "Politisches Bewußtsein in Deutschland vor 1789," in *Deutschland im 18. Jahrhundert: Politische Verfassung, soziales Gefüge, geistige Bewegungen* (Göttingen: Vandenhoeck & Ruprecht, 1987), 195; Charles Ingrao, "Introduction: A Pre-Revolutionary Sonderweg," *German History* 20/3 (2002): 282.
78. George P. Gooch, *Germany and the French Revolution* (London: Longman, 1920), 22–3.
79. Friedrich Carl von Moser, *Der Herr und der Diener, geschildert mit patriotischer Freyheit* (Frankfurt: Raspe, 1759); von Moser, ed., *Patriotisches Archiv für Deutschland*, 12 vols. (Frankfurt and Leipzig: C. F. Schwan, 1784–1790). On Moser, see Notker Hammerstein, "Das politische Denken Friedrich Carl von Mosers," *Historische Zeitschrift* 212 (1971): 316–38; John Gagliardo, *Reich and Nation: The Holy Roman Empire as Idea and Reality, 1763–1806* (Bloomington: Indiana University Press, 1980), ch. 4; Angela Stirken, *Der Herr und der Diener. Friedrich Carl von Moser und das Beamtenwesen seiner Zeit* (Berlin: Ludwig Röhrscheid, 1984); Wolfgang Martens, *Der patriotische Minister. Fürstendiener in der Literatur der Aufklärungszeit* (Cologne: Böhlau, 1996), III: 1.
80. *Landeshoheit* is commonly translated into English as "territorial sovereignty." However, Moser rejects the sovereign quality of the authority in question.
81. Friedrich Carl von Moser, *Patriotische Briefe* (n.p., 1767 [1765]), Zweyter Brief, 32–40, 232–3.
82. Michael Stolleis, "Reichspublizistik und Reichspatriotismus vom 16. zum 18. Jahrhundert," *Aufklärung* 4/2 (1989): 7–23; Karl Othmar Freiherr von Aretin, "Reichspatriotismus," ibid., 25–36. The standard treatment of the history of the waning Holy Roman Empire is still Karl Othmar Freiherr von Aretin, *Heiliges Römisches Reich 1776–1806: Reichsverfassung und Staatssouveränität*, 2 vols. (Wiesbaden: Steiner, 1967).

83. Johann Jakob Bülau, *Noch etwas zum deutschen Nationalgeist* (1766), cited in Gagliardo, *Reich and Nation*, 58.
84. Johann Jakob Moser, *Lebensgeschichte... von ihm selbst geschrieben* (1777–1783), cited in Walker, *Johann Jakob Moser*, 292.
85. Geoff Grundy, *The Emulation of Nations: William Robertson and the International Order* (PhD diss., University of Edinburgh, 2005), 140 ff.
86. Richard Pares, "American versus Continental Warfare, 1739–1763," *English Historical Review* 51 (1936): 436.
87. Jonathan Knudsen, *Justus Möser and the German Enlightenment* (Cambridge: Cambridge University Press, 1986), 99–109; Umbach, *Federalism and Enlightenment*, 134 ff.; Volker Press, *Das Reichskammergericht in der deutschen Geschichte* (Wetzlar: Gesellschaft der Reichskammergerichtsforschung, 1987).
88. Manfred Friedrich, *Geschichte der deutschen Staatsrechtswissenschaft* (Berlin: Duncker & Humblot, 1997), 131.
89. On the character of Pütter's legal scholarship, see Ulrich Schlie, *Johann Stephan Pütters Rechtbegriff* (Göttingen: Verlag Otto Schwarz, 1961); for a broader contextualization, see Friedrich, *Geschichte der deutschen Staatsrechtswissenschaft*, ch. 9.
90. Johann Stephan Pütter, *Teutsche Reichsgeschichte in ihrem Hauptfaden entwickelt* (Göttingen: Ruprecht, 1778), 5, 278. In discussing the age of Charles V in this work, Pütter's notes show a quite thorough familiarity with Robertson.
91. Pütter, *An Historical Development of the Present Political Constitution of the Germanic Empire*, 3 vols. (London: Payne and Son, 1790), II: 165. Cf. Pütter's original, *Historische Entwicklung des heutigen Staatsverfassung des Teutschen Reichs*, 3 vols. (Göttingen: Ruprecht, 1786–1787), II: 156.
92. Ibid., II: 168.
93. Robertson, *Geschichte Carls des Fünften* (1781–1783), I: 316, 369; II: 361.
94. Franz Xaver von Wegele, "Häberlin, Franz Dominicus," in *Allgemeine Deutsche Biographie*, vol. X (Leipzig: Duncker & Humblot, 1879), 274–5.
95. Franz Dominic Häberlin, *Neue Teutsche Reichs-Geschichte, Vom Anfänge des Schmalkaldischen Krieges bis auf unsere Zeiten*, 20 vols. (Halle: Gebauer, 1774–1790), I: iv–v.
96. Ibid., II: 430.
97. Robertson, *Geschichte Carls des Fünften* (1778–1789), II: 466.
98. *Geschichte Carls des Fünften* (1781–1783), II: 468.
99. Cf. above, ch. 1, p. 27, on the lack of demand for literary appeal in historical compositions.
100. Pütter, *Teutsche Reichsgeschichte*, vii. It has been suggested that the praise of Pütter, as well as of Gatterer, for Schmidt was explicitly expressed in favorably comparing him to Robertson, for which I have found no evidence. Peter Baumgart, "Michael Ignaz Schmidt (1736–1794). Leben und Werk," in *Michael Ignaz Schmidt (1736–1794) in seiner Zeit. Der aufgeklärte Theologe, Bildungsreformer und "Historiker der Deutschen" aus Franken in neuer Sicht*, ed. Baumgart (Neustadt an der Aisch: Verlag Degener & Co., 1996), 121.
101. Universitätsarchiv Göttingen, J57; Promotionsalbum der Juristischen Fakultät 1789.
102. Josiah Dornford to Georg Christoph Lichtenberg, August 22, 1791. Niedersächsisches Staats- und Universitätsbibliothek Göttingen, Cod. Ms. Lichtenberg III, 51. It is noteworthy that before his premature death, Dornford also contributed in a thoroughly Burkean spirit to the debate on the French revolutionary wars. Josiah Dornford, *The Motives and Consequences of the Present War Impartially Considered* (London: Pridden, 1793).
103. Pütter, *An Historical Development*, I: xiv.
104. For instance, Pütter, *Teutsche Reichsgeschichte*, iii–iv.

105. E.g., Pütter, *An Historical Development*, I: 3 (on ancient Germanic manners), 13 (on mode of subsistence and the Salic laws), 117–18 (on medieval urban communities), 169 (on the consequences of the Crusades), 380–1 (on the consequences of the discovery of America).
106. Michael Ignaz Schmidt, *Geschichte der Deutschen* (Ulm: Stettin, 1778–1783), I: "Vorrede," 11–16.
107. Ibid., V: 1–6.
108. Ibid., I: 3.
109. Ibid., I: 12–13, 22.
110. Recently, Schmidt has been explicitly put forward as a counterpart of Robertson in the following terms: he too is portrayed as a religious and ecclesiastical "moderate" who belonged to the broader family of enlightened narrative history, and sought to place the history of the clergy "within the history of civil society and manners" (a reference to Pocock, *Barbarism and Religion*, II: 282). Michael Printy, *Enlightenment and the Creation of German Catholicism* (Cambridge: Cambridge University Press, 2009), 198, and the whole of ch. 9. See also Michael Printy, "From Barbarism to Religion: Church History and the Enlightened Narrative in Germany," *German History* 23 (2005): 172–201. On Schmidt as a historian, see further Arnold Berney, "Michael Ignatz Schmidt. Ein Beitrag zur Geschichte der Historiographie in der deutschen Aufklärung," *Historisches Jahrbuch*, 44 (1924): 211–39; Hans-Wolfgang Bergerhausen, "Michael Ignaz Schmidt in der historiographischen Tradition der Aufklärung," in *Michael Ignaz Schmidt*, ed. Baumgart, 63–79.
111. O'Brien, *Narratives of Enlightenment*, 121.
112. Robertson, *History of Charles V*, esp. III: 393 ff.
113. Ibid., III: 14–15.
114. *Geschichte Carls des Fünften* (1778–1789), II: 417. Later on the balance is somewhat redressed. In Robertson's account, it was "the greatest dishonour" upon Charles's reputation to have refused the fulfillment of the promises he had made in return for free march across French territory against the Low Countries in early 1540, while he also dismissed the "credulous simplicity" which Francis displayed in this matter. Agreeing with Robertson's judgment on the emperor, Remer stresses the "noble" conduct of the French king. Robertson, *History of Charles V*, III: 187–8; *Geschichte Carls des Fünften* (1778–1789), II: 604.
115. Pütter, *An Historical Development*, II: 402. Cf. Pütter, *Historische Entwickelung*, II: 355.
116. Ibid., III: 167 in the English, and 158 in the German text.
117. Printy, "From Barbarism to Religion," 174–5.
118. Schmidt, *Geschichte*, V: 138–40, 179–85.
119. Ibid., chs. 23, 24; VI: 305 ff.
120. Even Robertson's central claim on Charles's measures being the result of "cool reflection" and "disposed into a regular system" (mentioned above) were called into question by "P," who suggested that Robertson himself shows Charles often following his passion. *Geschichte Carls des Fünften* (1778–1789), III: 546–9.
121. In the *History of Scotland*, I: 91, Robertson flatly claimed that Charles "openly aspired to universal monarchy." In the *History of Charles V*, IV: 288, the emperor's undoubtedly "insatiable" ambition is described in more nuanced terms, and while he is shown to have harbored "a desire of being distinguished as a conqueror," in Robertson's revised view "there seems to be no foundation for an opinion prevalent in his own age, that he had formed the chimerical project of establishing a universal monarchy in Europe."
122. Schmidt, *Geschichte*, VI: 282.

5 Maps of Mankind

1. *The Correspondence of Edmund Burke*, 10 vols., ed. Thomas W. Copeland (Cambridge: Cambridge University Press, 1958–1978), III: 350–1.
2. For an assessment of the significance of the two books in this sense, see Karen O'Brien, *Narratives of Enlightenment: Cosmopolitan History from Voltaire to Gibbon* (Cambridge: Cambridge University Press, 1997), 156–65.
3. Cf. above, 28; Geoff Grundy, *The Emulation of Nations: William Robertson and the International Order* (PhD diss., University of Edinburgh, 2005), 272–6. Cf. Troy Bickham, *Savages within the Empire: Representations of American Indians in Eighteenth-Century Britain* (Oxford: Clarendon Press, 2005), ch. 5, especially pp. 195–8.
4. The name of the Jesuit Raynal provided a cover for this undertaking of a host of iconoclastic authors in order to protect them from harassment by the authorities. Diderot's contributions are estimated at c. 700 pages in the ten-volume 1780 edition. First published in 1772 (with an imprint of 1770), one of the most popular "forbidden bestsellers" of the eighteenth century went through more than thirty editions by 1787. Robert Darnton, *The Forbidden Best-Sellers of Pre-Revolutionary France* (New York: Norton, 1996), 22–3. The literature on the *Histoire des deux Indes* is immense. See Gabriel Esquer, *L'Anticolonialisme au XVIIIe siècle: Histoire philosophique et politique des établissements et du commerce des Européens dans les deux Indes* (Paris: Presses universitaires de France, 1951); Michèle Duchet, *Diderot et l'Histoire des deux Indes: ou, L'écriture fragmentaire* (Paris: A. G. Nizet, 1978); Hans-Jürgen Lüsebrink and Anthony Strugnell, *L'Histoire des deux Indes: réécriture et polygraphie* (Oxford: Voltaire Foundation, 1995); Sankar Muthu, *Enlightenment against Empire* (Princeton: Princeton University Press, 2003), ch. 3; J.G.A. Pocock, *Barbarism and Religion*, vol. IV: *Barbarians, Savages and Empires* (Cambridge: Cambridge University Press, 2005), ch. 4.
5. The "four stages," while present in eighteenth-century language, are better understood as a loose heuristic scheme—not necessarily rigidly applied, and always presenting challenges of interpretation for those who attempted to apply it (including Robertson)—than the "system" which Ronald Meek's pathbreaking *Social Science and the Ignoble Savage* proposed it to be. For a recent, detailed treatment of the subject, including a critique of Meek, see Thomas Nutz, *Varietäten des Menschengeschlechts. Die Wissenschaften vom menschen in der Zeit der Aufklärung* (Cologne: Böhlau, 2009), ch. 3.
6. William Robertson, *The History of America* (London: Routledge/Thoemmes Press, 1996), I: 2–3.
7. Ibid., I: 4–5.
8. Ibid., I: 8, 12–13. Cf. 20 ff., 40 ff.; and William Robertson, *An Historical Disquisition Concerning the Knowledge which the Ancients had of India; and the Progress of Trade with that Country prior to the Discovery of the Passage to it by the Cape of Good Hope* (London: Routledge/Thoemmes Press, 1996), 6, 30 ff., 152 ff.
9. Robertson, *History of America*, I: 54–8.
10. On the sixteenth-century history of the company, see Douglas R. Bisson, *The Merchant Adventurers of England: The Company and the Crown, 1474–1564* (Newark: University of Delaware Press, 1993).
11. Robertson, *History of America*, I: 86, 95, 120.
12. See Pocock, *Barbarism and Religion*, IV: ch. 9.
13. See Jorge Cañizares-Esguerra, *How to Write the History of the New World: Histories, Epistemologies and Identities in the Eighteenth-Century Atlantic World* (Stanford: Stanford University Press, 2001).
14. Robertson, *History of America*, I: 253–4.

15. Ibid., II: 49–50. While devoted to the study of Robertson's Spanish sources, Lenman, "'From Savage to Scot' via the French and the Spaniards: Principal Robertson's Spanish sources," in *William Robertson and the Expansion of Empire*, ed. Brown, emphasizes the centrality of the stadial scheme to the History of America. See also E. Adamson Hoebel, "William Robertson: An 18th Century Anthropological Historian," *American Anthropologist* 62 (1960): 648–55; Stuart J. Brown, "An Eighteenth-Century Historian on the Amerindians: Culture, Colonialism and Christianity in William Robertson's History of America," *Studies in World Christianity* 2 (1996): 204–22.
16. Robertson, *History of America*, II: 56.
17. Ibid., II: 51.
18. Ibid., II: 30.
19. Cf. below, 332–3.
20. Ibid., II: 188.
21. Robertson, *Historical Disquisition*, 283.
22. In his *Histoire naturelle, générale et particulière* (1749–1788, in 36 vols.), Georges-Louis Leclerc, Comte de Buffon placed man in the center of his zoological investigations, radically historicizing the notion of race by attributing all diversity within the unitary human species to the variability of climatic and geographical circumstances (adversely affecting the development of animate organisms in the Americas). In the Dutch philosopher Cornelius de Pauw's *Recherches philosophiques sur les Américains* (1771) this perspective was flatly converted into an argument about the inferiority of native Americans. The topic is discussed extensively in Antonello Gerbi, *The Dispute of the New World: The History of a Polemic 1750–1900* (Pittsburgh: University of Pittsburgh Press, 1973); Roxann Wheeler, *The Complexion of Race: Categories of Difference in Eighteenth-Century British Culture* (Philadelphia: University of Pennsylvania Press, 2000). For echoes in the Scottish Enlightenment, see Robert Wokler, "Apes and Races in the Scottish Enlightenment: Monboddo and Kames on the Nature of Man," in *Philosophy and Science in the Scottish Enlightenment*, ed. Peter Jones (Edinburgh: John Donald, 1988), 145–68; Silvia Sebastiani, "Race and National Character in Eighteenth-Century Scotland: The Polygenetic Discourses of Kames and Pinkerton," *Studi settecenteschi* 21 (2001): 265–81; Silvia Sebastiani, *I limiti del progresso. Razza e genere nell'Illuminismo scozzese* (Bologna: Il Mulino, 2008), rev. Eng. ed., *The Scottish Enlightenment: Race, Gender and the Limits of Progress* (Houndmills, Basingstoke: Palgrave Macmillan, 2013). For Robertson's reliance on Buffon, see Robertson, *History of America*, II: 19 ff.
23. Ibid., II: 58–9.
24. Ibid., II: 62–3.
25. Ibid., II: 94–5.
26. Ibid., II: 54–5.
27. These are Robertson's own representations of the two theories. Ibid., II: 57.
28. Cf. below, 341.
29. Robertson, *History of America*, II: 26.
30. Ibid., II: 30–1.
31. Robertson, *History of Charles V*, IV: 304.
32. Robertson, *History of America*, III: 151, 154.
33. Ibid., III: 152.
34. Ibid., III: 153.
35. Ibid., III: 178 ff. and 200–1 (on writing); 189–90 (on money); 217 ff. (on roads and traffic).
36. Pocock, *Barbarism and Religion*, IV: 202. Cf. Christopher J. Berry, *Social Theory of the Scottish Enlightenment* (Edinburgh: Edinburgh University Press, 1997), 96. Similarly, narrative altogether has been claimed to "serve to confuse, correct or overturn

the supposed verities, or perhaps simplicities, of the stadial exposition." Neal Hargraves, "Enterprise, Adventure and Industry: The Formation of 'Commercial Character' in William Robertson's *History of America*," *History of European Ideas* 29 (2003): 36–7; Hargraves, "Beyond the Savage Character: Mexicans, Peruvians, and the 'Imperfectly Civilized' in William Robertson's *History of America*," in *The Anthropology of the Enlightenment*, ed. Larry Wolff and Marco Cipollini (Stanford: Stanford University Press, 2007), 114.
37. Another formulation by Edmund Burke, review of *History of America*, by William Robertson, *Annual Register* 19 (1777): 215.
38. Höpfl, "From Savage to Scotsman," esp. 23.
39. Alexander du Toit, "Who Are the Barbarians? Scottish Views of Conquest and Indians, and Robertson's *History of America*," *Scottish Literary Journal* 26/1 (1999): 34–5.
40. Robertson, *History of America*, I: 134, 139.
41. Ibid., I: 178–83.
42. Ibid., I: 185–6.
43. Ibid., I: 251, 333–4.
44. Ibid., I: 259–61.
45. Hargraves, "Enterprise, Adventure and Industry," 44.
46. Robertson, *History of America*, II: 242, cf. III: 5.
47. Ibid., II: 235, 260–1.
48. Ibid., II: 287–8, 319.
49. Ibid., II: 388–9.
50. Ibid., II: 403–4.
51. Ibid., III: 37, 41.
52. Guillaume-Thomas Raynal, *Histoire philosophique et politique des établissements et du commerce des Européens dans les deux Indes*, 10 vols. (Geneva: Jean-Leonard Pellet, 1780), IX: 1, cited in Muthu, *Enlightenment against Empire*, 74. For parallel arguments in contemporary Britain, in particular by Alexander Dow and Edmund Burke, see Abbattista, "Empire, Liberty and the Rule of Difference: European Debates on British Colonialism in Asia at the End of the Eighteenth Century," *European Review of History/Revue européenne d'histoire* 13/3 (2006).
53. Robertson, *History of America*, III: 48.
54. Ibid., III: 58.
55. Ibid., III: 58.
56. Ibid., I: 172. Cf. II: 317–18.
57. Ibid., II: 279–81.
58. Ibid., II: 252.
59. Ibid., II: 300.
60. Ibid., III: 12, 22–4. The point is echoed in bk. 7, 208.
61. Hargraves, "Beyond the Savage Character," 104–5.
62. Robertson, *Historical Disquisition*, 214, 230 ff.
63. It has been suggested that the criticism Robertson received for the negative portrayal of "savagery" (implicitly serving as an excuse for European cruelty) and the dismissive treatment of American cultures in the *History of America* played a part in his adopting an empathetic stance in the *Historical Disquisition*. In this, he relied heavily on early British "orientalist" scholars, but went further than most of them in his positive view on Indian culture and in his opposition to an interventionist imperial policy. Stuart J. Brown, "William Robertson, Early Orientalism and the *Historical Disquisition* on India of 1791," *The Scottish Historical Review* 88/2 (2009): 299–300. Cf. Jane Rendall, "Scottish Orientalism: From Robertson to James Mill," *The Historical Journal* 25/1 (1982): 43–69; Michael S. Dodson, *Orientalism, Empire and National Culture: India, 1770–1880* (Basingstoke: Palgrave Macmillan, 2007), 1–6.

64. Robertson, *Historical Disquisition*, 59.
65. Ibid., 63–4.
66. Ibid., 203.
67. Ibid., 215–18.
68. Ibid., 229.
69. Ibid., 233–4, 239.
70. Ibid., 241, 244, 246.
71. Ibid., 249–53.
72. Ibid., 264, 274. He later adds "that it is only among a people of polished manners and delicate sentiments that a composition so simple and correct could be produced or relished." Ibid., 278.
73. Ibid., 283–300. In the quoted passage Robertson moves freely between generic reference to the bulk of Indian science and specifically to astronomy (to which the last sentence seems to be confined).
74. Ibid. 307.
75. Ibid. 307 ff., 321–2.
76. Ibid., 327–30. It has been suggested that in these reflections Robertson was "coming very close to comparing the popular Hinduism of the masses of India with popular Christianity as it existed among the uneducated classes in much of Europe, including the popular Calvinism in Scotland." Brown, "Robertson, Early Orientalism and the *Historical Disquisition*," 308.
77. Ibid., 332–3.
78. Niedersächsische Staats- und Universitätsbibliothek, Göttingen. Bibliotheksarchiv, Ausleiheregister A. Mich. 1777. f. 43.
79. Ibid., Ost. 1792. f. 49.
80. Dietrich Hilger, "Industrie, Gewerbe," sections IV–V, in *Geschichtliche Grundbegriffe*, ed. Brunner, Conze, and Koselleck, III: 253–69.
81. William Robertson, *Geschichte von Amerika*, trans. Johann Friedrich Schiller (Leipzig: Weidmanns Erben und Reich, 1777), I: 294 or II: 399.
82. Cf. Robertson, *Historical Disquisition*, 124; and Robertson, *Historische Untersuchung über die Kenntnisse der Alten von Indien, und die Fortschritte des Handels mit diesem Landevor der Entdeckung des Wegesdahin um das Vorgebirge der guten Hoffnung*, trans. Georg Forster (Berlin: Voß, 1792), 159.
83. *Geschichte von Amerika*, I: 169, 210, 326.
84. Ibid., I: 42, 168; *Historiche Untersuchung*, 140, 161
85. For *Barbarey*, see *Geschichte von Amerika*, II: 344, 376–7; for *Unmenschlichkeit*, II: 160, 203; for *Grausamkeit*, II: 239.
86. *Geschichte von Amerika*, II: 311.
87. Cf. above, 206–7.
88. Cf. above, 213.
89. On this work, see Giovanna Ceserani, "Narrative, Interpretation, and Plagiarism in Mr. Robertson's 1778 History of Ancient Greece," *Journal of the History of Ideas* 66/3 (2005): 413–36.
90. Adam Smith, *Untersuchung der Natur und Ursachen von Nationalreichthümern*, trans. Johann Friedrich Schiller and Christian August Wichmann (Leipzig: Weidmanns Erben und Reich, 1776–1778), I: "Preface."
91. *Historische Untersuchung*, translator's "Preface," viii.
92. [Christian Gottlob Heyne], review of William Robertson's *History of America*, pt. 2, *Zugabe zu den GAgS*, I, no. 44 (November 1, 1777): 695, 699.
93. See Dalphy I. Fagerstrom, "Scottish Opinion and the American Revolution," *William and Mary Quarterly* 11 (1954): 216, 264 ff.; Richard B. Sher, *Church and University in the Scottish Enlightenment: The Moderate Literati of Edinburgh* (Princeton: Princeton University Press, 1985), 263, 270, 275; and Jeffrey Smitten, "Moderatism

and History: William Robertson's Unfinished History of British America," in *Scotland and America in the Age of Enlightenment*, ed. Richard B. Sher and Jeffrey R. Smitten (Edinburgh: Edinburgh University Press, 1990), 163–79.
94. Horst Dippel, *Germany and the American Revolution 1770–1800* (Wiesbaden: Harrassowitz Verlag, 1978), 13.
95. [Christian Gottlob Heyne], review of William Robertson's *History of America*, pt. 1, *Zugabe zu den GAgS*, I, no. 42 (October 18, 1777): 662–3.
96. *The Correspondence of Edmund Burke*, III: 350–1. Cf. *Annual Register* 19 (1777): 214–34.
97. Cf. above, 249.
98. [Heyne], review of *History of America* pt. 1: 665.
99. See Jeremy Black, "The Enlightenment Historian at Work: The Researches of William Robertson," *Bulletin of Hispanic Studies* 65 (1988); Mark Duckworth, "An Eighteenth-Century Questionnaire: William Robertson on the Indians," *Eighteenth-Century Life* 11 (1987); Jeffrey Smitten, "Robertson's Letters and the Life of Writing," in *William Robertson and the Expansion of Empire*, ed. Brown, 34–56; Lenman, "'From Savage to Scot' via the French."
100. On Behaim and the half-mythical and legendary character he assumed in later speculations, see Peter J. Bräunlein, *Martin Behaim. Legende und Wirklichkeit eines berühmten Nürnbergers* (Bamberg: Bayerische Verlagsanstalt, 1992), esp. 15–67.
101. Johann Reinhold Forster to Robertson (via an unidentified intermediary), London, December 16, 1777. The National Library of Scotland. Robertson-Macdonald papers, MS. 3943. ff. 54–8.
102. Quoted in Michael E. Hoare, "Preface," in *The Resolution Journal of Johann Reinhold Forster 1772–1775* (London: Hakluyt Society, 1982), I: ix. On Forster in general see the Introduction in the same edition of his *Journal*, and Michael E. Hoare, *The Tactless Philosopher: Johann Reinhold Forster 1729–1798* (Melbourne: Hawthorn Press, 1976).
103. Johann Reinhold Forster, *Enchiridion historiae naturali inserviens: quo termini et delineationes ad avium, piscium, insectorum et plantarum adumbrationes intelligendas et concinnandas, secundum methodum systematis Linnaeani continentur* (Halle: Hemmerde und Schwetschke, 1788), [4]. Quoted in Hoare, "Introduction," in *Resolution Journal*, 77.
104. *The Critical Review, or, Annals of Literature* 32 (April 1772): 340.
105. As far as Robertson is concerned, he was certainly aware of Cook's voyages, but he only used the account of the third one (1776–1780), mainly for making observations on climate and geography. See for instance *History of America*, bk. 4, note vi.
106. Johann Reinhold Forster, *Beobachtungen während der Cookschen Weltumseglung 1772–1775* (Stuttgart: Brockhaus Antiquarium, 1981), 254–531. Cf. the English edition, *Observations Made during a Voyage round the World*, ed. Nicholas Thomas, Harriet Guest, and Michael Dettelbach (Honolulu: University of Hawaii Press, 1996), 191–357. See also the lengthy passages on comparative ethnology in the *Resolution Journal*, esp. III: 392–405.
107. Forster, *Observations*, 155, 175; cf. *Resolution Journal*, III: 392–405.
108. The original was published as *Geschichte der Entdeckungen und Schiffahrten in Norden* in 1784 and was dedicated to Catherine the Great in recognition of Russia's increasing role in promoting exploration (and in an unsuccessful effort to obtain membership into the St. Petersburg Academy of Sciences).
109. Johann Reinhold Forster, *History of the Voyages and Discoveries made in the North* (Dublin: Luke White, 1786), xiv.
110. Ibid.
111. Ibid.
112. [Anon.], review of Johann Reinhold Forster's *History of the Discoveries and Voyages*, *The Critical Review* 62 (November–December 1786), 330.
113. Forster, *History of the Voyages*, 232–4.

114. Ibid., 234.
115. Ibid., 236.
116. Ibid., 236–58.
117. Hoare, *Tactless Philosopher*, and its "Introduction."
118. Robertson actually did so in later editions, explicitly acknowledging his debt to Forster. See *History of America*, I: 372.
119. See endnote 101.
120. "We are almost Englishmen," he wrote to his old friend Michaelis from London on August 24, 1775. Cod. Mich. f. 322. Niedersächsische Staats- und Universitätsbibliothek, Göttingen
121. Robertson-MacDonald papers, National Library of Scotland, MS. 3943. ff. 106–7.
122. *Thomas Pennants Reise durch Schottland und die Hebridischen Inseln*, trans. Johann Philipp Ebeling (Leipzig: Weygand, 1779–1780), I: translator's "Preface." Pennant was one of Forster's closest friends in Britain.
123. See Colin Kidd, "Teutonist Ethnology and Scottish National Inhibition, 1780–1880," *The Scottish Historical Review* 74 (1995): 45–68.
124. [Anon.], review of William Robertson's *Historical Disquisition*, *Annalen der Geographie und Statistik* 3 (1792): 112.
125. Ibid., 120.
126. Cf. above, 295–6.
127. Arnold Ludwig Herrmann Heeren, *Ideen über die Politik, den Verkehr und den Handel der vornehmsten Völker der alten Welt*, 2 vols. (Göttingen: Vandenhoeck & Ruprecht, 1793–1796).
128. Heeren, *Handbuch der Geschichte des Europäischen Staatensystems und seiner Colonien, von der Entdeckung beyder Indien bis zur Errichtung des Französischer Kayserthrons* (Göttingen: Vandenhoeck & Ruprecht, 1809). For a penetrating study of Heeren's scholarship and achievement, see Christoph Becker-Schaum, *Arnold Herrmann Ludwig Heeren. Ein Beitrag zur Geschichte der Geschichtswissenschaft zwischen Aufklärung und Historismus* (Bern: Peter Lang, 1993). See also Horst Walter Blanke, "Zwischen Aufklärung und Historismus: A.H.L. Heerens 'Geschichte des Europäischen Staatensystems,'" in *Aufklärung und Historik. Aufsätze zur Entwicklung der Geschichtswissenschaft, Kirchengeschichte und Geschichtstheorie in der deutschen Aufklärung*, ed. Horst Walter Blanke and Dirk Fleischer (Waltrop: Hartmut Spenner, 1991), 202–26.
129. Heeren was also Georg Forster's brother-in-law. Their India-related publications in the early 1790s (together with the announcement by both of them of books in the field never to be written) were suggested to have been elements of emulation between them for the reputation as India-experts. See Christoph Becker-Schaum, "Die Beziehungen zwischen Georg Forster und Arnold Heeren und ihr Niederschlag in Heerens Werk," *Georg-Forster-Studien* 12 (2007): 211–29.
130. "Commentatio de graecorum de India notitia et cum Indis commerciis" (January 16, 1790); "Commentatio de mercatura Indicae ratione et viis" (January 8, 1791); "Commentatio de Romanorum de India notitia" (August 4, 1792). The texts are published in the Society's periodical, *Commentationes societatis regiae scientiarum goettingensis*, vols. 10–11 (Göttingen, 1791–1793), X: 121–56, and XI: 63–90.
131. Arnold Herrmann Ludwig Heeren, review of William Robertson's *Historical Disquisition*, *Bibliothek der alten Litteratur und Kunst* 9 (1792): 120.
132. Ibid., 105–7.
133. Georg Forster, *Kleine Schriften. Ein Beytrag zur Völker- und Länderkunde, Naturgeschichte und Philosophie des Lebens*, vol. I (Leipzig: Kummer, 1789), ii.
134. Forster's centrality to the eighteenth-century universe of participating in and reporting on travel is a prominent theme in Harry Liebersohn, *The Traveler's World: Europe to the Pacific* (Cambridge: Harvard University Press, 2006)

135. Ludwig Uhlig, *Georg Forster. Lebensabenteuer eines gelehrten Weltbürgers (1754–1794)* (Göttingen: Vandenhoeck & Ruprecht, 2004), 282.
136. Georg Forster, "Neuholland und die brittische Colonie in Botany-Bay [1786]," in *Georg Forsters Werke. Sämtliche Schriften, Tagebücher, Briefe*, ed. Georg Steiner et al., Deutsche Akademie der Wissenschaften zu Berlin [from 1974, Akademie der Wissenschaften der DDR; from 2003, Berlin-Brandenburgische Akademie der Wissenschaften] (Berlin: Akademie Verlag, 1958–), vol. V: *Kleine Schriften zur Völker- und Länderkunde*, ed. Horst Fiedler, Hans-Georg Popp, Annerose Schneider, and Christian Suckow, 176.
137. Georg Christoph Lichtenberg, "Einige Lebensumstände vom Captain Jacob Cook, größtentheils aus schriftlichen Nachrichten einiger seiner Bekannten," *Göttingisches Magazin der Wissenschaften und Litteratur* 1/1 (1780): 243–96. Forster and Lichtenberg were co-editors of this journal.
138. Georg Forster, "Antrittsrede vor der Société des Antiquités de Cassel am 12. Dezember 1778," in *Werke*, VIII, *Kleine Schriften zu Philosophie und Zeitgeschichte*, ed. Siegfried Scheibe (Berlin: Akademie Verlag, 1991), 66.
139. For a contextualization of Forster's relevant ideas against the background of the late eighteenth-century German confrontation with the problem of European expansion and encounter with human diversity, see John K. Noyes, "Commerce, Colonialism, and the Globalization of Action in Late Enlightenment Germany," *Postcolonial Studies* 9/1 (2006): 81–98; John Gascoigne, "The German Enlightenment and the Pacific," in *The Anthropology of the Enlightenment*, ed. Wolff and Cipollini, 141–71.
140. Georg Forster, *James Cook, der Entdecker und Fragmente über Captain Cooks letzte Reise und sein Ende*, ed. Frank Vorpahl (Berlin: Eichborn, 2008), 24.
141. Ibid., 106–7.
142. Ibid., 109.
143. Robertson, *Historical Disquisition*, 276 ff.; *Untersuchung über Indien*, 298 ff.
144. Raymond Schwab, *The Oriental Renaissance: Europe's Rediscovery of India and the East, 1660–1860* (New York: Columbia University Press, 1984), 7–8.
145. See Jörg Esleben, "'Indisch lesen': Conceptions of Intercultural Communication in Georg Forster's and Johann Gottfried Herder's Reception of Kālidāsa's 'Śakuntalā,'" *Monatshefte* 95/2 (2003): 217–29; Nicholas A. Germana, "Herder's India: The 'Morgenland' in Mythology and Anthropology," in *The Anthropology of the Enlightenment*, ed. Wolff and Cipollini, 119–37; Germana, *The Orient of Europe: The Mythical Image of India and Competing Images of German National Identity* (Cambridge: Cambridge Scholars Publishing, 2009), ch. 1.
146. Georg Forster, *Geschichte der Englischen Litteratur vom Jahre 1791*, in *Werke*, vol. VII: *Kleine Schriften zu Kunst und Literatur. Sakontala*, ed. Gerhard Steiner (Berlin: Akademie Verlag, 1993), 253.
147. Georg Forster, review of William Robertson's *Historical Disquisition*, *GAgS* 49 (December 3, 1791), in *Werke*, vol. XI: *Rezensionen*, ed. Horst Fiedler (Berlin: Akademie Verlag, 1977), 295. Forster's other main objection is that at the end of the work, suggesting that by discovering the route to India Europe was saved from the great misfortune of being conquered by the Ottomans, Robertson abandoned sound history and engaged in mere speculation. Ibid., 301.
148. *Historische Untersuchung*, translator's "Preface," ix.
149. Forster to Christian Friedrich Voß, May 28, 1791, *Werke*, vol. XVI: *Briefe 1790 bis 1791*, ed. Brigitte Leuschner and Siegfried Scheibe (Berlin: Akademie Verlag, 1980), 293–5.
150. For instance, Sprengel translated a part of Cook's travel account, mentioned above—but Forster found the translation so poor that he revised it completely. Dalia Švambrytė, "Georg Forster in Vilnius: Reverberations of the Great Age of Ocean Navigation," *Acta Orientalia Vilnensia* 10/1–2 (2009): 153.

151. Matthias Christian Sprengel, *Geschichte der wichtigsten geographischen Entdeckungen bis zur Ankunft der Portuguisen in Japan 1542*, 2nd ed. (Halle: Hemmerde und Schwetschke, 1792), 6, 15.
152. Ibid., 23. The Germans, on account of their medieval swarming into the Baltic and Slav areas are also confidently mentioned among such nations, along with the ancient Phoenicians, Greeks, Romans, medieval Arabians and Norsemen, and modern Portuguese, Spaniards, Dutch, English, Russians and the papal missionaries. Behaim is also quite proudly referred to. Ibid., 42.
153. The literature on Forster is very extensive. In earlier scholarship, he was mainly appreciated as a dominant figure in the revolution of the Rhineland after the French invasion of 1792 and as a deputy to the French Convent—in other words as a leading German "Jacobin." Recently there has been more emphasis on his character as a "philosophical traveler," his intellectual achievement and his exchanges with dominant figures of contemporary German thought—Kant, Herder, Goethe, Wilhelm von Humboldt. See especially Ludwig Uhlig, *Georg Forster: Einheit und Mannigfaltigkeit in seiner geistigen Welt* (Tübingen: Max Niemeyer Verlag, 1965); Detlef Rasmussen, ed., *Weltumsegler und seine Freunde. Georg Forster als gesellschaftlicher Schriftsteller der Goethezeit* (Tübingen: Max Niemeyer Verlag, 1988); for a recent biography, see Uhlig, *Georg Forster. Lebensabenteuer*; all the diverse pursuits of Forster are set in a comparative context in the valuable studies in *Georg Forster in interdisziplinären Perspektive*, ed. Claus-Volker Klenke, Jörn Garber, and Dieter Heintze (Berlin: Akademie Verlag, 1994). A series, *Georg-Forster-Studien* (fifteen volumes and several special issues to date, edited by Horst Dippel and Helmut Scheuer) is published by the Georg-Forster-Gesellschaft with Kassel U. P.
154. Cf. David Armitage, "The New World and British Historical Thought: From Richard Hakluyt to William Robertson," in *America in European Consciousness*, ed. Karen Ordahl Kupperman (Chapel Hill: University of North Carolina Press, 1995), 68–70; Brown, "An Eighteenth-Century Historian on the Amerindians."
155. As most importantly in his sermon on the centenary of the Glorious Revolution in 1788. NLS, Robertson-MacDonald Papers, MS. 3979. For an analysis of the sermon, see Sher, "1688 and 1788."
156. Cf. Paul Hazard, *La crise de la conscience européenne* (Paris: Boivin, 1935), Eng. ed. *The European Mind 1680–1715* (Harmondsworth: Penguin, 1973).
157. Jeffrey Smitten, "The Shaping of Moderatism: William Robertson and Arminianism," *Studies in Eighteenth-Century Culture* 22 (1992), esp. 290–2.
158. Forster to Christian Gottlob Heyne, June 5, 1792, *Werke*, vol. XVII: *Briefe 1792 bis 1794 und Nachträge*, ed. Klaus-Georg Popp (Berlin: Akademie Verlag, 1989), 126. Cf. Uhlig, *Georg Forster*, 283 ff., and more broadly the whole of chs. 21–23 for Forster's revolutionary engagement.
159. Hans Erich Bödeker, "'l'instrument de la Révolution et en même temps son âme': 'L'opinion publique' chez Georg Forster," *European Review of History/Revue européenne d'histoire* 13/3 (2006): 373–83.
160. Georg Forster, "Über lokale und allgemeine Bildung," in *Werke*, vol. VII: *Kleine Schriften*, 48.
161. For a fuller treatment of this essay by Forster, see Joseph Gomsu, "Über lokale und allgemeine Bildung," in *Georg-Forster-Studien* 11/1 (2006): 323–34.
162. Christoph Meiners (1747–1810) was, precisely on account his racism, the most controversial figure of the famous Göttingen historical school in the later eighteenth century. Forster was not the only one to polemicize with the views expressed in his ethnographically and anthropologically informed works of cultural history whose topics ranged from general "histories of mankind" through the history of women and the history of constitutions, learning and language (mostly their

decline), and luxury in the states of classical antiquity, to comparative studies of "manners, constitutions, laws, crafts, commerce, religion, learning and education in the Middle Ages and in our times." See Lotter, "Meiners und die Lehre"; Susanne Zantop, *Colonial Fantasies: Conquest, Family and Nation in Precolonial Germany* (Durham: Duke University Press, 1997), 66–97; Martin Gierl, "Christoph Meiners, Geschichte der Menschheit und Göttinger Universalgeschichte. Rasse und Nation als Politisierung der deutschen Aufklärung," in *Die Wissenschaft von Menschen*, ed. Bödeker, Büttgen, and Espagne, 419–33; Carhart, *The Science of Culture*, chs. 6–8. On the Meiners-Forster debate, see further Luigi Marino, *Praeceptores Germaniae. Göttingen 1770–1820* (Göttingen: Vandenhoeck & Ruprecht, 1995), 110–20.
163. Importantly, however, the contrasting positions of the philosophical traveler and the sedentary scholar were already inherent in Forster's and Meiners's age, and soon became the object of an interesting debate between Georges Cuvier and Alexander von Humboldt: according to the former, the expeditionary scientist passed too quickly over a terrain to provide reliable testimony, and it is only the "bench-tied naturalist" who can calmly spread out species and specimens and reorder them into taxonomic clusters never visible in the field. See Dorinda Outram, "New Spaces in Natural History," in *Cultures of Natural History*, ed. Nicholas Jardine, James Secord, and Emma C. Spary (Cambridge: Cambridge University Press, 1996), 249–65; Outram, "On Being Perseus: New Knowledge, Dislocation, and Enlightenment Exploration," in *Geography and Enlightenment*, ed. Donald N. Livingstone and Charles W. J. Withers (Chicago: University of Chicago Press, 1999), 281–94. Robertson, of course, was a sedentary scholar too who has been shown to have made strenuous efforts to obtain primary evidence from "the field" but preferred to these the frameworks he developed on the basis of the narrative sources he perused. Duckworth, "An Eighteenth-Century Questionnaire." For a discussion of Forster and Meiners in these terms, see Michael Carhart, "Polynesia and Polygenism: The Scientific Use of Travel Literature in the Early 19th Century," *History of the Human Sciences* 22/2 (2009): 58–86.
164. See Jörn Garber, *Wahrnehmung–Konstruktion–Text. Bilder des Wirklichen im Werk Georg Forsters* (Tübingen: Max Niemeyer Verlag, 2000), 4–6, 12–16, 203–5.
165. Georg Forster, *A Voyage Round the World in His Britannic Majesty's Sloop, the Resolution, commanded by Capt. James Cook, during the Year 1772. 3, 4, and 5* (London: White, Robson, Elmsly and Robinson, 1777), I: 386.
166. Ibid., I: 417.
167. Ibid., I: 575.
168. Ibid., I: 211.
169. Ibid., I: 302.
170. Ibid., I: 177–8.
171. Ibid., I: 221–2.
172. Ibid., I: 173.
173. Ibid., II: 315.
174. Revised and made famous as *The Origin of the Distinction of Ranks* (1777).
175. Forster, *Voyage Round the World*, II: 324; cf. I: 510.
176. Robertson, *History of America*, II: 103, 105
177. Ibid., II: 146.
178. Ibid., II: 54. See also 88 ff.
179. Forster, *Voyage Round the World*, II: 507.
180. Ibid., II: 606.
181. Ibid., II: 503. Without being mentioned by name, Rousseau is obviously the targeted "philosopher."
182. Ibid., II: 606.

183. On the ethnological approach of the Forsters, see Hans Erich Bödeker, "Aufklärerische ethnologische Praxis: Johann Reinhold Forster und Georg Forster," in *Wissenschaft als kulturelle Praxis 1750–1900*, ed. Hans Erich Bödeker, Peter Hanns Reill, and Jürgen Schlumbohm (Göttingen: Vandenhoeck & Ruprecht, 1999), 227–53; Bödeker, "Die 'Natur des Menschen so viel möglich in mehreres Licht...setzen.' Ethnologische Praxis bei Johann Reinhold und Georg Forster," in *Natur–Mensch–Kultur. Georg Forster im Wissenschaftsfeld seiner Zeit*, ed. Jörn Garber and Tanja van Hoorn (Hannover: Wehrhahn, 2006), 143–70.
184. Forster, *Voyage Round the World*, II: 349.
185. Ibid., II: 350.
186. Ibid., I: 296. The implicit polemic with Rousseau is unmistakable again.
187. Ibid., I: 168.
188. Ibid., I: 256.
189. Ibid., I: 290.
190. Ibid., I: 308.
191. Ibid., I: xiii.
192. Kant first addressed the subject in lectures at Königsberg, published in 1775 ("Von den verschiedenen Rassen des Menschen"), but the targets of Forster's reaction were his "Bestimmung des Begriffs einer Menschenrasse" and "Mutmaßlicher Anfang der Menschengeschichte," published in the *Berlinische Monatsschrift* in 1786. (These essays were themselves responses to the views advanced by his former student Johann Gottfried Herder in the *Ideen zur Philosophie der Geschichte der Menschheit* in 1784, rejecting the very concept of race as ignoble and unworthy of humanity.)
193. The topics of the relevant issue of the *Göttingisches historisches Magazin* included the "differences between the Germanic and other Celtic peoples," "the nature of African Negroes," "the rightfulness of the slave trade," etc. It ought to be added that Forster's polemic with Meiners—with whom he had been personally acquainted and kept a relatively friendly contact since 1778—can also be traced back to the publication of the latter's *Grundriß der Geschichte der Menschheit* (1785). See Lotter, *Christoph Meiners*, 51–6, 64–75; Marino, *Praeceptores*, 111 ff.
194. See, among others, Robert Bernasconi, "Who Invented the Concept of Race: Kant's Role in the Enlightenment Construction of Race," in *Race*, ed. Robert Bernasconi (Oxford: Blackwell, 2001), 11–36; Bernasconi, "Kant as an Unfamiliar Source of Racism," in *Philosophers on Race*, ed. T. Lott and J. Ward (Oxford: Oxford University Press, 2002), 145–66; Muthu, *Enlightenment Against Empire*, ch. 4; Pauline Kleingeld, "Kant's Second Thoughts on Race," *The Philosophical Quarterly* 57/229 (October 2007), 573–92; Mark Larrimore, "Antinomies of Race: Diversity and Destiny in Kant," *Patterns of Prejudice* 42/4-5 (2008): 341–63; Irene Tucker, *The Moment of Racial Sight: A History* (Chicago: University of Chicago Press, 2009), ch. 1; Pauline Kleingeld, *Kant and Cosmopolitanism: The Philosophical Ideal of World Citizenship* (Cambridge: Cambridge University Press, 2011), ch. 4 on the debate with Forster.
195. Immanuel Kant, "Bestimmung des Begriffs einer Menschenrace," in *Gesammelte Schriften*, ed. Königliche Preußische (Deutsche) Akademie der Wissenschaften, vol. VIII: *Abhandlungen nach 1780* (Berlin: Georg Reimer, 1912), 91. In developing his system of philosophical anthropology, Kant virtually ignored a sizeable body of recent literature on ethnography/*Völkerkunde* and ethnology/*Volkskunde* in Germany (especially at the University of Göttingen) and Austria-Hungary. Han T. Vermeulen, "The German Invention of Völkerkunde: Ethnological Discourse in Europe and Asia, 1740–1798," in *The German Invention of Race*, ed. Sara Eigen and Mark Larrimore (Albany: State University of New York Press, 2006), 136–7.
196. Sonia Sikka, *Herder on Humanity and Cultural Difference: Enlightened Relativism* (Cambridge: Cambridge University Press, 2011), especially 26 ff., 47 ff., 143 ff.

197. John Zammito, *Kant, Herder, and the Birth of Anthropology* (Chicago: University of Chicago Press, 2002), 333–4; Frederick C. Beiser, *The German Historicist Tradition* (Oxford: Oxford University Press, 2011), 104.
198. Tucker, *Moment of Racial Sight*, 59. On Herder ("a Kantian of the year 1765") as fulfilling the path which Kant abandoned, and the conflict between the two figures in the 1780s as one between the critical and the pre-critical Kant, see Zammito, *Kant, Herder, and the Birth of Anthropology*, "Introduction" and passim.
199. "By the dawn of the twenty-first century, some skepticism has developed about what remains of Kant's transcendental ambitions. At the same time, many of us seek to discover and redeploy the hermeneutic strategies of the path he abandoned and Herder took up." Ibid., 13.
200. John Zammito, "Policing Polygeneticism in Germany, 1775. (Kames), Kant, and Blumenbach," in *The German Invention of Race*, ed. Eigen and Larrimore, 38 ff. The conflict between Meiners and Johann Friedrich Blumenbach, who took a position similar to Forster's in the later debate, may similarly be traced back to the time of Blumenbach's famous dissertation "On the Natural Variety of Mankind" (1775), when Meiners himself started to publish essays on ethnographic subjects. Ibid., 44–5; and Frank Doughterty, "Christoph Meiners und Johann Friedrich Blumenbach im Streit um den Begriff der Menschenrasse," in *Die Natur des Menschen: Probleme der Physischen Anthropologie und Rassenkunde (1750–1850)*, Soemmering Forschungen VI, ed. Günter Mann and Franz Dumont (Stuttgart: Gustav Fischer, 1990), 89–111.
201. See for details Carhart, *The Science of Culture*, "Introduction," and ch. 7.
202. Meiners, *Grundriß der Geschichte der Menschheit*, 13.
203. Ibid., 18.
204. Pocock, *Barbarism and Religion*, IV: 37–64.
205. This term was not consistently used to denote the theory that mankind takes its origins from several pairs of ancestors created by God through multiple separate acts until after it appeared as a counterpart of "monogenism/monogenist" in the work of the Philadelphia school of anthropology in 1857. However, the idea itself had been in currency since at least Isaac la Peyrère's *Pre-Adamitae* (1655), with sixteenth-century antecedents including the work of Paracelsus, Walter Raleigh, and Giordano Bruno. Claude Blanckaert, "Monogénisme et polygénisme," in *Dictionnaire du darwinisme et de l'évolution*, ed. Patrick Tort (Paris: PUF, 1996) II: 321–37; Sebastiani, "Race and National Characters."
206. Meiners, *Grundriß*, 20 ff.
207. Carhart, "Polynesia and Polygenism," 61.
208. Forster to Herder, January 21, 1787 (the former's first extant pronouncement on Meiners's views), quoted in *Werke*, vol. XI: *Rezensionen*, 416.
209. In the very opening sentence, Kames claimed that "[w]hether there are different races of men, or whether all men are of one race without any difference but what proceeds from climate or other external cause, is a question which philosophers differ widely about," and after a criticism of Buffon concluded that "effects so regular and permanent [in national character] must be owing to a constant and invariable cause" and that "the character of that greater part [of a nation] can have no foundation but nature." Henry Home Lord Kames, *Sketches of the History of Man*, ed. James A. Harris (Indianapolis: Liberty Fund, 2007), I: 30.
210. Forster set out his principles in a 1781 lecture, "Ein Blick in das Ganze der Natur," in *Werke*, vol. VIII: *Schriften zur Philosophie und Zeitgeschichte*, 77–97. It has been suggested that his outlook resembles that of Adam Ferguson, with whose German translator, Christian Garve, Forster became acquainted in the same year. See Annette Meyer, "Von der 'Science of Man' zur 'Naturgeschichte der Menschheit.' Einflüsse angelsächsischer Wissenschaft im Werk Georg Forsters," in *Natur–Mensch–Kultur*,

ed. Garber and van Hoorn, 47. For the contrast between the Forster and Kant in this regard, see Wolfdietrich Schmied-Kowarzik, "Der Streit um die Einheit des Menschengeschlechts. Gedanken zu Forster, Herder und Kant," in *Georg Forster*, ed. Klenke, Garber, and Heintze, 124 ff.
211. To be sure, in cases in which this approach was combined with a thesis of degeneracy, as it did in Buffon, it was still capable of supporting a theory of racial superiority/inferiority. See Phillip R. Sloan, "The Idea of Racial Degeneracy in Buffon's *Histoire Naturelle*," in *Racism in the Eighteenth Century*, ed. Harold E. Pagliaro (Cleveland: Case Western Reserve University Press, 1973), 293–321.
212. Georg Forster, review of *Göttingisches historisches Magazin*, vols. 4–7, *Allgemeine Literatur-Zeitung* 7 (January 8 and 10, 1791), in *Werke*, vol. XI: *Rezensionen*, 240.
213. Ibid., 246.
214. Ibid.
215. Georg Forster, "Noch etwas über Menschenrassen" (*Teutsche Merkur*, October and November 1786), *Werke*, VIII, *Schriften zu Philosophie und Zeitgeschichte*, 152–4. It has been suggested, though, that "privately" Forster shared Sömmering's opinion that blacks are more closely related to apes than to whites. Ulrich Enzensberger, *Georg Forster. Ein Leben in Scherben* (Frankfurt: Eichborn, 1996), 158.
216. Ibid., 141–2. Cf. Takahashi Mori, "Zwischen Mensch und Affe. Anthropologische Aspekte in Forsters *Reise um die Welt*," *Georg Forster Studien* 10/2 (2006): 359–72.
217. Schmied-Kowarzik, "Der Streit um die Einheit des Menschengeschlechts," 122 ff. Cf. Turner, *Moment of Racial Sight*, 56.
218. For an interesting discussion of this amalgamation and its relevance to Forster's method, demonstrated on a circumscribed subject, see Manuela Ribeiro Sanches, "Dunkelheit und Aufklärung–Rasse und Kultur. Erfahrung und Macht in Forsters Auseinandersetzungen mit Kant und Meiners," *Georg Forster Studien* 8 (2003): 53–82.
219. Ludwig Uhlig, "Theoretical or Conjectural History. Georg Forsters *Voyage Round the World* im Zeitgenössischen Kontext," *Germanisch-Romantische Monatsschrift* 53 (2003): 399–414; Uhlig, *Georg Forster*, 85–95; Meyer, "Von der 'Science of Man' zur 'Naturgeschichte der Menschheit,'" 35 ff.
220. Similarly, and quite astonishingly, Robertson's name is not even mentioned in most of the *Forsteriana* addressing "translation as intercultural communication," "processes of civilization and global commerce," or "Forster and India." Cf. Jörg Esleben, "Übersetzung als interkulturelle Kommunikation bei Georg Forster," *Georg Forster Studien* 9 (2004): 165–80; Ruth Stummann-Bowert, "Zivilisationsprozesse und Welthandel bei Georg Forster," *Georg Forster Studien* 10/1 (2006): 147–75; Jörg Esleben, "Forster und Indien," *Georg Forster Studien* 10/2 (2006): 407–26. For an exception, see Katsami Funakoshi, "Dupaty's Reisebeschreibung und Forsters *Ansichten vom Niederrhein*," *Georg Forster Studien* 10/2 (2006): 427–42.
221. Carhart, *Science of Culture*, 270–1.

Bibliography

Abbreviations

AhB   *Allgemeine historische Bibliothek vom Mitglieder der königlichen Instituts der historischen Wissenschaften zu Göttingen*
GAgS   *Göttingische Anzeigen vom gelehrten Sachen*

Archival sources

National Library of Scotland, Edinburgh
Robertson-MacDonald papers

Niedersächsische Staats- und Universitätsbibliothek, Göttingen
Bibliotheksarchiv, Ausleiheregister 1769–1793
Cod. Ms. Lichtenberg
Cod. Mich.

Universitätsarchiv Göttingen
J57; Promotionsalbum der Juristischen Fakultät 1789

Niedersächsisches Staatsarchiv in Wolfenbüttel
37 Alt 3643

Printed sources

Alexander, H. G., ed. *The Leibniz-Clarke Correspondence*. Manchester: Manchester University Press, 1956.
Anon. Review of Johann Reinhold Forster's *History of the Discoveries and Voyages*, *The Critical Review* 62 (November–December 1786): 330–7, 401–8.
Anon. Review of Ludwig Heinrich Nicolay's *Vermischte Gedichte und Prosaische Schriften* (including Robertson's *Entwurf des politischen Zustandes in Europa*), *Neue allgemeine deutsche Bibliothek* 7/1 (1793): 292–301.
Anon. Review of Ludwig Heinrich Nicolay's *Verse und Prose* (including Robertson's *Entwurf des politischen Zustandes in Europa*), *Allgemeine deutsche Bibliothek* 24/1 (1775): 104–8.
Anon. Review of William Robertson's *Historical Disquisition*, *Annalen der Geographie und Statistik* 3 (1792): 111–21.
Augustine. *Confessions*. Translated by R. S. Pine-Coffin. Chicago: Encyclopaedia Britannica, 1990.
Baumgarten, Siegmund Jacob. *Auszug der Kirchengeschichte, von der Geburt Jesu an*. Halle: J. A. Bauer, 1743.

---. *A Supplement to the English Universal History.* Lately published in London. London: Dilly, 1760.

---. *Übersetzung der Allgemeinen Welthistorie die in England durch eine Gesellschaft der Gelehrten ausgefertiget worden...Genau durchgesehen und mit häufigen Anmerkungen vermeret von Siegmund Jacob Baumgarten.* Halle: Gebauer, 1744.

---. *Untersuchung Theologischer Streitigkeiten. Mit einigen Anmerkungen, Vorrede und fortgesetzten Geschichte der christlichen Glaubenslehre,* 3 vols. Edited by Johann Salomo Semler. Halle: Gebauer, 1762–1764.

Bruns, J. P. "Etwas von dem Leben und den Verdiensten des de 26sten August 1803 zu Helmstedt verstorbenen Professors und Hofraths Julius August Remer." *Braunschweigisches Magazin* 37 (September 10, 1803).

Burke, Edmund. *The Correspondence of Edmund Burke,* 20 vols. Edited by Thomas W. Copeland. Cambridge: Cambridge University Press, 1958–1978.

---. *A Philosophical Enquiry into the Origin of Our Ideas of the Sublime and the Beautiful* [1757]. Edited by James T. Boulton. Oxford: Blackwell, 1987.

---. *Reflections on the Revolution in France* [1790]. In *The Writings and Speeches of Edmund Burke,* vol. 8: *The French Revolution 1790–1794.* Edited by Leslie Mitchell. Oxford: Clarendon Press, 1989.

---. "Review of William Robertson's *History of America.*" *Annual Register* 19 (1777): 214–34.

Cooper, Anthony Ashley, Third Earl of Shaftesbury. *Characteristics of Men, Manners, Opinions, Times, etc.* [1900]. Edited by John M. Robertson. Bristol: Thoemmes Press, 1997.

Dornford, Josiah. *The Motives and Consequences of the Present War Impartially Considered.* London: Pridden, 1793.

Ebeling, Johann Philipp. *Dissertatio medica iauguralis de Quassia et lichene islandico...pro gradu doctoratus...in comitiis Universitati Glasquensis. Eruditorum examini subjicit Joh. Theod. Phil. Christ. Ebeling, Luneburgensis...* Glasgow, 1779.

[Erskine, John], ed. *A Narrative of the Debate in the General Assembly of the Church of Scotland, May 25, 1779.* Edinburgh: n.p., 1780.

Ferguson, Adam. *An Essay on the History of Civil Society* [1767]. Edited by Fania Oz-Salzberger. Cambridge: Cambridge University Press, 1995.

---. *Institutes of Moral Philosophy.* Edinburgh: Kincaid and Bell, 1769.

Fletcher, Andrew. "Speeches by a Member of the Parliament which Began at Edinburgh on the 6th of May, 1703." In *Political Works,* edited by John Robertson. Cambridge: Cambridge University Press, 1997.

Forster, Georg. "Antrittsrede vor der Société des Antiquités de Cassel am 12. Dezember 1778." In *Werke,* vol. 8: *Kleine Schriften zu Philosophie und Zeitgeschichte,* edited by Siegfried Scheibe, 65–8. Berlin: Akademie Verlag, 1991.

---. "Ein Blick in das Ganze der Natur." In *Werke,* vol. 8: *Kleine Schriften zu Philosophie und Zeitgeschichte,* edited by Siegfried Scheibe, 77–97. Berlin: Akademie Verlag, 1991.

---. *Geschichte der Englischen Litteratur vom Jahre 1791.* In *Werke,* vol. 7: *Kleine Schriften zu Kunst und Literatur. Sakontala.* Edited by Gerhard Steiner, 228–71. Berlin: Akademie Verlag, 1993.

---. *James Cook, der Entdecker und Fragmente über Captain Cooks letzte Reise und sein Ende* [1787]. Edited by Frank Vorpahl. Berlin: Eichborn, 2008.

---. *Kleine Schriften. Ein Beytrag zur Völker- und Länderkunde, Naturgeschichte und Philosophie des Lebens,* vol. 1. Leipzig: Kummer, 1789.

---. "Noch etwas über Menschenrassen." In *Werke,* vol. 8: *Kleine Schriften zu Philosophie und Zeitgeschichte,* edited by Siegfried Scheibe, 130–56. Berlin: Akademie Verlag, 1991.

---. "Review of *Göttingisches historisches Magazin,* vols. 4–7." In *Werke,* vol. 11: *Rezensionen,* edited by Horst Fiedler, 236–52. Berlin: Akademie Verlag, 1977.

———. Review of William Robertson's *Historical Disquisition*. In *Werke*, vol. 11: *Rezensionen*. Edited by Horst Fiedler, 294–302. Berlin: Akademie Verlag, 1977.

———. "Über locale und allgemeine Bildung." In *Werke*, vol. 8: *Kleine Schriften zu Philosophie und Zeitgeschichte*, edited by Siegfried Scheibe, 45–56. Berlin: Akademie Verlag, 1991.

———. *A Voyage Round the World in His Britannic Majesty's Sloop, the Resolution, commanded by Capt. James Cook, during the Year 1772, 3, 4, and 5*, 2 vols. London: White, Robson, Elmsly and Robinson, 1777.

———. *Werke. Sämtliche Schriften, Tagebücher, Briefe*. Edited by Gerhard Steiner et al. Deutsche Akademie der Wissenschaften zu Berlin [from 1974, Akademie der Wissenschaften der DDR; from 2003, Berlin-Brandenburgische Akademie der Wissenschaften]. Berlin: Akademie Verlag, 1958.

———. *Werke*, vol. 16: *Briefe 1790 bis 1791*. Edited by Brigitte Leuschner and Siegfried Scheibe. Berlin: Akademie Verlag, 1980.

———. *Werke*, vol. 17: *Briefe 1792 bis 1794 und Nachträge*. Edited by Klaus-Georg Popp. Berlin: Akademie Verlag, 1989.

Forster, Johann Reinhold. *History of the Voyages and Discoveries Made in the North*. Dublin: Luke White, 1786.

———. *Observations Made During a Voyage Round the World* [1778]. Edited by Nicholas Thomas, Harriet Guest, and Michael Dettelbach. Honolulu: University of Hawaii Press, 1996.

———. Review of Isaak Iselin's *Über die Geschichte der Menschheit*. *The Critical Review, or, Annals of Literature* 32 (April 1772): 340–1.

———. *The Resolution Journal of Johann Reinhold Forster 1772–1775*. Edited by Michael E. Hoare. London: Hakluyt Society, 1982.

Gatterer, Johann Christoph. "Nähere Nachricht voin der neuen Ausgabe der gleichzeitigen Schriftsteller über die teutsche Geschichte." *AhB* 8 (1768): 3–22.

———. "vom historischen Plan, und der darauf sich gründenden Zusammenfügung der Erzählungen." *AhB* 1/1 (1767): 9–28.

———. "von der Kunst zu übersetzen, besonders in Absicht auf historische Schriften." *AhB* 1/2 (1767): 7–23.

[Haller, Albrecht von]. Review of William Robertson's *History of Scotland*, *GAgS* 8 (1760): 913–8.

———. Review of William Robertson's *History of Charles V*. *GAgS* 1/18 (1770): 551–3, 931–3, 996–9.

Häberlin, Franz Dominic. *Neue Teutsche Reichs-Geschichte, Vom Anfänge des Schmalkaldischen Krieges bis auf unsere Zeiten*, 21 vols. Halle: Gebauer, 1774–1790.

Heeren, Arnold Ludwig Herrmann. "Commentatio de graecorum de India notitia et cum Indis commerciis"; "Commentatio de mercatura Indicae ratione et viis." *Commentationes societatis regiae scientiarum goettingensis* 10 (1791): 121–56.

———. "Commentatio de Romanorum de India notitia." *Commentationes societatis regiae scientiarum goettingensis* 11 (1793): 63–90.

———. *Handbuch der Geschichte des Europäischen Staatensystems und seiner Colonien, von der Entdeckung beyder Indien bis zur Errichtung des Französischer Kayserthrons*. Göttingen: Vandenhoeck & Ruprecht, 1809.

———. *Ideen über die Politik, den Verkehr und den Handel der vornehmsten Völker der alten Welt*, 2 vols. Göttingen: Vandenhoeck & Ruprecht, 1793–1796.

———. Review of William Robertson's *Historical Disquisition*. *Bibliothek der alten Litteratur und Kunst* 9 (1792): 105–22.

[Heyne, Christian Gottlob]. Review of Georg Friedrich Seiler's translation of Demosthenes and Lysias. *GAgS* 16 (1768): 1209–12.

———. Review of William Robertson's *History of America*. Pt. 1. *Zugabe zu den GAgS*, 1/23 (1777): 657–67.

———. Review of William Robertson's *History of America*. Pt. 2. *Zugabe zu den GAgS*, 1/23 (1777): 689–99.
Home, Henry, Lord Kames. *Sketches of the History of Man*, 2 vols. Edited by James A. Harris. Indianapolis: Liberty Fund, 2007.
Hume, David. *Essays Moral, Political and Literary*. Edited by Eugene F. Miller. Indianapolis: Liberty Press, 1985.
———. *The Letters of David Hume*, 2 vols. Edited by John Young Thomson Greig. Oxford: Clarendon Press, 1932.
Julius August Remers weil. Herzogl. Braunschw. Lüneb. Hofraths und Professors der Geschichte und Statistik auf der Julius Karls Universität zu Helmstedt hinterlassene Büchersammlung, welche den 1sten November 1804 und folgende Tage zu Helmstedt öffentlich verkauft warden soll. Braunschweig: Waisenhaus, 1804.
Kant, Immanuel. "Bestimmung des Begriffs einer Menschenrace." In *Gesammelte Schriften*, vol. 8: *Abhandlungen nach 1780*, edited by Königliche Preußische (Deutsche) Akademie der Wissenschaften, 89–106. Berlin: Georg Reimer, 1912.
Lessing, Gotthold Ephraim. *Anti-Goeze*. In *Werke und Briefe*, vol. 9: *Werke 1778–1780*. Edited by Klaus Bohnen and Arno Schilson, 93–215. Frankfurt: Deutscher Klassiker Verlag, 1993.
———. *Axiomata*. In *Werke und Briefe*, vol. 9: *Werke 1778–1780*. Edited by Klaus Bohnen and Arno Schilson, 53–89. Frankfurt: Deutscher Klassiker Verlag, 1993.
———. *Die Erziehung des Menschengeschlechts*. In *Werke und Briefe*, vol. 10: *Werke 1778–1781*. Edited by Arno Schilson, Axel Schmitt, 73–99. Frankfurt: Deutscher Klassiker Verlag, 2001.
———. *Gegensätze des Herausgebers*. In *Werke und Briefe*, vol. 8: *Werke 1774–1778*. Edited by Arno Schilson, 312–50. Frankfurt: Deutscher Klassiker Verlag, 1989.
———. *Über den Beweis des Geistes und der Kraft*. In *Werke und Briefe*, vol. 8: *Werke 1774–1778*. Edited by Arno Schilson, 437–46. Frankfurt: Deutscher Klassiker Verlag, 1989.
———. *Werke und Briefe*, vol. 11, pt. 2: *Briefe von und an Lessing 1770–1776*. Edited by Helmuth Kiesel et al. Frankfurt: Deutscher Klassiker Verlag, 1988.
———. *Werke und Briefe*, vol. 12: *Briefe von und an Lessing 1776–1781*. Edited by Helmuth Kiesel et al. Frankfurt: Deutscher Klassiker Verlag, 1994.
———. *Werke und Briefe in zwölf Bänden*, 12 vols. Edited by Wilfried Barner et al. Frankfurt: Deutscher Klassiker Verlag, 1985–2003.
Locke, John. *An Essay Concerning Human Understanding*. Edited by Peter H. Nidditch. Oxford: Clarendon Press, 1975.
———. *Two Treatises of Government*. Edited by Pater Laslett. Cambridge: Cambridge University Press, 1988.
Mandeville, Bernard. *The Fable of the Bees and Other Writings*. Edited by Edward Hundert. Indianapolis: Hackett, 1997.
Meiners, Christoph. *Geschichte des weiblichen Geschlechts*. Hannover: Helwing, 1788.
———. *Geschichte der Ungleichheit der Stände unter den vornehmsten Europäischen Staaten*. Hannover: Helwing, 1792.
———. *Grundriß der Geschichte der Menschheit*. Lemgo: Meyer, 1785.
Mendelssohn, Moses. "Über die Frage: was heißt aufklären?" [*Berlinische Monatsschrift*, 1784]. In *Was ist Aufklärung? Thesen und Definitionen*, edited by Ehrhard Bahr, 3–8. Stuttgart: Reclam, 1974.
Michaelis, Johann David. *Einleitung in die göttliche Schriften des Neuen Bundes. Dritte und vermehrte Ausgabe*, 2 vols. Göttingen: Vandenhoeck, 1777.
———. *Erklärung der Begräbnis und Auferstehungsgeschichte Christi nach der vier Evangelisten. Mit Rücksicht auf die in den Fragmenten gemachten Einwürfe und deren Beantwortung*. Halle: Waisenhaus, 1783.
Moser, Friedrich Carl von. *Der Herr und der Diener, geschildert mit patriotischer Freyheit*. Frankfurt: Raspe, 1759.

———. *Patriotische Briefe* [1765]. n.p., 1767.
———, ed. *Patriotisches Archiv für Deutschland*, 12 vols. Frankfurt and Leipzig: C. F. Schwan, 1784–1790.
Newton, Isaac. *Mathematical Principles of Natural Philosophy*. Chicago: University of Chicago Press, 1952.
Pennant, Thomas. *Thomas Pennants Reise durch Schottland und die Hebridischen Inseln*, 2 vols. Translated by Johann Philipp Ebeling. Leipzig: Weygand, 1779–1780.
Pufendorf, Samuel von. *Die Verfassung des deutschen Reiches*. Edited by Horst Denzer. Stuttgart: Reclam, 1976.
Pütter, Johann Stephan. *An Historical Development of the Present Political Constitution of the Germanic Empire*, 3 vols. London: Payne, 1790.
———. *Historische Entwicklung des heutigen Staatsverfassung des Teutschen Reichs*, 3 vols. Göttingen: Ruprecht, 1786–1787.
———. *Teutsche Reichsgeschichte in ihrem Hauptfaden entwickelt*. Göttingen: Ruprecht, 1778.
Remer, Julius August, ed. *Amerikanisches Archiv*, 3 vols. Braunschweig: Waisenhaus, 1777–1778.
———. *Ausführliches Handbuch der ältern allgemeinen Geschichte; nebst einer Vorstellung der politischen, geistlichen, gelehrten und bürgerlichen Verfassung der Nationen in jedem Zeitpunkte*. Braunschweig: Waisenhaus, 1775.
———. *Handbuch der allgemeinen Geschichte*, 3 vols. Braunschweig: Waisenhaus, 1783–1784.
———. *Handbuch der Geschichte neuerer Zeiten, von der grossen Völkerwanderung bis zum Hubertusburgischen Frieden*. Braunschweig: Waisenhaus, 1771.
———. *Lehrbuch der Staatskunde der vornehmsten europäischen Staaten*. Braunschweig: Waisenhaus, 1785.
———. *Tabellen zur Aufbewahrubg der wichtigsten statistischen Veränderungen in der vornehmsten Europäischen Staaten*. Braunschweig: Waisenhaus, 1786–1794.
———. *Versuch einer Geschichte der französischen Constitutionen*. Helmstedt: Fleckeisen, 1795.
Robertson, William. *Dr. Wilhelm Robertsons, Vorstehers der Universität Edinburg, und königlichen Großbritannischen Geschichtsschreibers, Geschichte der Regierung Kaiser Carls des V*, 3 vols. Translated by Johann Martin von Abele, notes Julius August Remer et al. Kempten: n.p., 1781–1783.
———. *Entwurf des politischen Zustandes in Europa, vom Verfall der römischen Macht an bis auf das sechzehnte Jahrhundert. Aus Robertsons Einleitung in die Geschichte Karls des Fünften gezogen* [1773]. In *Vermischte Gedichte und prosaische Schriften von Herrn Ludwig Heinrich von Nicolay*. Berlin and Stettin: Friedrich Nicolai, 1793.
———. *Geschichte von Amerika*, 2 vols. Translated by Johann Friedrich Schiller. Leipzig: Weidmanns Erben und Reich, 1777.
———. *Herrn Dr Wilhelm Robertsons Geschichte der Regirerung des Kaiser Carls des Fünften. Nebst einem Abrisse des Wachstums und Fortgangs des gesellschaftlichen Lebens in Europa bis auf den Anfang des 16. Jhs*, 5 vols. Translated and reviewed by Julius August Remer. Vienna: Härter, 1819. Based on the edition at Braunschweig: Schulbuchhandlung/Waisenhaus, 1792–1796.
———. *Herrn Dr. Wilhelm Robertsons Geschichte der Regierung Kaiser Carls des Fünften. Nebst einem Abrisse des Wachstums und Fortgangs des gesellschaftlichen Lebens in Europa bis auf den Anfang des sechzehnten Jahrhundert* [1770], 3 vols. Translated by Theodor Christoph Mittelstedt, notes by Julius August Remer. 2nd ed. Braunschweig: Waisenhaus, 1778–1779.
———. *Herrn Wilhelm Robertsons Geschichte von Schottland unter den Regierungen der Königinn Maria, und des Königes Jacobs VI. bis auf dessen Erhebung auf den englischen Thron*, 2 vols. Translated by Theodor Christoph Mittelstedt. Braunschweig: Meyer; Leipzig: Breitkopf, 1762.

——. *An Historical Disquisition Concerning the Knowledge Which the Ancients Had of India; and the Progress of Trade With That Country Prior to the Discovery of the Passage to It by the Cape of Good Hope* [1791]. London: Routledge/Thoemmes Press, 1996.

——. *Historische Untersuchung über die Kenntnisse der Alten von Indien, und die Fortschritte des Handels mit diesem Lande vor der Entdeckung des Weges dahin um das Vorgebirge der guten Hoffnung*. Translated by Georg Forster. Berlin: Voß, 1792.

——. *The History of America* [1777], 2 vols. London: Routledge/Thoemmes Press, 1996.

——. *The History of Scotland During the Reigns of Queen Mary and of King James VI, till His Accession to the Crown of England* [1759], 2 vols. London: Routledge/Thoemmes Press, 1996.

——. *The History of the Reign of the Emperor Charles V. With a View of the Progress of Society in Europe, from the Subversion of the Roman Empire to the Beginning of the Sixteenth Century* [1769]. Routledge/Thoemmes Press: London, 1996.

——. *The Situation of the World at the Time of Christ's Appearance, and Its Connection with the Success of His Religion* [1755]. London: Routledge/Thoemmes Press, 1996.

——. *Wilhelm Robertsons Geschichte von Schottland unter den Regierungen der Königinn Maria und des Königs Jacobs VI. bis auf die Zeit, da der Letztere den englischen Thron bestieg*. Translated by Georg Friedrich Seiler. Ulm and Leipzig: Gaum, 1762.

——. *Der Zustand der Welt bey der Erscheinung Christi und sein Einfluß auf den Fortgang der Religion*. Translated by Johann Philipp Ebeling. Hamburg: Herold, 1779.

Schlözer, August Ludwig. "Review of *Übersetzung der allgemeinen Welthistorie*," pts. 1–2. *GAgS*, 14 (January 27, 1766): 90–3, and (April 10–12, 1766): 340–8.

——. *Stats-Gelartheit. Zweiter Theil: Theorie der Statistik nebst Ideen über das Studium der Politik überhaupt*. Göttingen: Vandenhoeck & Ruprecht, 1804.

——. *Vorstellung seiner Universal-Historie* (1772/73). Edited by Horst Walter Blanke. Hagen: Margit Rottmann Medienverlag, 1990.

Schmidt, Michael Ignaz. *Geschichte der Deutschen*, 6 vols. Ulm: Stettin, 1778–1783.

Semler, Johann Salomo. *Beantwortung der Fragmente eines Ungenanten insbesondere vom Zweck Jesu und seiner Jünger* [1779]. Edited by Dirk Fleischer. Waltrop: Hartmut Spenner, 2003.

——. *Neue Versuche die Kirchenhistorie der ersten Jahrhunderte mehr aufzuklären*. Leipzig: Weygand, 1788.

——. *Versuch den Gebrauch der Quellen in den Staats- und Kirchengeschichte der mittleren Zeiten zu erleichtern* [1761]. Edited by Dirk Fleischer. Waltrop: Hartmut Spenner, 1996.

——. "Vorrede." In Johann von Ferreras's *Algemeine Historie von Spanien mit den Zusätzen der französischen Uebersetzung nebst Fortsetzung bis auf gegenwärtige Zeit*, vol. 8. Halle: Gebauer, 1757.

Smith, Adam. *An Inquiry into the Nature and Causes of the Wealth of Nations* [1776]. Edited by Roy H. Campbell and Andrew S. Skinner. Indianapolis: Liberty Classics, 1981.

——. *Lectures on Jurisprudence* [1762–1763]. Edited by Ronald L. Meek, David D. Raphael and Peter G. Stein. Oxford: Clarendon Press, 1978.

——. *The Theory of Moral Sentiments* [1759]. Edited by David D. Raphael and Alec L. Macfie. Indianapolis: Liberty Fund, 1982.

——. *Untersuchung der Natur und Ursachen von Nationalreichthümern*, 2 vols. Translated by Johann Friedrich Schiller and Christian August Wichmann. Leipzig: Weidmanns Erben und Reich, 1776–1778.

[Spittler, Ludwig Timotheus]. Review of Julius August Remer's *Abriß des gesellschaftlichen Lebens in Europa...Nach dem ertsen Theile von Robertsons Leben Carl V. bearbeitet*. *GAgS* 41 (1793): II: 786–96.

Sprengel, Matthias Christian. *Geschichte der wichtigsten geographischen Entdeckungen bis zur Ankunft der Portuguisen in Japan 1542*. 2nd ed. Halle: Hemmerde und Schwetschke, 1792.

Stedman, Charles. *Geschichte des Ursprungs, des Fortgangs und der Beendigung des Amerikanischen Krieges*, 2 vols. Translated by Julius August Remer. Berlin: Voß, 1795.
Stewart, Dugald. *Biographical Memoirs of Adam Smith, L.L.D., of William Robertson, D.D, and of Thomas Reid, D.D.* Edinburgh: George Ramsay, 1811.
Stuart, Gilbert. *A View of Society in Europe in Its Progress from Rudeness to Refinement: Or, Inquiries Concerning the History of Law, Government, and Manners* [1778]. Basel: Tourneisen, 1797.

Literature

Abbattista, Guido. "Empire, Liberty and the Rule of Difference: European Debates on British Colonialism in Asia at the End of the Eighteenth Century." *European Review of History/Revue européenne d'histoire* 13/3 (2006): 473–98.
Ahnert, Thomas. "Fortschrittsgeschichte und religiöse Aufklärung. William Robertson und die Deutung außereuropäischer Kulturen." In *Die Aufklärung und ihre Weltwirkung*, edited by Wolfgang Hardtwig, 101–22. Göttingen: Vandenhoeck & Ruprecht, 2009.
———. "Religion and the Moderates' Enlightenment: The Historiography of William Robertson." Manuscript. Paper read at the conference, "Empire, Philosophy and Religion: Scotland and Central/Eastern Europe in the Eighteenth Century." Central European University, Budapest, June 23–26, 2005.
Allan, David. "Protestantism, Presbyterianism and National Identity in Eighteenth-Century Scottish History." In *Protestantism and National Identity: Britain and Ireland, c. 1650–1850*, edited by Tony Claydon and Ian McBride, 182–205. Cambridge: Cambridge University Press, 1998.
———. *Virtue, Learning, and the Scottish Enlightenment: Ideas of Scholarship in Early Modern History*. Edinburgh: Edinburgh University Press, 1993.
Aretin, Karl Othmar Freiherr von. *Heiliges Römisches Reich 1776–1806: Reichsverfassung und Staatssouveränität*, 2 vols. Wiesbaden: Steiner, 1967.
———. "Reichspatriotismus." *Aufklärung* 4/2 (1989): 25–36.
Armitage, David. "The New World and British Historical Thought: From Richard Hakluyt to William Robertson." In *America in European Consciousness*, edited by Karen Ordahl Kupperman, 68–70. Chapel Hill and London: University of North Carolina Press, 1995.
———. *The Ideological Origins of the British Empire*. Cambridge: Cambridge University Press, 2000.
Barber, Giles, and Bernhard Fabian, eds. *Buch und Buchhandel in Europa im achtzehnten Jahrhundert*. Wolfenbüttler Studien zur Geschichte des Buchwesens 7. Hamburg: Felix Meiner, 1981.
Baumgart, Peter, ed. *Michael Ignaz Schmidt (1736–1794) in seiner Zeit. Der aufgeklärte Theologe, Bildungsreformer und "Historiker der Deutschen" aus Franken in neuer Sicht*. Neustadt an der Aisch: Verlag Degener. 1996.
———. "Michael Ignaz Schmidt (1736–1794). Leben und Werk." In *Michael Ignaz Schmidt (1736–1794) in seiner Zeit. Der aufgeklärte Theologe, Bildungsreformer und "Historiker der Deutschen" aus Franken in neuer Sicht*, edited by Peter Baumgart, 115–33. Neustadt an der Aisch: Verlag Degener. 1996.
Becker-Schaum, Christoph. *Arnold Herrmann Ludwig Heeren. Ein Beitrag zur Geschichte der Geschichtswissenschaft zwischen Aufklärung und Historismus*. Bern: Peter Lang, 1993.
———. "Die Beziehungen zwischen Georg Forster und Arnold Heeren und ihr Niederschlag in Heerens Werk." *Georg Forster Studien* 12 (2007): 211–29.
Beiser, Frederick C. *The German Historicist Tradition*. Oxford: Oxford University Press, 2011.
Bergerhausen, Hans-Wolfgang, "Michael Ignaz Schmidt in der historiographischen Tradition der Aufklärung." In *Michael Ignaz Schmidt (1736–1794) in seiner Zeit. Der*

aufgeklärte Theologe, Bildungsreformer und "Historiker der Deutschen" aus Franken in neuer Sicht, edited by Peter Baumgart, 63–79. Neustadt an der Aisch: Verlag Degener, 1996.
Berlin, Isaiah. "Hume and the Sources of German Anti-Rationalism." In *Against the Current: Essays in the History of Ideas*, 162–87. Oxford: Oxford University Press, 1981.
Bernasconi, Robert. "Kant as an Unfamiliar Source of Racism." In *Philosophers on Race*, edited by T. Lott and J. Ward, 145–66. Oxford: Oxford University Press, 2002.
———. "Who Invented the Concept of Race: Kant's Role in the Enlightenment Construction of Race." In *Race*, edited by Robert Bernasconi, 11–36. Oxford: Blackwell, 2001.
———. ed. *Concepts of Race in the Eighteenth Century*. Bristol: Thoemmes Press, 2001.
Bernasconi, Robert, and Tommy Lee Lott, eds. *The Idea of Race*. Indianapolis: Hackett, 2000.
Berney, Arnold. "Michael Ignatz Schmidt. Ein Beitrag zur Geschichte der Historiographie in der deutschen Aufklärung." *Historisches Jahrbuch* 44 (1924): 211–39.
Berry, Christopher J. *Social Theory of the Scottish Enlightenment*. Edinburgh: Edinburgh University Press, 1997.
Bickham, Troy. *Savages Within the Empire: Representations of American Indians in Eighteenth-Century Britain*. Oxford: Clarendon Press, 2005.
Bieberstein, Johannes Rogalla von. *Die These von der Verschwörung 1776–1945*. Frankfurt: Peter Lang, 1976.
Bisson, Douglas R. *The Merchant Adventurers of England: The Company and the Crown, 1474–1564*. Newark: University of Delaware Press, 1993.
Bitterli, Urs. *Cultures in Conflict: Encounters between European and Non-European Cultures*. Cambridge: Polity Press, 1989.
Black, Jeremy. "The Enlightenment Historian at Work: The Researches of William Robertson." *Bulletin of Hispanic Studies* 65 (1988): 251–60.
Blanckaert, Claude. "Monogénisme et polygénisme." In *Dictionnaire du darwinisme et de l'évolution*, vol 2, edited by Patrick Tort, 321–37. Paris: PUF, 1996.
Blanke, Horst Walter. "Zwischen Aufklärung und Historismus: A.H.L. Heerens 'Geschichte des Europäischen Staatensystems.'" In *Aufklärung und Historik. Aufsätze zur Entwicklung der Geschichtswissenschaft, Kirchengeschichte und Geschichtstheorie in der deutschen Aufklärung*, edited by Horst Walter Blanke and Dirk Fleischer, 202–26. Waltrop: Hartmut Spenner, 1991.
Bollacher, Martin. *Lessing: Vernunft und Geschichte. Untersuchungen zum Problem religiöser Aufklärung in der Spätschriften*. Tübingen: Niemeyer, 1978.
Boockmann, Hartmut, and Hermann Wellenreuther, eds. *Geschichtswissenschaft in Göttingen*. Göttingen: Vandenhoeck & Ruprecht, 1987.
Bödeker, Hans Erich. "Aufklärerische ethnologische Praxis: Johann Reinhold Forster und Georg Forster." In *Wissenschaft als kulturelle Praxis 1750–1900*, edited by Hans Erich Bödeker, Peter Hanns Reill, and Jürgen Schlumbohm, 227–53. Göttingen: Vandenhoeck & Ruprecht, 1999.
———. "The Debates about Universal History and National History around 1800: A Problem-Oriented Historical Attempt." In *Unity and Diversity in European Culture c. 1800: Proceedings of the British Academy*, edited by Tim Blanning and Hagen Schulze, 135–70. Oxford: Oxford University Press/British Academy, 2006.
———. "'…l'instrument de la Révolution et en même temps son âme': 'L'opinion publique' chez Georg Forster." *European Review of History/Revue européenne d'histoire* 13/3 (2006): 373–83.
———. "Landesgeschichtliche Erkenntnisinteressen der nordwestdeutschen Aufklärungshistorie." *Niedersächsisches Jahrbuch für Landesgeschichte* 69 (1997): 247–79.
———. "Die 'Natur des Menschen so viel möglich in mehreres Licht […] setzen.' Ethnologische Praxis bei Johann Reinhold und Georg Forster." In *Natur–Mensch–Kultur*.

Georg Forster im Wissenschaftsfeld seiner Zeit, edited by Jörn Garber and Tanja van Hoorn, 143–70. Hannover: Wehrhahn, 2006.
——. "…wer ächte freie Politik hören will, muss nach Göttingen gehen." In *Die Wissenschaft vom Menschen in Göttingen um 1800*, edited by Hans Erich Bödeker, Philippe Büttgen, and Michel Espagne, 325–69. Göttingen: Vandenhoeck & Ruprecht, 2008.
Bödeker, Hans Erich, and Ulrich Hermann, eds. *Aufklärung als Politisierung, Politisierung der Aufklärung*. Hamburg: Felix Meiner, 1987.
Bödeker, Hans Erich, Philippe Büttgen, and Michel Espagne, eds. *Die Wissenschaft vom Menschen in Göttingen um 1800*. Göttingen: Vandenhoeck & Ruprecht, 2008.
Bödeker, Hans Erich, Georg G. Iggers, and Jonathan B. Knudsen, eds. *Aufklärung und Geschichte. Studien zur deutschen Geschichtswissenschaft im 18. Jahrhundert*. Göttingen: Vandenhoeck & Ruprecht, 1986.
Bödeker, Hans Erich, Peter Hanns Reill, and Jürgen Schlumbohm, eds. *Wissenschaft als kulturelle Praxis 1750–1900*. Göttingen: Vandenhoeck & Ruprecht, 1999.
Bräunlein, Peter J. *Martin Behaim. Legende und Wirklichkeit eines berühmten Nürnbergers*. Bamberg: Bayerische Verlagsanstalt, 1992.
Brockington, John L. "Warren Hastings and Orientalism." In *The Impeachment of Warren Hastings*, edited by Geoffrey Carnall and Colin Nicholson, 91–108. Edinburgh: Edinburgh University Press, 1989.
Brown, Stuart J. "An Eighteenth-Century Historian on the Amerindians: Culture, Colonialism and Christianity in William Robertson's History of America." *Studies in World Christianity* 2 (1996): 204–22.
——. "William Robertson and the Scottish Enlightenment." In *William Robertson and the Expansion of Empire*, edited by Stuart J. Brown, 7–35. Cambridge: Cambridge University Press, 1997.
——. "William Robertson, Early Orientalism and the *Historical Disquisition* on India of 1791." *The Scottish Historical Review* 88/2 (2009): 289–312.
——, ed. *William Robertson and the Expansion of Empire*. Cambridge: Cambridge University Press, 1997.
Brunner, Otto, Werner Conze, and Reinhart Koselleck, eds. *Geschichtliche Grundbegriffe. Historisches Lexikon zur politisch-sozialen Sprache in Deutschland*, 8 vols. Stuttgart: Klett-Cotta, 1972–1997.
Brückner, Jutta. *Staatswissenschaften, Kameralismus und Naturrecht. Ein Beitrag zur Geschichte der politischen Wissenschaft im Deutschland des späten 17. und frühen 18. Jahrhunderts*. Munich: C. H. Beck, 1976.
Bryson, Gladys. *Man and Society: The Scottish Inquiry of the Eighteenth Century*. Princeton: Princeton University Press, 1945.
Bulst, Neithard, Jörg Fisch, and Reinhart Koselleck. "Revolution." In *Geschichtliche Grundbegriffe. Historisches Lexikon zur politisch-sozialen Sprache in Deutschland*, vol. 5, edited by Otto Brunner, Werner Conze, and Reinhart Koselleck, 653–788. Stuttgart: Klett-Cotta, 1984.
Bury, John B. *The Idea of Progress: An Inquiry into Its Growth and Origin*. New York: Dover, 1955.
Cañizares-Esguerra, Jorge. *How to Write the History of the New World: Historiographies, Epistemologies and Identities in the Eighteenth-Century Atlantic World*. Stanford: Stanford University Press, 2001.
Carhart, Michael. "Polynesia and Polygenism: The Scientific Use of Travel Literature in the Early 19th Century." *History of the Human Sciences* 22/2 (2009): 58–86.
——. *The Science of Culture in Enlightenment Germany*. Cambridge: Harvard University Press, 2007.
Carlsson, Eric Wilhelm. "Johann Salomo Semler, the German Enlightenment, and Protestant Theology's Historical Turn." PhD Diss., University of Wisconsin, Madison, 2006.

Carpenter, Kenneth E. *Dialogue in Political Economy: Translations from and into German in the Eighteenth Century*. Boston: Kress Library Publications, 1977.

Carter, Jeremy J. "The Making of Principal Robertson in 1762: Politics and the University of Edinburgh in the Second Half of the Eighteenth Century." *Scottish Historical Review* 49/1 (1970): 60–84.

Ceserani, Giovanna. "Narrative, Interpretation, and Plagiarism in Mr. Robertson's 1778 History of Ancient Greece." *Journal of the History of Ideas* 66/3 (2005): 413–36.

Clark, Ian D. L. "From Protest to Reaction: The Moderate Regime in the Church of Scotland, 1752–1805." In *Scotland in the Age of Improvement*, edited by Nicholas Phillipson and Rosalind Mitchison, 200–24. Edinburgh: Edinburgh University Press, 1970.

Clark, William. *Academic Charisma and the Origins of the Research University*. Chicago: University of Chicago Press, 2008.

———. "On the Bureaucratic Plots of the Research Library." In *Books and the Sciences in History*, edited by Marina Frasca-Spada and Nick Jardine, 190–206. Cambridge: Cambridge University Press, 2000.

Clark, William, Jan Golinski, and Simon Schaffer, eds. *The Sciences in Enlightened Europe*. Chicago: University of Chicago Press, 1999.

Cornell Szasz, Margaret. *Scottish Highlanders and Native Americans: Indigenous Education in the Eighteenth-Century Atlantic World*. Norman: University of Oklahoma Press, 2007.

Crusius, Gabriele. *Aufklärung und Bibliophilie. Der Hannoveraner Sammler Georg Friedrich Brandes und seine Bibliothek*. Heidelberg: Universitätsverlag Winter, 2008.

Damme, Stéphane Van. "La grandeur d'Édimbourg. Savoirs et mobilization identitaire au XVIIIe siècle." *Revue d'Histoire Moderne et Contemporaine* 55/2 (2008): 152–81.

Danneberg, Lutz. "Siegmund Jakob Baumgartens biblische Hermeneutik." In *Unzeitgemäße Hermeneutik. Verstehen und Interpretation im Denken der Aufklärung*, edited by Axel Bühler, 88–157. Frankfurt: Klostermann, 1994.

Darnton, Robert. *The Forbidden Best-Sellers of Pre-Revolutionary France*. New York: Norton, 1996.

———. *The Literary Underground of the Old Regime*. Cambridge: Harvard University Press, 1982.

Daston, Lorraine. "Afterword: The Ethos of Enlightenment." In *The Sciences in Enlightened Europe*, edited by William Clark, Jan Golinski, and Simon Schaffer, 495–504. Chicago: University of Chicago Press, 1999.

Deppermann, Klaus. *Der hallesche Pietismus und der preußische Staat unter Friedrich III./I.* Göttingen: Vandenhoeck & Ruprecht, 1961.

Dippel, Horst. *Germany and the American Revolution, 1770–1800*. Chapel Hill: University of North Carolina Press, 1977.

Dodson, Michael S. *Orientalism, Empire and National Culture: India, 1770–1880*. Basingstoke: Palgrave Macmillan, 2007.

Dougherty, Frank. "Christoph Meiners und Johann Friedrich Blumenbach im Streit um den Begriff der Menschenrasse." In *Die Natur des Menschen: Probleme der Physischen Anthropologie und Rassenkunde (1750–1850)*. Soemmering-Forschungen, VI, edited by Günter Mann and Frany Dumont, 89–111. Stuttgart: Gustav Fischer, 1990.

Dreitzel, Horst. "Die Entwicklung der Historie zur Wissenschaft." *Zeitschrift für Historische Forschung* 8/3 (1981): 257–84.

Du Toit, Alexander. "Cosmopolitanism, Despotism and Patriotic Resistance: William Robertson on the Spanish Revolts against Charles V." *Bulletin of Spanish Studies* 86/1 (2009): 19–43.

———. "God Before Mammon? William Robertson, Episcopacy and the Church of England." *Journal of Ecclesiastical History* 54 (2003): 671–90.

———. "'A Species of False Religion': William Robertson, Catholic Relief and the Myth of Moderate Tolerance." *Innes Review* 52/2 (2001): 167–88.

———. "Who Are the Barbarians? Scottish Views of Conquest and Indians, and Robertson's *History of America.*" *Scottish Literary Journal* 26/1 (1999): 29–47.
Duchet, Michèle. *Anthropologie et histoire au siècle des lumières.* Paris: Albin Michel, 1971.
———. *Diderot et l'Histoire des deux Indes: ou, L'écriture fragmentaire.* Paris: A. G. Nizet, 1978.
Duckworth, Mark. "An Eighteenth-Century Questionnaire: William Robertson on the Indians." *Eighteenth-Century Life* 11 (1987): 36–49.
Dwyer, John. *Virtuous Discourse: Sensibility and Community in Late Eighteenth-Century Scotland.* Edinburgh: John Donald, 1987.
Ebel, Wilhelm. *Der göttinger Professor Johann Stephan Pütter aus Iserlohn.* Göttingen: Vandenhoeck & Ruprecht, 1975.
Eigen, Sara, and Mark Larrimore, eds. *The German Invention of Race.* Albany: State University of New York Press, 2006.
Eisenstein, Elizabeth. "Clio and Chronos: An Essay on the Making and Breaking of History-Book Time." *History and Theory* 5/6 (1966): 36–64.
Emerson, Roger. "The Enlightenment and Social Structures." In *City and Society in the 18th Century*, edited by Paul Fritz and David Williams, 99–124. Toronto: Hakkert, 1973.
———. "Scottish Universities in the Eighteenth Century." In *Studies on Voltaire and the Eighteenth Century*, vol. 167, edited by James A. Leith, 453–74. Oxford: Voltaire Foundation, 1977.
Enzensberger, Ulrich. *Georg Forster. Ein Leben in Scherben.* Frankfurt: Eichborn, 1996.
Ermarth, Michael. "Hermeneutics and History: The Fork in Hermes' Path through the 18th Century." In *Aufklärung und Geschichte. Studien zur deutschen Geschichtswissenschaft im 18. Jahrhundert*, edited by Hans Erich Bödeker, Georg G. Iggers, and Jonathan B. Knudsen, 193–221. Göttingen: Vandenhoeck & Ruprecht, 1986.
Esleben, Jörg. "'Indisch lesen': Conceptions of Intercultural Communication in Georg Forster's and Johann Gottfried Herder's Reception of Kālidāsa's "Śakuntalā." *Monatshefte* 95/2 (2003): 217–29.
———. "Forster und Indien." *Georg Forster Studien* 10/2 (2006): 407–26.
———. "Übersetzung als interkulturelle Kommunikation bei Georg Forster." *Georg Forster Studien* 9 (2004): 165–80.
Esquer, Gabriel. *L'Anticolonialisme au XVIIIe siècle: Histoire philosophique et politique des établissements et du commerce des Européens dans les deux Indes.* Paris: Presses universitaires de France, 1951.
Fabian, Bernhard. *The English Book in Eighteenth-Century Germany.* London: British Library, 1992.
———. "English Books and their Eighteenth Century German Readers." In *The Widening Circle: Essays on the Circulation of Literature in Eighteenth-Century Europe*, edited by Paul Korshin, 117–96. Philadelphia: University of Pennsylvania Press, 1976.
———. "Die Göttinger Universitätsbibliothek im achtzehnten Jahrhundert." In *Göttinger Jahrbuch*, 109–23. Göttingen: Heinz Reise Verlag, 1980.
Fagerstrom, Dalphy I. "Scottish Opinion and the American Revolution." *William and Mary Quarterly* 11 (1954): 252–75.
Fearnley-Sander, Mary. "Philosophical History and the Scottish Reformation: William Robertson and the Knoxian Tradition." *Historical Journal* 33 (1990): 323–38.
Fitzpatrick, Martin, Peter Jones, Christa Knellwolf, and Iain McCalman, eds. *The Enlightenment World.* London: Routledge, 2004.
Fleischer, Dirk. "Geschichte und Sinn. Johann Salomo Semler als Geschichtstheoretiker." *Zeitschrift für Geschichtswissenschaft* 56/5 (2008): 397–417.
———. *Zwischen Tradition und Fortschritt: Der Strukturwandel der protestantischen Kinchengeschichtsschreibung im deutschsprachigen Diskurs der Aufklärung.* Waltrop: Hartmut Spenner, 2006.

Force, Pierre. *Self-Interest before Adam Smith: A Genealogy of Economic Science*. Cambridge: Cambridge University Press, 2003.
Foucault, Michel. "Governmentality." In *Power*, edited by James D. Faubion, 201–22. New York: The New Press, 2000.
Fox, Christopher, Roy Porter, and Robert Wokler, eds. *Inventing Human Science. Eighteenth-Century Domains*. Berkeley and Los Angeles: University of California Press, 1996.
Francesconi, Daniele. "William Robertson on Historical Causation and Unintended Consequences." *Storia della Storiografia* 36 (1999): 55–80.
Fraser, Julius Thomas. *Of Time, Passion, and Knowledge: Reflections on the Strategy of Existence*. Princeton: Princeton University Press, 1990.
Friedeburg, Robert von, and Michael Seidler. "The Holy Roman Empire of the German Nation." In *European Political Thought 1450–1700. Religion, Law and Philosophy*, edited by Howell Lloyd, Glenn Burgess, and Simon Hodson, 119–72. New Haven: Yale University Press, 2007.
Friedrich, Manfred. *Geschichte der deutschen Staatsrechtswissenschaft*. Berlin: Duncker & Humblot, 1997.
Fulda, Daniel. *Wissenschaft aus Kunst. Die Entstehung der modernen deutschen Geschichtsschreibung 1760–1860*. Berlin: Walter de Gruyter, 1996.
Funakoshi, Katsami. "Dupaty's Reisebeschreibung und Forsters *Ansichten vom Niederrhein*." *Georg Forster Studien* 10/2 (2006): 427–42.
Funkenstein, Amos. *Theology and the Scientific Imagination from the Middle Ages to the Seventeenth Century*. Princeton: Princeton University Press, 1986.
Gagliardo, John. *Germany under the Old Regime 1600–1790*. London: Longman, 1991.
———. *Reich and Nation: The Holy Roman Empire as Idea and Reality, 1763–1806*. Bloomington: Indiana University Press, 1980.
Garber, Jörn. "Selbstreferenz und Objektivität: Organisationsmodelle von Mensch- und Weltgeschichte in der deutschen Spätaufklärung." In *Wissenschaft als kulturelle Praxis 1750–1900*, edited by Hans Erich Bödeker, Peter Hanns Reill, and Jürgen Schlumbohm, 137–85. Göttingen: Vandenhoeck & Ruprecht, 1999.
———. "Von der Menschengeschichte zur Kulturgeschichte. Zum geschichtstheoretischen Kulturbegriff der deutschen Spätaufklärung." In *Spätabsolutismus und bürgerliche Gesellschaft. Studien zur deutschen Staats- und Gesellschaftstheorie im Übergang zur Moderne*, edited by Jörn Garber, 409–33. Frankfurt: Keip Verlag, 1992.
———. *Wahrnehmung–Konstruktion–Text. Bilder des Wirklichen im Werk Georg Forsters*. Tübingen: Max Niemeyer Verlag, 2000.
Garber, Jörn, and Tanja van Hoorn, eds. *Natur–Mensch–Kultur. Georg Forster im Wissenschaftsfeld seiner Zeit*. Hannover: Wehrhahn, 2006.
Garner, Guillaume. "Politische Ökonomie und Statistik an der Universität Göttingen (1760–1820)." In *Die Wissenschaft vom Menschen in Göttingen um 1800*, edited by Hans Erich Bödeker, Philippe Büttgen, and Michel Espagne, 371–92. Göttingen: Vandenhoeck & Ruprecht, 2008.
Gascoigne, John. "The German Enlightenment and the Pacific." In *The Anthropology of the Enlightenment*, edited by Larry Wolff and Marco Cipollini, 141–71. Stanford: Stanford University Press, 2007.
Gawlick, Günter, and Lothar Kreimendahl. *Hume in der deutschen Aufklärung. Umrisse einer Rezeptionsgeschichte*. Stuttgart-Bad Cannstatt: Frommann-Holzboog, 1987.
Gawthrop, Richard L. *Pietism and the Making of Eighteenth Century Prussia*. Cambridge: Cambridge University Press, 1993.
Gerbi, Antonello. *The Dispute of the New World: The History of a Polemic 1750–1900*. Pittsburgh: University of Pittsburgh Press, 1973.
Germana, Nicholas A. "Herder's India. The 'Morgenland' in Mythology and Anthropology." In *The Anthropology of the Enlightenment*, edited by Larry Wolff and Marco Cipollini, 119–37. Stanford: Stanford University Press, 2007.

———. *The Orient of Europe: The Mythical Image of India and Competing Images of German National Identity*. Cambridge: Cambridge Scholars Publishing, 2009.
Gierl, Martin. "Christoph Meiners, Geschichte der Menschheit und Göttinger Universalgeschichte. Rasse und Nation als Politisierung der deutschen Aufklärung." In *Die Wissenschaft vom Menschen in Göttingen um 1800*, edited by Hans Erich Bödeker, Philippe Büttgen, and Michel Espagne, 419–33. Göttingen: Vandenhoeck & Ruprecht, 2008.
———. "Compilation and the Production of Knowledge in the Early German Enlightenment." In *Wissenschaft als kulturelle Praxis 1750–1900*, edited by Hans Erich Bödeker, Peter Hanns Reill, and Jürgen Schlumbohm, 69–103. Göttingen: Vandenhoeck & Ruprecht, 1999.
———. *Geschichte als präzisierte Wissenschaft. Johann Christoph Gatterer und die Historiographie des 18. Jahrhunderts im ganzen Umfang*. Stuttgart-Bad Cannstatt: Fromann-Holzboog, 2012.
Gilbert, Felix. *Machiavelli and Guicciardini: Politics and History in Sixteenth-Century Florence*. Princeton: Princeton University Press, 1965.
Goldsmith, Maurice M. "Liberty, Luxury and the Pursuit of Happiness." In *The Languages of Political Theory in Early-Modern Europe*, edited by Anthony Pagden, 225–51. Cambridge: Cambridge University Press, 1987.
Gomsu, Joseph. "Über lokale und allgemeine Bildung." In *Georg Forster Studien* 11/1 (2006): 323–34.
Gooch, George P. *Germany and the French Revolution*. London: Longman, 1920.
Gottlob, Michael. *Geschichtsschreibung zwischen Aufklärung und Historismus. Johannes von Müller und Friedrich Christoph Schlosser*. Frankfurt: Peter Lang, 1989.
Grell, Ole Peter, and Roy Porter, eds. *Toleration in Enlightenment Europe*. Cambridge: Cambridge University Press, 2000.
Grundy, Geoff. "The Emulation of Nations: William Robertson and the International Order." PhD Diss., University of Edinburgh, 2005.
Haakonssen, Knud. *Natural Law and Moral Philosophy. From Grotius to the Scottish Enlightenment*. Cambridge: Cambridge University Press, 1996.
———. *The Science of a Legislator: The Natural Jurisprudence of David Hume and Adam Smith*. Cambridge: Cambridge University Press, 1981.
Hamberger, Georg Christoph, and Johann Georg Meusel. *Das gelehrte Teutschland oder Lexikon der jetzt lebenden teutschen Schriftsteller*, 23 vols. Lemgo, 1796–1834. Repr. Hildesheim: Olms, 1965.
Hammerstein, Notker. *Ius und Historie. Ein Beitrag zur Geschichte des historischen Denkens an deutschen Universitäten im späten 17. und im 18. Jahrhundert*. Göttingen: Vandenhoeck & Ruprecht, 1973.
———. "Das politische Denken Friedrich Carl von Mosers." *Historische Zeitschrift* 212 (1971): 316–38.
———. "Reichshistorie." In *Aufklärung und Geschichte. Studien zur deutschen Geschichtswissenschaft im 18. Jahrhundert*, edited by Hans Erich Bödeker, Georg G. Iggers, and Jonathan B. Knudsen, 82–104. Göttingen: Vandenhoeck & Ruprecht, 1986.
Hardtwig, Wolfgang. "Die Verwissenschaftlichung der Geschichtsschreibung zwischen Aufklärung und Historismus." In *Geschichtskultur und Wissenschaft*, edited by Wolfgang Hardtwig, 58–91. Munich: DTV, 1990.
Hargraves, Neal. "Beyond the Savage Character: Mexicans, Peruvians, and the 'Imperfectly Civilized' in William Robertson's *History of America*." In *The Anthropology of the Enlightenment*, edited by Larry Wolff and Marco Cipollini, 103–18. Stanford: Stanford University Press, 2007.
———. "Enterprise, Adventure and Industry: The Formation of 'Commercial Character' in William Robertson's *History of America*." *History of European Ideas* 29 (2003): 33–54.

———. "National History and 'Philosophical' History: Character and Narrative in William Robertson's *History of Scotland*." *History of European Ideas* 26 (2000): 19–33.

———. "The 'Progress of Ambition': Character, Narrative, and Philosophy in the Works of William Robertson." *Journal of the History of Ideas* 63 (2002): 261–82.

———. "Resentment and History in the Scottish Enlightenment." *Cromohs* 14 (2009): 1–21. Accessed July 14, 2013. http://www.cromohs.unifi.it/14_2009/hargraves_resentment.html.

Hartmann, Karl Julius, and Hans Füchsel, eds. *Geschichte der Göttinger Universitäts-Bibliothek*. Göttingen: Vandenhoeck & Ruprecht, 1937.

Härter, Karl, ed. *Policey und Frühneuzeitlicher Gesellschaft*. Frankfurt: Vittorio Klostermann, 2000.

Hazard, Paul. *La crise de la conscience européenne*. Paris: Boivin, 1935; Eng. ed. *The European Mind 1680–1715*. Harmondsworth: Penguin, 1973.

Heier, Edmund. *L. H. Nicolay (1737–1820) and His Contemporaries*. The Hague: Martinus Nijhoff, 1965.

———. "William Robertson and Ludwig Heinrich Nicolay, His German Translator at the Court of Catherine II." *Scottish Historical Review* 41 (1962): 135–40.

Hilger, Dietrich. "Industrie, Gewerbe," sections IV–V. In *Geschichtliche Grundbegriffe. Historisches Lexikon zur politisch-sozialen Sprache in Deutschland*, vol. 3, edited by Otto Brunner, Werner Conze, and Reinhart Koselleck, 253–69. Stuttgart: Klett-Cotta, 1982.

Hinrichs, Carl. *Preußentum und Pietismus. Der Pietismus in Brandenburg-Preußen als religiös-soziale Reformbewegung*. Göttingen: Vandenhoeck & Ruprecht 1971.

Hirschman, Albert O. *The Passions and the Interests: Political Arguments for Capitalism before Its Triumph*. Princeton: Princeton University Press, 1977.

Hoare, Michael E. *The Tactless Philosopher: Johann Reinhold Forster, 1729–1798*. Melbourne: Hawthorn Press, 1976.

Hochstrasser, Timothy J. *Natural Law Theories in the Early Enlightenment*. Cambridge: Cambridge University Press, 2000.

Hoebel, E. Adamson. "William Robertson: An 18th Century Anthropological Historian." *American Anthropologist* 62 (1960): 648–55.

Hollinger, David A. "The Enlightenment and the Genealogy of Cultural Conflict in the United States." In *What's Left of Enlightenment? A Postmodern Question*, edited by Keith Michael Baker and Peter Hanns Reill, 7–18. Stanford: Stanford University Press, 2001.

Hont, Istvan. "The Early Enlightenment Debate on Commerce and Luxury." In *The Cambridge History of Eighteenth-Century Political Thought*, edited by Mark Goldie and Robert Wokler, 379–418. Cambridge: Cambridge University Press, 2008.

———. *Jealousy of Trade: International Competition and the Nation State in Historical Perspective*. Cambridge: Harvard University Press, 2005.

———. "The Language of Sociability and Commerce: Samuel Pufendorf and the Theoretical Foundations of the 'Four-Stages Theory.'" In *The Languages of Political Theory in Early-Modern Europe*, edited by Anthony Pagden, 253–76. Cambridge: Cambridge University Press, 1987.

Hont, Istvan, and Michael Ignatieff, eds. *Wealth and Virtue: The Shaping of Political Economy in the Scottish Enlightenment*. Cambridge: Cambridge University Press, 1983.

Horn, David Bayne. *A Short History of the University of Edinburgh, 1556–1889*. Edinburgh: Edinburgh University Press, 1967.

Hornig, Gottfried. *Die Anfänge der historisch-kritischen Theologie. Johann Salomo Semlers Schriftverständnis und seine Stellung zu Luther*. Göttingen: Vandenhoeck & Ruprecht, 1961.

———. "Orthodoxie und Textkritik. Die Kontroverse Zwischen Johann Melchior Goeze und Johann Salomo Semler." In *Verspätete Orthodoxie. Über D. Johann Melchior Goeze*

(1717–1786), edited by Heimo Reinitzer and Walter Sparn, 159–77. Wiesbaden: Harrassowitz, 1989.
Howard, Thomas Albert. *Protestant Theology and the Making of the Modern German University*. Oxford: Oxford University Press, 2006.
Höpfl, Harro M. "From Savage to Scotsman: Conjectural History in the Scottish Enlightenment." *Journal of British Studies* 17 (1978): 19–40.
Humphreys, Robin A. "William Robertson and His History of America" [1954]. In *Tradition and Revolt in Latin America and Other Essays*. New York: Columbia University Press, 1969.
Hundert, Edward. *The Enlightenment's "Fable": Bernard Mandeville and the Discovery of Society*. Cambridge: Cambridge University Press, 1994.
Hunter, Ian. "Multiple Enlightenments: Rival *Aufklärer* at the University of Halle, 1690–1730." In *The Enlightenment World*, edited by Martin Fitzpatrick et al., 576–95. London: Routledge, 2004.
———. *Rival Enlightenments: Civil and Metaphysical Philosophy in Early-Modern Germany*. Cambridge: Cambridge University Press, 2001.
Iggers, Georg G. "The European Context of Eighteenth-Century German Historiography." In *Aufklärung und Geschichte. Studien zur deutschen Geschichtswissenschaft im 18. Jahrhundert*, edited by Hans Erich Bödeker, Georg G. Iggers, and Jonathan B. Knudsen, 222–40. Göttingen: Vandenhoeck & Ruprecht, 1986.
Ingrao, Charles. "Introduction: A Pre-Revolutionary Sonderweg." *German History* 20/3 (2002): 279–86.
Israel, Jonathan. *Democratic Enlightenment: Philosophy, Revolution and Human Rights 1750–1790*. Oxford University Press, 2011.
———. *Enlightenment Contested: Philosophy, Modernity and the Emancipation of Man 1670–1752*. Oxford: Oxford University Press, 2006.
———. *Radical Enlightenment: Philosophy and the Making of the Modern World*. Oxford: Oxford University Press, 2001.
———. *A Revolution of the Mind: Radical Enlightenment and the Intellectual Origins of Modern Democracy*. Princeton: Princeton University Press, 2009.
Jäger, Hans-Wolff, ed. *Öffentlichkeit im Achtzehnten Jahrhundert*. Göttingen: Wallstein, 1997.
Jefcoate, Graham, Karen Kloth, and Bernhard Fabian, eds. *A Catalogue of English Books Printed before 1801 Held by the University Library at Göttingen*. Hildesheim: Olms-Weidmann, 1988.
Jordahn, Ottfried. *Georg Friedrich Seilers Beitrag zur praktischen Theologie der kirchlichen Aufklärung*. Nuremberg: Selbstverlag des Vereins für bayerische Kirchengeschichte, 1970.
Jüttner, Siegfried, and Jochen Schlobach, eds. *Europäische Aufklärunge(en): Einheit und nationale Vielfalt*. Hamburg: Felix Meiner, 1992.
Kidd, Colin. "The Ideological Significance of Robertson's History of Scotland." In *William Robertson and the Expansion of Empire*, edited by Stuart J. Brown, 92–121. Cambridge: Cambridge University Press, 1997.
———. "Subscription, the Scottish Enlightenment and the Moderate Interpretation of History." *Journal of Ecclesiastical History* 55 (2004): 502–19.
———. *Subverting Scotland's Past. Scottish Whig Historians and the Creation of an Anglo-British Identity, 1689–c. 1830*. Cambridge: Cambridge University Press, 1993.
———. "Teutonist Ethnology and Scottish National Inhibition, 1780–1880." *The Scottish Historical Review* 74 (1995): 45–68.
Kleingeld, Pauline. "Kant's Second Thoughts on Race." *Philosophical Quarterly* 57/229 (October 2007): 573–92.
———. *Kant and Cosmopolitanism: The Philosophical Ideal of World Citizenship*. Cambridge: Cambridge University Press, 2011.

Klenke, Claus-Volker, Jörn Garber, and Dieter Heintze, eds. *Georg Forster in interdisziplinären Perspektive*. Berlin: Akademie Verlag, 1994.
Knemeyer, Franz-Ludwig. "Polizei." In *Geschichtliche Grundbegriffe. Historisches Lexikon zur politisch-sozialen Sprache in Deutschland*, vol. 4, edited by Otto Brunner, Werner Conze, and Reinhart Koselleck, 875–98. Stuttgart: Klett-Cotta, 1978.
Knudsen, Jonathan. *Justus Möser and the German Enlightenment*. Cambridge: Cambridge University Press, 1986.
Kontler, László. "Beauty or Beast or Monstrous Regiments? Robertson and Burke on Women and the Public Scene." *Modern Intellectual History* 1/3 (2004): 305–30.
———. "Superstitition, Enthusiasm and Propagandism: Burke and Gentz on the French Revolution." In *Propaganda. Political Rhetoric and Identity 1300—2000*, edited by Bertrand Taithe and Tim Thornton, 97–114. Phoenix Mill: Sutton, 1999.
———. "Translation and Comparison: Early-Modern and Current Perspectives." *Contributions to the History of Concepts* 3/1 (2007): 71–103.
———. "Translation and Comparison II: A Methodological Inquiry into Reception in the History of Ideas." *Contributions to the History of Concepts* 4/1 (2008): 27–56.
Kors, Alan Charles, ed. *Encyclopedia of the Enlightenment*, 4 vols. Oxford: Oxford University Press, 2002.
Korshin, Paul, ed. *The Widening Circle: Essays on the Circulation of Literature in Eighteenth-Century Europe*. Philadelphia: University of Pennsylvania Press, 1976.
Koselleck, Reinhart. *Futures Past: On the Semantics of Historical Time*. Cambridge: MIT Press, 1985.
———. *Critique and Crisis: Enlightenment and the Pathogenesis of Modern Society*. Oxford: Oxford University Press, 1988.
———. "Geschichte, Historie," section V. In *Geschichtliche Grundbegriffe. Historisches Lexikon zur politisch-sozialen Sprache in Deutschland*, vol. 2, edited by Otto Brunner, Werner Conze, and Reinhart Koselleck, 647–78. Stuttgart: Klett-Cotta, 1975.
Krieger, Leonard. *The German Idea of Freedom: History of a Political Idea*. Chicago: University of Chicage Press, 1957.
———. "Germany." In *National Consciousness, History, and Political Culture in Early-Modern Europe*, edited by Orest Ranum, 67–97. Baltimore: Johns Hopkins University Press, 1975.
Kuehn, Manfred. *Scottish Common Sense Philosophy in Germany, 1768–1800: A Contribution to the History of Critical Philosophy*. Kingston and Montreal: McGill-Queens University Press, 1987.
Larrimore, Mark. "Antinomies of Race: Diversity and Destiny in Kant." *Patterns of Prejudice* 42/4–5 (2008): 341–63.
Laudin, Gérard. "Gatterer und Schlözer: Geschichte als 'Wissenschaft vom Menschen?'" In *Die Wissenschaft vom Menschen in Göttingen um 1800*, edited by Hans Erich Bödeker, Philippe Büttgen, and Michel Espagne, 393–418. Göttingen: Vandenhoeck & Ruprecht, 2008.
———. "Histoire de la civilization et histoire anthropologique. Adelung et la *Culturgeschichte*." *Le Texte et l'Idée* 17 (2002): 59–78.
LaVopa, Anthony. "A New Intellectual History? Jonathan Israel's Enlightenment." *Historical Journal* 52/3 (2009): 717–38.
Legaspi, Michael C. *The Death of Scripture and the Rise of Biblical Studies*. Oxford: Oxford University Press, 2010.
Lehner, Ulrich. "What Is the Catholic Enlightenment?" *History Compass* 8/2 (2010): 166–78.
Lehner, Ulrich, and Michael Printy, eds. *A Companion to the Catholic Enlightenment in Europe*. Leiden: Brill, 2010.
Lenman, Bruce. "'From Savage to Scot' via the French and the Spaniards: Principal Robertson's Spanish Sources." In *William Robertson and the Expansion of Empire*, edited by Stuart J. Brown, 196–209. Cambridge: Cambridge University Press, 1997.

Leyden, W. Von. "History and the Concept of Relative Time." *History and Theory* 2 (1963): 263–85.

Liebersohn, Harry. *The Traveler's World: Europe to the Pacific.* Cambridge: Harvard University Press, 2006.

Link, Christoph. "Johann Stephan Pütter (1725–1807). Staatsrecht am Ende des alten Reiches." In *Rechtswissenschaft in Göttingen. Göttinger Juristen aus 250 Jahren*, edited by Fritz Loos, 75–99. Göttingen: Vandenhoeck & Ruprecht, 1987.

Lotter, Friedrich. "Christoph Meiners und die Lehre von der unterschiedlichen Wertigkeit der Menschenrassen." In *Geschichtswissenschaft in Göttingen*, edited by Hartmut Boockmann and Hermann Wellenreuther, 30–75. Göttingen: Vandenhoeck & Ruprecht, 1987.

Lüsebrink, Hans-Jürgen, and Anthony Strugnell. *L'Histoire des deux Indes: réécriture et polygraphie.* Oxford: Voltaire Foundation, 1995.

McCarthy, John A., "Disciplining History: Schiller als Historiograph." *Goethe Yearbook* 12. Goethe Society of North America, Boydell & Brewer, 2004. 209–26.

McClelland, Charles. *State, Society, and University in Germany, 1700–1914.* Cambridge: Cambridge University Press, 1980.

Maier, Hans. *Die ältere deutsche Staats- und Verwaltungslehre (Polizeiwissenschaft). Ein Beitrag zur Geschichte der politischen Wissenschaft in Deutschland.* Neuwied and Berlin: Luchterhand, 1966.

Marino, Luigi. *Praeceptores Germaniae. Göttingen 1770–1820.* Göttingen: Vandenhoeck & Ruprecht, 1995. Italian original, Torino: Einaudi, 1975.

Marshall, Peter J. *The British Discovery of Hinduism in the Eighteenth Century.* Cambridge: Cambridge University Press, 1970.

Marshall, Peter J., and Glyndwr Williams, eds. *The Great Map of Mankind: Perceptions of New Worlds in the Age of Enlightenment.* Cambridge: Harvard University Press, 1982.

Martens, Wolfgang. *Der patriotische Minister. Fürstendiener in der Literatur der Aufklärungszeit.* Cologne: Böhlau, 1996.

Mason, Roger A. "Scotching the Brut: Politics, History and National Myth in Sixteenth-Century Britain." In *Scotland and England 1286–1815*, edited by Roger A Maso, 60–84. Edinburgh: Edinburgh University Press, 1987.

Mason, Sheila. "Montesquieu's Vision of Europe and Its European Context." *Studies on Voltaire and the Eighteenth Century* 341 (1996): 61–87.

Meek, Ronald L. *Social Science and the Ignoble Savage.* Cambridge: Cambridge University Press, 1976.

Melo Araújo, André de. *Weltgeschichte in Göttingen. Eine Studie über das spätaufklärerische universalhistorische Denken, 1756–1815.* Bielefeld: Transcript Verlag, 2012.

Meusel, Johann Georg. *Lexikon der vom Jahr 1750 bis 1800 verstorbenen teutschen Schriftsteller*, 15 vols. Leipzig, 1802–1816. Reprint: Hildesheim: Olms, 1967.

Meyer, Annette. "Von der 'Science of Man' zur 'Naturgeschichte der Menschheit.' Einflüsse angelsächsischer Wissenschaft im Werk Georg Forsters." In *Natur–Mensch–Kultur. Georg Forster im Wissenschaftsfeld seiner Zeit*, edited by Jörn Garber and Tanja van Hoorn, 33–52. Hannover: Wehrhahn, 2006.

———. *Von der Wahrheit zur Wahrscheinlichkeit. Die Wissenschaft vom Menschen in der schottischen und deutschen Aufklärung.* Tübingen: Niemeyer, 2008.

Mori, Takahashi. "Zwischen Mensch und Affe. Anthropologische Aspekte in Forsters *Reise um die Welt.*" *Georg Forster Studien* 10/2 (2006): 359–72.

Muhlack, Ulrich. *Geschichtswissenschaft im Humanismus und Aufklärung. Die Vorgeschichte des Historismus.* Munich: C. H. Beck, 1991.

———. "Historie und Philologie." In *Aufklärung und Geschichte. Studien zur deutschen Geschichtswissenschaft im 18. Jahrhundert*, edited by Hans Erich Bödeker, Georg G. Iggers, and Jonathan B. Knudsen, 49–81. Göttingen: Vandenhoeck & Ruprecht, 1986.

Munck, Thomas. *The Enlightenment: A Comparative Social History 1721–1794*. London: Edward Arnold, 2000.
Mundhenke, Herbert, ed. *Die Matrikel der Universität Helmstedt 1685–1810*. Hildesheim: Lax, 1979.
Muthu, Sankar. *Enlightenment against Empire*. Princeton: Princeton University Press, 2003.
Nippel, Wilfried. "Gibbon and German Historiography." In *British and German Historiography 1750–1950: Traditions, Perceptions, and Transfers*, edited by Benedikt Stuchtey and Peter Wende, 67–81. Oxford: Oxford University Press, 2000.
Nisbet, Robert F. *Social Change and History: Aspects of the Western Theory of Development*. Oxford: Oxford University Press, 1965.
———. *The History of the Idea of Progress*. New York: Basic Books, 1980.
Noyes, John K. "Commerce, Colonialism, and the Globalization of Action in late Enlightenment Germany." *Postcolonial Studies* 9/1 (2006): 81–98.
Nutz, Thomas. *"Varietäten des Menschengeschlechts." Die Wissenschaften vom menschen in der Zeit der Aufklärung*. Cologne: Böhlau, 2009.
O'Brien, Karen. "Between Enlightenment and Stadial History: William Robertson on the History of Europe." *British Journal for Eighteenth-Century Studies* 16/1 (1993): 53–64.
———. *Narratives of Enlightenment: Cosmopolitan History from Voltaire to Gibbon*. Cambridge: Cambridge University Press, 1997.
———. "The Return of the Enlightenment." *American Historical Review* 115/5 (2010): 1426–35.
Oestreich, Gerhard. "'Police' and Prudentia civilis in the Seventeenth Century." In *Neostoicism and the Early Modern State*, edited by Gerhard Oestreich, 155–86. Cambridge: Cambridge University Press, 1982.
Outram, Dorinda. *The Enlightenment*. Cambridge: Cambridge University Press, 1995.
———. "New Spaces in Natural History." In *Cultures of Natural History*, edited by Nicholas Jardine, James Secord, and Emma C. Spary, 249–65. Cambridge: Cambridge University Press, 1996.
———. "On Being Perseus: New Knowledge, Dislocation, and Enlightenment Exploration." In *Geography and Enlightenment*, edited by Donald N. Livingstone and Charles W. J. Withers, 281–94. Chicago: University of Chicago Press, 1999.
Oz-Salzberger, Fania. "The Enlightenment in Translation: Regional, Cosmopolitan and National Aspects." *European Review of History/Revue européenne d'histoire* 13/3 (2006): 385–410.
———. *Translating the Enlightenment: Scottish Civic Discourse in Eighteenth-Century Germany*. Oxford: Clarendon Press, 1995.
Pagden, Anthony. *The Enlightenment: And Why It Still Matters*. Oxford: Oxford University Press, 2013.
———. *European Encounters With the New World*. New Haven: Yale University Press, 1993.
———. *The Fall of Natural Man: The American Indian and the Origins of Comparative Ethnology*. Cambridge: Cambridge University Press, 1986.
———, ed. *The Languages of Political Theory in Early-Modern Europe*. Cambridge: Cambridge University Press, 1987.
Palladini, Fiammetta. *Samuel Pufendorf discepolo di Hobbes*. Bologna: Il Mulino, 1996.
Pares, Richard. "American versus Continental Warfare, 1739–1763." *English Historical Review* 51 (1936): 429–65.
Pascal, Roy. "Property and Society: The Scottish Historical School of the Eighteenth Century." *Modern Quarterly* 2 (1938): 167–79.
Pasquino, Pasquale. "Politisches und historisches Interesse. Statistik und historische Staatslehre bei Gottfried Achenwall (1719–1772)." In *Aufklärung und Geschichte. Studien zur deutschen Geschichtswissenschaft im 18. Jahrhundert*, edited by Hans Erich Bödeker, Georg G. Iggers, and Jonathan B. Knudsen, 144–68. Göttingen: Vandenhoeck & Ruprecht, 1986.

Pelters, Wilm, *Lessings Standort: Sinndeutung der Geschichte als Kern seines Denkens*. Heidelberg: Stiehm, 1972.
Phillips, Mark Salber. *Society and Sentiment: Genres of Historical Writing in Britain, 1740–1820*. Princeton: Princeton University Press, 2000.
Phillipson, Nicholas. "Commerce and Culture: Edinburgh, Edinburgh University, and the Scottish Enlightenment." In *The University and the City: From Medieval Origins to the Present*, edited by Thomas Bender, 100–16. Oxford: Oxford University Press, 1988.
———. *Hume*. London: Weidenfeld & Nicolson, 1989.
———. "Providence and Progress: An Introduction to the Historical Thought of William Robertson." In *William Robertson and the Expansion of Empire*, edited by Stuart J. Brown, 55–73. Cambridge: Cambridge University Press, 1997.
———. "Scottish Public Opinion and the Union in the Age of Association." In *Scotland in the Age of Improvement*, edited by Nicholas Phillipson and Rosalind Mitchison, 125–47. Edinburgh: Edinburgh University Press, 1970.
Pier, Bernhard. *William Robertson als Historiker und Geschichtsphilosoph*. Radbod: Weitfeld, 1929.
Pocock, John G. A. *Barbarism and Religion*, 5 vols. Cambridge: Cambridge University Press, 1999–2011.
———. "Clergy and Commerce: The Conservative Enlightenment in England." In *L'età dei lumi: studi storici in onore di Franco Venturi*, vol. 1, edited by Raffaele Ajello et al., 523–62. Naples: Iovene Editore, 1985.
———. "Conservative Enlightenment and Democratic Revolutions: The American and French Cases in British Perspective." *Government and Opposition* 24 (1989): 82–101.
———. "Enthusiasm: The Antiself of Enlightenment." *Huntington Library Quarterly* 60/1–2 (1997): 7–28.
———. "Enlightenment and Counter-Enlightenment, Revolution and Counter-Revolution: A Eurosceptical Enquiry." *History of Political Thought* 20 (1999): 125–39.
———. "Historiography and Enlightenment: A View of Their History." *Modern Intellectual History* 5/1 (2008): 83–95.
———. *The Machiavellian Moment: Florentine Political Thought and the Atlantic Republican Tradition* [1975]. Princeton: Princeton University Press, 2003.
———. *Virtue, Commerce, and History: Essays on Political Thought and History, Chiefly in the Eighteenth Century*. Cambridge: Cambridge University Press, 1985.
Press, Volker. *Das Reichskammergericht in der deutschen Geschichte*. Wetzlar: Gesellschaft der Reichskammergerichtsforschung, 1987.
Printy, Michael. *Enlightenment and the Creation of German Catholicism*. Cambridge: Cambridge University Press, 2009.
———. "From Barbarism to Religion: Church History and the Enlightened Narrative in Germany." *German History* 23 (2005): 172–201.
Prüfer, Thomas. *Die Bildung der Geschichte. Friedrich Schiller und die Anfänge der modernen Geschichtswissenschaft*. Cologne: Böhlau, 2002.
Rasmussen, Detlef, ed. *Weltumsegler und seine Freunde. Georg Forster als gesellschaftlicher Schriftsteller der Goethezeit*. Tübingen: Max Niemeyer Verlag, 1988.
Reill, Peter Hanns. "Anthropology, Nature and History in the Late Enlightenment." In *Schiller als Historiker*, edited by Otto Dann, Norbert Oellers, and Ernst Osterkamp, 243–65. Stuttgart and Weimar: J. B. Metzler, 1995.
———. "Das Problem des Allgemeinen und des Besonderen im geschichtlichen Denken und in in den historiographischen Darstellungen des späten 18. Jahrhunderts." In *Teil und Ganzes: Zum Verhältnis von Einzel- und Gesamtanalyse in Geschichts- und Sozialwissenschaften*, edited by Karl Acham and Winfried Schulze, 141–68. Munich: DTV, 1990.
———. *The German Enlightenment and the Rise of Historicism*. Berkeley: University of California Press, 1975.

———. "Science and the Science of History in the Spätaufklärung." In *Aufklärung und Geschichte. Studien zur deutschen Geschichtswissenschaft im 18. Jahrhundert*, edited by Hans Erich Bödeker, Georg G. Iggers, and Jonathan B. Knudsen, 430–50. Göttingen: Vandenhoeck & Ruprecht, 1986.

———. *Vitalizing Nature in the Enlightenment*. Berkeley: University of California Press, 2006.

Reinitzer, Heimo, and Walter Sparn, eds. *Verspätete Orthodoxie. Über D. Johann Melchior Goeze (1717–1786)*. Wiesbaden: Harrassowitz, 1989.

Rendall, Jane. "Scottish Orientalism: From Robertson to James Mill." *The Historical Journal* 25/1 (1982): 43–69.

Renwick, John. "The Reception of William Robertson's Historical Writings in Eighteenth-Century France." In *William Robertson and the Expansion of Empire*, edited by Stuart J. Brown, 145–63. Cambridge: Cambridge University Press, 1997.

Ribeiro Sanches, Manuela. "Dunkelheit und Aufklärung–Rasse und Kultur. Erfahrung und Macht in Forsters Auseinandersetzungen mit Kant und Meiners." *Georg Forster Studien* 8 (2003): 53–82.

Ricoeur, Paul. *Sur la traduction*. Paris: Bayard, 2004.

Robertson, John. "The Enlightenment above National Context." *Historical Journal* 40 (1997): 667–97.

———. *The Case for the Enlightenment: Scotland and Naples 1680–1760*. Cambridge: Cambridge University Press, 2005.

Romano, Antonella, and Stéphane Van Damme. "Sciences et villes-mondes: penser les savoirs au large (XVIe–XVIIIe siècle)." *Revue d'Histoire Moderne et Contemporaine* 55/2 (2008): 7–18. English version: "Science and World Cities: Thinking Urban Knowledge and Science at Large (16th–18th century)." *Itinerario* 33/1 (2009): 79–95.

Rosenzweig, Franz. "The Impossibility and Necessity of Translation." In *Translating Literature: The German Tradition*, edited by André Lefevere, 110–12. Assen: Van Gorcum, 1977.

Ross, Ian Simpson. *The Life of Adam Smith*. Oxford: Oxford University Press, 1995.

Schieder, Wolfgang, and Christof Dipper. "Propaganda." In *Geschichtliche Grundbegriffe. Historisches Lexikon zur politisch-sozialen Sprache in Deutschland*, vol. 5, edited by Otto Brunner, Werner Conze, and Reinhart Koselleck, 71–6. Stuttgart: Klett-Cotta, 1984.

Schilson, Arno. *Geschichte im Horizont der Vorsehung. G. E. Lessings Beitrag zu einer Theologie der Geschichte*. Mainz: Matthias-Grünewald-Verlag, 1974.

———. "Lessing and Theology." In *A Companion to the Works of Gotthold Ephraim Lessing*, edited by Barbara Fischer and Thomas C. Fox, 157–85. Woodbridge: Camden House, 2005.

———. "Offenbarung und Geschichte bei J.M. Goeze und G.E. Lessing. Hinweise zu einer offenbarungstheologischen Neuorientierung." In *Verspätete Orthodoxie. Über D. Johann Melchior Goeze (1717–1786)*, edited by Heimo Reinitzer and Walter Sparn, 87–120. Wiesbaden: Harrassowitz, 1989.

Schleiermacher, Friedrich. "On the Different Methods of Translating" [Über die verschiedenen Methoden des Übersetzens (1813)]. In *Translating Literature: Practice and Theory in a Comparative Literature Context*, edited by Andre Lefevere, 75–88. New York: Modern Language Association of America, 1992.

Schlie, Ulrich. *Johann Stephan Pütters Rechtsbegriff*. Göttingen: Verlag Otto Schwarz, 1961.

Schloemann, Martin. *Siegmund Jacob Baumgarten. System und Geschichte in der Theologie des Überganges zum Neuprotestantismus*. Göttingen: Vandenhoeck & Ruprecht, 1974.

Schmied-Kowarzik, Wolfdietrich. "Der Streit um die Einheit des Menschengeschlechts. Gedanken zu Forster, Herder und Kant." In *Georg Forster in interdisziplinären Perspektive*, edited by Claus-Volker Klenke, Jörn Garber, and Dieter Heintze, 115–32. Berlin: Akademie Verlag, 1994.

Schröder, Winfried. "Natürliche Religion und Religionskritik in der deutschen Frühaufklärung." In *Strukturen der deutschen Frühaufklärung 1680–1720*, edited by Hans Erich Bödeker, 146–64. Göttingen: Vandenhoeck & Ruprecht, 2008.

Schröter, Marianne. *Aufklärung durch Historisierung: Johann Salomo Semlers Hermeneutik des Christentums*. Berlin: De Gruyter, 2012.

Schwab, Raymond. *The Oriental Renaissance: Europe's Rediscovery of India and the East, 1660–1860*. New York: Columbia University Press, 1984.

Sebastiani, Silvia. *I limiti del progresso. Razza e genere nell'Illuminismo scozzese*. Bologna: Il Mulino, 2008.

———. "Race and National Character in Eighteenth-Century Scotland: The Polygenetic Discourses of Kames and Pinkerton." *Studi settecenteschi* 21 (2001): 265–81.

———. *The Scottish Enlightenment: Race, Gender and the Limits of Progress*. Basingstoke: Palgrave Macmillan, 2013.

Selle, Götz von. *Die Georg-August Universität zu Göttingen 1737–1937*. Göttingen: Vandenhoeck & Ruprecht, 1937.

———, ed. *Die Matrikel der Georg-August Universität zu Göttingen*. Hildesheim: Lax, 1937.

Sellin, Volker. "Politik." In *Geschichtliche Grundbegriffe. Historisches Lexikon zur politisch-sozialen Sprache in Deutschland*, vol. 4, edited by Otto Brunner, Werner Conze, and Reinhart Koselleck, 789–874. Stuttgart: Klett-Cotta, 1978.

Sharp, L. W. "Charles Mackie, the First Professor of History at Edinburgh University." *Scottish Historical Review* 41 (1962): 23–45.

Sheehan, Jonathan. *The Enlightenment Bible: Translation, Scholarship, Culture*. Princeton: Princeton University Press, 2005.

———. "Religion and the Enigma of Secularization." *American Historical Review* 108/4 (2003): 1060–80.

Sher, Richard B. "Charles V and the Book Trade: An Episode in Enlightenment Print Culture." In *William Robertson and the Expansion of Empire*, edited by Stuart J. Brown, 164–95. Cambridge: Cambridge University Press, 1997.

———. *Church and University in the Scottish Enlightenment: The Moderate Literati of Edinburgh*. Princeton: Princeton University Press, 1985.

———. "1688 and 1788: William Robertson on Revolution in Britain and France." In *Culture and Revolution*, edited by Paul Dukes and John Dunkley, 98–109. London: Pinter, 1990.

Sikka, Sonia. *Herder on Humanity and Cultural Difference: Enlightened Relativism*. Cambridge: Cambridge University Press, 2011.

Simon, Thomas. *"Gute Policey." Ordnungsleitbilder und Zielvorstellungen politischen Handelns in der Frühen Neuzeit*. Frankfurt: Vittorio Klostermann, 2004.

Skinner, Quentin. "Retrospect: Studying Rhetoric and Conceptual Change." In *Visions of Politics*, vol. 1: *Regarding Method*, 175–87. Cambridge: Cambridge University Press, 2002.

Sklair, Leslie. *The Sociology of Progress*. London: Routledge, 1998.

Sloan, Phillip R. "The Idea of Racial Degeneracy in Buffon's *Histoire Naturelle*." In *Racism in the Eighteenth Century*, edited by Harold E. Pagliaro, 293–321. Cleveland: Case Western Reserve University Press, 1973.

Smitten, Jeffrey. "Impartiality in Robertson's *History of America*." *Eighteenth-Century Studies* 19 (1985): 56–77.

———. "Moderatism and History: William Robertson's Unfinished History of British America." In *Scotland and America in the Age of Enlightenment*, edited by Richard B. Sher and Jeffrey R. Smitten, 163–79. Edinburgh: Edinburgh University Press, 1990.

———. "Robertson's Letters and the Life of Writing." In *William Robertson and the Expansion of Empire*, edited by Stuart J. Brown, 36–54. Cambridge: Cambridge University Press, 1997.

──────. "The Shaping of Moderatism: William Robertson and Arminianism." *Studies in Eighteenth-Century Culture* 22 (1992): 281–300.
Sorkin, David. "Reclaiming Theology for the Enlightenment: The Case of Siegmund Jacob Baumgarten (1706–1757)." *Central European History* 36/4 (2003): 503–30.
──────. *The Religious Enlightenment: Protestants, Jews, and Catholics from London to Vienna.* Princeton: Princeton Universty Press, 2008.
Spadafora, David. *The Idea of Progress in Eighteenth-Century Britain.* New Haven: Yale University Press, 1990.
Starr, Chester G. "Historical and Philosophical Time." *History and Theory* 6/6 (1966): 24–35.
Stephan, Horst. *Realencyklopädie für protestantische Theologie und Kirche*, vol. 21. Edited by Albert Hauck. Leipzig: Hinrichs, 1908.
Stewart, Larry. *The Rise of Public Science: Rhetoric, Technology, and Natural Philosophy in Newtonian Britain, 1660–1750.* Cambridge: Cambridge University Press, 1992.
Stirken, Angela. *Der Herr und der Diener. Friedrich Carl von Moser und das Beamtenwesen seiner Zeit.* Berlin: Ludwig Röhrscheid, 1984.
Stolleis, Michael. *Geschichte des öffentlichen Rechts in Deutschland. Erster Band: Reichspublizistik und Policeywissenschaft 1600–1800.* Munich: C. H. Beck, 1988.
──────. "Reichspublizistik und Reichspatriotismus vom 16. zum 18. Jahrhundert." *Aufklärung* 4/2 (1989): 7–23.
Stolleis, Michael, Karl Härter, and Lothar Schilling, eds. *Policey im Europa der Frühen Neuzeit.* Frankfurt: Vittorio Klostermann, 1996.
Stummann-Bowert, Ruth. "Zivilisationsprozesse und Welthandel bei Georg Forster." *Georg Forster Studien* 10/1 (2006): 147–75.
Švambarytė, Dalia. "Georg Forster in Vilnius: Reverberations of the Great Age of Ocean Navigation." *Acta Orientalia Vilnensia* 10/1–2 (2009): 139–64.
Tarabuzzi, Gianfranco. "Le traduzioni italiani settecentesche delle opera di William Robertson." *Rivista storica italiana* 91/2–3 (1979): 486–509.
Trevor-Roper, Hugh. "George Buchanan and the Ancient Scottish Constitution." *English Historical Review*, Supplement 3 (1966).
Tribe, Keith. "Cameralism and the Sciences of the State." In *The Cambridge History of Eighteenth-Century Political Thought*, edited by Mark Goldie and Robert Wokler, 525–46. Cambridge: Cambridge University Press, 2006.
──────. *Governing Economy: The Transformation of German Economic Discourse, 1750–1840.* Cambridge: Cambridge University Press, 1988.
Tuck, Richard. *Philosophy and Government, 1572–1651.* Cambridge: Cambridge University Press, 1993.
Turetzky, Philip. *Time.* London: Routledge, 1998.
Tucker, Irene. *The Moment of Racial Sight: A History.* Chicago: University of Chicago Press, 2009.
Tuveson, Ernest Lee. *Millennium and Utopia: A Study in the Background of the Idea of Progress.* New York: Harper & Row, 1946.
Uhlig, Ludwig. *Georg Forster: Einheit und Mannigfaltigkeit in seiner geistigen Welt.* Tübingen: Max Niemeyer Verlag, 1965.
──────. *Georg Forster. Lebensabenteuer eines gelehrten Weltbürgers (1754–1794).* Göttingen: Vandenhoeck & Ruprecht, 2004.
──────. "Theoretical or Conjectural History. Georg Forster's *Voyage Round the World* im Zeitgenössischen Kontext." *Germanisch-Romantische Monatsschrift* 53 (2003): 399–414.
Umbach, Maiken. *Federalism and Enlightenment in Germany, 1740–1806.* London: Hambledon Press, 2000.
Valera, Gabriella. "Statistik, Staatengeschichte, Geschichte im 18. Jahrhundert." In *Aufklärung und Geschichte. Studien zur deutschen Geschichtswissenschaft im 18. Jahrhundert*, edited by Hans Erich Bödeker, Georg G. Iggers, and Jonathan B. Knudsen, 119–43. Göttingen: Vandenhoeck & Ruprecht, 1986.

Vermeulen, Han F. "Göttingen und die Völkerkunde. Ethnologie und Ethnographie in der deutschen Aufklärung, 1710–1815." In *Die Wissenschaft vom Menschen in Göttingen um 1800*, edited by Hans Erich Bödeker, Philippe Büttgen, and Michel Espagne, 199–230. Göttingen: Vandenhoeck & Ruprecht, 2008.

———. "The German Invention of Völkerkunde: Ethnological Discourse in Europe and Asia, 1740–1798." In *The German Invention of Race*, edited by Sara Eigen and Mark Larrimore, 131–48. Albany: State University of New York Press, 2006.

Vierhaus, Rudolf. "Bildung." In *Geschichtliche Grundbegriffe. Historisches Lexikon zur politisch-sozialen Sprache in Deutschland*, vol. 1, edited by Otto Brunner, Werner Conze, and Reinhart Koselleck, 508–51. Stuttgart: Klett-Cotta, 1972.

———. *Deutschland im 18. Jahrhundert: Politische Verfassung, soziales Gefüge, geistige Bewegungen*. Göttingen: Vandenhoeck & Ruprecht, 1987.

———. "Historisches Interesse im 18. Jahrhundert." In *Aufklärung und Geschichte. Studien zur deutschen Geschichtswissenschaft im 18. Jahrhundert*, edited by Hans Erich Bödeker, Georg G. Iggers, and Jonathan B. Knudsen, 241–66. Göttingen: Vandenhoeck & Ruprecht, 1986.

Wachler, Ludwig. *Geschichte der Kunst und Wissenschaften seit Wiederherstellung derselben bis an Ende des 18. Jahrhunderts*, 2 vols. Göttingen: Vandenhoeck & Ruprecht, 1818.

Walker, Mack. "Johann Jakob Moser." In *Aufklärung und Geschichte. Studien zur deutschen Geschichtswissenschaft im 18. Jahrhundert*, edited by Hans Erich Bödeker, Georg G. Iggers, and Jonathan B. Knudsen, 105–18. Göttingen: Vandenhoeck & Ruprecht, 1986.

———. *Johann Jakob Moser and the Holy Roman Empire of the German Nation*. Chapel Hill: North Carolina University Press, 1981.

Walpole, Horace. *The Yale Edition of Horace Walpole's Correspondence*, 48 vols. Edited by W. S. Lewis et al. New Haven: Yale University Press, 1937–1983.

Waszek, Norbert. "Die Schottische Aufklärung in der Göttinger Wissenschaft vom Menschen." In *Die Wissenschaft vom Menschen in Göttingen um 1800*, edited by Hans Erich Bödeker, Philippe Büttgen, and Michel Espagne, 123–47. Göttingen: Vandenhoeck & Ruprecht, 2008.

Wegele, Franz Xaver von. *Geschichte des deutschen Historiographie seit dem Auftreten des Humanismus*. Munich and Leipzig: Oldenbourg, 1885.

———. "Häberlin, Franz Dominicus." In *Allgemeine Deutsche Biographie*, vol. 10, 274–5. Leipzig: Duncker & Humblot, 1879.

Wheeler, Roxann. *The Complexion of Race: Categories of Difference in Eighteenth-Century British Culture*. Philadelphia: University of Pennsylvania Press, 2000.

Whelan, Frederick G. *Edmund Burke and India: Political Morality and Empire*. Pittsburgh: University of Pittsburgh Press, 1996.

———. "Robertson, Hume, and the Balance of Power." *Hume Studies* 21/2 (1995): 315–32.

Wokler, Robert. "Apes and Races in the Scottish Enlightenment: Monboddo and Kames on the Nature of Man." In *Philosophy and Science in the Scottish Enlightenment*, edited by Peter Jones, 145–68. Edinburgh: John Donald, 1988.

Wolff, Larry, and Marco Cipollini, eds. *The Anthropology of the Enlightenment*. Stanford: Stanford University Press, 2007.

Womersley, David J. "The Historical Writings of William Robertson." *Journal of the History of Ideas* 47 (1986): 497–506.

Wood, Paul. "The Natural History of Man in the Scottish Enlightenment." *History of Science* 28 (1990): 89–123.

Yasumata, Toshimasa. *Lessing's Philosophy of Religion and the German Enlightenment: Lessing on Christianity and Reason*. Oxford: Oxford University Press, 2002.

Zachs, William. *Without Regard to Good Manners: A Biography of Gilbert Stuart 1743–1786*. Edinburgh: Edinburgh University Press, 1992.

Zammito, John. *Kant, Herder, and the Birth of Anthropology*. Chicago: University of Chicago Press, 2002.

———. "Policing Polygeneticism in Germany, 1775. (Kames), Kant, and Blumenbach." In *The German Invention of Race*, edited by Sara Eigen and Mark Larrimore, 33–52. Albany: State University of New York Press, 2006.

Zande, Johan van der. "August Ludwig Schlözer and the English Universal History." In *Historikerdialoge. Geschichte, Mythos und Gedächtnis im deutsch-britischen kulturellen Austausch 1750–2000*, edited by Peter Schuman, Stefan Berger, and Peter Lambert, 137–56. Göttingen: Vandenhoeck & Ruprecht, 2003.

———. "The Microscope of Experience: Christian Garve's Translation of Cicero's *De Officiis* (1783)." *Journal of the History of Ideas* 59 (1998): 75–94.

———. "Popular Philosophy and the History of Mankind in Eighteenth-Century Germany." *Storia della Storiografia* 22 (1992): 37–56.

———. "Statistik and History in the German Enlightenment." *Journal of the History of Ideas* 71/3 (2010): 411–32.

Zantop, Susanne. *Colonial Fantasies: Conquest, Family and Nation in Precolonial Germany*. Durham: Duke University Press, 1997.

Index

Numbers in **bold** indicate notes

Abbt, Thomas (1738–66), 5, 179
Abele, Johann Martin von (1753–1805), 106, 117–18, 149, **211**
Abenteuer (*abenteuerlich* and *Abenteurer*), 147. *Compare* adventure, conquistadors
Aberdeen, University of, 10
Academies of Science: Academy of Sciences of Padua, 4
  Imperial Academy of Sciences of Saint Petersburg, 5, 79
  Prussian Academy of Sciences, 173
  Real Academia de Historia de Madrid, 5
  Royal Society, 22, 152
Acosta, José de (1539–1600), 25
adventure (adventurer), 127–8, 132, 137–9, 147, 157, 161, 163. *Compare* Abenteuer
Adventurers' Act (1642), 128
Africa, 145, 152, 172
Agricola, Gnaeus Julius (40–93), 80
agriculture, 30, 127, 129, 136, 153, 168
Akbar I (1542–1605), Mughal Emperor, 143
Alans, 75
alchemy, 12
Alexander the Great (356–323 BCE), 127
Allgemeine Litteraturzeitung (journal), 172
Althusius, Johannes (1563–1638), 38, 86
American Revolutionary War (1775–83), 82, 150
Americans, native. *See* Indians
Anabaptists, 104, 122
ancient (Greco-Roman), 21, 49, 58, 70, 149, 154, 158–9, 165, 174, 178, **222**. *See also* antiquity, classical
Anglican. *See* England, Church of
Anglophile (Anglophilism), 8, 18, 39

Anglo-Scottish Union (1707); Union of Parliaments, 4, 10, 26, 33, 41, 97–8, **191**
Annalen der Geographie und Statistik (journal), 158
anthropology (anthropological), 22, 25, 28, 32, 52, 60, 76, 86–7, 132, 151, 153, 158, 160, 172, 174, 177–8, 182, **222**, **224–5**
anti-aristocratic, 97. *See also* aristocracy
anti-Catholicism, 110. *See also* Catholicism
anti-clericalism, 110. *See also* cleric
antihumanism, 175. *See also* humanism
anti-Jacobitism, 99. *See also* Jacobite
antipopery, 110. *See also* popery
antiquarian, 152, 158–9, 162
antiquity, 17, 69, 144, 159, **223**. *See also* ancient, classical
anti-scholastic, 11. *See also* scholastic
apocalypticism, 42, 53, **197**
apocatastasis, doctrine of, 12
Arabians, **222**
aristocracy (aristocratic), 23, 37, 76, 78, 97, **199**. *See also* anti-aristocratic
Aristotle (384–322 BCE) (Aristotelianism), 12, 14, 22, 86, 91, 167
artig, 107, 109. *Compare* polite, verfeinert
arts, 21, 24–5, 74–5, 77, 84–5, 90, 98, 127, 131–3, 133–5, 141, 153, 155–6, 159, 168, 175. *Compare* industry, crafts, trades
Atahualpa (1497–1533), Sapa Inca Emperor of Inca Empire, 139
Athens, classical, 72
Atlantic Ocean, 146, 151. *See also* Transatlantic
Augustine of Hippo (354–430), 43, 47, 65, **197**

251

252 Index

Australia (New Holland), 160
Austria (Habsburg Empire), 114, **224**
Austrian Succession, War of (1740–48), 114
Austro-Prussian dualism, 36
 antagonism, 115
Aztecs (Aztec Empire), 126, 148

Bahamas (San Salvador), 135
Baltic region, **222**
Banks, Joseph (1743–1820), 152
Barbarei (*Barbarey*), 79, 148. Compare
 barbarity
barbarity (barbarism, barbarous, barbarian) 25, 51–2, 73–7, 79, 84, 86, 90–1, 99, 134–6, 138–40, 142, 147–8, 154–5, 158, 163, 168–9, 171, 174. Compare Barbarei.
 See also primitive, savage
Baumgarten, Siegmund Jacob (1706–57), 56–62, 64, 66, 68, **200**, **202**
Bavarian Succession, War of (1778–79), 54
Beatoun, David (c. 1494–1546), Cardinal, 101
Becher, Johann Joachim (1635–82), 38
Behaim, Martin von (1459–1507), 151–2, 156–7, **219**, **222**
Benares (Varanasi), India, 144
Benyovszky, Móric (1746–86), Count, 157
Berlin, Prussia, 10, 62, 79
Bethencourt, John de (1362–1425), Baron, 128
Bible, 57–8, 63–4, 66–9, 122, 133
 New Testament, 56, 65–6, 69–70, 72, **202**
 Old Testament, 64, 68–9, 72, 158
Bildung, 12, 90–1, 148
blacks (Negroes), 175–6, **224**, **226**
Blair, Hugh (1718–1800), 10
Bossuet, Jacques-Bénigne (1627–1704), 6
Botany Bay (New Holland), Australia, 160
Bougainville, Louis-Antoine, Comte de (1729–1811), 151
Brahmins, 144–5
Brandenburg-Prussia, 36, 57. *See also* Prussia
Brandes, Ernst (1758–1810), **208**
British East India Company, 28, **192**
Bruni, Leonardo (1370–1444), 89
Bruno, Giordano (1548–1600), **225**
Brunswick (Braunschweig), city of, 81–2, 106
 Electorate of Brunswick-Lüneburg/ Hanover (Braunschweig-Lüneburg/ Hannover), Holy Roman Empire, 5, 11, 63, 83, 179, 181, **208**

Buchanan, George (1506–82), 96, **209**
Buffon, Georges-Louis Leclerc, Comte de (1707–88) (Buffonian), 25, 39, 131–2, 136, 153, 175, **216**, **225**, **226**
Bürger (*bürgerlich*), 86, 93
Burke, Edmund (1729–97), 25, 36, 60, 81, 93–4, 100, 125, 134, 140, 150, 165, 183, **208**, **213**, **217**
Burnet, Gilbert (1643–1715), 81
Büsching, Anton Friedrich (1724–93), 157

Cabot, Sebastian (c. 1474–c. 1557), 128
Caesar, Gaius Julius (100–44 BCE), 76
Calvin, Jean (1509–64), 44, 112
Calvinist Reformed Church (Calvinism), 20, 27, 44, 48, 111
Cambridge, University of, 13
cameralism (*Kameralwissenschaft*), 11, 32, 38
Canary Islands, 128
cannibalism, 135
Cape of Good Hope, 142
Carib people, 135
Casket Letters, 110
Castile, Kingdom of (Castilians), 103, 107, 138
Catherine II (1729–96), Romanov, Empress of Russia, 5, 16, 79, 151, **186**, **219**
Catholic Church, Roman (Catholicism), 30–1, 41, 48, 68, 92, 99, 108, 110–12, 118, 120–2, 135.
 See also anti-Catholicism
Caucasians, 174
Celts (Celtic), 94, 146, 157, 174, **224**
Chancellor, Richard (c. 1521–66), 128
Charlemagne (?747–814), Charles I, Carolingian King and Emperor, 88
Charles III (1716–88), Bourbon, King of Spain, 5
Charles V (1500–58), Habsburg, Holy Roman Emperor, Charles I of Spain, 29, 74, 76–7, 101–5, 107, 115, 118, 120–2, 129
chiliasm (Millennialism), 12
chivalry, 77, 93–4, 99, 128, **209**
churches. *See* Calvinist Reformed Church; Catholic Church; England, Church of; Lutheran Church; Scotland, Church of (Presbyterian)
Cicero, Marcus Tullius (106–43 BCE) (Ciceronian), 10, 12
cities, 50, 77, 85, 89, 92, 133–4, 143, 155–6.
 See also urban
civil society, 32, 35, 78, 129, **214**

civility, 3, 90, 138, 141
civilization (civilizational), 4, 6, 15–16, 25, 27, 30, 47, 49–50, 55, 68–9, 75–6, 86, 93, 125, 133–4, 136, 138–42, 144, 146–7, 151, 153–4, 157, 159–60, 164–5, 167–8, 170–1, 173–4, 180–1, **203**, **226**
civilized, 2, 25, 28, 51, 56, 85, 126–7, 135, 140–2, 144, 148, 153, 164, 167–70, 176, 183. *Compare* gesittet. *See also* uncivilized
classical, 26, 69, 84–5, 97, 107, **223**. *See also* ancient, antiquity
cleric (clerical), 10, 12, 69, 145
climate, 15, 30, 37, 127, 136, 170–1, **219**, **225**
Cocceji, Iohannes (1603–69), 65
Collegium Carolinum, Braunschweig, 82
Collingwood, Robin George (1889–1943) (Collingwoodian or "Cambridge" approach), 8
Collins, Anthony (1676–1729), 81
Columbus, Christopher (1450/51–1506), 29, 129, 135, 137–8, 152, 161
commerce (commercial, commercialism), 3–4, 6, 10, 21–5, 30, 32, 47–51, 53–6, 77–8, 85, 88–9, 92–3, 97–8, 100, 102, 107, 126–9, 137–8, 140–3, 147–8, 153–5, 158–9, 163, 168–9, 180, **223**, **226**. *Compare* Handel, Handlung
Company of the Merchant Adventurers of London, 128
conceptual history (*Begriffsgeschichte*), 2, 7–8, **186**
confederation, 21, 25
confessional, 68, 121
  de-confessionalization (*Entkonfessionalisierung*), 11–12
  non-confessional, 10, 69
  post-confessional, 11, 69
conjectural history. *See* stadial history
conquistadors (conquerors), 129, 132–3, 135, 138, 140–1, 148, 163, **214**. *Compare* Abenteurer
Conring, Hermann (1606–81), 37, 152
conservatism (conservative), 15, 60, 69, 72, 146, 157, 178, 183
Constantinople, 156
constitution (constitutional), 3, 76, 77, 82, 86, 88, 91, 148, **222–3**
  English, 26
  French, 82, 183, **208**

Imperial German, 9, 18, 33, 37–8, 86–7, 113–17, 119–23, 181–2
Indian, 159, 162
Scottish, 4, 10, 96, 98, 100, 182
United Provinces, 117
United States, 117
see also Verfassung
Cook, James (1728–79), 152–3, 159–61, **219**, **221**
Cooper, Anthony Ashley (1671–1713), Third Earl of Shaftesbury, 81, 100
Copernicus, Nicolaus (1473–1543), 53
Cortes of Castile, 103
cosmopolitan (cosmopolitanism), 3, 8, 10, 25–6, 29, 96, 98, 120, 123, 146, 149, 157, 166, 177
Counter-Reformation, 50
Cranmer, Thomas (1489–1556), 112
Creole, 129
cruelty, inhumanity (*Grausamkeit, Unmenschlichkeit*), 148
Crusades, 76–7, 89, 92–4, 155, **214**
culture, 1, 7, 13–14, 16, 20, 25, 29, 31–2, 35, 37, 68–9, 72, 75, 85, 90, 105, 122, 126, 129–30, 136, 140, 143, 145, 148, 153, 159–60, 162, 164, 169, 172, 174, 178, 182, **199**, **217**
custom, 25, 30, 37, 55, 58, 71, 76, 90–1, 107, 116, 121, 132, 151, 153–4, 167, **199**. *Compare* Gewohnheiten, Sitten. *See also* manners

d'Alembert, Jean-Baptiste le Rond (1717–83), 78
Danube River, 52, 131
Danzig (Gdansk), 152
decline, 23, 89, 130, 174, **223**. *See also* progress
de-confessionalization (*Entkonfessionalisierung*). *See* confessional
deists (deism), 59, 62–4, 70, **201**
Denkart, 90, 92. *Compare* mentality
Descartes, René (1596–1650) (Cartesianism), 12
despotic (despotism), 47, 49, 96–7, 111, 115, 117, 134, 143, 176
determinism, 20
Diderot, Denis (1713–84), 25, 78, 126, 138, 176, **215**
Doppelmeyer, Johann Gabriel (1677–1750), 152
Dornford, Josiah (1764–97), 118–119, **213**

Dunbar, James (d. 1798), 25, 174
Dusky Bay, New Zealand, 168
Dutch, 44, **216**, **222**
Dutch Republic. *See* United Provinces

Ebeling, Christoph Daniel (1741–1817), 67, 157
Ebeling, Johann Philipp (1753–95), 54–6, 67, 157, **199**
ecclesiastical, 3, 10, 13–14, 24, 41, 48, 57, 60, 69, 111, 120, 133, **214**
estates, 117
Edict of Nantes (1598), 20
Edinburgh Review (journal), 2, 48, 97
Edinburgh, Scotland, 2, 4, 9–12, 16, 22, 32, 38, 41, 54, 111, 128, 133, 138, 177, **190**, **193**, **204**, **210**
  University of, 2, 10–11, 13, 28–9, 30, **187**, **192**
Edinburgh Volunteers, 28
egalitarian (egalitarianism), 30, 172, 176
Elizabeth I (1533–1603), Tudor, Queen of England and Ireland, 108–9, 111
encounters, 15, 125, 129, 130, 132, 135, 139, 146–7, 150, 164, **221**
England, 4, 13, 26, 48, 53, 79, 82, 92, 97–9, 103, 111, 113, 157, 159, 167, 181
England, Church of (Anglican) (Episcopalian), 30–1, **211**
enterprise (enterprising), 15, 75, 127–9, 137–9, 147–8, 161. *Compare* Unternehmung
Episcopalian. *See* England, Church of
Erastus, Thomas (1524–83) (Erastianism), 10
Erlangen, University of, 110
estates, 20, 35–6, 79, 113, 115–17, 120, **212**
ethnic identity, 86, 94
ethnicity, 87, 90, 94, 156–7
ethnography, 5, 12, 32, 36, 130, 163, 171, 177, **194**, **222**, **224–5**
ethnology (*Völkerkunde*), 18, 32, 52, 160, 161, 166, 175, 178, **219**, **224**
evangelists, 66–7, 70, 72
  Matthew, 70
  Mark, 70
  John, 70
  Luke, 70

Falconer, William (1732–69), 174
Feder, Johann Georg Heinrich (1740–1821), 32
federalism, 33, 36–7
fein[sten], 109. *Compare* refined

Ferdinand (1721–92), Duke of Brunswick-Wolfenbüttel, Prince of Brunswick-Lüneburg, 62
Ferdinand II (1452–1516), King of Aragon, 137
Ferdinand III (1608–57), Habsburg, Holy Roman Emperor, 121
Ferguson, Adam (1723–1816), 2, 10, 67, 84–5, 94, 174, 177, **203**, **206**, **211**, **225**
feudalism, 4, 75–7, 86–7, 89, 91, 96–7, 99, 108, 122
Figueroa, Rodrigo de (c. 1471–1515), 136
fine arts, 143
Fleiß, 84, 86, 147, **206**. *Compare* ingenuity, industry
Fletcher, Andrew (1655–1716), of Saltoun, 96–7
Forster, Georg (1754–94), 8, 18, 39, 146–50, 152–3, 156–78, 180, 182–3, **220–6**
Forster, Johann Reinhold (1729–98), 18, 152–7, 159, 169, **219**, **220**, **224**
fragment controversy (*Fragmententstreit*), 63, 66–7, 70
France (French), 4–5, 16–17, 20, 25, 28, 35, 42, 71, 79, 81–2, 92, 99–101, 109–10, 114–15, 117, 121, 144, 148, 150–1, 153, 166, **206**, **208**, **214**, **216**, **222**
Francis I (1494–1547), Valois, King of France, 101, 103, 120–1, **214**
Frankfurt am Main, Holy Roman Empire, 54, 114
Frederick I (1657–1713), Hohenzollern, King of Prussia, Frederick III as Elector of Brandenburg, 11, 57
Frederick II (1712–86), Hohenzollern, King of Prussia, 54, 114
freedom, 12, 57, 68, 76, 92–3, 96, 98, 113–14, 121, 155, **207**. *See also* liberty
freethinkers, 15, 59, 62, **200–1**
French Revolution (1789–99), 3, 146, 165, 183, **208**, **213**

Gaelic, 96, 157
Garve, Christian (1742–98), 149, **225**
Gatterer, Johann Christoph (1727–99), 33–4, 60, 81–3, 88, 108, 158, **187**, **194–5**, **200**, **210**, **213**
Gemeinschaft, 56. *Compare* intercourse
gentry, Scottish (*lairds*), 97
Gentz, Friedrich von (1764–1832), 94
George II, King of Great Britain and Ireland, Duke of Brunswick-Lüneburg (Hanover), 11

German National Theater, Hamburg, 62
German political history (*Teutsche Staats-Historie*), 37
Germanic peoples (ancient), 76, 87–8, 93–4, 114, **214**, **224**
Germanization, 93
geschliffen (*gebildet, gesittet*), 56, 86, 148. *Compare* civilized, polished, polizirt
Geschmack, 90, 109. *Compare* taste
Gewohnheiten, 90, 107. *Compare* customs
Giannone, Pietro (1676–1748), 24
Gibbon, Edward (1737–94), 5–6, 25, 29, 35, 174
Glasgow, Scotland, 10, 54, 169
  University of, **192**
Glorious Revolution (1688), 20, 53, **222**
Goeze, Johann Melchior (1717–86), 63, **201–2**
Goguet, Antoine-Yves (1716–58), 174
Golitsin, Dmitry Mikhailovich (1721–93), Prince, 78
Gospel, 31, 45, 47–8, 50–1, 53, 57, 61, 66–7, 70–2, 111
Gothic, 93
Göttingen, Brunswick-Lüneburg, Holy Roman Empire, 9–10
  University of ("Georgia Augusta"), 10–13, 32–3, 35–6, 67–9, 81–2, 87, 94, 106, 108, 116–17, 119, 146, 157–60, 163, 174, 176, 178–9, 180–1, **186–7**, **196**, **203**
Göttingische Anzeigen von gelehrten Sachen (journal), 13, 32, 80, 88, 106, 111, 117, 146, 150, 160, 162, 179–80
Göttingisches historisches Magazin (journal), 172
Gottsched, Johann Christoph (1700–66), 71
Great Britain, 11, 28, 32–3, 79, 85, 90, 98, 110, 115, 144, 150, 152, 156, **203**, **217**, **220**
Great Chain of Being, 175
Greece (Hellas) (Greek), 65, 69, 71–2, 144, 149, 159, **222**
Grimm, Friedrich Melchior (1723–1807), Baron von, 78
Grotius, Hugo (1583–1645), 23, 102, 152
Guatimozin (Cuauhtémoc) (c. 1495–1522), Aztec Emperor of Mexico, 138
Guevara Vasconcelos, Ramón de, 5
Guicciardini, Francesco (1483–1540), 20

Häberlin, Franz Dominic (1720–87), 117–18, 121
Habsburg, House of, 6, 33, 114. *See also* Charles V, Ferdinand III, Joseph II
Halle, University of, 10–11, 56–7, 60, 67–8, 163, **199**
Haller, Albrecht von (1708–77), 88, 108–9, 111–12, 180, **210**
Hamburg, Holy Roman Empire, 62–3, 67
Handel, 85–6, 147. *Compare* commerce
Handlung, 56, 147. *Compare* commerce
Hanover (Hannover), Electorate of, Holy Roman Empire. *See* Brunswick-Lüneburg
Hanover, House of, 115. *See also* Brunswick-Lüneburg, George II
Hastings, Warren (1732–1818), 28, 143, 160, **192**
Hawley, Gideon (1727–1807), 151
Hebraisms, 71
Heeren, Arnold Hermann Ludwig (1760–1842), 146, 158–9, 164, 180, 182, **220**
Helmstedt, University of, 81–2, 117, **205**
Henry III (1379–1406), King of Castile, 128
Henry VIII (1491–1547), Tudor, King of England, 103
Henry the Navigator (1394–1460), 29, 128, 137–8
Herbert, Edward (1583–1648), Baron of Cherbury, 81
Herder, Johann Gottfried von (1744–1803), 90, 94, 162, 172–3, 175, **207–8**, **221–2**, **224–5**
hermeneutics, 35, 61, **225**
historical, 34
Herrera y Tordesillas, Antonio de (1549–1625/26), 132, 152
Heyne, Christian Gottlob (1729–1812), 35, 67, 146, 150–1, 153, 165, 180, **203**, **211**
Hindu law, 143
Hinduism, **218**
Hispaniola, 135–7, 139
historicity (historicist), 31–2, 64, 66–7, 69, 72, **195**
historische Staatslehre, 38
Hobbes, Thomas (1588–1679) (Hobbesian), 12, 23, 81, 102, **190**
Hollmann, Samuel Christian (1696–1787), 12

Holy Roman Emperors, 20. *See also* Charles V, Ferdinand III, Joseph II
Holy Roman Empire (German Empire), 6, 9, 18, 33, 36–7, 87, 113, 116, 123, **212**
Home, Henry, Lord Kames (1696–1782), 2, 133, 175, **209**
Hörnigk, Philipp Wilhelm von (1640–1714), 38
Huguenot, 44
human agency, 23, 44, 46–7, 52–3, 56
humanism, 20, 27, 34, 42, 96, 182, **195**. *See also* antihumanism, neo-humanism
Humboldt, Alexander von (1769–1859), **223**
Humboldt, Wilhelm von (1767–1835), **222**
Hume, David (1711–76) (Humean), 2, 4–5, 16, 22, 26, 29–32, 35, 44, 48, 60, 84, 94, 144, **192**
Hungarian, 5
Huns, 75
Hutcheson, Francis (1694–1746), 99
Hutchinson, Thomas (1711–80), Governor of Province of Massachusetts Bay, 16, 151

imperial free cities, 87. *See also* Frankfurt, Hamburg, Kempten, Ulm
Inca (Empire), 126, 134, 138, 140, 148
India (Hindostan) (Indians), 142–4, 159, 162
Indians, North American (native Americans), 76, 87, 102, 131–2, 135–7, 139–40, 143, 145, 151, 164, 169, 176, **216**
indolence, 132, 156–7
Industrie, 147
industry, 50, 52, 75, 84–5, 90, 100, 107, 131, 133–4, 136, 139–40, 142–3, 147, 155, **206**. *Compare* Fleiß, Industrie
ingenuity, 46, 136, 147. *Compare* Fleiß
intercourse, 28, 47, 50, 55–6, 74–5, 77–8, 85, 89, 91–4, 107–8, 125, 140–2, 148, 159–60, 164, 167. *Compare* Gemeinschaft
interests, 21–2, 26, 36, 38, 50, 114–15, 173
intolerance, 11, 49, 57. *See also* tolerance
investment, 128
irenicism, 11, 68, 72
Irish rebellion (1641), 128
Iroquois, 28
Isabella I (1451–1504), Queen of Castile and León, 136

Iselin, Isaak (1728–82), 153, 174
Israel, ancient (Israelites), 63–4, 68–9. *See also* Jews
Italy (Italian), 4, 79, 92, 100–1, 109

Jacobins, 165
  German, 8, 146, 165, **222**
Jacobite (Jacobitism), 28, 96, 120, **209**
  rebellion (1745), 52
  see also anti-Jacobitism
James V (1512–42), Stuart, King of Scotland, 101
James VI (1566–1625), Stuart, King of Scotland, James I of England and Ireland, 97, 109, 111
Japan, 162
Jena, University of, 10
Jesuits, 25, 110–11, **215**
Jews, ancient, 48–9, 66, 72. *See also* Israel
John II (1455–95), King of Portugal, 152
Jones, William (1746–94), 143, 162
Joseph II (1741–90), Habsburg, Holy Roman Emperor, 54, 79, 114
Justi, Johann Heinrich Gottlob von (1717–71), 11
Justinian I (c. 482–565), Byzantine Emperor, 143

Kant, Immanuel (1724–1804), 22, 110, 166, 172–7, **222**, **224–6**
Kassel, Hesse, Holy Roman Empire, 160
Kempten, Bavaria, 106, **211**
Kleinstaaterei (system of small states), 35–6, 38
Knox, John (1514–72), 112
Koselleck, Reinhart (1923–2006) (Koselleckian), 41–2, 53, **195**

La Chapelle, N. P. Besset de, 4
labor, division of, 75, 92, 140
Lafitau, Joseph François (1681–1746), 25
Lahontan, Louis-Armand, Baron de (1666–1716), 25
Landesgeschichte, 9, 33
Las Casas, Bartolomé de (c. 1484–1566), 129, 136
Last Judgment, 42, 53
law. *See* Hindu law, Roman law, Salic law
law, rule of, 6, 10, 24, 50, 78, 92, 100, 122, 168
Le Clerc, Jean (1657–1736), 44
Leibniz, Gottfried Wilhelm (1646–1716) (Leibnizian), 11, 46, 110, **198**, **202**

Leidenschaften, 109. *Compare* passions
Leipzig, Saxony, Holy Roman Empire, 146
  University of, 57
Lessing, Gotthold Ephraim (1729–81) (Lessingian), 62–7, 72, **201–3**
liberty, 25–6, 37, 41, 47–8, 50, 75, 90, 95–6, 98, 103–4, 111, 113–14, 116, 122, 130, 136–7, 156, 158, 176, 181. *See also* freedom
Lichtenberg, Georg Christoph (1742–99), 160
Limborch, Philippe van (1633–1712), 44
linguistic contextualism, 8, **186**
Linnaeus, Carl (1707–78), 25, 175
Lipsius, Justus (1547–1606), 86
Locke, John (1632–1704), 44, 46, **193**, **198**
London, England, 10, 149, 151, 160
Louis XI (1423–83), Valois, King of France, 103
Louis XIV (1643–1715), Bourbon, King of France, 14, 114
Louis XVI (1754–93), Bourbon, King of France, 54
Low Countries, **214**. *See also* United Provinces
Lüneburg, Saxony, Holy Roman Empire, 54
Luther, Martin (1483–1546), 42, 65, 104, 112, 121–2
Lutheran Church (Lutheranism), 11, 57, 110
luxury, 10, 48, 50, 77, 83, 85, 90, 127, 141–2, 168, **204**, **223**. *Compare* Ueppigkeit. *See also* wealth

Machiavelli, Niccolò (1469–1527) (Machiavellianism), 12, 20, 29, 110–11, 189
Mackie, Charles (1688–1772), 29
Madrid, Spain, 16, 151
Mainz, Republic of, 146, 165
Mandeville, Bernard (1670–1733) (Mandevillean), 23, 81, 102, 168, **190**, **199**
Manicheans, 70
Manieren, 107, 211. *Compare* manners, Sitten
manners, 6, 10, 21, 24–7, 29–30, 42–3, 47, 49–53, 55–6, 59, 71, 74–8, 84–6, 89–93, 96, 98, 100, 104, 107–8, 119–20, 125–7, 129, 131, 133, 135, 140–2, 144, 147, 150–1, 153–4, 157, 162, 165, 167, 169, **198**, **205**, **207**, **211**, **214**, **218**, **223**. *Compare* Manieren, Sitten. *See also* custom

Mary I (1542–87), Stuart, Queen of Scotland, 4, 6, 29, 99–101, 108–11, 120, **209**
Mary of Guise (1515–60), Queen of Scotland, 101
Massachusetts Colony, 16, 151
material culture, 72, 75, 143, 145, 153
  progress, 50, 163–4
materialist (materialism), 24, 44, 50, 60, 67, 181
Maurice (1521–53), Elector of Saxony, 29, 104–5
Mediterranean Sea, 146, 151
Meiners, Christoph (1747–1810), 94, 146, 158, 166, 172–6, 178, **203**, **208**, **222–6**
Mendelssohn, Moses (1729–86), 57, 90
mentality, 86, 90, 92, 165, **206**. *Compare* Denkart
Mexico (Mexicans), 29, 133–5, 137–40
Michaelis, Johann David (1717–91), 67–72, **203**, **220**
Middle Ages (medieval, Dark Ages), 11, 26, 29, 32, 50–1, 60, 74, 79, 82, 88, 90–2, 116–17, 154, **200**, **204**, **206**, **214**, **222–3**
middle class, 24, 86, 91–3
Millar, John (1735–1801), 2, 32, 119, 169, 174
missionaries, 25, 41, 131, 151, 163, **222**
Mississippi River, 52, 131
Mittelstedt, Theodor Christoph (1712–77), 1, 6, 81, 85–6, 106–7, 109, 149, **205**, **211**
Moderate Party (moderatist), 3, 10, 11, 28, 31, 41, 111, 119–20, 146, 165, **185**, **193**, **197–8**
moderation, 5–6, 9, 13, 48, 100, 109, 170
modernity, 1, 3, 6, 15, 21–3, 25, 32, 42, 49, 129, 165, 180
Monboddo, James Burnett, Lord (1714–99), 25, **216**
Mongols, 174
monogenism, 133, 172, **225**
monotheism, 144
Monrepos, estate, Russia, 79
Montesquieu, Charles-Louis de Secondat (1689–1755) (Montesquieuian), 23, 30, 36, 79, 120, 143, 192
Montezuma II (1466–1520), Aztec Emperor of Mexico, 138–9
Moser, Friedrich Carl von (1723–98), 113–16, **212**

258 *Index*

Moser, Johann Jakob (1701–85), 37–8, 113, 115, **196, 203**
Möser, Justus (1720–94), 114, 116
Müller, Johannes von (1752–1809), 36
Münchhausen, Gerlach Adolph von (1688–1770), 11, 68
Muñoz, Juan Bautista (1745–99), 5
Münster and Osnabrück, Peace of. *See* Westphalia
Murr, Christoph Gottlieb von (1733–1811), 152, 157
Muscovy Company, 128
Muslim (Saracen), 156

Nantes, Edict of (1598), 20
native Americans. *See* Indians
natural history of man, 2–3, 18, 38, 132, 134–5, 144, 159, 160, 177, 179, **193**
nature, state of, 30, 87
neo-humanism, 69. *See also* antihumanism, humanism
Neology, Protestant, 62–3, 66
New Holland (Australia), 160
New World, 5, 129, 131–2, 137, 139–40, 142, 148, 150–2, 156
New Zealand (native New Zealanders), 168
Newton, Isaac (1642–1727), 46, **198**
Nicolai, Christoph Friedrich (1733–1811), 62, 79
Nicolay, Ludwig Heinrich von (1737–1820), 5, 78–81, **204**
Nicole, Pierre (1625–95), 23, **190**
nobility, 79, 96, 117, 156
non-confessional. *See* confessional
Norsemen, **222**

Ochaita, Bartolomé, Father Olmedo, 137
Oriental languages, 62, 110
orientalist (Orientalism), 15, 68, **192, 217**
Osnabrück, Lower Saxony, Holy Roman Empire, 114
Ottoman Empire (Ottomans), 156, **221**
Ovando, Nicholas de (1460–1511), 137
Oxford, University of, 119

Pacific islands (inhabitants), 51, 153
Pacific Ocean (South Seas), 147, 153, 160–1, 167, 172, 175
Palibothara (Pataliputra), ancient Indian city of, 159
Panin, Nikita (1717–83), Count, 79
Paracelsus (1493–1541), **225**
Paris, France (Parisian), 15–16, 78, 160, 165

parliament, 97
British, 28, 157
Scottish, 52, 98
passions, 9, 22, 27, 50, 59, 75, 99, 101–4, 109–10, 129, 140, 155, 167–8, **192**. *Compare* Leidenschaften
patriotism, 26, 29, 97, 99, 113, 115, 157, **204**. *See also* Reichspatriotismus
Paul I (1754–1801), Romanov, Emperor of Russia, 5, 79–80
Paul, the Apostle, 70
Pauw, Cornelius Franciscus de (1739–99) (Pauwian), 25, 131–2, 136, 174, **216**
Peru (Peruvians), 29, 133–5, 138–40
Pharisees, 48
philanthropy (philanthropist), 154–5, 168
Philip I (1504–67), Landgrave of Hesse, 112
philosophical history, 4, 20, 29, 82, 150, 162
Phoenicians, 127, **222**
physiocrats, 43
Picts, 157
Pietism (Pietist), 11, 57, 62, 65
Pinto, Luis de, 151
Pizarro, Francisco (c. 1471–1541), 129, 138, 140
plagiarism, 155–6, **192**
Plato (427–347 BCE), 12
plurality, religious, 3–4, 9, 24, 36, 101
Poland (Polish), 5, 116
police, 50, 55–6, 84–6, 90, 101, 107, 130, 134, 139, 148, **196**. *Compare* Polizey
policy, 37, 51–2, 55–6, 74, 76, 85, 97, 100–1, 103–5, 107, 126–7, 136–7, 140, 148, 150, 163. *Compare* Staatsklugheit
polished, 50, 52, 55–6, 64, 77, 85–6, 90, 93, 100, 104, 107, 128, 133, 135, 139, 142, 148, 154, 163, 169, **218**. *Compare* geschliffen, polizirt
polite (politeness), 1, 10, 25–6, 50–1, 55–6, 78, 84–6, 90–1, 93, 100, 107–9, 118, 135, 138, 148, 162, **198, 204**. *Compare* artig, verfeinert
Politik, 86
Polizey (Polizei), 11, 38, 86, 148, **196, 207**. *Compare* police
polizirt, 148. *Compare* polished
Polybius (c. 200–c. 118 BCE), 70
polytheism, 144
popery, 41, 155, **198**. *See also* antipopery
Portugal (Portuguese), 128, 142, 151–2, 162, **222**
postcolonial, studies, 15
post-confessional. *See* confessional

Prague, Peace of (1636), 114
Price, Richard (1723–91), 81
priestcraft, 145
primitive, 24, 28, 31, 47, 49–50, 52, 75, 89, 129, 131, 132, 134, 139, 141, 147, 153, 169, 173.
    See also barbarian, savage
progress, 17, 23–4, 26–7, 29–31, 33, 41–3, 45–7, 49–51, 55–6, 61, 67, 69, 73–5, 78, 85, 94–8, 102, 104–5, 108, 120, 122, 126–7, 130–3, 136, 138, 140–5, 150, 153, 161, 163, 165, 168, 171, 173, 177, 181, **197**, **204**. *See also* decline
Protestant (Protestantism), 5, 7, 12, 20, 48, 62, 65, 68, 81, 99, 104, 108, 110–12, 114–15, 120–2, 180, **211**
providential (providentialism), 7, 17, 28, 44, 67, 110, 154, 164, 181, **191**, **200**
Prussia, Kingdom of, 114, 157.
    See also Brandenburg-Prussia
Pufendorf, Samuel von (1632–94) (Pufendorfian), 23, 37–8, 182, **193**
Pütter, Johann Stephan (1725–1807), 37, 71, 81–2, 87, 116–22, 182, **205**, **213**

Queen Charlotte Sound, New Zealand, 170

race, 18, 51, 59–60, 63–4, 66, 76, 87, 133, 142, 145, 153, 166–8, 171–3, 175–7, **208**, **216**, **224–5**
Raffinement, 109. *Compare* refined (refinement)
Raleigh, Walter (c. 1552–1618), Sir, **225**
Ramus, Petrus (1515–72) (Ramism), 12
Rasumovsky, Aleksei (Oleksiy Rozumovsky) (1748–1822), Count, 78–9
Rasumovsky, Kirill (Kyrylo Rozumovsky) (1728–1803), Count, 79
Raynal, Guillaume Thomas, Abbé (1713–96), 25, 126, 176, **211**, **215**
reconquista, 128
redemption, 43, 49, 51
refined (refinement), 13, 21–2, 24, 29–31, 34, 36, 43, 46–7, 49–51, 55–6, 60, 73–5, 77–8, 85, 90, 92–4, 98, 100, 103–4, 108–9, 118, 122, 127, 134, 138–9, 141–2, 144, 153–4, 156, 164, 167–9, 171, 175, 182.
    Compare feinsten, Raffinement
Reformation, 50, 68, 97, 104, 109–12, 120–2
Rehberg, August Wilhelm (1757–1836), **208**
Reichsgeschichte, 71, 81, 116
Reichshistorie (imperial history), 9, 33

Reichshofrat, 87, 113
Reichskammergericht, 116
Reichspatriotismus, 114. *See also* patriotism
Reichstag, 87
Reimarus, Hermann Samuel (1694–1768), 62–3, 65, **201**, **203**
relativism, 29, 43, 126, 172
    historical, 61, 66
Remer, Julius August (1738–1803), 1, 2, 5, 80–94, 106, 112–13, 116–18, 121, 147, 149, 151, 163, 179, **205**, **206**, **208**, **214**
Remer, Wilhelm Hermann Georg (1775–1850), 83
Renaissance, 77, 89
republican, 3, 6, 47, 96, 158
revelation, 6, 31, 42–3, 45, 47, 50–1, 55, 57, 59, 62–3, 65, 67, 69–70, 72, 96, 110
revolution. *See* American Revolutionary War, French Revolution, Glorious Revolution
Rezeptionsgeschichte (reception history), 8, 105, 146, **186**
Robespierre, Maximilien de (1758–94), 42
Rogerson, Dr. John (1740–1828), 5, 16, 151
Roman Empire (Romans), 47, 49, 65, 72, 74, 86, 89–90, 141, 155, 157, 159, **212**, **222**
Roman law, 77, 92, 116
Rousseau, Jean-Jacques (1712–78), 36, 131, 165, 177, **223**, **224**
royalists, 96, 157
Russia (Russian), 5, 78–9, 114, **219**, **222**

sacred history, 45, 56, 59
Sadducees, 48
San Salvador. *See* Bahamas
Saint Petersburg, Russia, 16, 151, **219**
Salic law, **214**
Sattelzeit, 6
savage (savagery), 52, 91, 126–7, 129, 131–5, 138–9, 141, 150, 153, 163, 167–70, 174, **217**. *See also* barbarian, primitive
Saxony-Coburg, Duchy of, Holy Roman Empire, 110
Schiller, Friedrich (1759–1805), 6, 36, 146–50, 179, **186**
Schlegel, August Wilhelm (1767–1845), 36
Schleiermacher, Friedrich (1768–1834), 7
Schleswig, 82
Schlözer, August Ludwig von (1735–1809), 32, 34–5, 38, 108, 113, 157–8, 163, 182, **187**, **194–5**
Schmalkaldic League, 122

Schmidt, Michael Ignaz (1735–94), 118–22, 182
scholastic, 12, 57. *See also* anti-scholastic
Schriftprinzip, 66
Schröder, Wilhelm von (1640–88), 38
science of man (*Wissenschaft vom Menschen*), 4, 17, 20, 22–3, 32, 36, 125, 133, 141, 153, 172–3, 177–8, 181–2, **193**
Scotland, Church of (Scottish Presbyterian Church), 3, 10, 14, 28, 30–1, 41, 44–5, 109, 145
　General Assembly of, 10, 28, 31, 111, **185**
Scottish Relief Bill, 48
Seiler, Georg Friedrich (1733–1807), 106–7, 109–11, 149, **211**
Select Society, Edinburgh, 2
Semler, Johann Salomo (1725–91), 56–7, 60–3, 66, 68, **200–2**
serfs, 76–7, 92. *See also* feudalism
Servet, Miguel (1509/11–53), 112
Seven Years' War (1756–63), 114–16
Siberia, Russia, 16
Sitten (*gesittet*), 56, 84, 89–93, 107, 119, 147–48, 150, **199**. *Compare* custom
Skelton, Philip (1707–87), 81
slave (slavery, slavish), 47, 49, 61, 97, 122, 145, 157, 176, **198**, 224
Slavs, 174, **222**
Smith, Adam (1723–90) (Smithian), 2, 22–3, 30–2, 42, 44, 47, 77, 88, 149, 154–5, 177, **192**, **197**, **204**
social history of ideas, 15
Société des Antiquités de Cassel, 160
Society Islands, French Polynesia, 171
Sonderweg theory, 35
Sozzini, Fausto (1539–1604) (Socinianism), 12
Spain (Spanish), 5, 20, 61, 101, 115, 128–9, 132–3, 135–9, 142, 148, 150–1, **202**, **216**, **222**
　Kings of, 20
　see also Charles V (I), Charles III
Speyer, Imperial diet of (1529), 20
Spinoza, Baruch (1632–77), **202**
Spittler, Ludwig Timotheus (1752–1810), 35–6, 89
Sprengel, Matthias Christian (1746–1803), 157, 162–4, **221**
Staatistik (*Statistik*) (statistics), 38, 82.
　See also state sciences
Staatsklugheit, 56. *Compare* policy
Staatsrecht, 81

stadial history (conjectural history), 3, 8, 18, 23–4, 27–30, 42–3, 45–7, 50–1, 55–6, 60, 67, 73, 75–6, 78, 87, 95, 105–7, 119, 126, 128–30, 132–3, 135, 139–41, 143, 145, 147–8, 150, 153–4, 157, 162–5, 172–3, 177, 181, **190–1**, **193**, **199**, **216–17**
St. Andrews, University of, 10
state sciences (*Staatswissenschaften*), 9, 32, 38, 82, 86
Stedman, Charles (1753–1812), 82
Sterne, Laurence (1713–68), 81
Stewart, Dugald (1753–1828), 53–4, 150, 177, **185**, **190**, **192**, **209**
Stewart, Henry (1545–67), Lord Darnley, First Duke of Albany, 110
Stewart, James (c. 1531–70), First Earl of Murray (Moray), 101, 110
Stoicism, 10, 22, 144
Strasbourg, University of, 78–9
Stuart, Charles Edward (1720–88), Jacobite "Young Pretender," 28
Stuart, Gilbert (1742–86), 35, 94, 119, **195**
Stuart, House of, 26, 99. *See also* James V, James VI, Mary I, Stuart, Charles Edward
Suard, Jean-Baptiste-Antoine (1732–1817), 4, 151
subsistence, mode of, 24, 46, 73–5, 78, 86, 127, 132, 134, 141, 168, **214**
superstition, 3, 41–2, 48–50, 52, 59, 77–8, 92, 139, 144–5, 155–6, 171
supranationalism, 98
Switzerland (Swiss), 44, 79, 88, 153, 180

Tacitus, Publius Cornelius (56–after 117) (Tacitean), 26, 51, 76, 80
Tanna Island, Vanuatu (Melanesia), 170
Tartars (Tatars), 87
taste, refined, 75, 90, 109, 155, 158, 162, 171. *Compare* Geschmack
Teutonism, 157
Teutscher Merkur (journal), 172
theism, 144
theology, 11–12, 28, 31–2, 43–5, 48, 56–8, 60–2, 65–9, 71–2, 81, 110, 157, 179, **198**, **201–2**, **206**, **211**
Thirty Years' War (1618–48), 6, 9, 33, 36, 114
Thomasius, Christian (1655–1728), 11, 57
Thucydides (c. 460–c. 395 BCE) (Thucydidean), 26, 70
Tierra del Fuego, 170, 176
time, secular, 49, 51
　sacred, 51

Tindal, Matthew (1657–1733), 81
Tlascalans (Tlaxcalans), 135, 137, 139
Toland, John (1670–1722), 81
tolerance (toleration), 3–4, 10, 30, 44, 51, 101, 112, 122, 137, 141, 164–6, 177.
   See also intolerance
Tory (Toryish), 26, 115
Transatlantic, 147, 156, 164.
   See also Atlantic Ocean
travelogues, 25, 131, 160, 177, **206**
treaties. *See* Prague, Utrecht, Westphalia (Münster and Osnabrück)
Tudor, House of, 26. *See also* Elizabeth I, Henry VIII
tyrant (tyranny), 49, 96–7, 115, 141, 155, 165, **202**

Ueppigkeit, 85. *Compare* luxury
Ulm, Holy Roman Empire, 118
uncivilized, 41, 51, 75–6, 154, 167, 169.
   See also civilized
Union of Crowns (1603), Scottish and English, 96–7
United Provinces, 20, 117
United States of America, 117
universal monarchy, 4, 6, 9, 20, 24–5, 37, 54, 101, 122, 135, **214**
Universalgeschichte (universal history), 6, 9, 29, 33–4, 81–2, 108, 123, 174, 179, **187**, **195**
universalism, 134, 166, 172, 176–7
universities. *See* Aberdeen, Cambridge, Edinburgh, Erlangen, Glasgow, Göttingen, Halle, Helmstedt, Jena, Leipzig, Oxford, St. Andrews, Strasbourg, Wittenberg, Würzburg
unpolished, 139. *See also* polished
unsocial sociability (*Ungesellige Geselligkeit*), 22–3, **199**
Unternehmung (*unternehmend*), 147–8.
   Compare enterprise
urban, 38, 50, 87, 94, **187**, **204**, **214**
Utrecht, Treaty of (1713), 15

vassalage, 113, 155–6. *See also* feudalism
Verfassung, 33, 89, 119, 148, 150.
   See also constitution
verfeinert, 86. *Compare* artig, polite
Vernet, Jacob (1698–1789), 57
Versailles, France, 79
Vienna, Austria, 78–9, 113, 118
violence, 9, 22–3, 50, 76, 100–3, 110, 129, 135, 138, 168

virtue, 9, 12, 20, 23, 26, 30–1, 41, 47–9, 74–5, 86, 91, 93, 97, 109, 132, 155, 174, 211
   civil (civic), 10, 12, 21, 211
vita activa, 21. *See* virtue, civil
Völkergeschichte, 33, 88
Voltaire [François-Marie Arouet] (1694–1778) (Voltairean), 5, 14, 24, 78, 96, 120, 158
Vyborg, Russia, 79

Waddilove (formerly Darley), Robert (1736–1828), 16, 151
Warburton, William (1698–1779), 57, 67, **203**, **211**
warfare, 88, 139, 153
   civil, 28, 59
   religious, 25
Warrington dissenting academy, 152
Wars. *See* American, Austrian, Bavarian, Seven Years', Thirty Years'
wealth, 23, 50, 77, 97, 138, 141–2, **204**.
   See also luxury
Wedderburn, Alexander (1733–1805), First Earl of Rosslyn, 97
welfare, 93, 119, 171, **207**
Werenfels, Samuel (1657–1740), 44
Westphalen, J., 82, 112
Westphalia, Peace of (1648) (Peace of Münster and Osnabrück), 6, 9, 20, 33, 36, 114, 117, 123, 182, **196**
Whigs (Whiggish), 26, 96, 99, 108, 115, 120
Whiston, William (1667–1752), 67
Wilkins, Charles (1749–1836), 143
Willoughby, Hugh (d. 1554), 128
Wilno (Vilnius), Poland-Lithuania, 160
Wissenschaft vom Menschen.
   See science of man
Wittenberg, University of, 57
Wolfenbüttel, city of, Duchy of Brunswick-Wolfenbüttel, Holy Roman Empire, 62
Wolff, Christian (1679–1754) (Wolffianism), 11, 56–8, 110, **199–200**, **211**
Würzburg, University of, 118

Xenophon (c. 430–354 BCE), 70

Yorkshire, County, England, 157

Zeno (c. 490–c. 430 BCE), 144

Printed and bound by CPI Group (UK) Ltd, Croydon, CR0 4YY